THE SELF-HELP COMPULSION

THE
SELF-HELP
COMPULSION

SEARCHING FOR ADVICE
IN MODERN LITERATURE

BETH BLUM

Columbia University Press

New York

Columbia University Press
Publishers Since 1893
New York   Chichester, West Sussex
cup.columbia.edu
Copyright © 2020 Columbia University Press

Library of Congress Cataloging-in-Publication Data
Names: Blum, Beth, author.
Title: The self-help compulsion: searching for advice in modern literature / Beth Blum.
Other titles: Searching for advice in modern literature
Description: New York : Columbia University Press, 2019. | Includes bibliographical
    references and index.
Identifiers: LCCN 2019023320 (print) | LCCN 2019023321 (e-book) |
    ISBN 9780231194921 (cloth) | ISBN 9780231551083 (e-book)
Subjects: LCSH: Fiction—History and criticism—Theory, etc. | Fiction—Psychological
    aspects. | Psychology in literature. | Psychology and literature. | Psychological literature. |
    Books and reading—Psychological aspects. | Reading interests. | Self-help techniques.
Classification: LCC PN3352.P7 B58 2019 (print) | LCC PN3352.P7 (e-book) |
    DDC 809/.93353—dc23
LC record available at https://lccn.loc.gov/2019023320
LC e-book record available at https://lccn.loc.gov/2019023321

Columbia University Press books are printed on permanent and durable acid-free paper.
Printed in the United States of America

Cover design and illustration: Lisa Hamm

Could the most complex and sophisticated works of art legitimately be considered somewhat as "proverbs writ large"?

Kenneth Burke

CONTENTS

ACKNOWLEDGMENTS

Everyone knows that the best acknowledgments manage to cannily relate the subject of the forthcoming book to the act of acknowledging at hand, and in my case this is an unjustly easy task. For the first and most obvious thing to say about self-help is that it is a fallacy that omits the invisible supporters who have enabled the individual to cope, perhaps even to succeed, whatever that may mean. Benjamin Franklin notoriously left out mention of his wife and servants, Dale Carnegie omitted some of his key textual precedents, and, though the achievement of my book seems modest in comparison, I have benefited no less than these "self-made" men from the conditions of support that have allowed me to think, write, and persevere.

The first omission of self-help, typically, is the parents, and I have to admit that, whatever kicking and screaming may have occurred, with perhaps a peak in the grunge-addled 1990s, I would probably not choose any others if I could do this life over again. From whom else could I have learned, as I did from my father, the commitment to scholarly risk-taking, nonconformity, and the deep and soul-sustaining joy of writing and the examined life? And whom else would have, like my mother, planted the idea of the writer's vocation so early in my mind, if even by naming me after my literature-obsessed aunt, and whom else's creativity and adventurousness could have provided the spirited counterweight to my own—too often brooding—groundedness? They are not only my parents but often my truest, and most complicated, friends.

I am no less indebted to my wider, extended family for the pleasures and consolations they provide: Elke Grenzer, who helped me work through this project's earliest iteration, and who is always up for a spirited discussion, and to Paula and Hannah—for the things that only they will ever understand. My love and gratitude to Estelle, Jean-François, Marieke, François, Félix, Floryanne, and Évelyne, for enthusiastically following the development of this book, and for giving me so many moments of laughter and warmth during the years of its composition.

Teachers are often given short shrift in narratives of self-making, but mine have been crucial and inexpressibly kind, so that I know that I will spend the rest of my career attempting to pay my pedagogic good fortune forward. It began with Mr. Charles Lavers at Huron Street Public School, who allowed me to type up my earliest poetic forays on the Commodore newly installed—to great commotion—beside his desk. I'm grateful to Dana Dragunoiu, who insisted I go to graduate school, and who instilled in me a lasting love of Russian literature; Mary Esteve, a bright star in Montreal's scholarly scene; Ariela Freedman and the faculty of that soulful gem of a program, Concordia's Liberal Arts College. I found there Miriam Israel, Marc-André Boisvert, and Charlotte Colbert, friends I will always treasure.

My streak of great teachers continued in graduate school, in particular with Damien Keane at SUNY Buffalo, who always offers crucial, careful feedback, and also with Michael Sayeau and Ruth Mack, who inspired me to brave the ice storms and "lake effects" to attend their wonderful classes.

I entered the program at UPenn the same year that Paul Saint-Amour arrived there, and much of this book is motivated by a desire to do justice to the true gift of his intellectual attention. I'm grateful to have had an advisor who shares my investment in the beautiful alchemy of a good sentence, and whose own work models more of these than I could count. His radical kindness has become a fixture for all of his students, and for many others in the profession. When, exhausted after a long day, I remember a student's last-minute recommendation request, I think of Paul's incredible generosity, dedication, and conscientiousness, and blearily open up my computer.

I leave every conversation with Jed Esty invigorated, abuzz with the energy of his infectious spirit. He is a fount of wisdom and good-naturedness. If you have ever so much as sat in a Q & A with Jed, you have likely marveled at his storied ability to spontaneously synthesize and contextualize a person's argument. My own project rarely appeared so lucid or full of interesting potential as when it was being reformulated back to me by him.

Heather Love has all my trust, admiration, and devotion. She has sustained me during some of the most difficult moments of my career, whether through the consolation of her unfailing mentorship or the inspiration of her dazzling writing. Ever since I first ran the idea for this project by her on a bench outside the McNeil center, confessing my fascination with Samuel Smiles and the history of self-help, which she urged me to pursue, Heather has been staunchly and sturdily there, and I'm so grateful for her humor, her good taste, and her sharp radar for nonsense.

One of the most important functions of advisors lasts long after the period in which they administer exams, serve on committees, and offer draft feedback. It is to forever become an imagined audience for one's writing, to be the eyes through which all new sentences and ideas must pass. I could not have asked for better filters than those I have received in the form of my graduate mentors. Their imagined responses will forever vet my inchoate formulations. I count it among the great gifts of my life to have crossed paths with these outstanding minds and exceptional humans.

Institutional support is another blind spot of the self-help canon. This has manifested itself for me in the form of a graduate fellowship from the Social Sciences and Research Council of Canada, a dissertation completion award from the American Council of Learned Societies, and a postdoctoral fellowship from the Andrew Mellon Foundation. I'm incredibly lucky for the institutional support I currently receive from Harvard, which has provided the material and also the intellectual conditions for the completion of this book. Thank you to the departmental staff, and especially to Anna McDonald, Sol Kim Bentley, Case Kerns, Henry Vega Ortiz, Lauren Bimmler, and Lauren Bauschard, for their essential assistance, as well as to Jennifer Ivers and Heather Lantz on the administrative side of things, for their readiness to help. Harvard's is a department of strong and independent thinkers, and I'm grateful for the courage of my colleagues' conviction in my perhaps unorthodox-seeming work. In particular, it is a blessing to have as wise a colleague and counselor as Deidre Lynch, who works harder than almost anyone, and also to have had a colleague as alert to bibliographic circulation and serendipity as Leah Price. For specific advice at various moments, my thanks also to David Alworth, Stephanie Burt, Amanda Claybaugh, Philip Fisher, Luke Menand, Derek Miller, Elaine Scarry, Marc Shell, James Simpson, John Stauffer, Nicholas Watson, Andrew Warren, and Leah Whittington. Long days in the Barker basement are made so much better by the camaraderie of the sagacious and inimitable Kelly Rich.

My studies of the ideology of success have convinced me that there may be few more entrenched beliefs than the idea that success is right. Nobody in a position of even minor professional prosperity wants to believe that the rewards they are enjoying for their labors are not earned. Though so much intellectual work addresses the injustices of historical and political power, the institutional structure of the academic labor market still clings like a dying man's last breath to outmoded, meritocratic conceptions of a just ratio between work and reward, talents and recognition. And so, amid this act of celebrating the professional and personal milestone of this monograph, it seems important to also pay heed to the contingencies of my situation, and the privileges enabling this book's production, and to pay tribute to the many colleagues I know and admire who, unfairly, do not have the security from which I currently, however precariously, benefit.

Some of my happiest discoveries at Harvard have been the wonderful graduate students: Alex Creighton's unbeatable research skills have been a great help, Rebecca Kastleman's exciting work and natural kindness have been a delight, Michelle Taylor's unparalleled knowledge of Bloomsbury esoterica and her rousing enthusiasm for all things modernist are a pleasure to witness. It has been a joy to work with Sarah Corrigan, Charlie Tyson, and Sophia Mao, and to see their ideas develop. I've also learned a great deal from the undergraduates I have worked with at UPenn and Harvard, and particularly those enrolled in my English 90HL seminar, *How to Live*, who have helped to keep me abreast of the latest self-help trends. Among these, I'm particularly grateful to Siqi Liu, who, in addition to being a brilliant student, provided me with invaluable research and translation assistance.

Like many of the professedly self-fashioned, when I began this project I imagined myself to be a lone wolf, toiling away in my solitary corner, but one of the great pleasures of the past years has been the discovery of many whose work intersects with mine in generative ways: Michaela Bronstein, Angus Brown, Andrew Goldstone, Lisa Mendelman, Becky Roach, Aarthi Vadde, Bob Volpicelli, and Merve Emre, who invited me to participate in the seminar that occasioned the first draft of my Coda. Len Gutkin has my appreciation for his terrific editing of the related *Chronicle* article, much of which made its way into this book. No one understands like Timothy Aubry does the slog that can be reading through some of self-help's more inane iterations. His work is my best and closest precedent, and it's been a pleasure to connect with one who not only shares my interest in bibliotherapy, but also my investment in the aesthetic. Warmest thanks to Matthew Sandler, whose own excellent study of self-help I vehemently recommend, to the learned Vincent Sherry for his much-appreciated kindness, and to Marshall Brown, who gave a young, determined, Joycean a chance. It's been wonderful to have the chance to get to know Jim English this past year; I only wish I had begun working with him sooner. James Pawelski has been a delight to connect with over our shared belief in the humanities and its measurable and immeasurable effects. My thanks also to my former peers at UPenn, and in particular, for various gestures and words of encouragement, to Rachel Banner, Kara Gaston, Phillip Maciak, Melanie Micir, and Rafael Walker. For commiseration and a crucial last-minute willingness to babysit, I owe Katie Price and Joe DeVitis.

One of the happiest turns of the past few years has been the friendship of Holden Green's genius-painter, Maya Brodsky.

Few self-help authors pay much heed to the vagaries of print history and production, but I've learned both through my research and experience how important editors, reviewers, and publishers can be. My appreciation extends to my remarkably generous and conscientious readers at Columbia University Press, to Philip Leventhal—who believed in this book from the beginning, patiently waited for its completion, and offered useful feedback and support throughout—and also to the delightfully organized and responsive Monique Briones, who keeps everything manageable.

My most consistent and deepest collaborator has been Jean-Christophe Cloutier. No one has believed in my writing more, or felt more viscerally and intimately the highs and lows that accompanied this project's completion. I couldn't endure these times without his utterly singular faith, lucidity, and energy, which I first discovered during a life-changing conversation about Diane DiPrima.

I thank my beloved Aimée, and our precious gift, Théodore, for granting me, together with JC, these little pockets of happiness.

● ● ●

Parts of chapter 4 previously appeared as "*Ulysses* as Self-Help Manual?: James Joyce's Strategic Populism" in *Modern Language Quarterly* 74, no. 1 (March 2013): 67–89, reprinted with the permission of Duke University Press. Portions of chapters 1 and 6 originally appeared in *PMLA* 133, no. 5 (2018) as "The Self-Help Hermeneutic: Its Global History and Literary Future," published by the Modern Language Association of America. An earlier version of chapter 3 was originally published as "Modernism's Anti-Advice," *Modernism/Modernity* 24, no. 1 (January 2017): 117–139. Reprinted by permission of Johns Hopkins University Press.

THE SELF-HELP COMPULSION

INTRODUCTION

SELF-HELP: A LITERARY HISTORY

Walk into a contemporary bookstore and self-help manuals are likely to be among the first books you'll see. In my local Barnes & Noble, a "self-improvement" section is featured in the vestibule, luring customers before they even open the store's main doors. Inside the store, the boundary between self-help manuals and literary fiction appears curiously blurred, with Paula Cocozza's novel *How to Be Human*, for example, displayed next to Heather Havrilesky's advice compendium *How to Be a Person in the World*.[1] Far from being particular to the era of the corporate bookstore chain, self-help's overlap with the literary has a long and varied history marked by negotiation, strife, influence, and imitation. Novels and success manuals have been competing for readers' attention at least since the late nineteenth century, when they vied for space on the same early best-seller lists.

Self-help and literature have historically been ambivalent shelf-fellows, but today the two industries appear to court and even encourage their mutual conflation. It can be difficult to discern from covers alone whether one is standing in the self-help section or among the new releases in fiction. The literary vanguard has taken to emulating self-help's language and packaging in works such as Sheila Heti's *How Should a Person Be?*, Charles Yu's *How to Live Safely in a Science Fictional Universe*, Mohsin Hamid's *How to Get Filthy Rich in Rising Asia*, Eleanor Davis's *How to Be Happy*, Terrance Hayes's *How to Be Drawn*, Jesse Ball's *How to Set a Fire and Why*, Ryan North's *How to Invent Everything: A Survival Guide for the Stranded Time Traveler*, and many more.[2] Serious literature has a reputation for resisting the vulgarity of use, and popular readers are known for shunning preachy lessons. But as I reveal in this book, rather than a deterrent, the prospect of a moral lesson has historically drawn readers from all over the world to even the most obscure and impractical narratives. The desire for self-help links such diverse reading cultures as samurai in Meiji Japan, late-Victorian French hobbyists, mid-twentieth-century Nigerian taxi drivers, and Reagan-era Dear Abby devotees.

Self-help's textual practice draws on the Renaissance tradition of the commonplace book: a scrapbook that assembled and recopied quotations for personal use and was meant to "lay up a fund of knowledge, from which we may at all times select what is useful in the several pursuits of life."[3] Book historian Robert Darnton explains how "early modern Englishmen read in fits and starts and jumped from book to book." This Renaissance practice of reading nonsequentially for personal use offers a window onto the way that reading and writing once "belonged to a continuous effort to make sense of things."[4] Over time, and with the rise of the modern research university, this classical view of literature as life preparation was gradually supplanted by specialized models of literary study, accompanied by what philosopher Michel Foucault has described as the subordination of self-care to self-knowledge.[5] However, this fragmentary and utilitarian approach to reading remains active in self-help. In her analysis of female self-help readers, Wendy Simonds discovered that "they are more likely to subvert the physical authority of the text than they would in fiction: they skip around, read halfway through and abandon the book, read only the chapters they think will pertain to them or their particular situation, or even use a book by reading the back cover and quickly skimming through it in the bookstore."[6] Such practices have found an outlet not only in self-help books but also in the "hyperlinked homilies" and "virtual verities" circulating in digital culture.[7] Self-help books are now "part of an extensive web of psycho-media."[8] As Boris Kachka, a journalist who covers literature and the publishing industry, complains, "today, every section of the store (or web page) overflows with instructions, anecdotes, and homilies."[9] This overflow into every genre, section, and web page is what makes recognizing self-help as a transmedia, cross-cultural reading practice so urgent.

Self-help's most valuable secrets are not about getting rich or winning friends but about how and why people read. All self-help, even Dale Carnegie's 1936 *How to Win Friends and Influence People*, advances a textual pedagogy. "*The great aim of education*," wrote Carnegie, quoting Herbert Spencer, "*is not knowledge but action*. And this is an *action* book."[10] Ever since its emergence out of Victorian working-class associations, self-help has operated as an alternative pedagogic space to the academy—one whose breezy, instrumental reading methods contrasted with the close, disinterested paradigms promoted by the modern research university. This modern university had little interest in Carnegie's proposed course on public speaking, which contained the seeds of his best-selling manual. His course was rejected by both Columbia and NYU, leading him to settle in 1912 on the Harlem YMCA as his venue. In the introduction to *How to Win Friends and Influence People*, Carnegie scoffed: "Wouldn't you suppose that every college in the land would conduct courses to develop the highest-priced ability under the sun?"[11]

Yet it was not just Carnegie's subject matter but also his reading and research methods that dissuaded academic institutions from securing his talents. His practice of liberal copying and unsignaled paraphrase was at odds with the originality and propriety prized by institutional academic culture. Described by a friend as "condensation's greatest zealot," Carnegie's manual repurposes the insights of thinkers from Lin Yutang to William James.[12] Even in person, it seems, Carnegie had a tendency to speak "in quotations, along with the qualifying phrases, mostly from his book, which he knows by heart."[13] His approach was in keeping with self-help's unapologetic derivativeness (in the 1883 self-improvement manual *Room at the Top*, author A. R. Craig humbly signs off as "The Compiler").[14] Long before theorists began announcing the "death of the author," self-help authors had abdicated the originality claim.[15] With their collating of wisdom literature from Confucius to Charles Schwab, self-help handbooks have historically supplied de facto syllabi for those excluded from elite educational institutions (indeed, many early guides included recommended reading lists as appendices). Above all, whether explicitly or implicitly, these guides modeled how to read.

In addition to Carnegie's practical methods, his research ethics also ostracized him from scholarly circles. A controversy erupted in 1919 after Carnegie submitted an article purportedly written by one of his business students touting the transformative effects of his public speaking course, "My Triumph Over Fears That Cost Me $10,000.00 a Year," when the journal editors of the academic *Quarterly Journal of Speech Education* discovered that Carnegie had fabricated the account.[16] But his penchant for invention soon found another, more literary outlet. In 1922, in the modernist pattern of Hemingway and Stein, Carnegie moved to France to pen his own Lost Generation epic, explaining that "in my early thirties, I decided to spend my life writing novels. I was going to be a second Frank Norris or Jack London or Thomas Hardy."[17] During the same period that James Joyce was in Trieste trying to re-create the Dublin of his youth, Carnegie journeyed to the French countryside to reconstruct his native Maryville, Missouri: "I am going to put that fountain with the gold fish back in Schumacher and Kirch's grocery, and the hitch racks back around the court house."[18] The novel, originally titled *The Blizzard* and later retitled *All That I Have*, participated in the same ironic portraits of pious, small town life that defined the modernist satires of Sherwood Anderson and Sinclair Lewis.[19]

When publishers rejected his novel, describing it as "worthless," Carnegie suffered a serious blow.[20] The rejection led to a crisis of self-reassessment and hastened his 1926 return to the United States, this time under his revised name (from Carnagey to Carnegie, after the

Dale Carnegie writing his novel in the European countryside.
Credit: Courtesy of the Dale Carnegie Estate.

entrepreneur-philanthropist), to resume his public education initiatives.[21] Although Carnegie came to accept that his talents lay elsewhere than in literature, he retained his admiration for the craft and power of the written word. "Genius is the creation of a cliché,"[22] wrote Charles Baudelaire, and Carnegie concurred, remarking that it is "easier to make a million dollars than to put a phrase into the English language."[23]

That "How to Win Friends and Influence People" has become a stock phrase, leading to parodies such as Lenny Bruce's *How to Talk Dirty and Influence People* and Toby Young's *How to Lose Friends and Alienate People*, suggests that Carnegie eventually attained his ambition.[24] But in a classic example of self-help's penchant for repurposing, the phrase has a longer history. Already in 1902 the expatriated Canadian hustler Victor Segno, who opened the "Segno School of Success" in Los Angeles, had used a variation of the saying in a chapter titled "How to Win Friends

"He is the richest man who enriches mankind most."

ABSOLUTELY FREE
TO YOU

Health or Success

A Month's Treatment
Free of Charge

This is the Opportunity
You Have Been Looking For

Promotional pamphlet for Victor Segno's *Mentalism* (Los Angeles: Inspiration Point, Echo Park, 1911).
Source: IAPSOP, www.iapsop.com.

and Affections" from his handbook *The Law of Mentalism*, which contains passages that anticipate those found in Carnegie's book. Segno writes, "if one should desire to win the affection of some particular person, I would advise him to proceed systematically to gain that desire . . . and if his thoughts are backed by sincerity, they will be accepted. . . . If he is insincere, he cannot hold the affection."[25] Segno's caveat was echoed in Carnegie's insistence that, contrary to appearances, he is not advocating flattery but rather "honest, sincere appreciation." "No! No! No! I am not suggesting flattery! Far from it. I'm talking about a new way of life. Let me repeat. *I am talking about a new way of life.*"[26] Like so much of self-help, Carnegie's quintessential slogan of American success possesses buried international origins—it may well have been inspired by an expatriated Canuck.

Though self-help appears to endorse the trope of self-making, the industry is defined by brazen textual recycling. More than a sheer manifestation of self-help's ruthlessly appropriative capitalist energies, this tendency offers a glimpse into its surprisingly collaborative textual ethos. Self-help's citation practices manifest our cultural interdependence in a manner analogous to how, according to Bruce Robbins, "reading upward mobility stories may be deviously teaching us not to be self-reliant and self-interested, as is usually taken for granted. It may be teaching us to think about the common good."[27] At its best, self-help is an extension of the advice tradition's commitment to a communal archive of human experience.

The self-improvement industry has been analyzed in a variety of academic disciplines, but its literary import has not received the attention it demands.[28] The omission is even more glaring in light of the fact that self-help guides are among the most lucrative book genres of the past thirty years, with approximately 150 new self-help titles published every week.[29] Uniting the majority of economic, historical, and sociological scholarship on self-help is the view that the industry is fueled largely by fear, anxiety, and insecurity. Although the literary angle does not disprove the influence of these motives, one of its most striking revelations concerns the affirmative impulses that compel self-help's readership. At a time when the value of literature is often called into question, self-help offers a reminder of the promises of transformation, agency, culture, and wisdom that draw readers to books.

Though reading for improvement has fallen into disfavor among academics, self-help provides a medium through which individuals can pursue self-betterment unfettered. This is, at least, one hypothesis of how the self-help compulsion came to flourish. In declining to endorse improvement as an end of reading, the professionalization of literary study, taking its cue from high-literary celebrations of impersonality and autonomy, may have inadvertently ceded an entire market to self-help.

There are other explanations, of course. Economists stress how late-nineteenth-century class mobility created new anxieties over self-presentation among the aspirational middle classes. Sociologists and scholars of religion outline the way the anomie of industrial modernity—urbanization, secularization, the division of labor—created a vacuum that self-help strove to fill.[30] Historians discuss these and others factors as part of "the turmoil of the turn of the century," which led to rise of the "therapeutic ethos."[31] But this book is about literature and, while I draw on these hypotheses throughout, I argue that the literary perspective offers crucial insight into the ongoing appeal and evolution of modern advice. The literary paradigm points to the emergence of self-help as a defense of a specific mode of reading—for agency, use, well-being, and self-change—that was being expelled from institutional spheres.

Scholars today are wringing their hands over the question of the nature of literature's influence and necessity. Self-help has no such qualms about its utility and insists on the singular appeal of literature to offer models for how to survive. Counterintuitive though it may seem to some, today it is possible to find a stronger defense of the charisma, singularity, and even autonomy of the literary in self-help than in most literary criticism. As Timothy Aubry puts it in *Reading as Therapy*, "scholars have challenged this special status [of the literary] by disputing the notion of the author as an individual genius, by treating novels and poems as if they were no different from other kinds of texts, and by analyzing them to uncover the ideological and economic forces responsible for their production. But readers outside of the academy have not surrendered their piety."[32] Likewise, Leah Price discovered in her interviews with the new breed of bibliotherapists, or what she wryly terms "biblio-baristas," that these professionals see their mission as "wresting literature out of the hands of the killjoys who make a living chaperoning booklovers' natural urges."[33] And so, rather than blithely negating the aesthetic, as some might assume, self-help has become an unlikely, vestigial sphere of literary veneration, however polemical or anti-intellectual its version of the literary may be.

AN ANCIENT PRACTICE, A MODERN INDUSTRY

This book employs a twofold understanding of self-help: on the one hand, as a historically specific cultural industry that emerged in the late nineteenth century out of all the historical factors I will address and, on the other hand, as a reading compulsion or hermeneutic that can be applied to any text from any time period. The self-help hermeneutic consists of strategically mining, collating, and adapting the textual counsel of the past for the purposes of self-transformation. While this practice finds a commercial apex in the American self-help manual, it transcends culture and genre and can be applied to the *Bhagavad Gita* or *Swann's Way*.

Although the turn of the twentieth century ushered in the rise of self-help as a full-fledged commercial genre and industry, there is no denying that the advice tradition has a much longer history. What is Boethius's *The Consolation of Philosophy* if not bibliotherapy *avant la lettre*, Ovid's *Ars Amatoria* but an ancient *Men Are from Mars, Women Are from Venus*, and Epictetus's Enchiridion if not cognitive behavioral therapy before its time?[34] Some trace the Western self-help tradition back to Cicero's *De Officiis*, but the golden age of advice is typically associated with the dissolution of the medieval church in the Renaissance, the period that saw the rise of parenting manuals such as Elizabeth Joceline's *The Mothers Legacie to Her Unborn Child* (1622) and Sir Walter Raleigh's *Instructions to His Sonne and to Posteritie* (1632), but also, as Rudolphe Bell has shown, the emergence of more contemporary-sounding guides such as sex manuals for middlebrow Renaissance Italians.[35] Most agree that the prescriptive writings of the Puritans, embodied by Cotton Mather's *Bonifacius: Essays to Do Good* (1710), laid the crucial groundwork for future, more secular advice.[36] Already in the eighteenth century such manuals inspired parodic ripostes: Joseph Alleine's 1689 *A Sure Guide to Heaven* was countered in 1751 by *A Sure Guide to Hell*, written by the devil himself.[37] As the eighteenth and nineteenth centuries progressed, the prescriptive rules of the

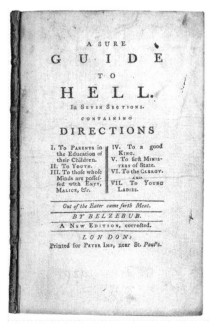

Early conduct guides: (*top*) Joseph Alleine, *A Sure Guide to Heaven*, 1689; (*bottom*) Belzebub, *A Sure Guide to Hell*, 1751.

New England settlers were translated into conduct or etiquette guides on matters such as household management, courtship, and parenthood (a prolific author of these was William A. Alcott, Louisa May's second cousin). Typically written for women and youth, these works vied with fictional novels for moral authority over readers.[38]

Self-help's seemingly indissoluble association with American nationalism is largely due to the influence of Benjamin Franklin, widely viewed as the grandfather of the field. Indeed, it will come as a surprise to precisely no one that Franklin created one of the earliest prototypes of the Western self-help manual. But this is not his *Poor Richard's Almanack*, the folksy hodgepodge of proverbs, jokes, and recipes typically cited as the genre's progenitor. Rather, it is in a passing mention in Franklin's *Autobiography* (1791) that one of the first American self-help manuals proper makes its appearance, where it is described, with just a touch of regret, as a mere might-have-been. After taking a short hiatus from his *Autobiography* to help found the United States of America, Franklin divulges his "scheme" to write a manual that, although "not wholly without religion," would not bear the marks of any particular sect. Although he claims to have jotted down a few ideas for the volume, Franklin demurely relates that some matters of private and public business have "occasioned my postponing it; for, it being connected in my mind with *a great and extensive project*, that required the whole man to execute . . . it has hitherto remain'd unfinish'd." As it could not be done today, Franklin's manual had to be put off until tomorrow, and the "great and extensive project" of self-help was introduced to America in the form of the conditional perfect—the wistful grammatical tense used for failed and aborted initiatives. "I should have called my book THE ART OF VIRTUE," he recounted,

> because it would have shown . . . that it was, therefore, every one's interest to be virtuous who wish'd to be happy even in this world; and I should, from this circumstance (there being always in the world a number of rich merchants, nobility, states, and princes, who have need of honest instruments for the management of their affairs, and such being so rare), have endeavored to

convince young persons that no qualities were so likely to make a poor man's fortune as those of probity and integrity.[39]

Franklin's précis strikingly anticipates the premise of Carnegie's *How to Win Friends and Influence People*, with its argument for the professional and economic benefits of earnest appreciation.[40] In addition, Franklin's unwritten manual provides a fitting keyhole into self-help's overlooked embroilment in speculation, imagination, the fantastical, and counterfactual: all those qualities more commonly associated with literature than with life-management guides.

Franklin's writings exemplify the way that the automatic association of self-help with rugged American individualism has obscured the industry's international prehistory. After acquiring a copy of the Latin work *Confucius Sinarum Philosophus* from his bibliophile friend John Logan in 1738, Franklin's *Pennsylvania Gazette* published a series called "From the Morals of Confucius."[41] It is these Confucius extracts, which reference "The Art of Being Virtuous," that sparked Franklin's idea for his unrealized self-help book, "The Art of Virtue." Confucius explains, "whatever is honest and advantageous, is amiable; and we are obliged to love Virtue, because it includes both these Qualities."[42] Franklin's borrowing from the sage reflected his admiration for the "industriousness of the Chinese" and his advice to his compatriots to emulate Chinese "arts of living."[43]

Through such examples, the chapters to follow complicate the engrained view that, as Steven Starker puts it, "American individualism . . . is the wellspring from which nearly all self-help materials flow" or that "the ambition to succeed," as Irving Wyllie has it, "is emphatically an American ambition."[44] As sociologist Eric Hendriks laments, "almost all research [into self-help] focuses on the US."[45] Rather than a unidirectional tool of Western imperialism, self-help emerges in this book as a crucial vector of cross-cultural exchange.

Once Franklin reluctantly put aside his manual, it took another full century for the self-help genre to gain steam. Its emergence was announced by the publication of the 1859 Victorian handbook *Self-Help:*

With Illustrations of Character, Conduct, and Perseverance by the Scotsman Samuel Smiles, who is often credited with establishing the term, although the idea of self-culture was percolating in other, lesser-known working-class improvement treatises of the day. Smiles was forced to partially self-finance his book when it was rejected by publishers, but it quickly became a colossal bestseller all over the world. In a fascinating kind of full circle, given the lineage from Confucius to Franklin to Smiles, it is reported that in 1871 Japanese samurai, who embraced the Confucian ideals, camped overnight to buy a copy of Smiles's *Self-Help*.[46]

Contrary to self-help's association with the uniquely American temperament, as Samuel Smiles exhorted, "the spirit of self-help, as exhibited in the energetic action of individuals, has in all times been a marked feature in the English character."[47] Some might be surprised to learn that the term *self-help* was popularized in the United Kingdom in guides to working-class radicalism such as G. J. Holyoake's *Self-Help by the People* (1857) and Timothy Claxton's *Hints to Mechanics on Self-Education and Mutual Instruction* (1833).[48] Although the phrase *self-help* had earlier appeared in *Sartor Resartus* by Thomas Carlyle (1834) and, in variant form, in Ralph Waldo Emerson's "Self-Reliance" (1841), it found an emissary in Smiles, whose 1859 *Self-Help* offered unprecedented proof of the market for practical advice.[49]

Due in part to the way it constellates vast networks of cross-cultural exchange, Smiles's *Self-Help* marks the beginning point of my inquiry. Espousing the Victorian tenets of industriousness, perseverance, honesty, and self-discipline, the book became an international sensation and an antecedent of the contemporary self-improvement guide. The manual discouraged working-class men from relying on institutions to secure their happiness and well-being, an argument that has contributed to its reputation as a handbook of laissez-faire liberalism, although its original politics were more radical. Smiles insisted that the self-help spirit could be found not only in the lives of famous generals, renowned authors, and celebrated inventors but also in the masses of common engineers, artisans, and day-laborers: "our progress has also been owing to multitudes of smaller and less known men."[50]

Smiles is also a logical starting point because it is in the period between the first oratorical iterations of his self-help philosophy in 1840 and his manual's eventual 1859 publication that self-help begins to assume the individualized form we know today. During these years, "what had been originally a working-class device to try to grasp some of those cultural and material benefits which were denied to them in the new industrial society, now became the middle-class reply to workers' demands for better social conditions."[51] At the same time, as I maintain in chapter 1, the particular realities of self-help's international reception do not always reinforce the genre's ideological mission.

It was only in the wake of the success of Smiles's work that self-help emerged as a formidable commercial industry—and the literary community, being in the book business, took notice. During this period, self-help authors looked upon literary entertainment with suspicion. With links to the asceticism of New England Puritanism, early self-help authors were wary of the diversion of novels, preferring to recommend biography and history. Although Victorian handbooks like Smiles's *Self-Help* were tapestries of literary anecdote and quotation, they repudiated fiction reading as a nefarious diversion. Smiles probably did more to disseminate the Western literary canon than any other author of his time, yet he also cautioned that novels could leave readers "perverted or benumbed."[52]

Fellow pedagogue William Robinson, who wrote the early handbook *Self-Education* in 1845, likewise warned readers "against contracting a taste for novel reading." He conceded that "*some* few novels or tales are worth pursuing; about one perhaps, in *two hundred*; but the chance is, whether you may happen to have that individual one thrown in your way." Due to these unlikely odds, he decided, "it will be better for you, in every respect, neither to taste, nor to handle such books."[53] In addition to its recommendations, the matter-of-fact style and tone of the self-help manual defined itself against the romance and the pomposity of fiction. In the preface to *How to Make a Living* (1875), George Eggleston proudly avers, in a typical proclamation, that "this little manual makes no literary pretensions whatever."[54]

With the arrival of the twentieth century, the growing antipathy between literature and self-help is evident in the new vehemence with which the slogan "art for art's sake" suddenly began to be brandished under the mantle of modernist autonomy, in part as a reaction to the perceived instrumentalism of the increasingly popular self-improvement handbook. But the rising cultural prominence of self-help also comes across in the use of the instructional, imperative mode by early twentieth-century novelists and poets as a literary gimmick. How many aspiring authors have purchased a copy of Gertrude's Stein's *How to Write* (1931) only to be discomfited by the book's gleeful, almost mocking, inutility? Autodidacts expecting a straightforward primer in Ezra Pound's *ABC of Reading* (1934) have no doubt met with similar degrees of perplexity. Never mind those earnest "common readers" who picked up Virginia Woolf's essay, "How Should One Read a Book?" (1925), only to then be chastised: "the only advice, indeed, that one person need give another about reading is to take no advice."[55]

Despite its robust prehistory in the early decades of the twentieth century, most assume self-help to be a mid- to late-century phenomenon.[56] This restricted understanding of self-help's provenance has led to an impoverished sense of the industry's reach and complexity. For instance, the narrow focus on self-help's late-century apex has obscured the cross-cultural exchange that was integral to the industry's development, from charismatic personalities such as Émile Coué and George Gurdjieff to the Eastern philosophy found in American handbooks such as Wallace Wattles's *The Science of Getting Rich* (1910), inspired by Hindu philosophy,[57] and Horace Fletcher's *Menticulture* (1897), which refers to Japanese culture as "a missionary of the art of true living."[58] (Fletcher also invented a faddish system of mastication, Fletcherism, that Henry James claimed, in a letter from March 15, 1910, "bedevilled my digestion to within an inch of its life."[59]) As my case studies make plain, self-help was already a major international print market in the first decades of the twentieth century, well before *How to Win Friends and Influence People* came along.

DIFFICULT WISDOM

Rather than offering an exhaustive inventory of every instance of histori-cal overlap between literature and self-help, I burrow into the moment of their most violent and radical opposition in the first decades of the twenti-eth century. It was during the early twentieth century that self-help began to more fully resemble the industry we know today; that is, it went from being a gamble in the nineteenth-century print market to a commercial juggernaut. A convergence of factors enabled the industry's coalescence at that time: the commercialization of the self-culture of the late Victorian era,[60] the rise of mass literacy spurred by nineteenth-century education legislation, the proliferation of semioccult mail-order schemes in which many self-help pamphlets originated, and, above all, the rise of the proto–New Age movement of New Thought, which marked the early twentieth century as a watershed moment for self-help.

A mind-healing movement that flourished between 1875 and 1920, New Thought argued for the universal divinity and spiritual power of all thought. It combined strains of Transcendentalism, Swedenborgism, Christianity, and Hindu philosophy to promote the individual's power to achieve health and prosperity through affirmative visualization. In the 1920s, books on what French New Thought pioneer Émile Coué called "autosuggestion" outsold those on psychoanalysis. Originally a chemist, Coué took a mail-order course in hypnotism, began seeing patients in his pharmacy and home, and eventually renounced hypnotism in favor of "suggestion," which, unlike hypnotism, could be self-induced. His teachings became known as the "New Nancy School" and attracted dis-ciples such as Roger Fry, Katherine Mansfield, and Italo Svevo. Coué's book *Self-Mastery Through Conscious Autosuggestion* instructed read-ers to repeat the affirmation "*Tous les jours, à tout point de vue, je vais de mieux en mieux*" [Every day, in every way, I'm getting better and better] twenty times in the morning and at night. It must be uttered with convic-tion, Coué instructed, and with the aid of a string with twenty knots to keep count, just as on a rosary.[61] During this time, some people, such as

Émile Coué cartoon, *The Bystander*, April 19, 1922.

the editors of *The Saturday Review*, saw Couéism as "a refreshing antidote to the heavy overdose of fashionable Freudianism from which the semi-intelligent are at present suffering."[62] New Thought's immediacy and optimism made it a more palatable alternative to Freud's dark and unsettling theories of human sexuality and desire. New Thought appeared to liberate readers from dependence on scientific authorities while also reassuring them that their unconscious desires could be funneled toward productive, even lucrative, ends.

Although self-help was no doubt abetted by the vulgarization of theories of the will and the unconscious taking place through American translations and adaptations of Freud, the first of which, by A. A. Brill, appeared in 1909, psychoanalysis, like high literature, distinguished itself from such therapies in its abstention from dispensing advice: "You are misinformed if you assume that advice and guidance in the affairs of life is an integral part of the analytic influence," Freud wrote. "On the contrary, we reject this role of mentor as far as possible . . . we require [the patient] to postpone all vital resolutions such as choice of a career, marriage, or divorce, until the close of the treatment."[63]

In light of their opposing methods, it is ironic that so many of the key concepts of psychoanalysis—for instance, the discourses of childhood trauma, self-destructive behavior, and wishful thinking—came to be absorbed and reanimated as clichés of self-help culture.[64] Though intellectuals tend to emphasize Freud's influence on modern conceptions of the self, with its infiltration of economic, corporate, advertising, and popular discourse, we have inherited New Thought's world. As professor of history Maury Klein comments, "within a remarkably short time the New Era [of the late 1920s American economy] became the application [of Coué's slogan] on a colossal scale long after Coué had been forgotten."[65]

Early twentieth-century bookstores did not yet house self-help or personal growth sections, an important aspect of the industry's complex and belated bibliographic self-identification, but they could have included such sections, which would have been well stocked with titles such as *How to Be Happy Though Married*; *The Scientific Elimination of Failure*; *Eat and Grow Thin*; *Are You You?*; *How to Analyze People on Sight*; *How to Live Life and Love It*; *The Conquest of Worry*; *It Works*; *What the Hell Are You Living For?*; *The Art of Thinking*; *Life Begins at Forty*; and far too many others to list.[66] These titles often appeared as installments of pocket philosophies such as Putnam's "handy books" and Emanuel Haldeman-Julius's Little Blue Books.[67]

As early as 1864, Charles Baudelaire's prose poem "Assommons les Pauvres" [Let Us Flay the Poor] reflected on the popularity of these early guides:

> For a fortnight I was confined to my room, and I surrounded myself with the books of the day (sixteen or seventeen years ago); I mean those volumes which treat of the art of making people wise, happy, and rich, in twenty four hours. . . . I was in a state of mind bordering on intoxication or stupidity. . . .
>
> And I went out with a great thirst. For a passionate taste for bad reading engenders a proportional need for fresh air and refreshments.[68]

Baudelaire's poetry here emerges precisely as the "fresh air" to self-help's stale nostrums, a point reinforced by Edith Wharton, Henry James, Gustave Flaubert, Flann O'Brien, James Joyce, Virginia Woolf, Samuel Beckett, and Nathanael West, who, as we shall see, defined their styles partly in recoil against self-help's instrumental materialism.

If self-help, like popular reading in general, was once premised on "a refusal of the refusal" of the aesthete, to quote sociologist Pierre Bourdieu, the aesthete's refusal has a whole new kind of cultural purchase now that the discourse of affirmation has been utterly co-opted and degraded.[69] It is because authors such as Proust, Kafka, Joyce, and Woolf refused to supply readers with the easy solutions the self-industry thought that they wanted (whether readers really wanted such facile answers is a question I address in later chapters) that modernism is now experiencing a revival as a source of useful countercounsel in our advice-saturated culture.

In recent self-help works, modernism has become an unlikely mascot for the embrace of resilience in the place of perfectionism, realism rather than "cruel optimism."[70] With their appeals to the most impractical of literary genres for advice, such guides strangely enact Marjorie Garber's contention that "the very uselessness of literature is its most profound and valuable attribute."[71] Alain de Botton's *How Proust Can Change Your Life* may be the most successful self-help reading of modernism to date, but it is far from an isolated phenomenon. In the past decade, countless self-help readings of modernism have emerged—*A Guide to Better Living Through the Work and Wisdom of Virginia Woolf*; *Why You Should Read Kafka Before You Waste Your Life*; *Ulysses and Us*; *The Heming Way*; *What W. H. Auden Can Do for You*; and *What Would Virginia Woolf Do?*[72] Together, these guides unwittingly disclose a history of generic reciprocity that literary criticism has largely overlooked.

Given our endless subjection to a barrage of unsolicited advice, the most reliable guides today appear to be the most reluctant ones. In *The 4-hour Workweek*, Timothy Ferriss turns Samuel Beckett's "fail better" quotation into an entrepreneurial catchphrase,[73] and in *The Last Self-Help Book You'll Ever Need*, Paul Persall coins the phrase "The Tono-Bungay Effect," from H. G. Wells's 1909 parody of quick-fix culture, to urge readers to resist overly credulous, compliant thinking.[74] Svend Brinkmann's recent life-management guide extols works that "lack illusions and focus on negative aspects." In particular, those difficult authors writing at the turn of the twentieth century now appear prescient for the way they expose the bad faith of the culture industry and "remind you how little control you have over your life, and also show you how it is inextricably entangled with social, cultural, and historical forces."[75]

Due to its resistance to Victorian moralism and its celebration of aesthetic autonomy, literary modernism is a canvas that brings the brushstrokes of self-help's utilitarian flourish into stark relief. Such difficult literature makes the compulsiveness of self-help to which my title refers particularly dramatic and visible. "Compulsion" is not meant to preclude the potentially generative or productive aspects of self-help reading, but refers to its undeterrable quality, its self-perpetuating persistence. Self-help reading participates in the way that "hyperbolic forms of control can bespeak their polar opposite, a deep anxiety about the chaos that seems to threaten," as Jennifer Fleissner describes compulsion.[76] Of course, modernism is neither the sole nor the most privileged object of self-help's compulsive attentions. Self-help readings of Shakespeare, Montaigne, and Jane Austen abound,[77] but the turn to modernism for advice is unique in the way that it undermines the authors' own vehemently antiutilitarian agendas. The deterrent complexity of avant-garde narrative forces readers to articulate, even reconsider, the expectations they bring to literary texts.

There is no denying that self-help appropriations of modernist insight, such as Ferriss's Beckett catchphrase, can easily be read as another depressing example of the way all gestures of negation and refusal are fated to be co-opted by the culture industry. It is with a grim irony indeed, as Raymond Williams observes, that "the painfully acquired techniques of significant disconnection are relocated" and "the isolated, estranged images of alienation and loss, the narrative discontinuities, have become the easy iconography of the commercials."[78] Self-help's preoccupation with modernism is symptomatic of the surplus desires that are not being met by commercial and conventional self-improvement discourse. These guides point to modernism's continued status as an irritation in self-help culture—and are a reminder of that culture's limits.

The rising status of literature in self-help also reflects the growing embrace of specialized knowledge in the commercial field, with guidebooks appealing to experts in science, sociology, economics, and medicine to substantiate their counsel. Authors like Carnegie drew upon the hardearned insights of intellectuals for inspiration and corroboration, but since his time the kind of knowledge self-help is invoking has only grown more technical and precise.[79] Instead of simply being set in opposition to useful generalization, the esoterica of a discipline or métier offer a resource of technical knowledge that self-help authors can translate for readers into pragmatic lessons. (This is what journalist Dwight Macdonald called the "alchemy in reverse" of popularizing abstruse works.[80]) As specialists in the most extreme and seemingly hermetic aspects of aesthetic experimentation, modernists take their place among the neurobiologists and social scientists as possessing arcane and therefore valuable knowledge about their particular literary office. Those very modernist tendencies that once made serious literature appear so elitist and remote—its hermetic linguistic experiments, disdain for mass satisfactions, and wariness of popular taste—are now its saving remnant: the key to its continued value and relevance. This is not despite but because of the fact that it is with literary modernism that the schism between commodity and aesthetic culture appears more unbridgeable than ever before. However, much like the New Critics and the poststructuralists who followed them, the modernists did not entirely eschew practical wisdom but developed a recursive, dialogic style of counteradvice.

Of course, the rise of self-help is inextricable from the issue of social class. Joan Rubin has suggested that late-Victorian self-culture invented the middlebrow as such, and this is even more specifically true of self-help.[81] Self-help played a significant but under-acknowledged role in the two key middlebrow polemics of the twentieth century: the first by Woolf in her 1932 piece on the "Middlebrow," a subset that for her was personified by her longtime adversary Arnold Bennett, who had offended her not only with his cutting reviews of her novels but also with the crudity of his practical "pocket philosophies," titles such as *How to Live on Twenty Four Hours a Day* and *Literary Taste: How to Obtain It.* As Woolf scoffs, "how dare the middlebrows teach you how to read—Shakespeare for instance? All you have to do is to read him."[82] The second middlebrow polemic for which self-help offered crucial subtext was instigated by *New Yorker* journalist Dwight Macdonald, who famously coined the pejorative "midcult." What links all of Macdonald's influential invectives against popular taste is his abiding disdain for self-help: from his 1952 contempt for Mortimer Adler's "Cashing in on Culture," to his 1954 takedown of the plague of "Howto" books invading America, to his 1960 "Masscult and Midcult" essay, which cites Norman Vincent Peale and Ella Wheeler Wilcox as examples of the midcult's "tepid ooze."[83]

As Macdonald's exasperation with the proliferating how-to guides suggests, the paperback revolution in publishing was another important factor contributing to self-help's ascent. *How to Win Friends* was an early test case of the controversial question of whether paperbacks would destroy demand for hardcovers of the same work, as some publishers feared (they did not). As a result of the success of Robert de Graff's pocket editions of Carnegie's books, publishers began developing lines of inexpensive fiction and nonfiction paperback books. Sales of pocket books rose from three million in 1939 to two hundred million in 1950.[84]

Macdonald's complaints also reflected the way that the growth of 1950s consumer culture and of that "other directedness" necessary for corporate success had abetted self-help's spread.[85] In his tirade against the "howto" mania sweeping American society during these years, Macdonald laments that "everything that was once a matter for meditation and retreat into the wilderness has been reduced to a matter of technique." He surmises that "as world issues appear increasingly hopeless of solution, people console themselves with efforts in spheres where solutions are more manageable—the practical and the personal."[86]

Although the ideas of self-help and the middlebrow used to be inextricable, as Macdonald's polemic and Aubry's *Reading as Therapy* elucidate,[87] it is increasingly the case that the omnivorous readers who peruse *The New Yorker* belong to the same educational strata as those who enjoy Elizabeth Gilbert's *Eat Pray Love*[88] or who seek therapeutic counsel from advice columnist Cheryl Strayed. Therapeutic culture offers a broader context for situating the intellectual tendency to "excoriate rather than to analyze" that has informed the reception of self-help. Both self-help and the therapeutic are thought to exacerbate the feelings of personal insufficiency and dissatisfaction upon which consumer capitalism feeds.[89] Nevertheless, this book is less concerned with self-help as a form of therapy than with self-help as an alternate *pedagogy*. Put differently, I am less interested in self-help's therapeutic agenda than in the cultural and literary labor the industry implicitly performs.

The growth of the "creative economy" in the latter half of the twentieth century has co-opted the jargon of well-being, self-optimization, and self-actualization for the liberal-managerial class.[89] Today the middlebrow stigma of self-help has been largely supplanted by corporate absorption of the wellness industry and the integration of self-care into Silicon Valley start-up culture. No longer just a pastime of the middlebrow, today we are witness to a new wave of "highbrow self-help."[90] These are "self-help books for the rest of us"[91] or, as one guidebook bluntly puts it, "life advice that doesn't suck."[92]

TRAVERSING THE JOKE

As these opening pages have outlined, self-help has a history of promoting itself as an antidote to intellectual bombast and aesthetic idealism. Conversely, serious literature has long defined itself against the instrumental pedantry of popular advice. But behind this polemical opposition, a relation of mutual intrigue and influence was also developing. The fluidity between the literature and self-help spheres is already discernable in the paratextual materials that bookended early self-help guides. Publishing houses like Henry A. Sumner & Company, which sold A. Craig's *Room at the Top, Or How to Reach Success, Happiness, Fame, and Fortune* (1883) as well as popular works of fiction, would use the same terms to promote their forthcoming novels in the endpapers as were sprinkled throughout the preceding self-help guides. For example, the novel *No Gentleman* is "The Success of the Year," while another title, *Her Bright Future*, was marketed to pique the success-hungry reader's interest.[93] Some novels would borrow from advice literature's instructional appeal, as in Peter Kyne's 1921 fictional *The Go-Getter: A Story That Tells You How to Be One*.[94] In other cases, as with James Joyce's *Ulysses* (1922), as I elucidate in chapter 4, or, later, Betty Friedan's 1963 *The Feminine Mystique*, a book would be disingenuously marketed as self-help even though this designation strayed from the text's real purpose or intention.[95] Conversely, the nebulousness of self-help, according to Viv Groskop, has enabled it to infiltrate best-seller lists under a variety of labels, a phenomenon Shinker has dubbed "self-help masquerading as 'big idea' books'": "Under the guise of modern philosophy and psychology, the self-help market has taken over the bestseller lists . . . These books are not overtly marketed as self-help, but on the sly that is what they are: they are manuals on how to live your life, and how not to."[96] In this respect, the self-help compulsion is partly an invention of the publishing industry, which encourages visual and conceptual continuity between distinct fields in their advertising materials and marketing tactics. The blurring is further intensified by internet platforms such as Amazon, in which "one and the same delivery system directs readers to *Mrs. Dalloway* as a canonical novel or as [an] arch-literary self-help book."[97]

These marketing strategies have methodological consequences, implying that the reading methods and expectations appropriate to the self-help guide can carry through to and find fulfillment in literature as well. This discursive overlap continues in the numerous how-to fictions emerging today (see chapter 6). As Mohsin's Hamid's narrator contends in *How to Get Filthy Rich in Rising Asia*, "all books, each and every book ever written, could be said to be offered to the reader as a form of self-help."[98] This is a sentiment with which the rising profession of bibliotherapist would vehemently agree.

In recent years, the field of "shelf-help" or "bibliotherapy" has exploded, spurred partly by the efforts of Alain de Botton, who opened his School of Life, an adult education center for London professionals, right next door to University College London. The School of Life produces its own publishing imprint, a series of "Toolkits for Life" on subjects from "How to Find Love" to "How to Be Bored." Another offshoot of the school is Ella Berthoud and Susan Elderkin's *The Novel Cure*, "an apothecary of literary solutions" that mines novels for advice on ailments from a stubbed toe to a midlife crisis.[99] Publishers have quickly jumped aboard the trend: Penguin Life is a new imprint marketing "authors who share a passion for living well," the UK's Yellow Kite Press has devoted itself to "books that help you live a good life," and even university publishers such as Princeton University Press are repackaging "Ancient Wisdom for Modern Readers," rebranding Cicero and Seneca in manuals such as *How to Keep Your Cool: An Ancient Guide to Anger Management*.[100] Leah Price's recent work surveys the growth of government-funded initiatives such as NHS Wales's Books Prescription program, as well as private bibliotherapy clinics catering to the "worried well off" in what she describes as "an upmarket alternative to what librarians have long done for free."[101]

The landscape has radically changed since handbooks like Smiles's and Robinson's warned against the effects of novel reading. In a striking about-face, contemporary self-help guides are commanding readers to put aside their how-to manuals and reach for fiction instead. "Read a novel—not a self-help manual or biography," advises Svend Brinkmann in his popular antiguide *Stand Firm*. "Unlike self-help books and most autobiographies," he notes, "novels present life more faithfully—as complex, random, chaotic and multifaceted."[102] This shift from the self-help industry's repudiation of novel reading to its celebration of literature's singular utility will form part of the story of the chapters that follow.

Just as contemporary self-help is becoming more interested in the practical uses of even the most rarefied fiction, novelists are growing increasingly attuned to self-help's literary potential. Where once Flaubert, Wharton, James, and Woolf looked suspiciously upon self-help's instrumental precepts, today the two fields are entertaining a cautious collaboration, as Hamid's comment indicates. A good example of this more complicated, generative literary engagement with self-help is found in Eleanor Davis's 2014 *How to Be Happy*, a graphic novel composed of vignettes that interrogate the different coping mechanisms to which modern individuals seek recourse, from self-help seminars to Prozac and biological reproduction. While the comic's serial form visualizes the repetitiveness of the self-help compulsion, its embrace of ambiguity and inconclusiveness stand in stark contrast to the self-help solutions it thematically depicts. Tightly enclosed panels juxtaposed with sprawling page bleeds dramatize the homology between life management and narrative containment.

One particular episode from the book makes this relationship explicit. In it, a character is attending a seminar led by a self-help guru for people who are unable to cry called "No Tears, No Sorrow." Attendees of the seminar are encouraged to practice crying because "without sorrow there is no joy."[103] To help them overcome their crying blockages, they are shown tragic slides of starving children, grieving family members, and dying pets. The monochrome moralism of these cartoons couldn't be further from Davis's colorful, uncontainable, and ambiguous aesthetic. In using

Page from Eleanor Davis, "No Tears, No Sorrow," in *How to Be Happy* (Seattle, Wash.: Fantagraphics, 2014), 134.

Credit: © Eleanor Davis, courtesy of Fantagraphics Books, www.fantagraphics.com.

these images to launch a metareferential commentary on the manipulative use of simplistic images in the service of ideological persuasion, Davis's comics, like most of the how-to fictions I discuss, initially appear to define themselves via their embrace of everything self-help is not.

However, there are also affinities between Davis's narrative methods and those of the self-help program. Loose hand sketches interspersed throughout her book incorporate motivational and therapeutic messages. Episodes depict with sympathy characters' quests for improvement, purity, security, community, and validation. Davis addresses her use of the mock self-help title in the front pages of her graphic narrative, where, in a considerate updating of the modernist faux primers by Stein and Pound, she cautions:

> This is not actually a book about how to be happy. I've read a lot of books about how to be happy, however, and if you're struggling, the following have been helpful to me.
>
> *Depressed and Anxious: The Dialectical Behavior Therapy Workbook for Overcoming Depression & Anxiety*
> BY THOMAS MARRA
>
> *Nonviolent Communication: A Language of Life*
> BY MARSHALL B. ROSENBERG[104]

When asked about her how-to title by interviewers, Davis begins by confessing that "the title of the book is sort of a joke because the stories in *How to Be Happy* tend not to be happy at all. They are often about people struggling to be happy and not being able to succeed. It's a painful joke. It's a joke that feels bad to make."[105] In another interview, she offers a more complex account: "I read a lot of self-help texts. I think the struggle to be happy is an important and a noble one. The stories are a pretty motley collection written over a course of seven years, but most are about the search for happiness, the desire to be our best selves, the need to connect with other people, the struggle to become good."[106]

A shifting relation to the "joke" of self-help is a common theme among contemporary writers. Hamid's *How to Get Filthy Rich in Rising Asia* began as a joke and then evolved into a more serious consideration of the self-help phenomenon.[107] This inability to maintain irony or skepticism toward popular advice discourse will sound familiar to readers of Nathanael West's *Miss Lonelyhearts*, whose protagonist stops being able to laugh when he realizes "he is the victim of the joke and not its perpetrator."[108] Flaubert, the supreme ironist, is not afraid to laugh at self-help, but the stance of superiority such humor entails is eroded by his universalizing of self-help's pathos, so that it ultimately applies to all "unfeathered bipeds"—whether autodidacts or university professors—seeking mastery and a way to pass the time.[109] The inability to laugh at self-help may be, in part, a consequence of maturity, which brings with it the realization of the precariousness of the laugher's superiority. In *Dept. of Speculation*, Jenny Offill looks back on her earlier impulse to mock those people with "their happiness maps and their gratitude journals and their bags made out of recycled tire treads." She continues, "But now it seems possible that the truth about getting older is that there are fewer and fewer things to make fun of until finally there is nothing you are sure you will never be."[110] Never that funny to begin with, the joke of the mock self-help frame, which might be akin to what Sianne Ngai has so usefully theorized as the "gimmick"— something that offends in the aesthetic because it seems simultaneously too easy and as if it is trying too hard[111]—evolves, for all of these authors, into something deeper: a manifestation of the "noble" spiritual search that consumes us all. In traversing the joke of self-help, these authors shift from satirists to accomplices in the quest for a meaningful existence.

JANUS-FACED SELF-HELP

Scholars of self-help would do well to follow the lead of contemporary authors in moving beyond automatic skepticism of the industry and recognizing, as Rita Felski puts it, that "the pragmatic . . . neither destroys nor excludes the poetic."[112] Instead, though, "between the one-sided exaltation of self-help literature on the part of authors with books to sell and the blasé rejection on the part of the intellectual elite, there is a vacuum."[113]

Self-help's ability to elicit such polarized responses may be due to its inherently "Janus-face[d]" character, as sociologist Micki McGee calls it.[114] Self-help became the target of a fairly sustained academic attack in the early twentieth century. Thinkers from Theodor Adorno to Michel Foucault have derided self-help as a form of narcissistic self-indulgence and as a "technology of the self" meant to depoliticize individuals for the sake of social control.[115] The question of whether self-help can spur subversive or revolutionary political practice has been at the core of academic debates over the genre. Scholars fall roughly into two opposed camps of critical theory and reader-response-based cultural studies.[116] In addition to Adorno and Foucault, subscribers to the former position, including T. J. Jackson Lears, Christopher Lasch, and Lauren Berlant, have been reluctant to acknowledge the idea that self-help could incite positive political change, arguing that it tends to domesticate, rather than inflame, transgressive appetites.[117] At times my research draws upon and indeed often corroborates such critiques, but it also builds upon the work of minority, feminist, and reader-response scholars who maintain that there is more to the story of self-help than its status as an index of a narcissistic, self-indulgent culture, as a force that paralyzes those it claims to help, and as an agent that fosters privatized solutions to systemic problems.

In contrast to the cultural theorists just mentioned, feminist critics, in particular, have been vocal about the genre's political potential. Following the work of Janice Radway, they have been suspicious of the scholarly construct of a passive, indoctrinated popular reader.[118] Arlie Russell Hochschild describes self-help "with optimism" as a "prepolitical stance," a view that McGee extends when she argues that "the ideas that self-improvement literature is premised on—self-determination and self-fulfillment—continue to hold political possibilities that might be tapped for a progressive, even radical, agenda."[119] Verta Taylor concurs, focusing specifically on the emancipatory potential of self-help for feminism; as she puts it, "self-help is the distinctively postmodern project that allows women to combine the tenets of feminism with the professional discourses of medicine, law, psychology, therapy, and the social sciences in the ongoing struggle to reconstitute the meaning of the female self."[120] In a comment that applies to self-help, Audre Lorde writes that "caring for myself is not self-indulgence, it is self-preservation, and that is an act of political warfare."[121] Although women are often cited as the historical victims of the cultural obsession with self-betterment, it is women critics who have most vocally defended the genre's influence, along with the working-class readers who repeatedly aver the constructive personal impact of self-help texts. Treating such positive accounts as a sign of the extent of these groups' indoctrination by the self-help ideology, rather than granting their perspectives insight into the genre's consequence, risks perpetuating self-help's own alleged co-optation of these voices.

In addition to feminist criticism, another sphere that invites a more nuanced approach to self-help is African diasporic studies, where the literature's Janus-faced status as both a necessary tool for self-reliance and a vehicle of oppressive pathologizing comes starkly into view. The status of self-help in African Anglo-American culture has been explored by scholars including Paul Gilroy and Henry Giroux and, to a degree, can be said to inform Afro-pessimism's negation of the affirmative, triumphalist, and redemptive rhetoric used to narrate black experience, such as is found in self-help. Articulating the standard critique, Giroux emphasizes the way self-help "displaces responsibility for social welfare from government to individual citizens," with the "discourses of self-help and demonization" together conspiring to pathologize and individualize the social causes of racial inequality.[122] Gayle McKeen complicates this reading by pointing out that "self-help has deep roots in and enduring importance for African-American culture. From the beginning of their life in America, blacks 'helped themselves' through church groups, secret societies, mutual aid and insurance societies, cooperative businesses, and benevolent societies."[123] Initially associated with the message of "uplift" advanced by Frederick Douglass, Booker T. Washington, and Marcus Garvey, among others, self-help became at once a tenet of black nationalist groups and, later, a motto of neoconservative African American thinkers such as Shelby Steele, Glenn Loury, and Thomas Sowell.[124] The multifaceted quality of self-help is evident in black literary engagements with the phenomenon as well, from W. E. B. Du Bois's endorsement of Emanuel Haldeman-Julius's series of self-help pamphlets, known as the Little Blue Books, which became a key resource for African American autodidacts, and for which Du Bois himself wrote two booklets,[125] to Richard Wright's calls for "self-help in negro education."[126] My final chapter addresses the tradition of African American self-help in relation to the contemporary writings of Baratunde Thurston and Terrance Hayes, but in general this book pursues a global diasporic trajectory—from the Onitsha pamphlets and Chris Abani's *GraceLand* to considering self-help's Middle Eastern, Chinese, and Japanese manifestations.[127]

Self-help has been a target not only of academic scorn but also of the public-intellectual polemicists who have extensively documented the industry's shortcomings. Todd Tiede, Wendy Kaminer, Barbara Ehrenreich, and Steve Salerno, for example, have all launched cutting invectives against the consequences of self-help's startling ascent.[128] To begin, they cite self-help's contribution to our culture of anxiety and over-work, which leads to what McGee calls the "belabored self" of modernity.[129] Even more troubling is self-help's erasure of the systemic and subsequent dampening of the people's ardor for social reform, a move with the worst consequences for the poor and disenfranchised. For instance, self-help embodies the ethos of individual accountability that must be overcome in order for the welfare state to prove its necessity. In the writings of Adorno and West, it often appears as a harbinger of the transition from democracy to fascism, a lineage that now seems a little too real in view of Donald Trump's long-standing devotion to Norman Vincent Peale's Marble Collegiate Church in Manhattan. (In *The Power of Positive Thinking* [1952], Peale advises his readers to "*always* picture 'success' no matter how badly things seem.") It is Peale whom Trump credits with instilling his "positive" outlook and unbridled confidence in the idea that he could become anything he desired.[130] Probably Ehrenreich herself could not have invented better proof that positive thinking has ruined America.

My own approach to self-help's history hinges upon an insight that is essentially sociological: that situated practice is worth pursuing as an object of inquiry regardless of whether the research authorizes this practice or not. In so doing, it builds on the dialectical understanding of self-help advanced by African American and feminist critics. Though the term *dialectic* can seem like a euphemism for a problem that is simply unresolved, it is the most apt description of my method of engaging with the Janus-faced character of self-help as both a tool of ideological oppression and a potentially productive vector of consolation, community, and self-transformation, much like many other popular media.

Without undermining the value of the anti-self-help polemics, my own focus is on the question of what *else* self-help accomplishes and what is left out of these dominant accounts of the industry. Chiefly, commentators have neglected to take account of self-help's role as a purveyor of a literary counterhistory in which reading is not cataloged according to historical period or genre but according to personal need. By examining a slew of popular self-help authors from the nineteenth century to the present day—those typically overlooked by cultural histories of the development of modern subjectivity—this book presses on the academic suspicion toward discourses of agency and self-cultivation that has until recently defined the overwhelming current of scholarship on this topic.

Self-help is a vehicle for the romance of upward mobility, but it also designates a mode of reading and appropriating the wisdom literature of the past. *Wisdom literature* may sound a little archaic to some scholars, and that is part of the point. At a time when moral humanism has fallen out of academic fashion, self-help readers and writers have become custodians of the canon of practical thought. The cultural work self-help performs is fraught with political consequence. Self-help's emulative reading methodology has a surprising political history of inspiring the formation of radical readers in countries across the globe, from U Nu, the first prime minister of Burma, who translated Carnegie's *How to Win Friends and Influence People* into Burmese, to the young Iranian feminists reading pirated copies of John Gray's *Men Are from Mars, Women Are from Venus*.[131] Far from passively assimilating capitalist values and hierarchies, readers around the world have pivoted from encounters with classic self-help texts to agitating for political independence and contributing to nationalist cultural initiatives. By putting on hold the standard critique of the genre's homogenous influence, this book is a step toward recalibrating the scales by which we measure self-help's literary and political relevance.

Of course, saying that the influence of a group of texts is universally good is as hyperbolic as saying that it is universally bad, an important reminder for humanists as well as ideology critics. For every U Nu, in other words, there is a Charles Manson, who was also apparently a Carnegie fan.[132] This inquiry suspends the question of whether self-help is inherently good or bad to explore how it is received and implemented in specific cultural contexts. In practice, most readers approach self-help relationally, and with a grain of salt. This is not to deny that self-help is guilty of all of the charges laid against it but to point out that we are reluctant to attribute to it the heterogeneous cultural influence allotted to many other cultural forms. If advertising, cinema, television, genre fiction, and comic books are worthy of nuance and attention, the same may be true of self-help. At least some of our most lauded contemporary authors, from Zadie Smith to Mohsin Hamid, believe as much.[133] Scholarship lags far behind their aesthetic considerations of the industry's global and personal consequence.

ARCHIVE OF A NONEXISTENT GENRE

Research for this book has confronted, on the one hand, an unceasing deluge of new self-help guides to everything under the sun and, on the other, complete disorder and inconsistency in cataloging procedures for archival self-help materials, many of which have been lost as a result. Gotham Books publisher William Shinker, discoverer of *Men Are from Mars, Women Are from Venus*, notes as late as 2013 that "there isn't even a category officially called 'self-help.'"[134] The nebulousness of the genre has led self-help's archive to be arbitrarily filed under psychology, religion, finance, nutrition, business, and home design.

The preservation of self-help's archive is so patchy, disorderly, and complex that two academic librarians use the New Thought movement as a case study of the challenges facing acquisitions librarians seeking to establish a new university collection. As John Fenner and Audrey Fenner note, "libraries . . . have routinely weeded their New Thought collections, treating the material as popular genre or polemical literature of passing interest." In addition, "many early volumes of New Thought periodicals have been lost through the failure of libraries to maintain continuous subscriptions or to purchase back issues."[135] Needless to say, all of these challenges facing acquisitions librarians also confront literary scholars who are conducting inquiries into this incredibly ubiquitous and yet diffuse movement.

One cannot simply type "self-help" into a finding aid with the date parameters in question and be presented with relevant material, so this research has often been guided by the bespoke archival initiatives of hobbyists, by leads in advertisements to books that can no longer be found, and by references to lecturers whose ideas were so popular and pervasive that no transcripts have been saved. It is a culture pieced together though literary allusions, correspondence course ephemera, family scrapbooks, and back-page mail-order advertisements.

Other obstacles also exist to reconstructing self-help's early circulation and reception. Among them is the fact that "the lives of most non-professional readers remain unpreserved by the archive," as Amy Blair observes.[136] Added to this is the stigma associated with self-help reading, which was typically relegated to the individual's "Secret-Shelf collection"[137] and often was not reported in surveys of reading habits.

Our current knowledge of self-help's history represents a division of labor among select sociologists, Americanists, and scholars of cultural studies and religion. The nationalized silos of academic scholarship have impeded the study of self-help's history. Specialists in American studies have written the most useful extant histories of self-help, which unsurprisingly tend to focus on an American canon, a trend that perpetuates engrained omissions of the *longue durée* cross-cultural exchange that was integral to the industry's formation. The popularity of self-help in the

United States should not obfuscate its international manifestations, which even in English exist under several designations: self-culture, aspirational culture, conduct literature, personal growth, and the literature of success. In China, where self-help dominates the shelves of local bookstores, one finds references to "chicken soup books," after Jack Canfield's popular series;[138] in France, self-help guides can be found under the headings "vie pratique" (practical life) or "développement personnel" (personal development).

Even the index of the massive *A History of the Book in America*, the ostensive birthplace of the industry, skips from "self-censorship" to "Sendak (Maurice)" with nary a mention of self-help. This omission is even more puzzling when we learn that volume four of this series, covering the years of self-help's consolidation, seeks to explain how "in our period, contending parties sought to broaden and diversify literacy training and education and to exploit new mass production technologies in order to challenge the traditional connection between books and educated elites"—precisely the causes and conditions of self-help's ascension.[139]

Literary critics and book historians have remained largely quiet on the subject of self-help, but scholars have come up with a variety of terms to describe the strategies of the aspirational reading classes: Darnton's "segmental" reading, Mortimer Adler's "action reading," Michel de Certeau's "poaching," Louise Rosenblatt's "efferent reading," and Amy Blair's "reading up."[140] The self-help compulsion bears affinities with all of these methods. In the name of pragmatism, self-help books gamely pluck passages from their historical context and implicitly encourage readers to do the same. In this respect, self-help models a mobility and textual agency that has been relegated to the margins of professional literary criticism.

THE SELF-HELP COMPULSION IN SIX STEPS (OR CHAPTER SUMMARIES)

This book's trajectory is guided in part by the temporal and geographic nimbleness of the self-help readers it describes. It impudently traverses vast terrains of time and space, like the readers it studies, finding common patterns of experience and attention in reading communities from disparate locales. I do this partly in an effort to keep up with the globetrotting history of self-help itself. Self-help is a medium in which, as Jeffrey Kenney puts it, "the Qur'an and Michel Foucault contribute to the discovery of the self," and "a motivational epigram from Gandhi can be followed a few pages later by a quote from 'Ali b. Abi Talib, and still later by one from Jean-Paul Sartre."[141]

I engage in temporal leaps as well as geographic ones. This is in part due to the uneven delays of travel and importation, as exemplified in the deferred global reception of Smiles's *Self-Help* (see chapter 1). In pursuing such leaps, *The Self-Help Compulsion* is an experiment in imagining and enacting alternatives to a strictly chronological methodology, and, to a degree, it can be aligned with the growing chorus of scholars questioning the usefulness of periodization in literary study.[142] I was spurred to adopt this approach less out of any strict methodological conviction than out of the realization that the historical and geographic dynamism of self-help would be impossible to capture through any narrowly chronological or nationalist approach. Although the brazen textual leaps and unlikely cultural connections self-help brings to view may initially feel disconcerting, I hope my readers can countenance a little bit of choppiness as a necessary induction to—and immersion in—self-help's irreverent method.

As I argue, handbooks such as Smiles's *Self-Help* and Carnegie's *How to Win Friends and Influence People* have historically operated as cultural ambassadors, introducing readers around the world to the intellectual tradition through their hodgepodge of citations. Chapter 1 introduces the cultural wormhole that is self-help's collapsing of period, nation, and genre by demonstrating the way Smiles's work specifically, and the self-help hermeneutic more broadly, were adopted and popularized throughout the world—with particular analysis of Smiles's influence in Japan, China, and Nigeria. It argues, through a concluding discussion of Tash Aw's *Five Star Billionaire*, that the patchwork, utilitarian method of the industry's early readers continues to inform self-help's global circulation.

Chapter 1 outlines self-help's overlooked cultural influence, and this influence is precisely what made the rising industry so threatening to the staunch aesthete Gustave Flaubert as early as the late nineteenth century. Flaubert's final novel, *Bouvard and Pécuchet* (1881), offers one of literary history's most merciless takedowns of the pathos of self-help's pseudo-activity, bringing the class dynamics of self-help's aspirational promises into full view. After inheriting a sudden windfall, Flaubert's middle-class characters quit their day jobs as copy clerks to move to the country and pursue their hobbies full time; they dabble in landscaping, philanthropy, canning, homeopathy, and more, always with abysmal results. Through a close reading of Flaubert's novel and its neglected guidebook intertexts, chapter 2 examines a key moment in self-help's history, when the industry shifted away from its working-class, radical origins to become a domestic pastime of the bourgeoisie. Described as a great "how not to" book, *Bouvard and Pécuchet* sets the pattern for future literary engagements with self-help discourse and practice.[143]

Chapter 3, "Negative Visualization," broadens the focus to survey a variety of early twentieth-century responses to self-help's consolidation into a formidable textual industry. In particular, I revisit Henry James's "The Jolly Corner" (1908), Virginia Woolf's *Mrs Dalloway* (1925), Edith Wharton's *Twilight Sleep* (1927), and Flann O'Brien's *The Third Policeman* (1939) to lay bare the commitment to unsettling early self-improvement axioms that underlies these authors' diverse textual pedagogies. Though the rarified ambitions of these novelists seem diametrically opposed to self-help's instrumental materialism, I suggest that they both sprang from similar efforts to cope with the competition and overstimulation of urban experience. Moreover, each movement was responding to the other's version of textual counsel, and I argue that it is impossible to fully understand the pedagogic impetus of either the modern novel or self-help without reference to the competing movement's didactic and philosophic practice.

Chapter 4, "Joyce for Life," uncovers a tradition of populist commentators who advocate approaching James Joyce's *Ulysses* as nothing less than a self-help manual. Like Joyce's populist critics, the characters in

Ulysses read books not for pure aesthetic enjoyment but for practical use. The problem of reading for use versus for appreciation was a hotly contested issue in Ireland during Joyce's day. This chapter uses Joyce's oeuvre to reveal self-help reading methods as a continuum that unites critics and lay readers, entrepreneurs and aesthetes, politicians and revolutionaries.

Chapter 5, "Modernism Without Tears," explores three unlikely examples of the convergence of high, serious literature and self-help: first, Alain de Botton's and Theodor Adorno's surprisingly complementary readings of Marcel Proust; second, the interpretations of Nathanael West's experimental story *Miss Lonelyhearts* by practicing advice columnists Dear Abby and Ann Landers; and third, readings of Samuel Beckett as a model for corporate creativity. I ask what happens when modernism meets with contemporary readers who refuse to accept its antididactic pose.

The piecemeal methodology of self-help's early readers around the world, who mined authors from Shakespeare to Ibsen for their practical insights, has become a structural device of the contemporary fiction of Mohsin Hamid, Tash Aw, Sheila Heti, Charles Yu, and more, as I address in chapter 6. These authors are attracted to the self-help focalization for precisely what previous authors disliked—the way it implicates the reader in the story being told. Contemporary novelists have caught on to the point made by one of the readers in Simonds's study of self-help for women: "With the novel, you can forget yourself a little bit, it's like watching a movie. . . . The self-help book is piercing right into you. . . . You're always—you're reading the book—but you're looking at the book separately and objectively, saying, 'How does this impact on me?' "[144] These authors continue the critiques of self-help that Flaubert and his modernist successors began, but they resist the stance of superiority, impersonality, and disinterestedness that earlier authors adopted toward the industry. For them, self-help becomes a vehicle for posing important questions about how to most fully embody and appreciate transient experience.

The novels and works of self-help discussed in this book offer a new textual genealogy of modern selfhood that departs from received, canonized, intellectual histories. My alternate history does not begin with the "father of evolution," Charles Darwin, but with his market rival Samuel Smiles, the father of self-help; it focuses less on Sigmund Freud than on the contemporaneous positive thinking pioneer Émile Coué; not on Chinua Achebe but on the lesser-known self-help pamphlets that came out of Onitsha, Nigeria, in the 1960s. This alternate genealogy describes individuals who repeatedly affirm the transformative agency of the text. Such a reframing of intellectual history and unsettling of orthodox reading and pedagogy is what the study of self-help can open up, particularly when it moves beyond stale and polarizing polemics regarding the industry's neoliberal influence. Particularly germane to those of us in the teaching professions is self-help's unwavering pedagogical optimism; from attractiveness to taste and charisma, there is nothing that cannot be taught.

1

SELF-HELP'S PORTABLE WISDOM

A "THIN CULTURE"

When discussing self-help, intellectuals tend to begin with the bad: self-help as an instrument of neoliberal governance, a tool of systemic oppression, or an agent of colonial subjection. For a change, this chapter begins with the good. In addition to being a "technology" used to discipline citizens and manage populations (see Foucault and Rimke),[1] self-help has historically served another, curatorial function: to mine, collate, and reorganize the archive of textual counsel for the purposes of inspiring self-transformation. If the literary text is a "tissue of quotations,"[2] then the self-help book is even more so. The genre's manic citational practice is already operative in the case of Samuel Smiles's 1859 *Self-Help*, the central case study of this chapter, which uses quotations from authors as various as William Shakespeare, John Milton, John Keats, Walter Scott, John Ruskin, and John Stuart Mill, and it carries through to Dale Carnegie's zealous collating of the life advice of thinkers from Sigmund Freud to John Dewey, Dorothy Dix, William James, and Lin Yutang. As I'll show, Smiles's *Self-Help* offers a keyhole into self-help's embroilment in translation, popularization, and canon formation. In a striking example of self-help's cultural authority, countless readers in Britain and beyond first encountered the classic literature of the West through Smiles's Victorian handbook. In late nineteenth-century Meiji Japan, for example, *Self-Help* was so influential that the authors it praised became instant sensations, whereas the authors it neglected to mention remained largely untranslated.[3]

Patricia Neville laments that "perhaps one of the most glaring omissions from the self-help book canon has been the absence of globalization, either as a theorizing construct or operational framework against which we could chart, plot, and measure the breadth and width of contemporary self-help book culture."[4] In the interest of redressing this gap, I have assembled a motley community of readers who have used self-help texts such as Smiles's as occasions to articulate a critical perspective of Western modernity's key tenets. Early self-help, and the patchwork, didactic hermeneutic it advocates, defined individuals' first experiences with literary works and acquired the status of a gateway to cultural literacy around the world. Self-help's globalized presence has only intensified over time. *New York Times* writer Azadeh Moaveni observes that, in Iranian bookstores, "self-help books and their eclectic offshoots, on topics like Indian spirituality and feng shui, enjoy the most prominent position."[5] In Egypt, notes Jeffrey T. Kenney, the self-help industry has grown "dramatically" since 2000, with both Islamic self-help authors and translations of works by Carnegie, Tony Robbins, and Rhonda Byrne, among many others, stocked on local shelves.[6]

Research into self-help's global reception reveals that "culture in action"[7] does not operate through a unilateral movement from source to recipient—as reception theory traditionally claimed—but through a complex and ongoing process of negotiation, qualification, and selection. Sociologist Paul Lichterman proposes the term *thin culture* to describe the "shared understanding" among self-help readers that "the words and concepts put forth in these books can be read and adopted loosely, tentatively, sometimes interchangeably, without enduring conviction."[8] In opposition to accounts of the genre's homogeneous neoliberal influence, he explains that we should not "assume in advance that we know how strong or how unified an ideological message it is that self-help book readers read out of

Self-help books in a street market in old Delhi.
Credit: Leah Price, 2018.

their books, nor that they are passive receivers of what "ideologies" they may read out."[9]

The self-help hermeneutic binds this global community of utilitarian readers, whose first encounters with such popular manuals often occur at critical historic junctures when traditional cultural values are upended.[10] To give just a few examples, self-help activity spiked in Japan following the 1867 collapse of the Tokugawa shogunate, which created an urgent demand for shortcuts to the modernization that the country had closed itself off from for over two hundred years; it flourished in Ghana and Nigeria in the years leading up to independence (1957 and 1960, respectively); and it is exploding today in the post-socialist People's Republic of China, where the ideology complements the society's intensely competitive market economy.[11] It would be easy to bemoan self-help's influx during such transitional periods as the opportunism of Western capitalism inserting itself into a vulnerable and impressionable populace. Yet for such nonsynchronous communities of readers, self-help culture is not received in the form of a monolithic and authoritarian ideology to replace the political ones only just overcome, but adopts the portable, objectified status of an "objet trouvé."[12]

It is time to bring together the wealth of sociological data regarding self-help reading practices around the world, practices that raise germane issues of bibliography, reception, circulation, and cultural exchange, and to place this data in conversation with literary studies. In this chapter, I argue that Smiles's *Self-Help* initiated a pattern of cultural transmission through self-help literature that continues to be strong into the present day. The book's reception furnishes a portal onto the mechanisms of literature's transmission through vernacular genres around the globe. Self-help not only transmits literary culture but also introduces an element of taxonomic confusion into preexisting institutional bibliographic arrangements. This unsettling of generic and cultural classifications implemented by self-help's early readers has become a formal strategy of contemporary novels, or what I call "how-to fictions," and is exemplified by Tash Aw's *Five Star Billionaire* (2013), the subject of this chapter's concluding sections. Hybridized novels like Aw's reveal that the pastiche methodology of self-help's first readers has become a mainstream conceit of contemporary novelists. Self-help has become a transmedia industry that implicates us all—aesthetes and entrepreneurs, critics and lay readers—in its expanding cultural matrix.

THE SMILES HEARD ROUND THE WORLD

When Smiles self-financed *Self-Help* in 1859 (the same year Charles Darwin's *On the Origin of Species* appeared), it quickly became an international sensation even though, Smiles confessed, "there was nothing in the slightest degree new in this counsel, which was as old as the Proverbs of Solomon, and possibly quite as familiar."[13] Samurai in Japan reportedly camped out overnight to buy a copy, earning *Self-Help* the moniker "The Bible of the Meiji."[14] And Smiles loved to recount that the khedive of Egypt inscribed his maxims on his harem walls, right beside lines from the Qur'an.[15]

The choppy structure of Smiles's text, composed of more than three hundred biographical sketches, maxims, and anecdotes, invited the portable, serendipitous reading methods more commonly associated with biblical *sortes* (chance selections of the Bible). But perhaps the most striking feature of Smiles's text is its unabashed reliance on very long and tedious lists that rival anything found, for example, in Joyce's *Ulysses*. *Self-Help* includes endless catalogs of successful men (only men) who rose from obscure origins to achieve professional recognition:

> The common class of day-laborers has given us Brindley the engineer, Cook the navigator, and Burns the poet. Masons and bricklayers can boast of Ben Johnson, who worked at the building of Lincoln's Inn, with a trowel in his hand and a book in his pocket, Edwards and Telford the engineers, Hugh Miller the geologist, and Allan Cunningham the writer and sculptor; whilst among distinguished carpenters we find the names of Inigo Jones the architect, Harrison the chronometer-maker, John Hunter the physiologist, Romney and Opie the painters, Professor Lee the Orientalist, and John Gibson the sculptor.[16]

Contemporary readers may be incredulous that a book so popular could contain so many dry and lengthy catalogs. But Smiles's readers found these inventories anything but dull; their sheer quantity intensified and substantiated *Self-Help*'s thrilling promises of upward mobility. Smiles's emulative heuristic, which resonated so forcibly around the world, is communicated as much through the book's form as through its content. Indeed, self-help's almost mystical veneration of the transcendent power of the list to conjure one's desires is already germinating in Smiles's inventories. This power of the list eventually came to be exploited by cult best-sellers such as R. H. Jarrett's 1926 "little red book" *It Works*, which guides readers toward making their "dreams came true" through the composition of successive lists of their goals that they are then instructed to review and repeat several times a day.[17] From Franklin's list of virtues to Smiles's inventories to Reddit's listsicles, the list has become a staple of self-help discourse.

Though Smiles's book helped to lay the groundwork of the contemporary improvement handbook, it was also very much a product of the self-culture of its time, whose other proponents included G. J. Holyoake's *Self-Help by the People* (1857) and Timothy Claxton's *Hints to Mechanics on Self-Education and Mutual Instruction* (1833), among others.[18] Although self-help is typically assigned Anglo-American origins, an important precedent being John Lillie Craik's 1830 *The Pursuit of Knowledge Under Difficulties, Illustrated by Anecdotes*,[19] two of Smiles's most influential models were French: Louis Aimé-Martin's *Education des Meres de Famille* [*The Education of Mothers*] (1840) and Baron de Gérando's *Du Perfectionnement moral, ou de l'Éducation de soi-même* [*Self-Education: Or the Means and Art of Moral Progress*] (1833), which was also a key influence on the New England transcendentalists.[20] In addition, as Vladimir Trendafilov's careful genealogy indicates, the phrase "self-help" had precedents in the writings of Carlyle and Emerson, and likely was coined in an editorial by Smiles's predecessor Robert Nicoll in the *Leeds Times* of September 3, 1836.[21]

Self-Help's serial pedagogy and investment in the drama of upward mobility found parallel expression in the Victorian *Bildungsroman* which sometimes extended (*Adam Bede*) and sometimes parodied (*Great Expectations*) Smiles's approach.[22] But one of many significant differences between *Self-Help* and the period's fiction concerns their opposing stances on the aesthetic merit of failure. Early critics of Smiles's book objected to its focus on men who have succeeded and its neglect of those who have floundered: "Why should not Failure," they asked, "have its Plutarch as well as Success?" Smiles responded: "Readers do not care to know about the general who lost his battles, the engineer whose engines blew up, the architect who designed only deformities, the painter who never got beyond daubs,"[23] a point that key practitioners of the novel genre, such as Gustave Flaubert and George Eliot, seemed determined to disprove.

For this reason, Victorianists often read Smiles's book as a foil for the period's success-wary fiction. A striking example of this dynamic is Dickens's "anti-Cinderella story," as Jerome Meckier calls *Great Expectations*, which is read as an inquiry into the moral quandaries and inevitable disappointments raised by the dramatic social ascent *Self-Help* promises. Tellingly, as Meckier notes, *Self-Help* sold twenty thousand copies in its first year, compared to the 3,750 copies sold of *Great Expectations*.[24] Smiles's sales "far exceeded those of the great nineteenth-century novels," Asa Briggs observes.[25] There are numerous intriguing examples of rivalry and exchange between Smiles's *Self-Help* and the period's fiction, but a lesser-known Smiles rebuttal is found in H. G. Wells's 1894 story "The Jilting of Jane," about a servant girl whose fiancé William, a second porter in a draper's shop, reads a copy of "'Smiles' 'Elp Yourself'" given to him by his employer, which inspires him to adopt the posture of a gentleman and abandon his promise to poor Jane in favor of a better match with a piano-playing milliner.[26]

Many are quick to point out that modern-day self-help bears little in common with the Victorian ethos espoused by the genre's Scottish forefather. Unlike most contemporary self-help handbooks, Smiles advocated prosaic labor above magical solutions and extolled hard work in the name of civic progress rather than material gain. In a recent biography, John Hunter asks, "What significance has Smiles's work in generating the self-help movement so pervasive today?" He concludes that "a quick examination of the titles on Amazon (and there are thousands) suggests the answer 'not much.'"[27] The character ethic *Self-Help* promotes initially seems worlds apart from the culture of personality that informs contemporary commercial advice. Smiles argued that "we must seek elevation of character without which capacity is worthless and worldly success is naught."[28] Rather than affirming the remoteness of Smiles to the contemporary industry, however, deeper comparison reveals the extent to which

Victorian values of character and perseverance, for example, continue to inform self-help culture in ways that scholars of consumer culture have neglected to fully recognize. David Brooks's *The Road to Character*, Daniel Pink's *Drive*, and Malcolm Gladwell's *Outliers* all, in different ways, extend the neo-Victorian celebration of character, perseverance, and determination.[29] Such correspondences go a long way toward complicating Warren Susman's characterization of modernity as a shift from "character" to "personality."[30] Explaining the emergence of neo-Victorian self-help discourse in the late twentieth-century United States, Alison Booth reads the renewed interest in self-help as part of a "conservative revival" of the Victorian celebration of "rules" and personal accountability. She urges, "while Victorianists have been doing what they want with cultural studies lately, cultural studies would do well to recall the Victorians, to add historical dimensions beyond the decades of the twentieth century and to glance across the Atlantic."[31]

This lineage between Smiles's work and contemporary self-help merits consideration. Smiles's writings give voice to the anti-institutional energies that continue to impel self-help's program. For example, he vehemently repudiated the practice of competitive examinations. As Lauren Goodlad notes, he "insisted on the 'thoroughly demoralizing' effects of 'cramming' for examinations," and he warned against the deleterious effects of leaving "so 'little room left' for 'free' mental action."[32] Even as a child Smiles bristled against academic orthodoxies. He recalls, of a formative clash with a school librarian, "when I took out Gibbon's Decline and Fall, he havered a bit to me in his dictatorial way, as to how I was to read it. I did not like this, and went to other libraries."[33]

Smiles's first advice book was a manual for mothers on childrearing, which contains the seeds of his bias against compulsory learning. It argued that children's physical health was being neglected in the service of forced studies and forced labor. According to Hunter, Smiles's early foray into parental guidance was overshadowed by a much better book on the same subject that appeared at the same time—Dr. Combe's *Treatise on the Physiological and Moral Management of Infancy*—which left Smiles with the final hundred unbound copies that he gave away to a London bookseller. In fact, *Self-Help* was in Smiles's mind a mere side-project and diversion from his more important biographies of engineers and cotton spinners; he reportedly tore up the pages of the original *Self-Help* manuscript to use as waste paper.[34] His private correspondence suggests that Smiles interpreted *Self-Help*'s success not as the beginning of a new and lucrative trend but largely as heartening proof of a potential market for his beloved biographies of engineers. He wrote, "the men who have most moved the world have not been so much men of genius, strictly called, as men of intense mediocre abilities and untiring perseverance."[35] Smiles enjoyed the aesthetic challenge posed by seemingly quotidian subjects; such pedestrian material demanded a deft rhetorical touch. This inclination predates literary modernism's use of average people and the mundane as occasions for extravagant displays of aesthetic prowess. No less a writer than Ford Madox Ford described Smiles's *The Life of a Scottish Naturalist* in 1924 as "*sui generis* the most beautiful book in the world."[36]

Scholars have squabbled and split over the problem of how to reconcile Smiles's socialist and conservative inclinations: his advocacy of working-class autodidacts and his defense of some of the most pernicious tenets of laissez-faire governance. "Far from poverty being a misfortune," he wrote, "it may, by vigorous self-help, be converted into a blessing."[37] Smiles's reputation as an apologist for free market capitalism was cemented by a business edition of *Self-Help* endorsed by Margaret Thatcher's education secretary, Sir Keith Joseph, in 1986, that excised the text's more socialist leanings.[38] At the same time, as many have pointed out, Smiles was a Scottish-born radical whose book began as lectures to the society for working men in Leeds after Smiles came to see that no working-class politics would be possible without a solid grounding in self-education. According to intellectual historian Jonathan Rose, *Self-Help* had a catalyzing effect on scores of working-class readers when it first appeared:

> Smiles's fans included Labour MPs William Johnson and Thomas Summerbell. Ramsay Macdonald enjoyed his biographies of working-class

naturalists. Even A. J. Cook, who became a Communist miners' leader, started out with *Self-Help*.[39]

But Rose's favorite example is George Gregory (b.1888), who came from an illiterate mining family and was introduced to Smiles's book by a clerk. Smiles's stories of men who rose, as Gregory put it, "phoenix-like from the ruins of their plans and the collapse of their expectations to find a way to success" stirred ambitions which he channeled into educating himself in the history of religion and capitalism. Gregory went on to become "a socialist, a trade union organizer, a Co-operative society manager, an anti-war activist, a branch secretary for the Workers' Educational Association and for the League of Nations Union, a Congregational minister and the owner of more than a thousand books." Rose notes, "That is what *Self-Help* set in motion."[40]

The list of political readers *Self-Help* set in motion outside Britain is even more impressive: the first Nigerian president, Nnamdi Azikiwe, a socialist whose life story "owes more in outline to Horatio Alger or Samuel Smiles than Karl Marx";[41] the Iranian senator, author, and scholar Ali Dashti, who translated *Self-Help* into Persian in 1926 and commented that the book "shook me up, tore me away from the sleep, idleness, lack of obligations, and laziness";[42] and the Korean historian, poet, and independence activist Ch'oe Namson, who published serialized Korean translations of Smiles's text, work that in turn influenced his drafting of the 1919 Korean Declaration of Independence.[43]

One particularly enthusiastic reader was Jurji Zaidan (1861–1914), a prominent Arab nationalist author of the early twentieth century, whose intellectual trajectory was galvanized by the "enthusiastic impact" of Smiles's book.[44] Zaidan went on to become "the most productive and versatile Arab writer of modern times."[45] He read Ya'qub Sarruf's "wildly popular" 1880 translation of Smiles's book,[46] and he described the effect of these inventories on an ambitious Syrian youth such as himself:

> I had read parts of the book *The Secret of Success* which Dr. Sarruf had translated into Arabic. Vigor and zeal sprang up in me. I read, as I said, some of it

but was unable to finish the rest. Too great was the enthusiastic impact it had upon me to read about the lives of men who reached highest achievements by their own diligence and efforts and selfreliance. Amongst them, barbers and shoemakers, servants, artisans and maids who rose through their eagerness and vigilance to the station of great people. If I read a few pages I would be so agitated that I could not sleep any longer or be calm, and, finding myself tied down, pity would overcome me and I would get depressed. So I would put the book aside and till today I have not finished reading it.[47]

As Donald Reid explains, like Zaidan, Smiles's translator Sarruf was also a Syrian Christian, and he was the first to translate Smiles's book into Arabic, in 1880. He attempted to make Smiles's tales more palatable to a Middle Eastern audience by inserting indigenous rags-to-riches stories into his translation. Smiles's stories likely appealed to Syrian Christians because of the way they valorized the types of professions such as merchants and shopkeepers to which the Christian minority was relegated as a result of being excluded from more prestigious Muslim offices in government and bureaucracy. Reid comments:

The British American success story, with its stress on individual initiative and free enterprise, was made to order for the Syrian Christian entrepreneur. It expressed in a bold and highly developed ideology thoughts he had long felt instinctively. For generations he has been instilling in his children the delicate mixture of shrewdness and ambition, industry and thrift necessary for financial success in the few careers open to them. In the late nineteenth century, when he encountered the Western rags-to-riches story which extolled these same virtues, he eagerly made it his own.[48]

Though he may have been inspired by Smiles to pursue his education, *Self-Help* (or *The Secret of Success*, as he knew it) did not make Zaidan uniformly accepting of westernization or modernization. After medical school, he went on to found one of the oldest arts and culture journals in the Arab world, الهلال (*Al-hilal*: "The Crescent" magazine), and he became a vocal proponent of pan-Arabic nationalism who "attacked the British repeatedly in the pages of his magazine for their language policy," which aimed to replace Arabic with English as the language of business and instruction.[49]

Smiles's African readers were similarly selective about the messages they adapted from his text. Stephanie Newell describes how *Self-Help* "was listed by West African schoolchildren as a 'favourite book' in the 1930s and quoted extensively by local authors in order to justify their writing activities." The locals may have internalized Smiles's ethic of self-culture, but Newell contends that they "were interpreting and utilising 'western' education, English literacy, mission Christianity, and colonial power structures for their own ends."[50]

An important example of the selective agency enacted by Smiles's early readers is their circumvention of his warnings against novel reading. Smiles cautioned that "the habitual novel-reader indulges in fictitious feelings so much, that there is great risk of sound and healthy feeling becoming perverted or benumbed."[51] However, rather than heed his injunction to eliminate novels, most of his disciples interpreted this admonishment as an invitation to approach narrative with a didactic prism, an approach encouraged by their mission educations. By 1935, Newell explains,

> students from mission schools had been trained to interpret all fiction as "helpful" and edifying, to seek didactic plots and moral advice in secular as well as religious novels. In the students' view *Morte d'Arthur* is as much a "penny-helpful" as *What a Young Woman Ought to Know* and *How to Catch a Girl*. Clearly, these readers have been trained to regard all "good" literature as self-helping, moral and useful, and to select favourites on that basis.[52]

In their treatment of every work of literature as a "penny helpful," whatever its provenance or intentions, the zealously prescriptive reading protocols of these Ghanaian pupils anticipate today's "bibliotherapy boom," as Leah Price calls it.[53]

To be sure, other accounts of Smiles's colonial influence are considerably less enthusiastic. The self-help reader's leveling of the discourses of novel and handbook is depicted in V. S. Naipaul's *A House for Mr Biswas* (1961), which coins the term "Samuel Smiles depression" to describe the effect of Smiles's book on the protagonist:

> [Mr. Biswas] had bought one of [Samuel Smiles's] books in the belief that it was a novel, and had become an addict. Samuel Smiles was as romantic and satisfying as any novelist, and Mr. Biswas saw himself in many Samuel Smiles heroes: he was young, he was poor, and he fancied he was struggling. But there always came a point where resemblance ceased. The heroes had rigid ambitions and lived in countries where ambitions could be pursued, and had a meaning. He had no ambition, and in this hot land, apart from opening a shop or buying a motorbus, what could he do?[54]

Biswas confuses *Self-Help* for a novel and is never fully disabused of this "mistake." After all, the genres invoke the same narrative tropes: identification, heroic struggle, and resolution through happy social integration. For Naipaul, the power of self-help's narrative arc hit close to home; the character of Mr. Biswas was based on his father, Seepersad, a journalist whose writing—and career—were modeled after Smiles's blueprints for success.[55]

In a fairly straightforward depiction of the way self-help depoliticizes and privatizes social inequity, Mr. Biswas admonishes himself with "What would Samuel Smiles think of him right now?" when he feels overwhelmed by circumstance. At the same time, as Nehring and his coauthors explain, there is a self-help culture indigenous to Trinidad and Tobago, where *Mr Biswas* is set, that is different although not entirely antithetical to the Anglo-American style of self-help associated with Smiles. They write of "longstanding forms of self-help in Trinidad and Tobago" such as the indigenous historic cultures of "sou sou (community savings) gayap (informal housing) and 'lend hand.' " They continue:

> Self-help has a long history and importance locally as a practical solution for many low-income families in the Caribbean, including Trinidad and Tobago. It was a solution to the needs of certain populations rather than waiting for nascent or absent state organizations to assist. And while this notion of self-help is not the same definition of self-help travelling in the therapeutic discourses arriving from the Global North, the two do share some elements, including a vision of independence, self-determination and self-respect. Furthermore, the traditional local understanding of self-help and the more contemporary transnational definition do meet here and elsewhere in the region.[56]

Sociologist Lichterman has explained how self-help's "thin culture" operates not as a uniform world system but through readers' continual negotiation and qualification of self-help's ideology vis-à-vis other moral systems prevalent in their cultural environments. Self-help's portable ethic is even more apparent when tracing its global circulation. As this circulation reveals, self-help's practical pedagogy had long-standing antecedents in the cultures into which it was imported. For example, in West Africa, Smiles's "promotion of achievement through hard work and through the emulation of great men and women meshed perfectly with Akan conceptions of the self-made individual."[57] In Japan, "Smiles's concept of a gentleman [was seen] as essentially identical to the Confucian-samurai ideal," whereas in Iran, Dashti's translation of Smiles extended the "urge to instruct" that informed the Persian literary tradition.[58] In these cases, the intermingling of ancient and modern advice traditions, often inseparable from the violence of the imperial encounter, resulted in new, nonelite reading practices. As the following brief excursion into the case of the Onitsha Market pamphlets makes clear, enterprising readers around the world strategically appropriated Anglo-American improvement discourse for personal, political, and aesthetic ends.

THE "MASTER OF LIFE"

The pattern of global knowledge transfer that Smiles helped to initiate applies to his self-help disciples, such as Dale Carnegie, as well. It is possible to trace a direct line from Smiles to Carnegie via the mediating figure of Orison Swett Marden, one of Carnegie's most important idols. Marden was a tremendously prolific early American self-help author who penned best sellers such as *Pushing to the Front or Success Under Difficulties* and *The Conquest of Worry*, and also founded *Success* magazine in 1897.[59] Marden himself enacted the quintessential "rags-to-riches" trajectory; he grew up an orphan and credited his rebirth as a self-improvement author with his chance discovery of Smiles's *Self-Help* in the attic of a household where he was employed as hired help. He wrote that "the little book was the friction which awakened the spark sleeping in the flint."[60] Marden, in turn, "played a central role in [Dale] Carnagey's writings on public speaking, where he was frequently quoted and fulsomely praised," and introduced Carnegie to the American New Thought tradition, which would prove formative to Carnegie's self-help philosophy.[61]

By 1954, Carnegie's American popularity and method had so escalated that *New Yorker* journalist Dwight Macdonald could lament, "the country is in the grip of a howto mania comparable to the dancing mania that swept over Europe in the fourteenth century. There has always been something in the American soul that responds to the howto book."[62] However, closer examination reveals that the period's how-to hysteria extended well beyond the borders of the United States and allows us to redress "self-help's understudied transnational presence in a globalized world."[63]

For example, noticing the same "howto mania" in Nigeria in 1964, not long after Macdonald published his invective, Chinua Achebe describes his nation's preoccupation with turning all literature into "a how-for-do" book, as it is called in Nigerian pidgin, a trend that extends to the region's intellectuals, whom Achebe ruefully describes as too busy with self-improvement to bother much about fiction. He recounts receiving a letter from an earnest youth from northern Nigeria who related that "your novels serve as advice to us young," and another reader from Ghana complained that "there were no questions and answers" appended to Achebe's novel *Things Fall Apart*.[64] Stephanie Newell describes the prevalent view that "reading for personal achievement rather than for fantasy or pleasure, Africans have what T. Gyedu terms a 'textbook mentality,' selecting educational texts in the hope of acquiring knowledge for social or professional advancement."[65] Rather than turn up his nose at this utilitarian reading impulse, however, Achebe noted the link between this how-for-do mania and the moral messages of Hausa folktales, averring his commitment to an "applied art" that does not shirk the project of national "re-education" and "regeneration." If you think the didactic message of self-improvement is "naïve," Achebe wrote in 1965, "then you cannot know very much about Africa."[66]

At the same time, for authors who had rallied for the right to aesthetic autonomy and disinterestedness, the self-help hermeneutic could feel oppressively regressive. Kenyan author Ngũgĩ wa Thiong'o articulates this counterperspective in his memoir when he described the composition of his first short story, "My Childhood," which he eagerly shared with Kīmani Mūnyaka, an acquaintance who had a reputation for being well read. This reputation stemmed from the fact that Kīmani never went anywhere without his books. However, Ngũgĩ was soon disillusioned to discover that these books Kīmani so faithfully transported were both by Dale Carnegie: *How to Make Friends and Influence People* and *How to Stop Worrying and Start Living*. He describes his peer's hermeneutic: "Kīmani had a habit of reading a text, restating it in his own words, and then reinterpreting it by quoting instances from the same passage. His advice was always through quotes or paraphrases from this guru of wisdom, achievement, and success." Eventually, Ngũgĩ decided to avoid Kīmani because "I really did not want to hear my story being used as a bridge to Carnegie."[67]

Self-help's circulation in the Global South is of course inseparable from the violent history of colonial hegemony. Ever since the late nineteenth-century spread of British mission schools, which trained students to mine literature for moral messages, the self-help hermeneutic has been used by imperial powers to domesticate and discipline indigenous peoples.

Like other imports such as the bildungsroman (Esty) and the spaghetti western (Jaji),[68] self-help's African appropriations manifest "a continual process of working through European categories in order to displace them from the locus of their original signification."[69] Its reception is marked by the "doubly anxious yet nonetheless fervent aspiration" that Karin Barber associates with the broader field of African "tin-trunk literacy," or the effort to improve oneself through immersion in newspapers, diaries, self-help books, book clubs, and other discourses.[70] In this way, the study of self-help's international circulation touches upon concerns that have long occupied colonial scholars regarding the agency and paradoxes of cultural appropriation (e.g., Bhabha and Tiffin).[71]

Perhaps the most striking example of this strategic and creative use of self-help discourse is found in the Onitsha Market pamphlets, a didactic pidgin literature named after the famous open-air market in the Igbo-speaking region of southeastern Nigeria where they were produced and sold by locals from the 1940s until the Nigerian Civil War (1967–1970) destroyed most of the physical market. Onitsha was a historic site of commerce on the banks of the Niger River that had "always attracted the exceptional, the colorful and the bizarre," as Achebe writes.[72] The Onitsha pamphlets were produced on local printing presses and composed in pidgin English by authors who usually held day jobs as taxi drivers, guitar players, and schoolboys. With titles including *Why Harlots Hate Married Men and Love Bachelors*, *How to Avoid Corner Love and Win Good Love from Girls*, and *Money Hard to Get but Easy to Spend*, these "brochure masterpieces" were grounded in Igbo oral traditions but were inspired by the "howto mania" in the West.[73] Although the pamphleteers were channeling the parabolic style of authors like Carnegie and Smiles, the "high life" artistic culture they created was far from sententious: "It is a way of life that believes in pleasure, music, drinking, free love, and the ostentatious spending of money" and that promoted the movements of Africanization and nationalization.[74]

One of the more prolific Onitsha pamphleteers, Okenwa Olisah, who humbly dubbed himself "Master of Life," offers his readers the advice that

"No condition is permanent, in the world but fools do now know . . . One could rejoice in the morning and cry in the afternoon . . . because things are not what they seem, and life you see, is nothing but an empty dream," along with more prosaic warnings such as "it is one of the greatest mistake to marry a wrong somebody."[75] The chapbooks included collage images from American popular culture, vibrant cartoons drawn in the style of African folk art, lists of warnings and what-not-to-dos, and pulp noir tales of love and adventure. This literature's outlook is poetically summarized by Frank E. Odili, author of the pamphlet "What Is Life?": "If life is to be endured perfectly, and in a more enlightening way than burden-like occupancy, it is a rule of general importance that we should apply a solutional thought into it."[76]

Some Nigerian intellectuals regarded the pamphlets as an embarrassing record of the "sudden inundation" of the "false values" of the West.[77] In a contrasting effort to convey the Onitsha pamphlets' literary legitimacy, Emmanuel Obiechina compares them with didactic Elizabethan pamphlets that were similarly exuberant products of the novelty of printing presses.[78] Nevertheless, the pamphlets are unmistakably modern, containing phrases that could almost have been torn from Carnegie's pages: "Time is money and waits no body" and "When starting to associate with somebody, one first of all impress him. This shall make you win him."[79] Like their Western self-help counterparts, these texts exhibit a "mania for quotations." One best-selling pamphlet, Ogali A. Ogali's *Veronica My Daughter*, sold more than sixty thousand copies upon its release in 1956

(*Opposite*) Covers of Onitsha Market pamphlets.

Felix N. Stephen, *How to Play Love*, Stephen's Drama Series. (Onitsha: Njoku & Sons, [ca. 1962?]); Rufus Okonkwo, *How to Make Friends with Girls*. (Onitsha: J. C. Brothers Bookshop, [ca 1963?]); Raja Raphael, *How to Start Life and End it Well*. ([Onitsha: Gebo Brothers, 1964?]); Sunday Okenwa Olisah, *How to Live Better Life and Help Yourself*. ([Onitsha: Okenwa Publications, ca 1963?]); J. C. Abikam, *How to Speak in Public and Beware of Women?* (Onitsha: J. C. Brothers Bookshop, [1964?]); Nathan Njoku, *Beware of Women*. (Onitsha, Nigeria, Njoku & Sons Bookshop, [1960?])

Credit: Courtesy of Special Collections, Kenneth Spencer Research Library, University of Kansas Library.

and references "quotations from Richard Whately, William Shakespeare, G. A. Gallock, Rudyard Kipling, Benjamin Harrison, William Ernest Henley, and Henry Longfellow" within the span of three pages.[80]

In his novel *GraceLand*, about a teenage Elvis Presley impersonator from Lagos, Chris Abani describes the chapbooks as "the Nigerian equivalent of dime drugstore pulp fiction crossed with pulp pop self-help books. They were morality tales with their subject matter and tone translated straight out of the oral culture." Although Abani's protagonist "Elvis" had read scores of the books, "he wouldn't admit it publicly. These books were considered to be low-class trash, but they sold in the thousands."[81]

Although Elvis usually enjoys the high literary writings of Ralph Ellison, James Baldwin, and Fyodor Dostoyevsky, he is lured by a bookseller's call: "Come and buy de original Onitsha Market Pamphlet! Leave all that imported nonsense and buy de books written by our people for de people. We got plenty. Three for five naira!"[82] A letter from the most famous of these, *Mabel the Sweet Honey That Poured Away*, is used to introduce chapter twelve of Abani's novel. After buying the pamphlet, Elvis hides his new purchase between the more reputable Dostoyevsky and Baldwin volumes before continuing on his way. But if Elvis is ashamed of the pamphlets, the novel's reliance on them suggests that their aesthetic stigma has waned. Abani cites two in particular—J. Nnadozie, *Beware of Harlots and Many Friends* (1960), and Speedy Eric, *Mabel the Sweet Honey the Poured Away* (1965)—as "invaluable resource[s]," and so underscores self-help's new aesthetic cachet and legitimacy.[83]

Readers have drawn attention to the avant-garde content of the Onitsha pamphlets' stylistic innovations, likening them to jazz, pop art, surrealism, and even the "aleatoric Joyceanism" of *Finnegans Wake*.[84] The collector and publisher Kurt Thometz identifies a parallel between the Onitsha experiments and the contemporaneous art-making techniques emerging out of Warhol's New York Factory: "One wonders if there was any way Andy Warhol could have seen the Master of Life's *The Way to Get Money: The Best Wonderful Book for Money Mongers* before appropriating the identical image of Troy Donahue (nine times), coincidentally in the same pale yellow hue as the pamphlet, for his first one man exhibition at the Eleanor Ward Gallery."[85]

Indeed, the pamphlets' mixed typefaces, mash-ups of American iconography, grammatical experiments, and handmade drawings resemble the guerilla aesthetic of avant-garde magazines like *Blast*. Édouard Glissant compares the linguistic possibilities that attend the passage from oral to written culture—possibilities that the Onitsha pamphlets so palpably manifest—to the deconstructions of modernist texts.[86] Modernist works by Ezra Pound, André Breton, and Gertrude Stein similarly exploit the frame of the how-to manual and also play with the conventions of English grammar and syntax. This view of aspirational and elite readers operating on a critical continuum has for too long eluded critics dismissive of self-help's reading methods. The Ontisha authors enact Michel de Certeau's description of "reading as poaching," or what Wendy Simonds describes as the tendency of self-help readers to "subvert the physical authority of the text" by grazing, skipping, and handling-at-will.[87] By disrupting narrative teleology, rejecting the construct of authorial originality, and asserting their frenetic citational politics, self-help readers can unsettle the pieties of orthodox reading protocols as effectively as the most radical avant-gardists.

The formal experiments of the Onitsha Market literature are but one example of self-help's remarkable cultural mobility. In post–Soviet Russia, authors developed complex "ways of negotiating the normalizing power of self-help." As one interviewee put it, they take foreign self-help and "rework it all . . . for the needs of our reality."[88] In the Middle East, popular "literature on 'caring for oneself' is put into practice and brings about real social facts in suitable conditions."[89] And although self-help books are "often ignored by Japan anthropologists," according to Laura Miller they are "obvious instruments for the dissemination of culture," and sites where the country "grapples with contemporary transformations in women's roles and identities."[90] In fact, Japan's rich history of engagement with self-help goes back much further and warrants particular attention.

SELF-HELP FOR SAMURAI, CONFUCIUS FOR CAPITALISTS

The cultural and political activity that Smiles's book "set in motion" is probably nowhere as striking as in Japan, where, according to sociologist Earl Kinmonth, its reception "provides a prime example of what can happen to the meaning of ideas in their transition from one culture to another."[91] After two hundred years of being a closed, feudal society, in the 1870s Meiji Japan opened itself to Western influences. Having missed out on two hundred years of modernization, the country felt it had a great deal of catching up to do, and Smiles's *Self-Help*, the first English book translated into Japanese, became a cheat sheet for this purpose. Japanese scholars agree that it is virtually impossible to overestimate the influence of Smiles's book as it "served positively as a guidebook for the industrialization of Japan." The book was discovered and imported by the Confucian-trained scholar Nakamura Masanao (alias Keiu), whose 1871 Japanese translation of *Self-Help*, 西國立志編 [*Saikoku risshi hen*; Success Stories in the West] would go on to become "the most influential single Western book translated into Japanese."[92]

Nakamura's edition appeared following the Meiji Restoration of 1868, when Japan—struggling against the unequal treaties imposed by the West—believed that selectively adopting the practices of other countries, from baseball to military strategy, offered a path to national sovereignty. Amid this climate, Nakamura's translation had a remarkable influence on the leaders of Japanese modernization, from the pioneering romantic-naturalist author Kunikida Doppo to Sakichi Toyoda, who grew up as the son of a poor village carpenter to become the founder of Toyota.[93]

The precocious Nakamura was appointed a full-fledged Confucian scholar at the young age of twenty-nine, a position usually reserved for those over sixty.[94] Although officially trained as a Confucian, throughout his youth Nakamura nursed a fascination with England and the West (he purportedly hid Western texts between the covers of Confucian ones). But his interest in Smiles may have been less of a departure from his academic training than it appears, for Smiles himself extended the

Confucian tendencies of the authors who inspired him, and who used Eastern philosophy as a resource for forging their transcendental philosophy.[95] Smiles's book probably resonated with Nakamura in part because of the way it channeled Confucian forms of advice via its emulation of Franklin and Ralph Waldo Emerson. The popularity of Smiles in China and Japan is not only due to his status as a symbol of Western imperial capital, as it is usually understood, but also is a result of the way his work unwittingly extends and loops back to the advice traditions indigenous to the nations into which it was imported. Part of the reason self-help guides such as Smiles's proved so portable, in other words, is because they were an inherently hybridized form whose style and ethics readers could recognize.

In 1866, Nakamura volunteered to supervise young students on a trip to London sponsored by the Tokugawa government. While in London, Nakamura asked his friend H. U. Freeland what he could bring back to Japan to teach people about the West, and Freeland gave him a copy of *Self-Help*. Nakamura memorized Smiles's text on the ship back home, and then translated it upon his return in 1871. Nakamura's translation was quickly staged as a Kabuki play and even used as an ethics textbook in primary schools. The following figure shows a Japanese color print based on the 1871 edition of Smiles's book, acquired by ethnographer and curator of the Brooklyn Museum Stewart Culin on one of his expeditions to Japan in the early twentieth century. The woodblock prints were part of a Japanese series illustrating anecdotes from Smiles's book, depicting scenes meant to inspire resilience, such as Thomas Carlyle's manuscript engulfed in flames, ornithologist John James Audubon's sketches destroyed by rats, Benjamin Franklin conducting an electrical experiment with lightning, and James Watt tending a teapot on the fire. As the accession card notes, "people took an interest in Smiles' view of utilitarian morality which they related to traditional Confucian stoicism and samurai self-reliance. Franklin became the most well-known American in Meiji Japan because of Smiles' book."[96] Following the tremendous success of *Self-Help*, Nakamura next translated *On Liberty* by John Stuart Mill (which he was introduced to via

Illustration showing Thomas Carlyle's manuscript engulfed in flames,
from Japanese edition of Samuel Smiles, *Self-Help*, woodblock print ca. 1890.
Credit: Courtesy of the Brooklyn Museum.

Smiles), and later in life he also translated Emerson's essay "Compensation" (encountered by Nakamura in Smiles's book on *Character*).

The challenge confronting Nakamura as a translator was considerable,
for Japan did not yet have a term for "individualism," which he translated as *dokuji ikko naru mono* [that which makes each one distinct], let
alone one for "self-help," translated as *jijo*. Kinmonth makes the important observation that "because of the time lag between 'humble origins'
and ultimate accomplishment, the actual models in *Self-Help* were not

nineteenth-century factory workers but eighteenth-century artisans, craftsmen, and petty functionaries."[97] Like the genre of biography with which it is so deeply entwined, self-help narrative temporality is deeply invested in the unit of the individual life. The eighteenth-century craftsmen Smiles described were figures Japanese readers could recognize.

The list of concepts Nakamura's handbook is said to have introduced to Japan is "almost beyond imagination"[98]; they included the philosophies of liberty and individualism, women's rights, and even patent law.[99] In an intriguing twist of bibliographic history, scholars even suggest that William Shakespeare has Nakamura (and Smiles) to thank for his Japanese importation, an idea traced to the words of Shakespeare's character Polonius in the epigraph opening Smiles's chapter "Money— Use and Abuse."[100] Because Japan had been a closed society under the Tokugawa shogun for more than two centuries, Shakespeare arrived on the island alongside modernists such as Anton Chekhov and George Bernard Shaw, and "his poetic dramas were studied alongside and produced in much the same ways as the plays of Ibsen."[101] With its modernist Shakespeare, Meiji Japan offers a microcosm of the cultural wormhole that is the self-help hermeneutic's collapsing of period, nation, and genre. Moreover, according to the scholar Keiko Kockum, Smiles's praise directly correlates with the period's best-selling foreign novels in Japan.[102] The alternative literary history implemented in Japan through Smiles dramatically exemplifies self-help's historical role in reordering and recategorizing the intellectual tradition. Despite Self-Help's seemingly Western imperialist agenda, the Japanese readers it influenced funneled Smiles's principles into the project of nationalism. In addition to becoming "a political tract for disgruntled samurai,"[103] Smiles's book transformed the younger generation in Japan: "Self-cultivation did not stop at the personal level for Meiji youths but became associated with preserving Japan's independence in the face of Western encroachment."[104] His readers could become so infused with Self-Help's message of independence that overly literalized adherence to the politics of its source culture began to appear counter-progressive.

Smiles's reception in Japan was part of a broader cultural effort under way in eastern Asia to reconcile the modern success ethic with Confucian ideals. In 1918, Shibusawa Eiichi, the founder of the modern banking system in Japan, wrote his *Seminar on Self-Cultivation*, which described how Confucian principles could be adapted for business success. He was "influenced in both form and content by the genre of Western self-help books which enjoyed huge popularity in Meiji Japan, starting with the very influential book by Samuel Smiles *Self-Help*." At the same time, Shibusawa had local advice manuals to emulate, such as Matsudaira Sadanobu's 1823 "Record of Spiritual Exercises" and Yukichi Fukuzawa's *An Encouragement of Learning* (*Gakumon no Susume*) (1872–1876). According to Kiri Paramore, Shibusawa's hybridized work "walked a tightrope" between competitive Smilesian individualism and his Confucian view of the inherently social nature of human beings.[105]

Self-help's international circulation furnishes a classic case of what Eric Hayot, following Rey Chow, calls the "geography of mimetic desire," which describes the cross-cultural yearning for "recognition by the other as an equal."[106] Hayot cautions that the force of European counter-transference must not be underestimated, as self-help's mimicking of ancient wisdom traditions from Confucianism to the Qur'an corroborates. For evidence of this reciprocal desire for validation, one need simply recall Smiles's boasts about his words being inscribed on the khedive's harem walls.

Across the Pacific, other authors soon followed in Nakamura's steps and applied themselves to reconciling Confucian and Western wisdom traditions, but this time for American audiences. The early twentieth-century Chinese intellectual Lin Yutang (1895–1976), who counted Dale Carnegie among his admirers, made his name by shuttling between American and Eastern advice. In 1938, Yutang's *The Importance of Living* took the top slot on the national best-seller list from Carnegie's *How to Win Friends and Influence People*, which had been the number one best-seller of the previous year but was now bumped to sixth place.[107] Yutang was born the son of a Chinese Presbyterian minister in Fujian Province, China; he traveled to the United States to work with Irving Babbitt and pursue doctoral studies at Harvard in 1920, but financial issues eventually forced him to relocate to France as secretary for the YMCA. After he gained the endorsement of Pearl S. Buck and Richard Walsh, he became known as "the most influential and prolific Asian writer/intellectual in America and the world from the 1930s to the 1960s."[108]

Yutang's career embodied the perils and possibilities of cross-cultural mediation that attend self-help's global history. In China, his simplifications and Westernizations of Chinese philosophy garnered ridicule and critique, but in America they were celebrated:

> "Your book, The Importance of Living, has become my bible," writes a lady from Wallace, Idaho; "I keep it near my bed and I could not imagine living without it." "Your books have changed my life," says a soda clerk from Flatbush Avenue, Brooklyn; "I have been commuting for years, being in a mad rush practically all the time. Now I think that something is wrong. I am reading your books and I think I am beginning to understand life." "That chapter on the thirty-three Happy Moments," a big industrialist in Pittsburgh has his secretary type—"I read it every evening before retiring. Thank you for having written it: it makes me feel thirty-three times more wisely about life."[109]

The chapter "Thirty-Three Happy Moments" to which the "big industrialist" alludes was the "most popular bit of writing" Yutang ever produced, although it would be more accurate to say Yutang "transcribed" rather than "wrote" the happiness list. In truth, as Yutang himself freely disclosed, the passage was a translation of the writing of seventeenth-century Chinese scholar and member of the xingling school Jin Shengtan. Shengtan advised the incorporation of simple but "happy moments" into one's life, which Yutang enumerated as "a sudden shower on a hot stuffy day, meeting an old friend unexpectedly, tearing up old I.O.U.s from people who were either dead or unable to repay the money," etcetera.[110]

The importance of translation to the history and emergence of self-help is evident in the very conceptualization of Yutang's book. Initially, he explained that he did not plan to write an original book but "merely to translate several classics that are sufficient to represent Chinese art of life and cultural spirit."[111] His friend Richard Walsh dissuaded him from undertaking a strict translation, but the practice and philosophy of translation undergirds his guide and methodology.

This tradition of cross-cultural negotiation and exchange that Yutang's and Smiles's careers encapsulate continues to flourish in self-help culture today.[112] Chinese personalities such as Zen Shi Qiang advocate a Confucian-based approach to modern management, whereas Taiwanese entrepreneur Kai-Fu Lee strives to combine Chinese ethical traditions with Western educational reforms, and TV personality Yu Dan's New-Age "Confucius From the Heart" reiterates tenets of American self-help discourse. As Nehring et al. observe, in addition to its Western influences, "Chinese self-help possesses unique content features emerging from a creative interplay with native Chinese traditions of life advice, particularly those associated with Confucianism, Daoism, Buddhism and Chinese medicine."[113] It is not uncommon for Americanized renditions of Chinese idioms to be retranslated back into the source culture, where they may replace or obscure the nuances of original Chinese sayings. This messy and multilayered process of cultural hybridization is the topic of Tash Aw's 2013 novel *Five Star Billionaire*, which uses the clumsiness of its self-help translations as a means of depicting the awkwardness of reconciling Eastern and Western philosophies of living.

TRANSLATING SELF-HELP, ONE PROVERB AT A TIME

Self-help's international circulation is inextricable from the practice of translation, and it is through translation that the gritty labor of reconciling indigenous and imported advice traditions is most visible. The dilemmas of translation echo the perils of self-invention: the need to balance assimilation and estrangement, to either reproduce or subvert global-imperial power dynamics. With the advent of the twenty-first century, translations of Carnegie's *How to Win Friends and Influence People*, John Gray's *Men*

Are from Mars, Women Are from Venus, Spencer Johnson's *Who Moved My Cheese,* and other American self-help titles skyrocketed, particularly in mainland China, where self-help has an approximate annual revenue of RMB 18.2 billion (US $3 billion).[114] Translations of these books deploy elaborate strategies of idiomatic hybridization. Their solutions to reconciling Chinese and American advice traditions can produce beautiful and poetic results, finding ingenious solutions to translation challenges in the ancient resources of the cultural lexicon.

It is striking how many seminal self-help texts were initially envisaged not as original creations but as modest projects of translation, from Lin Yutang's translations of Shengtan's "Happy Moments" list for an audience of American housewives, to Nakamura's reconciling of the discourse of Smilesian self-making with Meiji terminology, all the way back to Benjamin Franklin's adaptations of Confucius. Speaking of Franklin's Confucius-inspired self-help experiments, David Weir explains:

> The fragments from the classic text that Franklin quotes in the *Gazette* are probably translated from *Confucius Sinarum Philosophus* (1687), a Latin work by the Jesuit Philippe Couplet. The fact is remarkable in itself, since the first English translations of Confucius are usually dated from the early nineteenth century.

Although the exact provenance of the Confucius translations remains difficult to pinpoint, Weir raises the possibility that "Franklin could have been not only the first American publisher of Confucius but the first American translator (from Latin, not Chinese)." Remarkably, as Weir notes, "no American after Franklin attempted another translation of Confucius until Ezra Pound did so in the twentieth century."[115] Both Franklin and Pound honed their authorial identities in Philadelphia, whose sharing of the same latitude as Peking, Weir argues, lent the city a special affinity for Chinese agricultural and philosophical practices, from Philadelphia proposals for the harvesting of Ginseng and Chinese tea to the founding of Fairmount Park's "Temple of Confucius." As Franklin wrote, "we could be so fortunate as to introduce the industry of the Chinese, their arts of living and improvements in industry, as well as their native plants."[116]

Weir sees Franklin's "use of Confucius [as] an early instance of a general pattern in the growth of the American Orient: time and again, Eastern values, beliefs, and ideas are used to supplement American political, theological, or aesthetic interests."[117] This trend continues in the writings of the New England transcendentalists such as Emerson and Thoreau, whose exhortations of autonomy and independence were tremendously influential in the rise of self-help, and all the way up to Pound's Confucius translations, which, according to Weir, visibly inherited Franklin's selective reading of the Chinese sage as an emissary of American individualism and self-reliance. For example, Weir explains, Pound tellingly translates certain Chinese characters as "support oneself" rather than the more conventional "subdue oneself." By exchanging submission for self-reliance, "Pound utilized Confucian doctrines in a rather 'opportunistic' manner that characterizes his overall dealings with Confucianism," which tended to stress "Confucius' constant emphasis on the value of personality."[118] Although modernists such as D. H. Lawrence blasted Franklin and his moralizing tradition,[119] the connection between Pound's and Franklin's appropriations of Confucius suggests that there may be other methodological and formal affinities between the two industries of modernism and self-help that have been obscured by such polemical oppositions.

In updating Franklin's Americanized adaptation, Weir observes that "Pound's return to the Confucian classics recapitulates the earliest manifestations of the American Orient." For Weir, as for many others, this tradition is not characterized by productive influence but by the more sinister "contamination." Weir states that its culmination in New-Age Orientalism is alarming, to say the least: "when Western consumerism contaminates Eastern spiritualism to the degree that it has done in contemporary culture—there is no hope of improvement, no hope for the self. And there is no stronger proof of this claim than the fact that transcendental meditation, yoga, and the rest are securely branded now as sectors of the self-help industry."[120]

However, it is not always easy to disentangle Western influence from local practice. Researcher Gregory Ornatowski's cautionary statement about neo-Confucianism in contemporary Japan might apply to the cultural tendencies Weir is concerned with as well:

> The application of the tradition of self-cultivation to economic life in Japan cannot be viewed *solely* as an institutional means for boosting economic production or efficiency but also must be seen as an attempt, at least in some cases, by thoughtful individuals and groups to integrate at the deepest level the "spiritual" values and "secular" goals of a society.

Likening this phenomenon to early formulations of the Protestant ethic in the United States, Ornatowski argues that because today "the Western orientation is to view secular goals such as economic production as separate from spiritual life and ultimate meanings, it seems more difficult for Western theorists to accept such spiritualization of secular goals as being truly legitimate."[121] In other words, the merging of Confucian philosophical and modern economic practices reflects not just a tool of political domestication but also the spiritual project of finding meaning in one's labor.

Novelist Tash Aw is similarly interested in resisting a purely dismissive or negative reading of the spread of the self-help diaspora in eastern Asia. Aw relates in an interview, "They were everywhere I went in China. In bookshops, eight of the 10 best sellers would be self-help books. In street stalls, they would be selling counterfeit self-help books, on the metro in the morning, all these people were reading self-help books." Aw's novel describes the scrappy, sometimes inelegant process by which Western and Chinese ideals of self-making are combined. He was inspired to write *Five Star Billionaire* after he witnessed the popularity of Chinese translations of texts such as Sherry Argov's American relationship guide, *Why Men Love Bitches* (2000). The popularity of such titles occasioned Aw's realization that "Americans and Chinese often think of themselves as polar opposites to each other, and yet they are bounded by the notion that you can improve every aspect of your life by reading a book."[122] Sociologists provide a materialist context for Aw's point: "even the deep-seated cultural and historical differences between China and the US were no match for the growing socio-economic similarities between the two countries as a result of China's pro-market reforms during the eighties and nineties."[123] But rather than sheer manifestations of the economic shifts that link these cultures, Aw finds commonality in the desire for connection and meaning to which, at best, self-help's global popularity gives voice.

Aw's book was published in 2013, the same year as Mohsin Hamid's *How to Get Filthy Rich in Rising Asia*, which similarly explores the merging of ancient counsel (in Hamid, Sufi love poetry) and American self-help ideals (see chapter 6). Both novels use self-help "rules" or imperatives as a structural device and chapter organization (in Aw: "Move to Where the Money Is," "Forget the Past, Look Only to the Future," and "Be Prepared to Sacrifice Everything"). But in contrast to Hamid's toned prose, which reproduces the ascetic ideal of the novel's body-building protagonist, Aw's narrative is sprawling, messy, and a little bit out of control, much like the thwarted plans of his characters. Despite their differences, both texts are products of Asia's economic boom and resultant urban migration. Both are also working through the problem of whether the Western self-help idiom can be meaningfully combined with autochthonous folklore traditions (the term "Chinese Dream" has even become a slogan of Chinese president Xi Jinping). But it is in Aw's novel that the problem of translation as it pertains to self-help receives the most sustained attention.

The status of translation as a window into self-help's cultural hybridization is formalized in Aw's conspicuously creative translations of American and Chinese maxims in his chapter titles.[124] The chapters of *Five Star Billionaire* are headed by English imperatives—"Choose the Right Moment to Launch Yourself" or "Always Rebound with Each Failure"— with a Chinese translation underneath undertaken by Aw himself. As the novel advances, it alternates the Western-sounding self-help mantras with English translations of ancient Chinese proverbs and sayings. The heading to chapter 3, "Bravely Set the World on Fire," comes from a line that first appears in a poem by the renowned poet of the Tang Dynasty Bai Juyi,

"惊天动地," and refers to momentous events that "shock the sky and shake the earth." The heading to chapter 14, "Even Beautiful Things Will Fade," is translated as "明日黃花," a phrase coined by the poet from the Song Dynasty, Su Shi (1037–1101), that refers to withered, yellowed flowers, or a topic that is stale and out of fashion. In chapter 19, Aw translates "箭在弦上" [the arrow is set on the bow], a saying from the Three Kingdoms period (184–220 CE), as "There Can Be No Turning Back."

Such granular moments of linguistic reconciliation contain microcosms of the plot's larger interest in the convergence of Chinese and Western arts of living. But they also enact the dual directionality of self-help's recursive cross-cultural history. Proverbs are translated back and forth and back again, often resulting in a form of "recycled Orientalism" that makes identification of an original source culture for the self-help maxims impossible.[125]

In addition to its depiction of self-help's embroilment in practices of cultural translation, Aw's novel is interested in the consequences of the industry for fiction. *Five Star Billionaire* opens with businessman and self-help author Walter Chao's first-person account of his childhood in rural Malaysia, specifically his youthful viewing of his favorite show, a legal drama set in the United States:

> I'm not certain I could tell you what happened in a single episode of that soap opera, and besides, I do not care for the artificial little conflicts that took place all the time, the emotional ups and downs, men and women crying because they were falling in love or out of love; the arguing, making up, making love, et cetera. I had a sensation they were wasting time, that their days and nights could have been spent more profitably . . . the only thing I really remember is the opening sequence, a sweeping panorama of metal-and-glass skyscrapers glinting in the sun. . . . All I cared for were these introductory images; the show that followed was meaningless to me.

Plot is tangential for the aspiring Walter, who sees in the soap-opera opening only a mirage of Western capitalist prosperity. All narrative details are subordinate to his emulation agenda: "every time I sat down in front of the TV I would think: One day, I will own a building like that, a whole tower block filled with industrious clever people working to make their fantasies come true." This account is an inauspicious way for a novel to begin its 379 pages of emotional drama; character, plot, and setting are all considered inessential—in Walter's words, so much "wasted time."[126] The passage invokes self-help's long-standing ambivalence toward the "diversion" of fiction, from Smiles's and his peers' cautions about the influences of novels to the wariness of self-made men such as Benjamin Franklin and Booker T. Washington toward any reading material other than biography and historical nonfiction. Conversely, from a literary perspective, self-help's offensiveness has to do with its functionalist impatience with the ornamental and aesthetic (recall the description of Carnegie as "condensation's greatest zealot").

Like Walter, like Mr. Biswas, the Shanghai women of New China in Aw's novel zealously adopt the self-help hermeneutic, reading "mere novels" with the same "steely," emulative spirit as Walter approaches his television drama:

> Often these impressive-looking women would take out papers or a book from their sleek bags and read them in the bus with an air of purpose, and even if they were reading mere novels, Phoebe could see that they were absorbing the contents of the words the way high-acting achieving people do, all the time working, in a way that was steely yet elegant. It reminded her of a girl at school who always came first in class, the way that girl read books with a determination that no one else had.[127]

Aw's text is an inquiry into whether self-help and the literary can ever be reconciled. His narrative oscillates between self-help's hackneyed steps to success and moments of irrational sentimentality, emotion, connection, and nostalgia that punctuate and disrupt each character's achievement arc.

The theme comes across most forcefully in the character of Phoebe Chen Aiping—a factory girl from Malaysia who comes to Shanghai in search of a better life and who embodies the impressionable, ambitious demographic the self-help manuals exploit. She devours the guidance found in books like *Why Men Love Bitches* and *Sophistify Yourself,* whose rules she copies and memorizes, such as how to seduce a man or comport oneself at a fancy restaurant. She records "how to use the cutlery, what to do with the little baskets of bread that arrived before the meal, how to deal with olives." Phoebe determines her self-invention project to be a success when she realizes at a restaurant that she "did not even need to look in her handbag for the piece of paper on which she had written: *1. Soup (+ bread). 2. Fish (flat knife). 3. Meat. 4. Cheese. 5. Dessert. 6. Coffee.*"[128]

Although she is wholly consumed by her improvement program, Phoebe allows herself a fleeting moment of sentimentalism in the narrative. When creating her profile on a dating website, she decides against the "cartoon" or "neutral" images typically used in favor of a more natural photograph of herself in which "her eyes were glowing with laughter and promise, and the vegetation behind her was so lush it reminded her of home." This unfashionably sincere and natural picture is what draws another struggling character, Gary, to Phoebe's profile. Amid China's culture of "copycat power," "it is rare to see a photo of a real face on these chat sites. The last time Gary saw it, he decided that it must be a fake—no girl would place a picture on the Internet that showed her smiling straight into the camera." This argument for the sincerity of the sentimental or nostalgic recurs in the novel when another achievement-obsessed character, the businesswoman Yinghui, cannot explain why she is reluctant to throw out the business card of an old friend, Justin: "why she had not been able to cut away the association with her past, why she was not being her usual ruthless self."[129]

Justin, a businessman suffering from a nervous breakdown, also experiences an inexplicable moment of sentimentalism during a spontaneous connection with an ice-cream-loving neighbor, who happens to be Phoebe's roommate. The encounter disconcerts him because

he did not know why he was providing a solemn undertaking to buy ice cream, why he was taking the trouble to ask what flavors she liked, why he was pretending to share her love of red-bean ices when he didn't even like ice cream, why he cared about what was written in that diary or if her roommate's life was heading for disaster, why he was concerned that they were two hapless girls from the provinces who thought that the rich men they were going out with were going to leave their wives and marry them.[130]

Each of these moments celebrates the authenticity of the digressive and nontransactional. The romantic dramas of "two hapless girls from the provinces"—those "artificial conflicts" self-help guru Walter Chao derided as superfluous in the novel's opening scene—ultimately operate as portals to the real. The heart of Aw's narrative hinges on such moments that valorize the very categories absent from self-help's agenda: nostalgia, benevolence, the possibility of genuine understanding, and self-expression. At the same time, the novel refrains from passing a final judgment on self-help as just another example of capitalist corruption or cultural contamination. Rather, it finds in the act of translating self-help an expression of the desire for the human, cross-cultural, even sentimental connection that forms the core of the book's narrative ethics.

Aw's book also effectively captures one other important aspect of self-help, the reality of its transmedia presence. Phoebe's first encounter with self-help in *Five Star Billionaire* is not via a printed book but via a DVD of an inspirational "self-help master" that she spots in a noodle shop in Guangzhou. For her, the seduction of the self-help program is initially visual: "Phoebe liked the way the woman looked straight at her, holding her gaze so steadily that Phoebe felt embarrassed, shamed by her own failure." Although the woman seems to be an endless fount of wise sayings, "now she cannot remember much except the feeling of courage that the woman had given her." Phoebe decides on the spot, "I am going to buy your words of wisdom and study them the way some people study the Bible."[131] We have already seen this same selective recall at play in the novel's *mise en scène* when Walter details his childhood self-help reading of the *Law & Order*–style legal drama on television. Walter's experience is couched in similarly forgetful terms: "I'm not certain I could tell you what happened in a single episode of that soap opera."[132] What both characters retain is not any particular advice or content but rather a feeling of desire and a stirring of ambition.

The determination with which the New Shanghai women strategically mine their literature on the bus is an extension of these same methods. Through such associations, Aw depicts self-help not as a deliberate, hermetic activity but as an endless stream of intake, filtering, and application. What Hunter called the "pick-and-mix quality" of Smiles's self-help method is ideally suited to Shanghai's fast-paced urban and visual culture.[133]

Self-help's status as a mode of reading that does not differentiate between manuals and novels applies to its refusal to discriminate between different media as well. Neville's discussion of self-help's "product diversification" is useful here:

> There is a tendency in the research to conceptualize self-help book consumption as a "special" life event, and to conceive that these popular cultural products "float" around the marketplace only to "appear" in the private spheres at times of personal difficulty. Not only are countless publishing companies around the world involved in producing and printing vast volumes of self-help books for the global audience, but such is the extent of their cultural penetration that self-help books are featured in the newspapers and magazines we read, the talk shows and situation comedies we watch on TV, and even the films we view. As a consequence it is fair to assert that self-help books have become integrated into our daily lives . . . whether we purposely seek these products or not.[134]

Self-help's influence can be more atmospheric than deliberate in a way that troubles academic efforts to distinguish between self-help readers and non-self-help readers *tout court*. In addition, self-help's transmedia overflow into different platforms represents another kind of translation in which the industry is invested. Self-help is not confined to print but is spread through memes, talk shows, greeting cards, podcasts, apps, and many other representational forms. An example of this phenomenon is the trend in China and Japan of adapting self-help into comic book form.

In Japan, "many American self-help books . . . have been made into comic books." Shunsuke Ozaki explains that Stephen Covey, Napoleon Hill, and Dale Carnegie have all been adapted into comics form.[135] For example, a Japanese adaptation of Dale Carnegie's *How to Stop Worrying and Start Living*, published in 2015, recasts Carnegie's anecdotes as comic panels and inserts Japanese referents, such as a picture of the regional dish *omuraisu*, to make the American handbook more accessible.[136] Such graphic renditions of self-help are modern extensions of those early Japanese woodblock illustrations of the stories in Smiles's *Self-Help* preserved by Stewart Culin, the former curator of the Brooklyn Museum. This transmedia adaptation is a robust area of self-help's translation and diversification, with manga versions of classic self-help on the rise, such as Marie Kondo's *The Life Changing Manga of Tidying Up*.[137] The sequentialism of graphic narrative reinforces the step-by-step proceduralism of the self-help manual, and the comic panel's emphasis on framing and simplification complements the self-help genre's investment in life management and containment.[138]

As the varied examples from this chapter have shown, the self-help hermeneutic binds in unexpected ways a nonsynchronous, cross-cultural community of practical readers, whose first encounters with self-help manuals tend to occur at critical historical junctures when traditional social and economic hierarchies are upended. My concern with the reserves of both textual and individual agency elided by academic critiques of self-help echoes similar warnings on the part of some scholars regarding those potentially valuable categories, such as ethical-humanism and self-cultivation, that the wholesale dismissal of liberalism throws out. Like the broader philosophy of English liberalism it manifests, self-help partakes of what Uday Singh Mehta describes as the "flavor of romanticism" attending the belief that social good can come from individual initiative.[139] Both self-help and liberalism depend on the construct of the autonomous, self-determining individual who is seen as the condition of possibility for

Panel from Marie Kondo and Yuka Uramoto, *The Life Changing Manga of Tidying Up.*

democratic self-governance, and many of the objections waged against the two discourses are the same. They are jointly condemned for their individualism, voluntarism, emphasis on temperamental accountability above state welfare, and simultaneously universalizing and exclusionary logic. Recent powerful expositions of liberalism's complicity in colonial and masculinist agendas and self-justifications (for example, Mehta and Pateman) have contributed to the equation of self-cultivation with hegemony.[140] In response, scholars including Lauren Goodlad, Amanda Anderson, and David Wayne Thomas have sought to provide what Thomas describes as a "measured but generally redemptive account of modern liberal agency."[141] Such interventions participate in the broader disciplinary recoil against the increasing automatism of poststructuralist paradigms of critique. As I explain more fully in chapter 6, "Practicality Hunger," the same wish to reanimate the possibilities of self-transformation, cross-cultural connection, and especially textual agency motivates the turn to self-help in contemporary fiction. In this respect, contemporary literature has moved beyond the polarizing reception studies/ideology critique impasse with regard to the subject of self-help, even if academic scholarship has not.

Chapter 2 takes up Gustave Flaubert's derisive stance on the self-culture of his time, engaging some of the critiques of the industry that were put on hold here. Today self-help is everywhere, but it has been in the cultural atmosphere for much longer than most believe. It is time to attend to the cultural, pedagogic, and aesthetic needs that self-help's popularity manifests.

2

BOUVARD AND PÉCUCHET

FLAUBERT'S DIY DYSTOPIA

SELF-HELP'S PSEUDOACTIVITY

The behemoth of self-help individualism grew out of the minority cooperative tradition of nineteenth-century "mutual improvement societies," which were spontaneous clubs organized by working-class laborers desperate to educate themselves and improve their conditions. It was in the center of this activity in the newly industrialized city of Leeds that Smiles began offering lectures to working societies while he was serving as editor of the *Leeds Times*. The seeds of Smiles's *Self-Help* were planted in 1845, when he was invited to give a lecture to a workingman's educational society located, due to the discounted rent, in an abandoned cholera hospital. Smiles regarded the mutual improvement society he met there as "one of the most gratifying signs of social progress" he had ever witnessed:[1]

> No tenant could be found for the place, which was avoided as if a plague still clung to it. But the mutual-improvement youths, nothing daunted, hired the cholera-room at so much a week, lit it up, placed a few benches and a deal table in it, and began their winter classes. . . . The teaching may have been, as no doubt it was, of a very rude and imperfect sort; but it was done with a will.

> Those who knew a little taught those who knew less—improving themselves
> while they improved others; and, at all events, setting before them a good
> working example.[2]

To be sure, the grim reality of working-class living conditions in Leeds
at the time somewhat deflates the optimism of the Smilesian account.
Most families were crammed into rooms averaging 9 by 14 feet, with no
ventilation or sanitation, and laborers and their families worked between
twelve and fourteen hours a day and had an average mortality age of nine-
teen.[3] In light of these figures, it is easy to dismiss self-help as a tool for
quashing and redirecting class conflict. Yet, as J. F. C. Harrison explains
in his history of the adult education movement, the mutual improvement
group began as "a rudimentary organization set up by working men to do
something which they could not, as individuals, do so well alone."[4] These
two strains of self-help—as a tool of depoliticization and a collective, self-
directed coping strategy—continue to compete and coexist.

But what happens when Smiles's gritty working-class radicalism is
imported into the bucolic countryside of the French bourgeoisie? For an
answer, and to understand the tremendous shift self-help underwent at
the end of the nineteenth century, we can compare Smiles's moving *mise
en scène* of working-class self-education undertaken in drafty choleric
rooms to the bathetic amateurism of Gustave Flaubert's retired hobbyists
Bouvard and Pécuchet.

Flaubert's final novel, *Bouvard and Pécuchet* offers one of literary history's most merciless demonstrations of the pathos of self-help's
"pseudo-activity," as Theodor Adorno would later call it.[5] Published in
1881, one year after his death, Flaubert's narrative recounts the schemes of
two Parisian copy clerks who, thanks to a sudden inheritance, pack up their
belongings and move to the country to pursue their hobbies full time. Written in the wake of Smiles's tremendous success, Flaubert's novel exhibits
remarkable prescience regarding the spread and overflow of self-help into
every genre, discipline, and sphere of human activity. It anticipates self-
help's inexorable product diversification, describing the infiltration of the

self-help ethic into all disciplines and activities, from jam making to philosophy and politics. Frances Ferguson describes Bouvard and Pécuchet as "committed to self-improvement and to improvement in all things."[6] If Smiles's global reception testifies to self-help's overlooked cultural influence, it is precisely this rising cultural consequence that made the new ethos so threatening to an aesthete like Flaubert.

"Self-help" is a term perched upon the reticent tip of Flaubertian criticism's tongue. As the *Gustave Flaubert Encyclopedia* puts it (a construction whose perversity would not have been lost upon the author), "while instructional manuals seek to codify information and instruct the reader, Flaubert uses many how-to books to produce *Bouvard et Pécuchet*, a great 'how-not-to' book." Rita Felski notes that Emma Bovary "reads literally, and out of pure self-interest," and for Leo Bersani, the "eminently practical" Bouvard and Pécuchet are risible because "they would put knowledge to use."[7] Most strikingly, Flaubert described the *Dictionary of Clichés*, which he planned to append to his narrative, as an amalgamation of "everything one should say if one is to be considered a decent and likable member of society." "If properly done," he continued, "anyone who read it would never dare open his mouth again, for fear of spontaneously uttering one of its pronouncements."[8] When constellated in this way, *Madame Bovary*'s disdain for textual escapism and *Bouvard and Pécuchet*'s relentless instrumentalism appear as a cohesive, unified commentary on the cultural rise of the self-help compulsion.[9] Essentially, self-help is aestheticism's worst nightmare and the apotheosis of processes Flaubert anticipated with dread: the reduction of literature to use, the mass-production and commodification of print, and the vulgarization of knowledge and art. Flaubert's representation of early do-it-yourself (DIY) culture offers a fresh context for two key tenets of modernist practice: autonomy and experiment.

Bouvard and Pécuchet records the process by which the mutual improvement society's investment in "cooperative reorganization for mutual benefit," as Alison Booth puts it, evolved into the fetishism of "solitary initiative" and self-making associated with the self-help industry today.

In Smiles's early self-help, singular achievement is always subordinate to the promise of recurrence. Although it perpetuates a form of modern hagiography, self-help also depends on the accretion of biographical examples, which is evident in the Smilesian repetition of inventories and lists (see chapter 1). His reliance on the list manifests his preference for the imitable life story above the "long shot" or exception.[10] Rather than a celebration of charismatic individualism, as one might assume, Smiles's book is initially a romance of prosaic and collective determination. He insisted that "the education of the working classes is to be regarded, in its highest aspect, not as a means of raising up a few clever and talented men into a higher rank of life, but of elevating and improving the whole class—of raising the entire condition of the working man."[11] But far from an assertion of autonomous choice, Flaubert's narrative depicts self-help as an addiction, and in so doing paints a very different lineage from my previous chapter's description of politicians and activists who found productive stimulus in Smiles's book. If chapter 1 surveyed some of the best possible applications of self-help—as a catalyst of national independence and a tool for self-learning—Flaubert presents us with the worst. The episodic formula of anticipation, frustration, and substitution that his characters endlessly repeat pathologizes the ethos of aspirational sequentialism embodied in the Smilesian list. The dependence of early success literature on inventories of self-makers and imitable examples finds parodic expression in the compulsive, episodic failures of his hapless clerks.

MIDDLE-CLASS MALAISE

Fed up with muggy Paris, tired of their insufferable officemates, Bouvard and Pécuchet yearn for the simpler pleasures of village life. Modern middle-class city dwellers will empathize with their fantasy of early retirement in some rural abode: "They would awake with the meadowlark's song to follow the plows, would go with their basket to pick apples, watch butter being churned, grain being threshed, sheep being shorn. . . . No more writing! no more bosses!" However, the reality is not quite so picturesque:

> Up at dawn, they worked until nightfall, rush baskets around their waists. In the cold spring mornings, Bouvard wore his woolen jacket beneath his coveralls, Pécuchet his old frock coat under his apron, and the people passing by the lattice fence could hear them coughing in the fog.
>
> Sometimes Pécuchet pulled his manual from his pocket and studied a paragraph, standing, with his spade beside him, in the pose of the gardener decorating the book's frontispiece. He found the resemblance quite flattering, and his respect for the author increased.

"Coughing in the fog" with their Parisian constitutions, Bouvard and Pécuchet are ill equipped for the hardships of agricultural labor.[12] When Pécuchet "studies a paragraph," he is not reading but posing, and what he is thinking about is not receiving new knowledge but his received idea of himself. Far from a pedagogic object, the text becomes a mere stage prop in this gardening tableau. A pantomime of the DIY mentality, Pécuchet's posture with his manual encapsulates Flaubert's concern with the utilitarian future of the text. The clerks apply the same pragmatic reading methodology to gardening handbooks, astronomy textbooks, romance novels, and Hegelian philosophy—with equally abysmal results. Contemporary DIY handbooks are not all that different from the Roret manuals on hygiene, home libraries, and gardening that Flaubert scrupulously consulted in composing *Bouvard and Pécuchet*.[13] Flaubert's transtextual critique is not directed at a particular field but at the self-help hermeneutic more broadly. Like the fungus that will eventually ruin the copy clerks' apricot trees, for Flaubert instrumentalism is a parasite corrupting the purest of expressions. *Habent sua fata libelli* [every book has its destiny], but Flaubert warns that this destiny may be self-help.

The contrast between Smiles and Flaubert suggests how easily the self-improvement project can shift from rousing to ridiculous. In a startlingly short span of time, as the comparison suggests, adult education went from a vehicle of working-class protest to a tool of social accommodation. Yet even with Flaubert's petit bourgeois hobbyists, vestiges of the old, political impulse of self-help persist. "The instability of Bouvard and Pécuchet as characters," Leo Bersani observes, "points to a kind of resistance to strategies of power."[14] Self-help's meaning underwent substantial changes in the short period between Smiles's tenure as editor of the *Leeds Times*, where he developed his sympathy for the workingmen's associations, and the publication of *Self-Help*, which was soon deployed as a tool for defusing social unrest. In addition, the mutual improvement societies that Smiles describes flourished during a short and transient window, "between 18th century private study and education by an expert."[15] Flaubert is interested in this window when the culture of spontaneous self-education begins to take root as the leisure pastime of the middle classes.

The centrality of the practices of modeling and imitation to early self-help comes across explicitly in the French term for the mutual improvement societies, which were called "emulation societies"; they were also referred to as "learned societies" and "*sociétés savantes*."[16] In 1846, Charles Louandré poked fun at the emulation societies for giving a forum to "la curiosité oisive des rentiers désoeuvrés" [the idle curiosity of pension-fund retirees], indicating just how typical Bouvard and Pécuchet were for their time. He laments that the societies are usually composed of

> lost children of haphazard theories of political economy, law, history, science, and literature. Magnetism, phrenology, fourierism, homeopathy, humanitarian progress, all these things that there have their tribunal, each is allowed to share his ideas, and to contradict those of others.[17]

With titles that would not be out of place at a Modern Language Association conference, savants at the Emulation Society of Doubs composed papers on subjects such as "Inscription on a Stone Needle of the Ornans Territory"; "Note on an Error in Péclet's *The Sharing of Heat*"; "An Unedited Letter by Voltaire"; "On Deformities, Infirmities, and Maladies

Reproduced in Artworks"; and "What Is Music?"[18] Despite their prolific output, however, the general historical consensus is that the savant societies did little or nothing to advance the development of knowledge in their fields, antagonizing both the government and the academy. Fox describes their contributions to science as "decidedly patchy," and Harrison observes that "learned societies in general contributed very little to the progress of science or letters in nineteenth-century France."[19] Savant societies were particular irritants to the Ministry of Public Instruction, which attempted to assimilate them, copy them, and quash them. Fox notes that "the sociétés savantes became the focus for one of the most intense of mid-century debates about the proper extent of ministerial prerogatives."[20]

In Flaubert's hands, the suspicion of institutional learning one finds in Smiles becomes paranoia, the collective spirit of the improvement societies becomes petty competitiveness, and the sincere pursuit of adult education devolves into a misguided and frenetic amateurism. Once Bouvard and Pécuchet realize that contradictions and weaknesses can be found in all intellectual systems, they decide, in the very pattern of the early self-help associations, to open their own school of adult education:

> A magnificent dream consumed them. If they succeeded with their pupils' education, they would found an institution whose purpose would be to rectify minds, straighten our personalities, ennoble hearts. They were already talking about subscriptions and building new wings.[21]

Flaubert's preoccupation with savant culture predates *Bouvard and Pécuchet*, going back to *Madame Bovary*'s town chemist, Homais, an "apostle of progress and a local patriot" who adds to his signature "member of several learned societies. (He belonged to one.)" Emma's sentimental romances are the explicit targets of the text, but Homais's clichéd manuals and treatises are the subtler villains of *Madame Bovary*. "The happiest of fathers and luckiest of men," "whom everything conspired to bless,"[22] Homais is responsible for almost every misfortune that occurs in the narrative. The fallout zone of Homais's "success" is ever increasing.

It is Homais's disquisition on the benefits of art that inspires Charles to take Emma to the opera, where she sees Léon and renews her acquaintance with him. The disaster of Charles's club foot surgery occurs at Homais's instigation, and Homais plants the idea of arsenic in Emma's head. When the savant societies are mentioned by Flaubert scholars, it is almost always in regard to Homais's sign-off, although the copy clerks are more fully fleshed-out versions of this same provincial type. It was Flaubert's friends Maxime Du Camp and Louis Bouilhet who convinced him to make a suicidal housewife the subject of his text, but the character of Homais steals the spotlight as soon as he appears. As *Madame Bovary* progresses, Emma's readings appear increasingly as an alibi for interrogating the alternate future for applied literature embodied by Homais.

According to Fox, "the proliferation of the *sociétés savantes* is one of the most startling and neglected cultural phenomena of nineteenth-century France."[23] These provincial societies were voluntary, exclusively male associations, related to the gentleman's club or "*Cercle*," and as Flaubert sarcastically notes in his *Dictionary of Clichés*, "one must always belong to one."[24] Self-taught and often explicitly utilitarian, these groups displayed a "determined, aggressive independence" amid the authoritarian educational context of the Second Empire regime.[25] Stressing fieldwork above formal education and research, these dilettantes were less interested in novel or unprecedented theses than in the immersive pleasure of firsthand observation.

These voluntary associations of male autodidacts are a strikingly neglected context for *Bouvard and Pécuchet*, which evokes the theme of emulation in the very occupations of its protagonists (copyists). Emulation is a "lost cliché of nineteenth-century French society," as Carol Harrison explains, which, "as a rhetoric of competitive and collaborative achievement, participated in the bourgeois process of self-invention."[26]

Flaubert first describes the acquisitive social type of the savant in a paragraph recounting the exploits of Homais:

> Now for a book, an opus! Accordingly, he compiled a *Statistical Survey of the Canton of Yonville, with Climatological Observations*. Statistics led him into

philosophy. He turned his mind to the questions of the day, to social problems, to the "moralization" of the lower classes, to fish-breeding, rubber, railways, and so on. He began to feel ashamed of being a bourgeois; he aped the artistic temperament; he smoked! And he bought a smart pair of Pompadour statuettes to grace his drawing room.[27]

A cascade effect links Homais's dabbling with lower-class benevolence to his forays with rubber and railways, just as Bouvard and Pécuchet will not only experiment with chemistry and geology but will also dabble in education, village politics, and medicine. Notably, social justice is just another item in the list of Homais's self-serving ambitions; charity has no nobler a motive than fish breeding, and benevolence is not exempt from the callousness of the dilettante. From the perspective of the savant, Pompadour statuettes and problems of social class are equivalent; poverty is merely one more subject to check off the list.

This same pattern of restless acquisitiveness and perennial dissatisfaction punctuates the arcs of Bouvard and Pécuchet and Emma Bovary as well. Like Pécuchet with his gardening manual, Emma also practices a form of talismanic identification, and she is similarly susceptible to the influence of the pictorial. Emma decides that "she wanted to become a saint. She bought rosaries, wore amulets, and asked for a little reliquary set in emeralds to be placed at the head of her bed, that she might kiss it every night."[28] Emma's fantasy of acquiring sainthood by imitating it resonates with the modern injunction to "dress the part" or "dress for success." A similar sensibility is associated with the character Martinon in *Sentimental Education*, "wishing already to present a dignified exterior, he wore his beard cut like a collar around his neck."[29] Emma's focus on ornament rather than ideals is an example of what Jonathan Culler calls her "misplaced concreteness,"[30] a disorder the copy clerks suffer from as well. Her fixation on accessories reflects her superficiality, but it also represents Emma's wish for a shortcut to the rewards and markers of meaningful experience. If "Madame Bovary, c'est moi," as the famous sentence goes,[31] this may be less of a reference to her amorous proclivities than to her passion for self-learning. Flaubert also confessed, "How often I have regretted not being a savant, and how I envy their calm existences spent studying the feet of flies, stars or flowers!"[32]

Like the savants, "Emma wanted to learn Italian: she bought dictionaries, a grammar book, and a provision of white paper. She tried serious reading, history, and philosophy."[33] The constructions of the sentences about sainthood and Italian are almost identical. Both sentences begin with an abrupt declaration of desire (in the French, in both cases, "Elle voulut . . ."), and then proceed to list the acquisitions imagined to be necessary for its fulfillment. Discussed in isolation, such narrative moments appear almost inconsequential; the reader might even applaud the character's resolve. When compiled and compared, however, and by sheer virtue of their multiplicity, the declarations adopt a kind of Sisyphean fatalism in which their very familiarity belies the resolution being described. The same formula appears with only slight variations (from the passé simple to the imperfect "Ils voulaient . . .") in *Bouvard and Pécuchet*. On ancient history: "They wanted to read the original sources, Grégoire de Tours, Monstrelet, Commines, all those authors with strange and enticing names." Or later, speaking of Bouvard, "He wanted to learn, to further his knowledge of mores. He reread Paul de Kock, skimmed through an old copy of *The Hermit of the Chaussée-d'Antin*."[34] The effect of this structure is to highlight the belatedness of the textual aids, which, as in the scene with the gardening manual, are consigned to an afterthought because they are always dependent upon the desires they serve. In addition, the aesthetic object's singularity is nullified by virtue of the listlike sequence in which it appears. As with Emma, the clerks' future projects are driven not by choice but by a kind of accidental necessity; they need new exploits to distract them from previous failures, and from the ontological emptiness that their projects are meant to conceal. Such episodic repetition prefigures the compulsive or addictive quality of self-help, what Micki McGee calls its "contagion of insufficiency" and Steve Salerno describes as the "eighteen-month rule" of self-help publishing: "the most likely customer for a book on any given topic was someone who had bought a similar one within the preceding eighteen months."[35] With his refusal to accept the progressive politics of the bespoke, Flaubert's critique is more relevant than ever today.

EARLY SELF-EXPERIMENTERS

As Flaubert warns, the insufficiency fostered by DIY stems in large part from its blurring of the line between autonomy and dependence. You are rarely as dependent on external sources as when you attempt to "do-it-yourself." The genre is premised on the paradoxical promise of an autonomy only attainable via a radically dogmatic subservience to someone else's textual—and, increasingly, visual—aid.

According to Adorno, the danger of the DIY spirit is the way it threatens to induce a false feeling of emancipation and subversion. In a passage worth quoting in full, he muses:

> "Do it yourself," this contemporary type of spare time behaviour fits however into a much more far-reaching context. More than thirty years ago I described such behavior as "pseudo-activity." . . . Pseudo-activity is misguided spontaneity. Misguided, but not accidentally so; because people do have a dim suspicion of how hard it would be to throw off the yoke that weighs upon them. They prefer to be distracted by spurious and illusory activities, by institutionalized vicarious satisfactions, than to face up to the awareness of how little access they have to the possibility of change today. Pseudo-activities are fictions and parodies of the same productivity which society on the one hand incessantly calls for, but on the other holds in check and, as far as the individual is concerned, does not really desire at all.[36]

Pseudoactivities, says Adorno, are daydreams borne of middle-class malaise. *Bouvard and Pécuchet* is an experiment in what would happen if one had the opportunity to render the DIY imaginary real: What if you were granted that sudden windfall, that early retirement, the country house you had been yearning for? It is possible that, just as for Flaubert's characters, the desk job would acquire a whole new kind of appeal and that you would soon be plotting your return to the shackles of menial labor. Adorno would argue that DIY is a paradigmatic expression of the desire for self-expression that capitalism produces but can never fulfill.

But there is another name for the seemingly inconsequential spare-time spontaneity that Adorno dubs pseudoactivity: experiment. The savants' spirit of observation and play corresponds to Pericles Lewis's account of "the immersion of modernist literature in a culture of experiment."[37] In contrast to attendees of institutional universities and museums, savants preferred to catch their own butterflies, find their own shells, and dig their own fossils rather than purchase them from external collectors. Rather than relying on the expertise of authorities, Bouvard and Pécuchet insist upon testing all knowledge firsthand, and so they are sometimes read as rebelling against the narrowness of disciplinary stratification. Marx might say that Bouvard and Pécuchet's DIY projects reflect their frustration with the "one-sided development" of the division of labor: "If the circumstances in which the individual lives allow him only the one-sided development of a single quality at the expense of all the rest, if they give him the material and time to develop only that one quality, then this individual achieves only a one-sided, crippled development."[38] Sentenced by their jobs to copy all day long, the clerks yearn to express their autonomy through their leisure.

In Flaubert's hands, however, the heroism of the DIY method of capitalist subversion is questionable at best. As he depicts it, when DIY enters the modern home, it is not as an undermining of the relations of production but as the elusive quest for the perfect, purest product. Experimenting first with making their own liquor, then with preserving food in tins, the clerks "began to suspect fraud in all food products. . . . They quibbled with the baker on the color of his bread. They made an enemy of the grocer by claiming that he adulterated his chocolate."[39] Today DIY reflects a wariness of assembly line anonymity and of the toxic substances routinely infiltrating our goods, but within the context of nineteenth-century France, the clerks' complacency is an insult to the craftsmen, experts, and specialists who have devoted their lives to the fields and trades the clerks so haphazardly appropriate. "They cast doubt on the integrity of men, the chastity of women, the wisdom of the government, the common sense of the people—in short, they undermined the foundations of society."[40]

The clerks proudly invite some villagers over to taste their homemade wares, but the response is distressing. In a preview of many similar scenes to follow in the wake of the twenty-first-century Brooklyn artisanal movement, Flaubert recounts the outcome of the clerks' experiments in home preserving:

> Pécuchet opened a bottle of his Malaga, less out of generosity than in hopes of hearing it praised. But the laborer made a grimace and said it was "like licorice syrup." And his wife, "to get the taste out of her mouth," demanded a glass of brandy. . . . Pécuchet, tormented by the mishap with the Malaga, took the tins from the armoire, opened the lid of the first, then a second, then a third. He tossed them aside in a rage and called Bouvard over . . .
>
> Their disappointment was complete. The slices of veal looked like boiled shoe soles. A murky liquid had replaced the lobster. The fish stew was beyond recognition. Mushrooms were growing on the soup. And the entire laboratory reeked with an intolerable stench.[41]

According to Marx, the bespoke impulse reflects the desire for "self-assertion" that life under capitalism produces; alienated from the outcome of their labor, in their leisure people want to stamp their individuality on the objects they produce. However, as long as economic exchange under capitalism continues, Marx warns that this desire for self-assertion will be futile. In Marx's ideal communist society, every individual would be well rounded and proficient in different fields, an ideal of which Bouvard and Pécuchet are the sad and inadequate reality. But this productive, generative form of autodidacticism would only be possible in a society driven by community rather than self-interest, where people's skills are freely developed rather than imposed by the economy as necessary respite from alienated labor. Marx states that "within communist society, the only society in which the original and free development of individuals ceases to be a mere phrase, this development is determined precisely by the connection of individuals," and it is a product of "the necessary solidarity of the free development of all."[42] This free development cannot be willed by the individual in her leisure time; it must be a well roundedness that the empirical conditions of social life demand. Marx believes that it is only when communism has arrived that anything like true self-help would be possible. However, the revolution can only occur through the autonomous efforts of the people, a position that leads to the well-known contradiction between the need for action and the insistence upon economic determinism in Marx's thought.

With their paranoid recoil from professional axioms, Bouvard and Pécuchet appear to be precursors of the modern wave of "self-experimenters" embodied by figures such as contemporary self-help celebrity Timothy Ferriss.

> Ferriss's self-experimentation has not been without its risks: in 2009, he landed in the emergency room with a joint infection after getting a series of human-growth-factor injections at a sports-medicine facility in Arizona. And once, in Cape Town, after megadosing on resveratrol, which may extend life in laboratory mice, he discovered that the tablets also contained a laxative.[43]

"I am a human guinea pig and a professional dilettante," boasts Ferriss in an interview.[44] More than idle pseudoactivity, this extreme DIY is hazardous business indeed.

In her study of French emulation societies, Carol Harrison recounts an amusing anecdote that helps to historicize this type of social behavior. The story concerns a paper submitted to the savant society of Jura by an amateur scientist, titled "Singular Inflammation of Phosphorous in the Body of a Chicken." During a celebratory Mardi Gras supper, the author, father of the family, sat down to carve a chicken at the table.

When he cut into the chicken, plumes of smoke emerged, along with an odd smell. He recounts:

> O great prodigy! With what great astonishment we saw a brilliant phosphorous flame rise from the upper region of the insertion of the neck and spread itself in an instant from one end to another, with a few atoms falling in flames on the table. This sad apparition killed the appetite. . . . Most of the diners refused to eat this infernal dish. Some of the more courageous (myself included) hazarded a taste and finding neither the odour nor the taste of phosphorous, but, on the contrary, a tender and succulent meat, ate with pleasure.[45]

After proceeding to dissect the chicken at the dining room table, the author of the paper describes his astonishment at finding no abnormalities in the carcass. The mystery is explained when the author finally remembers an experiment he conducted a few days earlier with some phosphorous, whose smell offended him, and which he threw out the window in disgust. He deduces that a chicken in the yard must have found the phosphorous and eaten it, and he uses the incident to present some hypotheses regarding phosphoric acid and its effect on the alimentary system to his local emulation society.

If this episode of the infernal chicken did not actually exist, Flaubert would have had to invent it. Bouvard and Pécuchet yearn to undertake their own phosphorous experiment with a local mutt: "They could inject the dog with phosphorus, then shut it in a cellar to see if it would breathe fire through its snout. But how would they inject it? And besides, no one would sell them phosphorous." Their experiments seem sadistic enough when the guinea pig is the village mongrel: "They thought of trapping it under an air pump, having it breathe various gasses, making it drink poison. That might be so much fun!"[46] But the ease and rapidity with which the clerks move from testing on dogs to the town locals is even more troubling. Despite their interventions, "the hunchback did not stand any straighter. The tax collector quit inhaling, as it was making his wheezing twice as bad. Foureau complained about the aloe pills, which gave him hemorrhoids. Bouvard developed stomach cramps and Pécuchet had terrible migraines."[47] The clerks have no qualms about meddling with others' health for the sake of their "science," even developing their own kidney and liver conditions from the medical fads they entertain.[48] What's more, the dog they had experimented upon breaks free, and they live in fear of its rabid retaliation. Because many of their experiments are undertaken for the sake of science or the "public good," these questionable experiments serve to undermine the philanthropy of their more explicitly charitable enterprises.

Indeed, the savants had little tolerance for any art, group, or lifestyle that did not directly contribute to their modernizing agenda; like Homais, they did not hesitate to imprison beggars in order to "improve" the village. The clearest expression of Homais's ruthless instrumentalism occurs at the end of *Madame Bovary*, when his ointments fail to cure a blind local beggar of his facial sores, and the chemist desperately seeks to conceal the evidence of his failure. Inventing stories for the local *Beacon* about the blind man's threat to village serenity, describing his "leprous and scrofulous diseases" as blights upon village life, Homais finally succeeds in getting the blind man imprisoned for life.[49]

Bourdieu points out that in *Sentimental Education* Flaubert's detached bemusement with aesthetic rules and social power gives life the quality of a game.[50] Bouvard and Pécuchet treat their town as their personal laboratory. Flaubert's different texts share a common concern with the casualties of uncommitted study.[51] In a fairly mordant critique of the virtuousness of the homemade, Bouvard and Pécuchet do not transcend consumerism through their projects but become all the more indebted and enslaved. Flaubert maintains that it is when the DIY spirit becomes privatized as selfish individualism that it is most pernicious.

Sentimental Education, *Madame Bovary*, and *Bouvard and Pécuchet* are all defined by a refusal to hierarchize the fields of human endeavor. Part of Flaubert's agenda in setting *Bouvard and Pécuchet* thirty years in the past was to document the retrospective futility of revolutionary hopes. Although the early decades of the nineteenth century in France were characterized by discoveries and aspirations, by 1870, when Flaubert was writing, the country had seen defeat at the Battle of Sedan and the rise of the Paris Commune, and "enthusiasm dropped, institutions vegetated, decadence began to take hold in historical and social thought." As Claudine Cohen recounts, *Bouvard and Pécuchet* became for Flaubert "a kind of observatory from which it was possible . . . to judge with a certain cynicism the revolutionary, romantic hopes placed in the success of science and the progress of the human spirit."[52] Flaubert's universalizing of the self-improvement compulsion takes some of the bite out of his parody, which ultimately evolves into a panoramic meditation upon the farcical futility of all human efforts at warding off the inevitable omnipotence of the natural world. Indeed, Bouvard and Pécuchet's deranged literalism shows up the dogmatism of even the most established disciplinary fields. In a statement sadly corroborated by the increasing evidence of climate change, Flaubert confessed to Guy de Maupassant, "I want to show that education, no matter what it is, does not signify much, and that nature does everything, or almost everything."[53] Driven by the desire to master the vagaries of the market, the body, and the social world, the self-help spirit appealed to Flaubert's interest in the pathos of "human aspiration: the age-old desire to be more than oneself, to reach fulfillment, to find happiness."[54]

RECONTEXTUALIZING MODERNIST AUTONOMY

Bouvard and Pécuchet points to the textual codependency perpetuated by early self-help manuals as an overlooked referent for modernist autonomy. The narrative suggests that modernist negation emerges in part as a reaction to the commodification of the self-improvement instinct through print. As a savant from the period melodramatically exclaimed, "There is no longer an office of the mind, but an office of recipes; the products of thought are priced like merchandise in a boutique."[55] It was in this climate

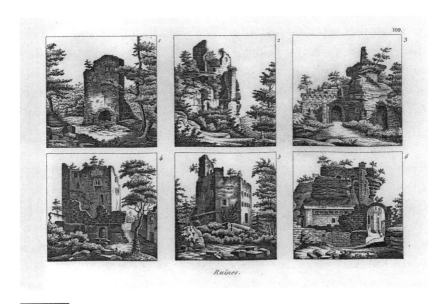

Plate from M. Boitard, *Manuel de L'Architecte des Jardins: L'art de les composer et de les décorer* (Paris: Chez Leonce Laget, 1834), 32.

of fraught instrumentalism that Flaubert wrote his final narrative. As Cohen observes, "Bouvard and Pécuchet are great consumers of guides and manuals of practical science, which they use like books of recipes."[56]

The influence of the self-help guide on the rise of modernist autonomy becomes clearer upon closer examination of Flaubert's response to one of the specific how-to manuals he consulted for his narrative, Pierre Boitard's *The Garden Architect*, a Roret guide to different landscaping styles. (Flaubert consulted a different Boitard manual, his guide to taxidermy, the *Nouveau Manuel du Naturaliste-Préparateur* [1839] when composing "A Simple Heart".[57])

Initially it is not the Roret landscaping manual but a fruit-farming guide that captures the clerks' imaginations: "they spoke constantly of sap and cambium, of fencing, breakage, disbudding." But after a great storm destroys their farming efforts, tearing their latticework and fruit to the ground, the manual's authority is undermined, and its prescriptions adopt a questionable air:

> The authors recommend stopping up the ducts. If not, the sap gets blocked and the tree suffers. To thrive, it really shouldn't bear fruit at all. Still, the ones that are never pruned or manured produce better fruit—smaller, maybe, but more flavorful. I demand that someone tell me why that is! And it's not just each variety that requires specific care, but each individual tree depending on the climate, the temperature, and God knows what else! So then, where's the rule? And what hope do we have of any success or profit?[58]

Flaubert's deconstruction of the instruction manual has two grounds. First, the manual can't account for the infinite particularities of real life— it can't anticipate all the contingencies of temperature, locale, and reader that may arise. Second, the manual needlessly meddles with the natural order; what little advantage it provides simultaneously creates more problems that need to be solved. By unnaturally forcing a tree to produce fruit, you create an excess of sap, which in turn needs to be managed or stopped, reflecting self-help's complicity in producing the demand for even more manuals, consumption, and work.

Disillusioned with the fruit-farming manual whose cover he had so admired, Pécuchet attempts to conceal his barren fruit trees, the embarrassing reminders of his horticultural inadequacy, with the help of yet *another* manual, *The Garden Architect*, in which Boitard divides gardens into different types: the "Melancholic or Romantic" garden, which incorporates ruins and tombs; the "Dreadful" type of landscape, which uses hanging rocks and shattered trees; and the "Exotic," "Pensive," "Fantastic," "Majestic," and "Mysterious" styles of gardens.[59] In Boitard's section "On Conventions and Scenes," which Flaubert carefully consulted and transcribed in writing *Bouvard and Pécuchet*, he remarks that "it is necessary to establish a principle that applies to all, without which we would create only ridiculous or absurd compositions: we want to speak about the rule of convention."[60] One can imagine how this schooling in conventionality would have appeared to the author of the *Dictionary of Clichés*! Later on, though, Boitard admits, "If we wanted to preview and describe every convention or more this chapter would be too long, and even had we chosen to turn it into a thick volume, it would still be incomplete, for there are a thousand conventions for each state, for each position in the world, and maybe for each man."[61] It is the inherent inability of the instruction manual to anticipate every contingency that Bouvard and Pécuchet's disastrous pastimes bring to the fore.

Flaubert's protagonists are characterized by their susceptibility to passing fads, and Boitard's landscaping "moods" present no exception. Their DIY initiatives are conformity masquerading as spontaneity. Settling on the "Dreadful" style of landscape, due to the regional accessibility of rocks and moss, Pécuchet even incorporates a fallen tree into his landscaping tableau. Once finished, he proudly displays his garden to a crowd of the village elite:

> In the light of dusk, it was something terrifying to behold. The mountainous boulder occupied the entire lawn, the tomb formed a cube in the middle of the spinach, the Venetian bridge made a circumflex over the beans—and beyond that, the cabana was a huge black blot, for they had scorched its roof to render it more poetic.

The villagers are not impressed. "Madame Bourdin burst out laughing, everyone else followed suit. The priest emitted a kind of clucking, Hurel coughed, and the doctor had tears in his eyes. . . . So much disparagement was due to the blackest envy," the copy clerks surmise.[62]

Pécuchet is oblivious to the inappropriateness of the setting of the vegetable garden for the poeticism of his landscaping art; his garden is the monstrous outcome of the attempt to combine functionalism and aesthetics. One cannot plop a gothic tomb in the middle of a bed of spinach or merge the lyricism of the Venetian bridge with pedestrian pods of beans without regard for the unsightly commingling of the utilitarian and the poetic. This scene parodies the role of the garden in self-improvement culture as a site of indecision over the proper function of aesthetics.

Ridicule is the risk haunting Boitard's every instruction; it is the punishment for not following his instructions well, the fine line separating a successful and a failed emulation. "Never risk a grand picturesque composition," Boitard warns, "for, if by the force of art, you evade local improprieties and ridicule, you will end up necessarily with the monotonous, particularly if you are without water."[63] Far from encouraging independence of mind and spirit, Boitard's emphasis is on pandering to trend, propriety, and the irrational whims of patrons.

Boitard continues, "In all decorations, you must submit to the taste of the day, to the trends of the moment. These trends are not always very reasonable, we know, but nevertheless, like with a despotic queen: one must obey."[64] Flaubert's famous *Dictionary of Clichés*—the sarcastic guide to social conformity that was to conclude *Bouvard and Pécuchet*[65]—adopts a targeted and timely relevance when read in the context of Boitard's normalizing prescriptions. Read alongside Boitard, Flaubert's *Dictionary of Clichés* acts as a critique of self-help's schooling in the "despotic queen" of social conformity. Flaubert constructed this work as a parody of the homogeneity and false autonomy that he believed the self-help manual exploits.

FLAUBERT'S WHAT-NOT-TO-DO

The title "Dictionary" for Flaubert's little volume is something of a misnomer. Instead of the denotative explanations of clichés one might expect from a dictionary, Flaubert's entries assume a sardonically prescriptive form. Under the entry for "Olive Oil" the reader is advised, "Never good. You should have a friend in Marseille who sends you a small barrel of it." Under "Newspapers" the *Dictionary* instructs,

> You must leave them about in your drawing room, taking care to cut pages before hand. Marking certain passages in blue is also impressive. In the

morning, read an article in one of these grave and solid journals; in the evening, in company, bring the conversation around to the subject, and shine.[66]

A critique of the guidebook's ideological complicity, the *Dictionary* parodies self-help's affirmation of the status quo. "MONOPOLY: Thunder against"; "SELFISHNESS: Complain of other people's; overlook your own"; "YAWNING: Say, 'Excuse me, it's not the company, it's my stomach' "; etcetera.[67] As Jacques Barzun observes, "the cliché, as its name indicates, is the metal plate that clicks and reproduces the same image mechanically without end. This is what distinguishes it from an idiom or a proverb."[68] But rather than supporting this distinction, Flaubert's *Dictionary* reveals the inextricable complicity between the two modes: many of the clichés Flaubert incorporates are indisputably proverbial, grounded in the superstitions of the people (e.g., "BACK: A slap on the back can start tuberculosis").[69] The trajectory of Flaubert's narrative from description to prescription formally documents the self-help fate of the literary, or the prescriptive destination of the aesthetic, that so tormented his late thinking.

The *Dictionary*'s ironic engagement with the self-help manual also vulgarizes the novel form's classical investment in generalities and prescriptions. Although the *Dictionary* sarcastically registers the proximity between the novel and the guidebook, it is far from a passive concession to the inexorable didacticism of the text. Flaubert concludes his epic critique of textual instrumentalism by offering a heap of clichés where, in a different kind of work, a moral might reside. Denaturalizing the ritual of proverbial summation, the dictionary of clichés parodies the conceit of the concluding message, turning the proffering of a moral prize into a buffet of vapid utterances. The trajectory of *Bouvard and Pécuchet* from narrative to manual, like that of *Madame Bovary* from Emma to Homais, seems to enact language's instrumental fate. It offers a sarcastic retort to the classical desire for textual wisdom, documenting what Flaubert saw as the utilitarian degradation of the literary, the shift from the art of the self to the art of self-management.

In stark contrast to self-help's insistence upon "mind-power," or the capacity of the will to influence circumstance ("By considering the thing easy it becomes so for you," writes Flaubert's compatriot Émile Coué, who would become the founder of positive thinking shortly after Flaubert's death),[70] Flaubert's narrative documents the futility of human agency and control before the dictates of nature and time. *Bouvard and Pécuchet* is the ruin's ironic retort to the utilitarian interpretations imposed upon it. Imagining the perspective of the rain, rebuking the gardener's false mastery, it voices chance's guffaw at the merchant's string of good luck, or the fire's disdain for a bountiful harvest of wheat. His sense of the paltriness of human aspiration bleeds into Flaubert's insistence that every aesthetic utterance risks complicity with the worst possible interpretation of it that can arise. He commented that books "are made like pyramids. There's some long-pondered plan, and then great blocks of stone are placed one on top of the other, and it's back-breaking, sweaty, time-consuming work. And all to no purpose! It just stands like that in the desert! But it towers over it prodigiously. Jackals piss at the base of it, and bourgeois clamber to the top of it, etc."[71] Describing his impression of the ruins of Carnac on a trip to Brittany, Flaubert returns to the problem of art and utility:

> We understood perfectly then the irony of these granite boulders that, since the age of the Druids, have laughed in their green lichen beards at seeing all the imbeciles that came to stare at them. Savants have spent their lives in attempting to determine their past usages; don't you admire this eternal preoccupation of the unfeathered biped with finding some sort of usefulness for everything? Not content with distilling the ocean to salt his stew, and assassinating elephants to make knife-handles out of them, his egotism is again provoked when he is faced with some debris or other whose utility he can't figure out.[72]

Flaubert's fantasy of liberating art from the practical appropriations of savants and other "unfeathered bipeds" reflects the influence of Immanuel Kant.[73] The inability to ascertain an object's use is, for Kant, a precondition for appreciation of the beautiful.[74] Thus self-help is threatening for Flaubert because its insistence on use robs us of a precious opportunity for beauty. At the same time, the possibility is raised that this ostensive expulsion of the instrumental and utilitarian from modernism (and, as a corollary, from the discipline of literature, which, with the rise of New Criticism, was increasingly premised on modernist tenets), instead of countering self-help, may have abetted its growth by surrendering to self-help an entire demographic of readers in search of the practical guidance modernism refused to supply. But "history is a boomerang," to quote Ralph Ellison, and, as demonstrated in subsequent chapters, self-help today is desperate for the appearance of moral authority and commercial disinterestedness that modernist autonomy has come to signify.[75] Flaubert's dictionary, and the broader narrative to which it is attached, represent an early foray into the explosively popular subgenre of anti-self-help self-help, or of narrative pseudoadvice, which receives sustained attention in chapter 6.

Flaubert's narrative-as-negative-exemplar turns Smilesian emulation on its head. His use of the imperative, second-person voice in his pseudo-manual predates not only modernist mock manuals by Stein, Pound, and Woolf but also the popularity of the "how-to narration" that emerged in the master of fine arts (MFA) writing of the 1980s and flourishes among the prestige literature of the present day. The lead story from Lorrie Moore's 1985 collection *Self-Help*, for some time the frontrunner of this trend, and a continued influence on texts like Jessica Anne's *A Manual for Nothing* (2017), makes this Flaubertian lineage explicit. In Moore's "How to Be an Other Woman," the main character meets her paramour while furtively reading *Madame Bovary* on a bus.

> You climb on together, grab adjacent chrome posts, and when the bus hisses and rumbles forward, you take out a book. A minute goes by and he asks you what you're reading. It is *Madame Bovary* in a Doris Day biography jacket. Try to explain binding about warpage. He smiles, interested.
>
> Return to your book. Emma is opening her window, thinking of Rouen.

"What weather," you hear him sigh, faintly British or uppercrust Delaware.

Glance up. Say: "It is fit for neither beast nor vegetable."

It sounds dumb. It makes no sense.

But it is how you meet.[76]

The allusion is revealing in part because, much like her precursor, Emma, Moore's character operates as if she were acting out a prewritten adultery tale. She is following the script for how to be "an other" woman, or a mistress, but also for how to be just *another* woman, a walking cliché. But the allusion is also notable because it intimates the literary debt owed by this new cadre of self-help parodists to Flaubert's what not to do, his *Dictionary of Clichés*, from its second-person focalization to its use of imperatives as a vehicle for cautionary lessons.

Around the time of the publication of Moore's celebrated collection, the second-person focalization began to gain steam, a turn that attracted the ire of some reviewers. Jonathan Holden wrote an essay bemoaning its prevalence in poetry: "The Abuse of the Second Person Pronoun."[77] Likewise, as a *New Yorker* reviewer snapped, "the gimmick of writing a how-to story in the imperative mood should have been retired after Pam Houston used it (to better effect) in her 1989 story 'How to Talk to a Hunter.'"[78] In contrast, Brian Richardson maintains that the second-person voice is "arguably the most important technical advance in fiction narration since the introduction of the stream of consciousness," that other modernist innovation.[79] The self-help subtext of the second-person mode was not lost on the narrative theorists of Moore's stories, who described their "pseudo-guide book" style[80] and "how-to narration,"[81] and compared their voice to those of "the cookbook, the travel guide, and the self-help manual."[82] "In using the second-person address to invite her actual readers to adopt multiple positionings," James Phelan comments, "Moore implicitly comments on the simplistic assumptions about readers operating in self-help books." In particular, "Where the standard narrative in the self-help genre always leads its audiences (actual and authorial) onward and upward toward Self-Fulfillment and the Better Life . . . Moore's narratee-protagonist is on a slow course to nowhere,"[83] a trajectory also encapsulated by Anne's *A Manual for Nothing*, but before either of these by *Bouvard and Pécuchet*.[84]

This is not the place to review the fascinating mimetic possibilities the literary use of the second person opens up (I treat that more fully in chapter 6), but simply to note that Flaubert's *Dictionary of Clichés*, with its pseudoguidebook of "everything one should say if one is to be considered a decent and likable member of society," presents an early case of the use of specious imperatives in the service of a cautionary tale. Before the second person became a "program-era" gimmick, Flaubert was experimenting with the use of how-to narration to disincentivize the action described.[85]

From a historical perspective, Flaubert's narrative documents a crucial moment of social change, when the communal improvement spirit becomes privatized as a form of domestic, leisure activity, when the locus of self-help shifts from the public square to the private garden. It depicts how this privatization of self-help corresponds to its textualization, for what Flaubert's novel indicates above all is the literary import of this newly instrumentalized reading method. Thoroughly attuned to the earliest glimmers of the self-improvement craze, Flaubert, a founder of high modernist aestheticism, feared the brute, assimilative power of bourgeois utilitarianism to absorb even the most recalcitrant of literary and philosophical objects. His giant "what not to do" paved the way for the tradition of call and response between popular advice and intellectual counterguidance, which I will proceed to disentangle, and that runs from the modernist parodies of Gertrude Stein, Ezra Pound, Henry James, Edith Wharton, Virginia Woolf, and Nathanael West through to the many contemporary narratives that use self-help as a structural and ethical frame.

3

NEGATIVE VISUALIZATION

SUSTAINABLE SELF-HELP

One of the most scathing appraisals of the self-help ethos ever set on paper was written by Marshall McLuhan in an unpublished 1939 essay, "Dale Carnegie: America's Machiavelli." McLuhan takes issue with Carnegie's "morally malignant" text on multiple levels, such as the way it "exploits the weaknesses of [one's] fellows" and endorses "the passion for irresponsible power over others." But the aspect that most rankles is Carnegie's account of his system as a "way of life."[1] In *How to Win Friends and Influence People*, published three years before McLuhan's piece, Carnegie tries to fend off critiques that he is fashioning flatterers: "No! No! No! I am not suggesting flattery! Far from it. I'm talking about a new way of life. Let me repeat. *I am talking about a new way of life.*"[2] But far from assuaging a reader like McLuhan, Carnegie's account of his system as a "new way of life" is even more distressing. If Carnegie's suggestions about withholding criticism and exploiting the inherent egotism of individuals are used merely as short-term strategies to climb a little higher up the company ladder, they are still ethically problematic, to be sure, but the sphere of their damage is potentially restricted to the corporate workplace. If Carnegie's methods become a life philosophy that extends into all spheres of existence, however, from friendship to childrearing and intellectual or political debate, the fallout would be impossible to contain. Ironically, then, those measures Carnegie adds to reassure readers of his conscientiousness are in fact what, for McLuhan, make his philosophy so socially pernicious.

Although McLuhan does not use this phrase, what he takes issue with is that Carnegie's self-help is not sustainable, if we take "sustainable" to designate measures that "meet the needs of the present without compromising the ability of future generations to meet their own needs."[3] To the contrary, McLuhan maintains that Carnegie's legacy wreaks havoc on the ability of future generations to "meet their needs," let alone to flourish. Indeed, this is the crux of Lauren Berlant's critique of the cruelty of optimism, whereby "a person or a world finds itself bound to a situation of extreme threat that is, at the same time, profoundly confirming."[4] Better, perhaps, to approach *How to Win Friends* not as a "way of life" but as a "kludge"—tech slang for "a workaround or quick-and-dirty solution that is clumsy, inelegant, inefficient, difficult to extend and hard to maintain."[5] Carnegie-style self-help may have a short-term utility in select situations, but as McLuhan cautions, it should never be more than a kludge.

This leaves us, however, with the question of what a more sustainable version of self-help would look like.[6] Some forays are found in the work of Adorno and Foucault. In *Minima Moralia*, Adorno composes what Jakob Norberg calls a book of "advice for the vanishing individual."[7] As Norberg comments, "*Minima Moralia* participates in known discursive formats—giving and taking advice—in order to disclose a world that renders these formats obsolete." But Adorno goes beyond sheer demystification to uphold the advice tradition's "appeal to reason" and "faith in the capacity of fellow individuals."[8] Like Adorno, Foucault was highly critical of self-help, but he spent his last lectures outlining the necessity for a return to counsel and self-care.[9] In a more recent contribution to this Continental tradition, German philosopher Peter Sloterdijk argues in *You Must Change Your Life*, a dense tome that takes its title from Rilke, that the global environmental crisis necessitates a renewal of ancient and religious "practices" of self-discipline, but with the aim of establishing a "horizon of universal co-operative asceticisms."[10] These intellectual forays into self-help celebrate didactic restraint, moral ambiguity, individual humility, and negative capability. As they intimate, the sustainable self-help of the future might look a lot like modernism.

In this chapter, I look at four instances of serious, early twentieth-century authors responding to the popular advice of the day in their fictions, and even experimenting with their own, more sustainable versions of counter-counsel: Flann O'Brien, Edith Wharton, Henry James, and Virginia Woolf. Each of these authors expresses skepticism toward the persuasive tactics and universalizing directives that have come to be associated with commercial advice. At the same time, close analysis reveals that their writings also make visible the troubling affinities between charismatic literary authorship and the spiritual manipulation of popular guides. As we shall see, part of the reason self-help was so troubling to them is not because of the degree to which it departs from their understanding of experience but because of how it exploits their own spiritual investments in affinity, kinship, intuition, coincidence, and the unconscious.

FLANN O'BRIEN VS. DE SELBY

In modeling the utility of negative visualization, modernism presages the affirmative backlash currently rattling the self-help industry. Whether in the viral online articles on "The Art of No," circulated by well-intentioned office colleagues, or in guides such as Oliver Burkeman's *The Antidote: Happiness for Those Who Can't Stand Positive Thinking*, the consensus is clear: "we chronically undervalue negativity and the 'not-doing' skills."[11] As Svend Brinkmann, another contributor to the anti-self-help movement, maintains, "if you have integrity, you will often have to say no because so much of the accelerating culture deserves to be renounced."[12] Even Marie Kondo's secret to tidying up urges us to say "no" to capitalism's accumulative, maximalist ethic.[13] We need to be more selective about our allotment of yeses, the new self-help maintains, for their indiscriminate allocation has not made us any happier or better off.

But before any of these, Flann O'Brien observed that "there is a lot to be said for No as a general principle." In his surreal novel *The Third Policeman* (written 1939, published 1967), the ghost of the murdered Old Mathers explains that he came to embrace the philosophy of No when he realized that most of the sins he committed were due to the pernicious influence of other people:

> I therefore decided to say No henceforth to every suggestion, request, or inquiry, whether inward or outward. It was the only simple formula which was sure and safe. . . . It is now many years since I said Yes. I have refused more requests and negativized more statements than any man living or dead. I have rejected, reneged, disagreed, refused, and denied to an extent that is unbelievable.[14]

Mathers's summation that "No is a better word than Yes"[15] is not just O'Brien's backchat to the affirmative conclusion to *Ulysses*. It is also a defense against the public credulity that enables Manus's mail-order schemes to prosper in O'Brien's late work, *The Hard Life* (1961), and that allow the character de Selby's philosophy to wreak havoc in the lives of his disciples. Harold Bloom has described the "anxiety of influence" as a driving force of literary production.[16] For O'Brien, this anxiety of influence is not just about how to follow on the heels of geniuses like Joyce but also about how to defend oneself from the pernicious manipulations of charlatans and savants. As the epigraph to *The Hard Life* from Pascal contends, "all the trouble of the world comes from not staying alone in one's room."[17]

In this respect, O'Brien's novels join Melville's *The Confidence-Man*, Twain's portraits of scoundrels and swindlers, Wells's *Tono-Bungay*, West's *Cool Million*, and the whole cadre of modern literature devoted to depicting and unraveling the huckster mythology. The scourge of irresponsible advice is a concern threaded throughout many of O'Brien's works, perhaps most explicitly in *The Hard Life*, where Manus's schemes could be torn right out of the quack treatments advertised in the pages of *Ireland's*

Own. One such questionable philosophy of the period belonged to Émile Coué, the French pioneer of positive thinking. In his influential *Self-Mastery Through Conscious Autosuggestion* (1922), Coué uses the example of the ease of walking a plank one foot off the ground versus the difficulty of walking one suspended between two cathedral towers to demonstrate the power of the mind to determine reality. "Why is it," he writes, "that you would not fall if the plank is on the ground, and why should you fall if it is raised to a height above the ground? Simply because in the first case you imagine that it is easy to go to the end of this plank, while in the second case you *imagine* that you *cannot* do so."[18] Vertigo, insomnia, uncontrollable giggles—for him each offers proof of the power of fantasy to govern our lives: "When the will and the imagination are opposed to each other, it is always the *imagination* which *wins, without any exception whatever.*"[19]

Coué's example is echoed almost verbatim by Manus as he explains the theory behind his mail-order course on high wire-walking to his brother in *The Hard Life*:

> What's the difference if you're an inch or a mile up? The only trouble is what they call psychological. It's a new word but I know what it means. The balancing part of it is child's play, and the trick is to put all the idea of height out of your mind. It *looks* dangerous, of course, but there's money in that kind of danger. Safe danger.[20]

When one of Manus's zealous pupils attempts to tightrope walk across the Liffey, only to panic hallway through and plummet into the river, hitting his head on a rock, Sergeant Driscoll comes round to the brothers' house to make inquiries. The sergeant explains how a young man almost died from falling off "a sort of death machine" perched above the river.[21]

Such schemes were able to prosper in early twentieth-century Ireland in part because the compulsory Education Act of 1892 had produced a whole new demographic of literate and ambitious readers. As a result of the universal education legislation, most children remained (at least nominally) in school up to eleven to fourteen years of age, giving them the benefit of minimal literacy without the more advanced training in critical thinking that would have helped to defend them against the propaganda of the culture industry, which targeted precisely the ambitions and anxieties of this emergent clerical class. The rapid increase in literacy (by 1902, 86 percent of the Irish population was deemed literate) brought a new "clerkly readership with a basic education, a taste for leisure reading, and the disposable income to buy cheap publications."[22] Worried about appearing weak, undistinguished, and effeminate, and ground down by the rote drudgery of office labor, this demographic formed the target audience of entrepreneurs such as Sydney Flower, who authored handbooks on personal magnetism, willpower, and success. Flower published a self-help guide to *establishing* a self-help operation called *The Mail-Order Business: A Series of Lessons* (1902). Using a "hair restorer" product as a case study, which he

20   The Mail-Order Business.

The composite ad to reach both agents and the general public, should run like this:

BALDNESS A CRIME!
Cantharin grows hair on
BALD HEADS.
Price, $1.00, postpaid. Trial Treatment, 10c silver. We will ship $1.00 worth for 25c to agents. A money maker. All readers of this paper should write for our free booklet. Address Cantharin Mfg. Co., Main St., Chicago.

You can now inclose this last advertisement in your letter to the journal whose offer you accepted, and you have now about ten days' time on your hands to be devoted to getting up your circulars. If you examine the pages of the journals which have been sent you you will find an advertisement something as follows:

CIRCULARS! Size 3x6, any 200 words, 500 printed and postpaid, 50 cents. Every eight extra words, 1 cent. Gummed labels for use on envelopes, note heads, packages, etc., 2,000 for $1. Samples free.

What you want, however, is not a 3x6 circular, but a 3x6 folder, making four pages of printing in place of two. You will get these for about $2 for 500 copies.
Here is your circular matter. The effort should be to be convincing and frank, using a

Page from Syndey Flower, *The Mail-Order Business* (Chicago: Mclurg, 1912), 20.
Source: IAPSOP, www.iapsop.com.

dubs "Cantharin," after the chemical thought to stimulate hair growth, he offers advice on everything from buttering up the local pharmacist to pacifying angry clients: "A soft answer turneth away wrath, and the probability is that this customer, after exploding in the manner aforesaid, will not be hard to appease."[23] One of his magazines posed the question: "If matter is but a manifestation of mind; if mind forms the body; if mind is only thought with purpose; if thought changes matter at will; why do some of our most advanced metaphysicians permit themselves to be afflicted with baldness?" Some of Flower's other projects included dietetic supplements to improve longevity and a "scheme to transplant goat glands into men (and women) to increase vigor."[24]

Handbooks like Flower's served as precedents for Manus's own long-distance learning endeavors. Undeterred by the tightrope incident, he concocts one scheme after another to make his fortune, from discount volumes of Cervantes to his "Gravid Water," a tonic that is supposed to cure rheumatoid arthritis:

THE GRAVID WATER

The miraculous specific for the
complete cure within one
month of the abominable
scourge known as Rheumatoid
Arthritis.
Dose—one t-spoonful three
times daily after meals.
Prepared at
LONDON ACADEMY LABORATORIES[25]

Such moments insert O'Brien into a familiar tradition of novelistic parodies of "humbuggery," in which Wells's *Tono-Bungay* also belongs, with its titular sham tonic advertisement in the evening paper: "HILARITY—TONO-BUNGAY. Like Mountain Air in the Veins," which inquires, "Are you bored with your Business? Are you bored with your Dinner? Are you bored with your Wife?"[26]

After Manus "prescribes" gravid water for his guardian Collopy's initially minor rheumatism, Collopy succumbs to a gruesome "premature and rapid decomposition of the body" brought about by the pernicious liquid.[27] It is easy enough to read *The Hard Life* as a simple satire of the gullible Irish reading public, but there is a deeper concern underlying O'Brien's text, about the co-optation of the imagination such manuals performed. His works pose the question of what separates constructive from pernicious textual influence. As Musil puts it, "prophets and charlatans rely on the same phrases, except for certain subtle differences no busy man has the time to keep track of."[28]

Another death-by-bad-advice takes place in *The Third Policeman*. The book's orphaned narrator—whose name we never learn—has devoted his life to completing a scholarly index on a made-up philosopher/scientist called de Selby. Lacking the funds to support the publication of his de Selby research, the narrator is convinced by his malevolent acquaintance Divney to help murder their wealthy neighbor Mathers in order to steal his box of cash. He relates how Divney made his case after he "read portions of my 'de Selby index' (or pretended to) and discussed with me afterwards the serious responsibility of any person who declined by mere reason of personal whim to give the 'Index' to the world."[29] But when the narrator is plunged into the novel's nightmarish fourth dimension, his de Selby specialization leaves him in the lurch.

The true crime of *The Third Policeman* is not Mathers's murder but the narrator devoting his life to a writer with no good advice. As O'Brien explains, "in the *Layman's Atlas* [de Selby] deals explicitly with bereavement, old age, love, sin, death and the other saliences of existence. It is true that he allows them only some six lines but this is due to his devastating assertion that they are all 'unnecessary.'" The novel details at length the shortcomings of de Selby's philosophy when it comes to practical insight. "Like all the greater thinkers, he has been looked to for guidance on many of the major perplexities of existence," O'Brien relates. However, "the commentators, it is to be feared, have not succeeded in extracting from the vast store-house of his writings any consistent, cohesive, or comprehensive spiritual belief and praxis." For example, although de Selby has developed an elaborate theory about the association between water and happiness, his account of this "hydraulic elysium" neglects to specify "whether the reader is expected to infer that a wet day is more enjoyable than a dry one or that a lengthy course of baths is a reliable method of achieving peace of mind."[30] The nightmarish impenetrability of *The Third Policeman* is what it looks like to live in a world of theory without praxis.

The best example of de Selby's bad advice is conveyed in an anecdote from one of his commentators. The narrator relates the story of a lovelorn man who appeals to de Selby for advice about a woman with whom he is obsessed. De Selby has earned the reputation of town savant, counterintuitively, because of the mystique surrounding the fact that he never reads the newspaper. His eccentricity leads people to believe he must have secret knowledge or wisdom. But "instead of exorcising this solitary blot from the young man's mind, as indeed could easily have been done, de Selby drew the young man's attention to some fifty imponderable propositions each of which raised difficulties which spanned many eternities and dwarfed the conundrum of the young lady to nothingness." As a result of de Selby's intervention, the young man forgets about his love and hatches a plan to commit suicide instead. When, by a lucky accident, the suicide plan is thwarted, he settles for a life of crime and is eventually imprisoned for larceny and "offences bearing on interference with railroads." O'Brien writes, "So much for the savant as a dispenser of advice."[31] As one writer observes, O'Brien's narrator is in love with the wisdom of de Selby "the way the man on the American street might love the wisdom of, oh, say, L. Ron Hubbard."[32]

Leo Tolstoy, the nineteenth-century moralist, demanded: What good is science if it cannot teach me how to live?[33] O'Brien, an author not typically associated with moral sententiousness of any kind, asks the same of de Selby. His novel opens with two epigraphs:

> Human existence being an hallucination containing in itself the secondary hallucinations of day and night (the latter an insanitary condition of the atmosphere due to accretions of black air) it ill becomes any man of sense to be concerned at the illusory approach of the supreme hallucination known as death.
>
> (de Selby)

> Since the affairs of men rest still uncertain,
> Let's reason with the worst that may befall.
>
> (Shakespeare)[34]

As many have observed, O'Brien here places an invented author and a canonized one on the same ontological plane. The form of the epigraph itself holds a crucial place in the literary history of self-help (as recounted in my discussion in chapter 1 of the legacies of Smiles's *Hamlet* epigraph in Japan). The literary politics of self-help are in many ways the politics of the epigraph: brazenly decontextualized citations for the sake of personal use (exemplified, to use another Shakespeare example, by *Ulysses*'s Mr. Deasy's quoting of racist villain Iago as a prescription for financial behavior).[35]

But these epigraphs also stage two clashing textual ethics. The first expresses a relativist disengagement from worldly anxieties. Whether the target is Berkeley's idealism or Humean skepticism, the quote shows how intellectual specialization has come to depend upon the renunciation of common sense. As Philip Coulter puts it, "The philosopher has given the narrator, the critic, a system which cannot be readily understood and by which it is impossible to live."[36]

The second epigraph articulates the Stoic practice of *praemeditatio malorum*, the preparation for future evils. In the early modern period, this was absorbed into the Renaissance view that philosophy should be about "learning how to die." The relevance of this second epigraph to the ensuing narrative tends to be overshadowed by de Selby's provocation.

However, it points to what we might call "negative visualization" as the nexus where stoic and modernist practice converge. The neo-stoical and neo-modernist tendencies of contemporary self-help are linked by the way their investments in negative visualization—in imagining the worst that may arise—operate as potential correctives to the industry's affirmative tunnel vision.

But there is one place in *The Third Policeman* where the novel appears to productively court the reader's desire for advice: the execution scene. We find the narrator standing on the scaffold for a crime he does not understand, in a world he does not recognize, and with a name he can't remember, and de Selby's paltry theories are nowhere to be found. Instead, the narrator copes with the imminence of death by turning his thoughts to the natural world, and the tone of the narration abruptly shifts. The art of gallows wisdom is unfortunately almost its own genre in Irish history; think of the rousing execution speeches of Roger Emmet and Wolfe Tone. The scaffold is not only an important site for political persuasion but also an occasion to articulate the moral legacy of a life.

The narrator's own contribution to this tradition of gallows wisdom presents some of the most beautiful writing of the entire modernist canon. The narrator is on the scaffold, about to be executed, and begins to imagine what might happen after death:

> Down into the earth where dead men go I would go soon and maybe come out of it again in some healthy way, free and innocent of all human perplexity. I would perhaps be the chill of an April wind, an essential part of some indomitable river or be personally concerned in the ageless perfection of some rank mountain. . . . Or perhaps a smaller thing like movement in the grass on an unbearable breathless yellow day, some hidden creature going about its business—I might well be responsible for that or for some important part of it. Or even those unaccountable distinctions that make an evening recognizable from its own morning, the smells and sounds and sights of the perfected and matured essences of the day, these might not be innocent of my meddling and my abiding presence.[37]

Hugh Kenner called these the most "deeply felt" sentences in all of O'Brien's work.[38] In contrast to the boisterous anomie of *The Third Policeman*'s absurdist universe, we're presented here with a scene of serene integration: to become part of the essence of things. Although the improvement economy obliges individuals to constantly prove themselves professionally indispensable, equanimity is here associated with transcending the necessity of self-justification. The narrator dreams of an occasion to just simply *be*, to exist outside of the endless loop of goals and rewards. And, significantly, in this moment he does not turn to de Selby but to Wordsworth's account of "the light that never was, on sea or land"[39] for consolation. During this crisis, it is literature and not quack advice or pseudophilosophy that comes to his aid.

In contrast to the manipulations of de Selby and Manus, this passage models a nontransactional version of worldly influence. It continues, "Or perhaps I would be an influence that prevails in water, something seaborne and far away, some certain arrangement of sun, light and water unknown and unbeheld, something far-from-usual." Throughout the novel, O'Brien establishes a link between the spiritual ideal of ego transcendence depicted in the nature imagery and the ethos of artistry "for its own sake," which finds expression in the policeman MacCruiskeen's aesthetic endeavors, from his tiny, invisible chests too small for the human eye to see, to his miniature piano that plays music on vibrations that elude the human ear.[40] Against de Selby's bombastic obfuscations, O'Brien here outlines an ethics of the autotelic.

For Kenner, these passages offer evidence of the ongoing importance of religion to O'Brien's thought. But O'Brien's celebration of nature as a potential key to a more sustainable form of advice not only links this moment to Catholicism but also grounds his approach in the methods of the Stoics, whom his Shakespeare epigraph invokes, and who advised individuals to learn to live in accordance with nature.[41] This goal may help to explain the appeals to stoicism in so much contemporary self-help, as more fully detailed in chapter 6, which is finally recognizing the error and futility of efforts to control the natural world (a theme, as we saw, also raised by Flaubert's *Bouvard and Pécuchet*). In fact, O'Brien wrote his master's thesis on "Nature in Irish Poetry" at University College Dublin in 1934. His works indicate the extent to which neo-stoical and neo-modernist inclinations of contemporary self-help are linked, not just by their shared recognition of the limits of human agency before nature but also by their joint investment in the value of negative visualization as a potential corrective to anthropocentric hubris.

EDITH WHARTON VS. GURDJIEFF

The case of O'Brien exemplifies how textual advice becomes a new kind of problem for twentieth-century authors. Plenty of scholars have explored how the modernists resisted Victorian didacticism, but I am interested in the status of modernism's countercounsel as a forward-looking reaction to the increasing commercialization of advice. Moreover, this problem of irresponsible advice is not just a charge that modernism slings at the self-help industry but one to which modernist authors are themselves susceptible. De Selby's eschewal of common sense, for example, his ability to beguile his disciples, who mistake the incomprehensible for the wise, was not just a tendency of the period's gurus but also of modernist icons like Joyce. "Your talk," exclaims O'Brien's protagonist, "is surely the handiwork of wisdom because not one word of it do I understand."[42] In addition to a warning against the mail-order credulity depicted in *The Hard Life*, it is difficult not to read O'Brien's critique of "deselbiana" in *The Third Policeman* as in part a takedown of the early Joyce industry. Both novels strive to deflate and parody charismatic language by describing discipleship as a unilateral devotion that does not give back.

Like O'Brien, Edith Wharton is concerned with the public credulity that links the worship of modernist icons such as Joyce with devotion to spiritual leaders or gurus. She also draws a correspondence between modernism's eschewal of common sense and self-help's deployment of vague and impenetrable language. In 1927, Wharton wrote an entire novel, called

Twilight Sleep, lampooning the pseudospirituality of the age.[43] Wharton stood "apart from modernism," as the title of Robin Peel's monograph about her indicates,[44] and her joint aversion to the fads of self-help and modernism brings out these movements' shared ambitions: to harness the processes of free association, liberate readers from the automatism of habit, and urge individuals to use their time well. *Twilight Sleep* centers around the oblivion of matriarch Pauline Manford, who is so busy fawning over the latest trendy self-improvement gurus—whether the mystic Mahatma, with his "School of Oriental Thought," or, later, the "Inspirational Healer" Alvah Loft, author of *Spiritual Vacuum Cleaning* and *Beyond God*—that she fails to notice her husband falling in love with her daughter-in-law Lita under her own roof.[45] Her packed regimen is reminiscent of Jay Gatsby's, another self-improvement fanatic.[46] As Mrs. Manford's secretary has transcribed, "7.30 Mental uplift. 7.45 Breakfast. 8. Psycho-analysis. 8.15 See Cook. 8.30 Silent Meditation. 8.45 Facial Massage. 9. Man with Persian miniatures. 9.15 Correspondence. 9.30 Manicure. 9.45 Eurythmic exercises. 10. Hair waved. 10.15 Sit for bust. 10.30 Receive Mother's Day deputation," and so on. The ongoing joke of the narrative is that Mrs. Manford needs a stress reliever to unwind from her numerous relaxation therapies; she is "agitated by the incessant effort to be calm." Indeed, "one might as well have tried to bring down one of the Pyramids by poking it with a parasol as attempt to disarrange the close mosaic of Mrs. Manford's engagement list."[47]

One of *Twilight Sleep*'s most ardent admirers was Aldous Huxley, who applauded its depiction of the rather "more magical than religious" quality of modern superstition, citing the book as a precedent for *Brave New World*.[48] Although Huxley played his own significant role in the development of the New Age philosophy as a founder of the "Human Potential" movement and speaker at Esalen, he had little tolerance for the improvement trends that Wharton's novel depicted:

With her customary acuteness, Edith Wharton has laid her finger on the essential fact about modern superstitions. They give results here and now;

and if they don't give results, they fail. People turn to the supernatural for some particular and immediate benefit—such as slender hips, freedom from worry, short cuts to success, improved digestions, money. They want, not truth, but power.[49]

Along the same lines, theorists of modernity have suggested that modern culture replaces meaning with information, value with technique.[50] However, the reconsideration of modernist secularism undertaken by Pericles Lewis and others brings into relief self-help's status as an extension of, rather than as a substitute for, religious thinking.[51] Early New Thought pamphlets read like sermons and abound with references to God, the Universal Mind, and Creation, which is why William James counted the movement among the twentieth-century's new "varieties of religious experience."[52] Even today, self-help is not a rejection of religion *tout court* but something like secularism with benefits. Mrs. Manford's self-improvement rituals resemble a form of meditation or prayer; with repetition, seemingly vacuous self-improvement clichés, such as Coué's famous sentence, adopt the meaningless sonority of a Buddhist mantra, or an incantation from an ancient religious rite.

As *Twilight* helps us to see, both modernism and self-help were deeply invested in what Aaron Jaffe and Jonathan Goldman describe as the early twentieth-century culture of celebrity.[53] The *annus mirabilis* of modernism—1922—marked both the international tour of the self-help guru Émile Coué, the French pioneer of the positive thinking industry, and the founding of George Gurdjieff's New Age "Institute for the Harmonious Development of Man" at Fontainebleau. Men like Gurdjieff and Coué were causes célèbres for the day's elite, an excuse for the wealthy to rally and congregate. They were also a last resort of the desperately ill; a tubercular Katherine Mansfield died in a damp room in Gurdjieff's institute in 1923,[54] and the modernist artist Roger Fry traveled in vain to Coué's institute in Nancy, France, in hopes of finding a cure for his illness.[55] The qualities Wharton condemns in self-help correspond to the qualities she resists in modernism: the cultishness, the primitivism, the fetishism of obscurity and difficulty, the linguistic bravado, even the dependence of the male "genius" upon a network of enabling and supportive women.

Mrs. Manford's devoted patronage of the gurus of the day eventually leads, through a clumsy series of events, to her daughter Nona being shot after she discovers her father and sister-in-law together in bed. Some critics have speculated that the real-life inspiration for one of the self-help gurus in the novel, the character of the Mahatma, was the Armenian mystic George Gurdjieff (1872–1949).[56] Purportedly trained as both a priest and a physician, Gurdjieff founded a highly influential New Age institute in 1922 that taught students how to transcend the situation of what he called "waking sleep" (thus Wharton's "twilight sleep") in which most people live. Only by undertaking the "Fourth Way" of his spiritual exercises could individuals hope to break free of this automatism and realize their full potential. In Wharton's novel, when news of a scandal erupts regarding Mrs. Manford's daughter-in-law's sojourn at the Mahatma's School, including a newspaper picture of her participation in the school's nudist tribal dances, the novel replicates contemporaneous headlines regarding the Gurdjieff institute's sacred "gymnasium," described by Sinclair Lewis as "a cross between a cabaret and a harem" and by Vivienne Eliot (T. S.'s first wife) as "where [Lady Rothmere] does religious naked dances with Katherine Mansfield."[57]

Gurdjieff had a transformative influence on a group of queer expatriate women authors in France, including Margaret Anderson and Jane Heap, the founders of the *Little Review*. Introduced through Djuna Barnes to Kathryn Hulme, Solita Solano, and Georgette Leblanc, they created the "Rope Group," which was devoted to expounding his teachings.[58] Anderson and Heap were inspired by their time with Gurdjieff to terminate the *Little Review*; his philosophy had convinced them of modernism's irrelevance. But his writings have more in common with those published in the *Little Review*'s pages than they were willing to recognize. Indeed, John Bennett's description of Gurdjieff's literary style could almost be a description of Joyce's:

Many who encounter Gurdjieff for the first time in Beelzebub's Tales are disconcerted by the strange style, and by his use of strange neologisms which often seem quite unnecessary for conveying his intention. There are several reasons why Gurdjieff decided to create his own literary style. In this first place, he was well aware that clarity and consistency in speech and writing nearly always result in the sacrifice of flexibility of expression and depth of meaning. When he spoke or lectured he paid no attention to the rules of grammar, logic, or consistency. After he learned some French and English, he mixed them indiscriminately, regardless of the linguistic limitations of his hearer.[59]

Editing opaque sentences, unpacking neologisms, and promoting genius, just as they had with Joyce, Eliot, and others, the Rope Group women's work with Gurdjieff was not so different from their modernist endeavors. The same wish to shed automatism, or what Gurdjieff calls man's "hypnotic state," and to resurrect the "inner life," attracted Anderson and Heap to both the misunderstood mystic and to the relatively unknown and unpublished Joyce.[60] Conversely, the same "exploration of the subliminal" that Wharton resisted in Woolf's stream of consciousness, and that she disdained in Joyce's "turgid welter" of "uninformed and unimportant" "sensation," made her suspicious of figures like Gurdjieff.[61]

A vociferous critic of stream of consciousness and the new "slice of life" literature of Joyce and Woolf,[62] Wharton warned the younger novelists against embracing what she viewed as a pathological inward turn, a trend she despised even in the later writings of Henry James, a friend with whom she otherwise sympathized.[63] She disapproved in particular of the modernists' indiscriminate notation of every passing thought: "The mid-nineteenth century group selected; the new novelists profess to pour everything out of their bag."[64] For Wharton, the fickleness of modernism and self-help are linked through their shared disregard for form, history, and selection. Much as Gurdjieff urged his followers toward intense "self-observation and self-remembering" (always carried out, however, under the supervision of a "Man Who Knows"),[65] modernism appears to embrace the unsorted, unfiltered, and subconscious. It is their "egoistic consciousness and self absorption" that, for Wharton, links Mrs. Manford and Stephen Dedalus.[66]

Even more than with Joyce and Eliot, the discipleship with Gurdjieff instigated a significant shift in the Rope Group women's vocations from editors to writers, from fiction to memoir, from transcribers to independent producers. Indeed, what is most remarkable is the tremendous literary output that the Rope discipleship engendered: enough to fill an entire library shelf. As one of the group's members, Kathryn Hulme, author of *The Nun's Story* (1956), later a film starring Audrey Hepburn, recounts:

> In the Paris of the Thirties the great adventure of my life began, the only event in it which seems worth recording in personal narrative form—a form, incidentally, which I love to read but dread to write. The event which compels me into this book was my meeting with the celebrated mystic, teacher, and philosopher, George Ivanovitch Gurdjieff, whom I encountered as if by chance and came to love as if by design. . . . He uncovered in me a hidden longing I never knew I had—the desire for an inner life of the spirit—and taught me to work for it as one works for one's daily bread.[67]

The group published a total of seventeen books.[68] As Hulme describes, Gurdjieff offered an occasion to contemplate the inner life, just as modernist stream of consciousness does. In addition to the women of the Rope Group, Gurdjieff influenced writers and artists such as Jean Toomer, Mabel Dodge Luhan (D. H. Lawrence's patron), and Frank Lloyd Wright. In contrast, modernists such as Ezra Pound, Wyndham Lewis, and W. B. Yeats were dismissive of Gurdjieff's teachings.[69]

As with de Selby (and Joyce), Gurdjieff forces us to confront the uncomfortable proximity between wisdom and humbug. As Geoffrey Hartman notes: "What we appreciate as exemplary in art, we admire and fear as 'charismatic' in public life. If it is hard enough to tell charlatan from genius in art, it often seems impossible to distinguish between creative and destructive portions of the spirit in a significant politician or religious leader."[70] According to Tobin Siebers, in response to this "dilemma of charisma" Hartman "recommends a healthy dose of skepticism and negative thinking about art." As Siebers sees it, beyond Hartman alone, the "argument for the self-destructive text, with its celebration of literary strangeness, hesitancy, and stuttering," stems from a desire to defeat "the monolith of charismatic power." Although he is specifically referring to Cold War criticism, Siebers's point also applies to the modernism from whence so much postwar, deconstructive criticism emerged. Both modernists authors and Cold War critics posit "learning how to read"[71] as a means of defending oneself against the dangers of charismatic persuasion, all the while deploying their own charismatic personalities and methods. It is not difficult to see how this skeptical legacy has resulted in the tradition of "suspicious," "critical, and negative" hermeneutics that has recently come under attack by proponents of "surface" reading and "post-critique."[72] As Siebers notes, in a sentiment many have recently echoed, "to be skeptical about skepticism is either the most reactionary of philosophies or the most radical. But how are we to tell which?"[73]

HENRY JAMES VS. WILLIAM JAMES

Twilight pokes fun at the period's charismatic gurus, but "The Jolly Corner" (1908), by Wharton's friend Henry James, offers a more somber assessment. Henry's reservations toward the industry are inextricable from his brother William's endorsement of it at a time when few intellectuals would deign to give self-help serious consideration. William James's discussions of the power of habit and will inspired countless early self-help handbooks, such as Frank Channing Haddock's *The Power of Will*, Annie Payson Call's *Nerves and Common Sense*, and Carnegie's *How to Win Friends and Influence People*, to name a few.[74] In light of this significant influence on the self-help literature to come, William's explicit and implicit debates with his brother over the genre's merits have a great deal of contemporary consequence. Self-help today increasingly mediates between William's motivational account of human potential and Henry's skeptical perspective on the interminable process of self-betterment. New antihandbooks such as Burkeman's *The Antidote* and Neel Burton's

The Art of Failure: The Anti-Self-Help Guide suggest that, after reaching an affirmative apex, the self-help tide may be turning toward Henry's position.[75]

Scholars have long suggested that Henry may have provided the model for the "sick soul" described by his brother William James as the "nerveless sentimentalist and dreamer, who spends his life in a weltering sea of sensibility and emotion, but who never does a manly concrete deed."[76] But little work has been undertaken on the reciprocal question of how William's promotion of the early self-help philosophy of mind-cure inspired Henry's critique of popular strategies of self-realization. When William lamented the "mustiness" of *The Golden Bowl* in a letter on October 22, 1905, it provoked Henry's irked response, in what can only be a reference to William's endorsement of self-help across America during these years: "Let me say, dear William, that I shall be greatly humiliated if you *do* like it, & thereby lump it, in your affection, with things, of the current age, that I have heard you express admiration for & that I would sooner descend to a dishonoured grave than have written."[77] As Henry wrote in a letter to Grace Norton, and which applies to William's prescriptions as well, "don't, I beseech you, *generalize* too much . . . remember that every life is a special problem which is not yours but another's, and content yourself with the terrible algebra of your own."[78]

More than one hundred magazines and newspapers were dedicated to the New Thought phenomenon by the time Henry composed "The Jolly Corner."[79] The story describes Spencer Brydon's trip from Europe back to America to inherit his childhood home. Seeing his old house inspires in Brydon a taste for remodeling, which starts him thinking about what would have happened if he had stayed in America to be a businessman or an architect, and if he had married his childhood sweetheart Alice Staverton, rather than emigrating to Europe to pursue his "selfish frivolous scandalous life" in the arts. Henry writes, "He found all things come back to the question of what he personally might have been, how he might have led his life and 'turned out,' if he had not so, at the outset, given it up."[80]

This theme of lost potentiality was preoccupying William as well during this same period, when he was advocating the benefits of mind-cure at universities across the country. In his popular treatise *The Energies of Men*, William describes how he was inspired by the everyday phenomenon of the "second wind" to examine the individual's overlooked energy reserves.[81] He observes, "Compared with what we ought to be, we are only half awake. Our fires are damped, our drafts are checked. We are making use of only a small part of our possible mental and physical resources." And he exhorts, "the human individual thus lives usually far within his limits; he possesses powers of various sorts which he habitually fails to use."[82] Carnegie quotes this line from James some thirty years later in his introduction to *How to Win Friends and Influence People*, in which he exclaims, "Those powers which you 'habitually fail to use'! The sole purpose of this book is to help you discover, develop, and profit by those dormant and unused assets."[83] The most successful self-help book ever written, then, is but a gloss on William James; and the controversy over modernism's ontological authority continues, via the legacy of William's refutation of Henry's representational strategies to obliquely inform self-help's trajectory.

Decontextualized, William's quotation reads like a motivational speech, but his observation about human potential originally occurs in a chapter with the downbeat title "Failure to Do All That We Can." In its original setting, the passage quickly shifts from a tone of inspiration to one of rebuke. Unlike the "hysteric," William says, who at least has an excuse for his narrow and "contracted" vision of his own potential, the rest of us have no one to blame for our failures but ourselves. In his 1914 preface to *The Energies of Men*, William had to exasperatedly defend the work from charges that its "gospel of overstrain" encourages individuals "to drive themselves at all times beyond the limits of ordinary endurance" and to "use . . . alcohol and opium as stimulants."[84]

Although his work often overlapped with the self-help discourse he analyzed, William was well aware of the movement's limitations.

He lamented how "the mind-cure principles are beginning so to pervade the air that one catches their spirit at second-hand. One hears of the 'Gospel of Relaxation,' of the 'Don't Worry Movement,' of people who repeat to themselves, 'Youth, health, vigor!' when dressing in the morning, as their motto for the day."[85] But unlike other philosophers, from Theodor Adorno to Michel Foucault, whose contempt for cliché distracts them from self-help's potential political or palliative social function, William argued that its reductionism should not dissuade us from taking the benefits of mind-power seriously.[86] Rather, he argued, in part *because* of its "crudity," New Thought might be destined "to play a part almost as great in the evolution of the popular religion of the future as did those earlier [religious] movements in their day."[87]

Casting a backward glance at the discoveries of the New Thought method in 1917, Orison Swett Marden, one of the movement's most prolific authors, explained that "the finding of the larger possibilities of man, the unused part, the undiscovered part, is the function of the New Philosophy." He urged his readers to shake out the "possible man" inside: "It is the man you are capable of making, not the man you have become, that is most important to you. . . . Try to bring out *that possible man. . . .* Why don't you use him . . . why don't you call him out, *why don't you stir him up*?"[88] "The Jolly Corner" tells us why. While the New Thought literature was lamenting the individual's quotidian estrangement from his innermost potential, Henry's story intimates that such estrangement might be preferable. Spencer Brydon is tormented by the specter of surplus potentiality that self-help dangles before its readers. As Brydon puts it, "it's only a question of what fantastic, yet perfectly possible, development of my own nature I mayn't have missed."[89] And this dormant possibility is manifest in Brydon's imagination in the form of his billionaire alter ego who stayed in New York to accumulate capital rather than moving to Europe to pursue a life in the arts. Brydon's equation of money with potential reflects the trends of his time; as McGee notes, the first definition of success as wealth occurred in the 1891 *New Century Dictionary*.[90] Brydon's refrain rings throughout Henry's story: "What would it have made of me, what would it have made of me? I keep for ever wondering, all idiotically; as if I could possibly know!" This pounding anaphora of the counterfactual motif is conspicuous:

> If he had but stayed at home he would have anticipated the inventor of the sky-scraper. If he had but stayed at home he would have discovered his genius in time really to start some new variety of awful architectural hare and run it till it burrowed in a goldmine.[91]

Brydon's thought patterns demonstrate the consequences of internalizing the ideology of unlimited potentiality. As Bruce MacLelland's 1907 *Prosperity Through Thought Force* declared, "you make your own misery; you make your own unhappiness," and further, "anyone can make of himself whatever he chooses."[92] "You are the architect of your own career," similarly urges Haddock in *The Power of Will*, also published in 1907, which makes copious use of William James's *Habit* and purports to teach both "supreme personal wellbeing and Actual Financial Betterment" through self-direction. Haddock advises, "You can so develop your [power of] will that it will command the luxuries, the accomplishments, the marked successes, which potentially lie dormant in every human being."[93]

With its screeds against wasted potential, mind-cure's "gospel of relaxation" transforms leisure into a new kind of work and invites a fresh reading of modernist interiority as representing the immaterial labor of compulsory self-betterment. The visualization techniques advocated by mind-cure guru Henry Wood exemplify the after-hours commitment New Thought demanded of its practitioners. Henry James encountered Wood's handbook through his 1902 reading of his brother's *Varieties*, which quotes Wood at length.[94] His protagonist Brydon's practice of "project[ing] himself all day, in thoughts . . . into the other, the real, the waiting life" strikingly evokes the visualization techniques Wood advocated, to the extent that Wood's leading mind-cure handbook, *Ideal Suggestion Through Mental Photography, A Restorative System for Home and Private Use* (1893), almost furnishes a blueprint for Henry's fictional text.

Wood recommends that his reader retire each night alone to a corner of his house to stare at select suggestions printed in block letters at the end of his book:

PRACTICAL DIRECTIONS FOR IDEAL SUGGESTION

Instructions for the use of the Suggested Ideals [contained in the following pages]:

FIRST.—Retire each day to a quiet apartment, and be alone IN THE SILENCE.

SECOND.—Assume the most restful position possible, in an easy-chair, or otherwise. . . .

THIRD.—Bar the door of thought against the external world. . . .

FOURTH.—Rivet the mind upon the "meditation" . . . and by careful and repeated reading absorb its truth. . . . Do not merely look upon it, but wholly GIVE YOURSELF UP TO IT. . . .

Ideals will be actualized in due season.[95]

As Steven Starker comments, "The after-images produced by all that staring must have been startling, even convincing to some."[96] Such after-images go a long way toward explaining the climax of "The Jolly Corner," which takes place when, after a great deal of meditation and repetition, Brydon's "ideal" is finally "actualized," and he comes face-to-face with the apparition of the person he could have been if he had never left America. Brydon's conjuring of the "black stranger"—that "mental photograph" of himself, to use Wood's term—is the result of nights of concentrated practice: "He had known fifty times the start of perception that had afterwards dropped; he had fifty times gasped to himself 'There!' under some fond brief hallucination." Finally, one night, Brydon feels the "central vagueness diminish," and he conjures his wretched "other self," the negative-image of the "triumphant life."[97] But instead of mind-cure's "possible man," brimming with dormant potential, Brydon's deformed, greedy alter ego bears a closer resemblance to Freud's unsightly id. "Thoughts are things," noted New Thought proponent Prentice Mulford in 1899; Brydon's hallucination is a mind-cure meditation gone awry.[98]

Although premised on the dramatic opposition between aesthetic and entrepreneurial ambition, "The Jolly Corner" also draws attention to the wishful thinking that unites both types of endeavor. As Freud argues, all creative writing springs from unsatisfied wishes, including that class of "ambitious wishes, serving to exalt the person creating them." According to him, aesthetic form is essentially an alibi for the author's enactment of the conflicting desires of "His Majesty the Ego."[99] Put differently, narrative may be merely the author's circuitous, devious form of self-help.[100] But if "The Jolly Corner" is Henry's form of oblique personal self-help, for example, as the persuasive queer readings of the story by Eve Sedgwick and Eric Savoy indirectly suggest, this is not self-help in the form of New Thought's consolatory mantras but about using the alternate reality of fiction as a forum for confronting difficult personal questions.[101] In this way, reading Henry's story for its self-help subtext is not incompatible with the interpretations influentially advanced by these queer theorists. After all, part of Henry's resistance to self-help is his aversion to its normalizing, domesticating discourse, whether in terms of aesthetics, sexuality, or politics. In contrast to what he saw as his brother's Procrustean typologies, (Henry) Jamesian self-help does not reduce or simplify difficult truths but is closer to Philip Weinstein's view of modernist knowledge as an unraveling of the Enlightenment conceit of a coherent subject and stable world.[102]

"The Jolly Corner" culminates in a loss of agency rather than in glorious self-realization, and in so doing it undermines not only mind-cure's promise of self-control but also the broader American myth of self-fashioning. New Thought had important international allies, influences, and affiliates such as Coué, Charles F. Haanal, Annie Besant, and Thomas Troward (the inspiration for Australian author Rhonda Byrne's *The Secret*), but it found an ideal habitat on American soil due, in part, to the foundation-laying works of Phineas Quimby, a clockmaker whose early witnessing of French mesmerism in his home town in southern Maine inspired him to help found the movement.[103] Henry's engagement with New Thought philosophy probably reflects the impact of his 1904 visit to the United States, which inspired many of the works belonging to this late phase of his career. He said that he returned to his native land in order "to make myself a notion of how, and where, and even *what*, I was."[104] But if Henry did "make himself" during his voyage to America, the self he made is defined by its rejection of American improvement discourse. Henry tellingly relates his retort to American industry and urbanization, "the great monotonous rumble of which seems forever to say to you: 'See what I'm making of all this—see what I'm making, what I'm making!' " To which he responds, "I see what you are *not* making, oh, what you are ever so vividly not; and how can I help it if I am subject to that lucidity?—which appears never so welcome to you, for its measure of truth, as it ought to be!"[105] With their digressive indirection and complexity, Henry's works strive to articulate precisely what is left out of American improvement rhetoric.

As for Spencer Brydon, the reader is left with the suspicion that no amount of feminine caress will permanently quash his beleaguered refrain: "Do you believe then—too dreadfully!—that I *am* as good as I ever might have been?"[106] The modernist inheritance of this burden of self-determinism can be seen in Leopold Bloom's endless reveries about alternate professions (farmer! mayor! Zionist!), in the indecision of Beckett's characters, in the subjunctive musings of Woolf's married pairs. In this way, mind-cure and modernism represent two different methods of coping with the frustrating, tantalizing proximity of success and fulfillment in modern middle-class life. As they both show, to different ends, self-help ideology is lived as misplaced guilt for failing to inhabit life's seemingly infinite possibilities.

WOOLF VS. BENNETT

Perhaps the most striking example of the enmity between "high" literature and self-help positions concerns a famous literary debate of the modernist period: the feud between Virginia Woolf and Arnold Bennett. Considered a crucial moment of modernism's self-formation, ongoing assessments of this dispute have largely failed to address the subtext of Bennett's work with self-help and the role of self-help in shaping both his and Woolf's aesthetic strategies.

Today Bennett is mainly known for his realist novels set in his home district of the Potteries, an industrial area that was a center for English ceramics production in the eighteenth century. But as Robert Squillace observes, "No writer of any period even a fraction so highly regarded as Bennett wrote a single self-help book, let alone the six or eight Bennett produced."[107] Bennett published several tremendously popular self-help guides, or "pocket philosophies" as he described them, including *How to Live on Twenty-Four Hours a Day*; *Literary Taste: How to Form It*; *Mental Efficiency*; *The Human Machine*; *Self and Self-Management*; and *How to Make the Best of Life*.[108] His texts advance less scientific versions of the argument for mental discipline espoused by William James, and it is surprising that the two contemporaries had so little to say about each other's work. Both writers advised readers to cultivate good habits, to minimize time wastage, and to forge their ideal character through minor acts of will. Bennett's writings were "at once a reproof and an inspiration," as the *Bristol Daily Mercury* noted, a descriptor that, as we have seen, applies to William's works as well.[109]

The similarities between the two authors may be partly attributable to the fact that they were both influenced by the same timeworn classical wisdom on the art of life.[110] Bennett described his pocket guides in a letter as "nothing but Marcus Aurelius & Christ assimilated & excreted by me in suitable form."[111] However, his account of his *Philosophy of Living* series was not always so flippant:

> When I proposed to republish them in book form I was most strongly urged not to do so, and terrible prophecies were made to me of the sinister consequences to my reputation if I did. I republished them. "How to live on twenty-four hours a day" sold very well from the start; it still has a steady

sale, and it has brought me more letters of appreciation than all my other books put together. I followed it up with a dozen or more books in a similar vein. And I do not suppose that my reputation would have been any less dreadful than it is if I had never published a line for plain people about the management of daily existence.[112]

His self-help guides achieved such monumental success that Henry Ford is reputed to have passed out five hundred copies of *How to Live on Twenty-Four Hours a Day* to his employees.[113] Even before the recent resurgence of his literary reputation, e-readers have been repackaging and popularizing Bennett's time-management tips for overtaxed contemporary readers.

Bennett explains the book's premise:

Newspapers are full of articles explaining how to live on such-and-such a sum. . . . I have seen an essay, "How to live on eight shillings a week." But I have never seen an essay, "How to live on twenty-four hours a day." Yet it has been said that time is money. That proverb understates the case. Time is a great deal more than money. If you have time you can obtain money— usually. But though you have the wealth of a cloak-room attendant at the Carleton hotel, you cannot buy yourself a minute more time than I have, or the cat by the fire has.[114]

For Bennett, social inequalities are neutralized by temporality's inherent democracy (rather than exacerbated by workday discrepancies). His handbook boasts that it can help readers save seven extra hours per week by convincing them that time is more of a commodity than money. However, Bennett's egalitarian premise is belied by his first order of business; he provides detailed instructions on how to set up one's tea and biscuits each night so that one can rise two hours before the servants: "These details may seem trivial to the foolish, but to the thoughtful they will not seem trivial." He continues, "The proper, wise balancing of one's whole life may depend upon the feasibility of a cup of tea at an unusual hour."[115]

Bennett promised to make his reader a "millionaire of minutes," and William James similarly invoked the economic terminology of "energy-budgets" and "efficiency-equilibriums" to advance his potentiality doctrine.[116] These practical treatises fully internalize the Protestant ethic's equation of good living with good budget-balancing. In turn, their modernist critics respond by dramatizing what Weber described as the "iron cage" of individual responsibility that this capitalist ideology engenders.[117] The Protestant ethic of industrious asceticism was all the more troubling to novelists because it entailed intolerance for fiction. Just as William had little patience for Henry's narrative digressions, Bennett's time-management philosophy bleeds into annoyance at the profligacy of modernist prose. It "beat me. I could not finish it," he admitted of *Mrs Dalloway*, and remarked that Joyce turned novel reading into a form of "penal servitude."[118] Bennett's essays on the art of living mount a challenge against modernism's disdain for the crude utilitarianism of public taste. Deriding aesthetic contemplation without action, he observed that "the man who pores over a manual of carpentry and does naught else is a fool. But every book is a manual of carpentry, and every man who pores over any book whatever and does naught else with it is deserving of an abusive epithet."[119] Imagine how Flaubert—the grandfather of high-modernist aestheticism—would have received such a pronouncement!

Bennett's ostracized status among the modernists was cemented by Woolf's essay "Mr. Bennett and Mrs. Brown" (delivered 1923, published 1924), a text that lays bare self-help's role in modernism's ethnogenesis. Woolf's denunciation of Bennett's materialism coincides with her proclamation of modernism's arrival; novelists need new representational strategies because "on or about December, 1910, human character changed."[120] Tellingly, the definition of novelistic character that Woolf advances in this essay is explicitly formulated against the "skill of character reading" demanded by the "practical business of life." "Character" was, of course, a loaded term in the self-help lexicon of the time. Samuel Smiles published an entire volume on the subject, and both James and Bennett discuss character as a product of habit, and therefore malleable to change.[121]

The strategic approach to character advanced by their advice manuals is for Woolf the very antithesis of the aesthetic: "Novelists differ from the rest of the world because they do not cease to be interested in character when they have learnt enough about it for practical purposes." In short, it is precisely that attention which exceeds instrumentalism, surpassing the needs of "happiness, comfort, or income" (precisely the province of self-help) that, for Woolf, defines the novelistic gaze.[122]

The context of self-help calls for a reappraisal of Woolf's style, defined, in part, by its inspired rebuttal of Bennett's practical philosophies. Although she renounces his moralizing impulse, Bennett's writings bring into relief the contours of a Woolfian counterpedagogy premised upon enactment rather than prescription, "steeping" rather than "sidling," to use her own terms.[123] Essays such as *A Room of One's Own* (1929) and "On Not Knowing Greek" (1925) position Woolf as a precursor of the feminist, prepolitical strain of self-help that seeks to imagine alternatives to the patriarchal status quo. Woolf's essays to the *Common Reader* (1925), written during the same period as the notorious feud, can hardly be considered apart from Bennett's directives for the "Plain Man and His Wife" (1913). Essays like her "How Should One Read a Book?" (1926) operate as concerted rewritings of Bennett's instructional texts such as *Literary Taste: How to Form It* [1909]. Woolf opens *her* essay, "In this first place, I want to emphasize the note of interrogation at the end of my title. Even if I could answer the question for myself, the answer would apply only to me and not to you. The only advice, indeed, that one person can give another about reading is to take no advice, to follow your own instincts, to use your own reason, to come to your own conclusions."[124] The difference between Bennett and Woolf is the distinction between the declarative and the interrogative; it is the difference that a question mark makes.[125]

Woolf converts the "how-to" into a question, an approach that also motivates her fiction. What unforeseen events, asks *Mrs Dalloway* (which famously occurs within the span of twenty-four hours), might interfere with Bennett's fantasy of mastering a single day? After all, Clarissa is just as intent on stanching the intractable flow of time with her party as Bennett is with his tea and biscuits. Modernists were just as attuned to the power of habit as were their more practical, "middlebrow" counterparts; Woolf bemoans the amount of one's day devoted to the monotonous routines of "non-being."[126] However, to transcend habit for her requires a surrendering of the self to the sway of the moment (as when Septimus Smith senses the "exquisite beauty" of "leaves being connected by millions of fibres with his own body") rather than the vehement reassertion of time-mastery that Bennett and William James recommend.[127]

A character like Septimus throws a wrench into Bennett's account of the power and reach of mental discipline. Spencer Brydon's counterfactual alter ego is a billionaire skyscraper mogul, and Septimus could have been a Bennett acolyte if certain contingencies, such as the First World War, had not intervened:

> To look at, he might have been a clerk, but of the better sort . . . might end with a house at Purley and a motor car, or continue renting apartments in back streets all his life; one of those half-educated, self-educated men whose education is all learnt from books borrowed from public libraries, read in the evening after the day's work, on the advice of well-known authors consulted by letter.[128]

Septimus could have led a perfectly deferential, semieducated life if not for the unforeseen influence of battle and illness, those bothersome impediments to even the most rational of life plans. (Actually, the First World War ushered in the term "bibliotherapy," which acquired cultural currency through the hospital libraries in which novels stood "row upon row like phials in a pharmacy.")[129] The conveyers of moral insights in *Mrs Dalloway* are either villains, like Dr. Bradshaw, or suffering from PTSD, like Septimus, who fancies himself the appointed bearer of "supreme secret" signals and messages ("that trees are alive," "there is no crime," "There is a God," "Change the world," "No one kills from hatred") and is convinced he knows "the meaning of the world" (not entirely unlike the way thinkers such as William James advertised that they knew the "meaning of truth").[130]

Such moments call to mind Lionel Trilling's lament that modernism aligns madness with authenticity, while also pointing to the fundamental irrationality and megalomania of the practice of dispensing advice.[131] (As we shall see in chapter 5, Adorno develops a similar idea in *The Stars Down to Earth*, his assessment of the totalitarianism underlying the *Los Angeles Times* advice column.) *Mrs Dalloway* enacts Woolf's disillusionment with the moral authority of the text in its oft-discussed skywriting scene, where, in the place of the exigent or profound dispatch they expect, pedestrians piece together the spelling out of an ad for toffee.

Woolf lays out her resistance to philosophical dogmatism in a comment on D. H. Lawrence, which also applies here:

> Its [*sic*] so barren; so easy; giving advice on a system. The moral is, if you want to help, never systematise—not till you're 70: & have been supple & sympathetic & creative & tried out all your nerves & scopes. . . . Art is being rid of all preaching: things in themselves: the sentence in itself beautiful.[132]

Woolf's exhortation that "art is being rid of all preaching" is, of course, a performative contradiction. Like James with his insistence on the universal singularity of every life's "terrible algebra," the only piece of counsel Woolf will permit herself is the injunction to disregard universalizing advice. Yet for someone recommending inconclusiveness, Woolf sounds like she has art's proper role very settled. Echoing the Flaubertian stance, she elsewhere laments that "we pin [words] down to one meaning, their useful meaning, the meaning which makes us catch the train, the meaning which makes us pass the examination."[133] The obsession with use drains language of its lifeblood. In the wake of Pierre Bourdieu, it is impossible to ignore the class prejudice underwriting such modernist celebrations of disinterestedness, and it is usually either through the lens of class or gender that this famous debate is discussed, with the critics focusing on the former tending to favor Bennett's position, and those invested in the latter defending Woolf's stance.[134] Bourdieu reminds us that only someone who has all of their necessities met can afford to champion art's uselessness.

Likewise, Bennett's patronizing assessments of women's writing no doubt informed his critiques of Woolf's work and inspired her reciprocal aversion. Beyond confirming their already well-established oppositions, the subject of self-help makes visible the authors' shared concern with how to capture and communicate life's intensity.

Today's critics do not have much to say about literature's stance on "life," at least, not without scare quotes, but it is around the nebulous question of literature's "life-impulsion" (as F. R. Leavis termed it)—or "spirit," "zest," "vigor"—that the Woolf/Bennett debate pivots.[135] As Edwin J. Kenney effectively posits, the debate centered on that difficult issue of "what is real in human life and how the novelist is to represent it."[136] Even more than "character," "life" is what Bennett believes Woolf's writing is missing, from as early as that incendiary review of *Jacob's Room* (1922): "there is an absence of vital inspiration. Some novelists appear to have no zest; they loll through their work as though they were taking a stroll in the Park."[137] In her turn, Woolf finds the same "vitality" absent from Bennett's works: "Life escapes. . . . Whether we call it life or spirit, truth or reality, this, the essential thing, has moved off."[138]

This debate—and its self-help subtext—underscores the inextricable relation between the representational problem of how to describe life and the philosophical problem of how to live it. The authors' reciprocal appraisals reflect what Lears describes as the pervasive "dread of unreality" and the yearning to "experience intense 'real life' in all its dimensions" that give rise to both the therapeutic ethos and also to modernist practice.[139] Bennett returns to the problem of "zest" in his handbooks and his novels, and even published a volume of essays called *The Savour of Life*, but his fiction is less confident that zest acquisition is teachable.[140] Although he repeatedly advises his self-help readers to sharpen their minds by reading a "little chapter of Marcus Aurelius or Epictetus" a day, Bennett's protagonist Edwin in *Clayhanger* undermines this counsel:

> He had diligently studied both Marcus Aurelius and Epictetus; he was enthu-
> siastic, to others, about the merit of the two expert daily philosophers; but

what had they done for him? Assuredly they had not enabled him to keep the one treasure of this world—zest.[141]

It seems that even the classics cannot solve the troublesome problem of zest retention.

In 1925, the same year *Mrs Dalloway* appeared, physician Abraham Myerson published a self-help book called *When Life Loses Its Zest.*[142] Myerson helped to popularize the term "anhedonia," which he learned from William James's discussion of the healthy-mindedness doctrine in *The Varieties of Religious Experience* (1902).[143] Citing James as a key influence, Myerson was also, in 1935, one of the first to advocate antidepressants; he was a pioneering prescriber of the amphetamine Benzedrine for the treatment of depression, anhedonia, and simple discouragement.[144] The vicious circle of self-improvement, exacerbated by the pharmacological turn, which at once causes feelings of insufficiency and claims to cure them, had already reached a crisis in the character of Spencer Brydon in a way that evinces the continued relevance of modernism's self-help revisionism to contemporary therapeutic culture. In his 1914 preface, William denied he was advocating the use of stimulants for exploiting the latent "energies of men" that his manual so persuasively outlined, but the pharmacological turn in therapeutic culture is one interpretation of his ideas about self-betterment. Already sensing this cultural consequence, both Henry James and Woolf document how easily the healthy impulse of self-improvement can morph into self-reproach.

RESILIENT MODERNISM

In this chapter I have traced a series of disputes between literary and self-help perspectives: O'Brien against mail-order hacks, Wharton against spiritual gurus, Henry James against the "potentiality" movement his brother William endorsed, and Virginia Woolf against Arnold Bennett. Yet rather than confirming the steadfastness of the distinction between serious literature and self-help methods, these case studies unsettle the steadfastness of their opposition.[145] Perhaps the most obvious point of convergence between modernist and self-help agendas concerns their joint fascination with the resources of the unconscious.

An example can help to illustrate this overlap. In *The Law of Mentalism*, the Los Angeles trickster Victor Segno invited subscribers to join his success clubs, which were devoted to the mutual transmission of positive "thought waves." The one-dollar admission fee was guaranteed to attract success. Segno explains the book's premise:

> Marconi, the inventor of Wireless Telegraphy, says that a word or its equiva-lent creates a vibration in the air just as a pebble thrown into a pond creates a ripple in the water, and that this vibration travels with the speed of lightening to the terminus, however distant, and makes itself known and felt by every telegraph instrument that is tuned in harmony with the sender. In the same manner a thought from the brain of one person travels on despite all resis-tance until it is taken up by the brain or brains that are in harmony with the mind from which it was sent.[146]

Segno argued that other people's thoughts change our constitution and experience. As fellow self-help author Prentice Mulford corroborated, "you are, to a certain extent, a different person through conversing an hour yesterday with A, than if you had interchanged thoughts with B. You have then grafted on you a shade of A's nature, or quality of thought."[147] One thinks of *Mrs Dalloway*'s "Fear no more the heat of the sun," one of several thoughts that "travel" between Septimus and Clarissa.[148] As Alex Zwerdling notes, "there is an uncanny quality in Woolf's characters that enables them to communicate telepathically."[149] Along similar lines, in *Ulysses*, Stephen and Bloom have uncanny mental exchanges, and Norpois and Marcel share an unspoken intuitive understanding in Proust's *In the Shadow of Young Girls in Flower*.[150]

Modernism's investment in interiority and the individual unconscious rendered it vulnerable to charges of solipsism and individualism similar to those laid against self-help. This position was perhaps most forcefully advanced by Georg Lukács, who argued that modernism is too concerned with the individual's mind to effect any social change.[151] In their efforts to counteract the forces of industrial atomization and standardization, both modernism and self-help risk implying that the individual mind is all that exists. As Wyndham Lewis wrote, in his irascible yet perceptive fashion, like *Mrs Dalloway*, like Bennett's *How to Live on Twenty-Four Hours a Day*, "the world in which Advertisement dwells is a one-day world." He maintains, pointing to the affinities between the seemingly polarized ideologies of self-help and modernism, that "*time is money*" is the hackneyed, relativist proverb that "Bergson's durée always conceals beneath its pretentious metaphysic."[152] Yet this did not stop Lewis himself from using the tongue-in-cheek title *The Art of Being Ruled* for his 1926 "manual of survival in what he saw as an apocalyptic situation."[153] In his own foray into sustainable self-help, Lewis wrote:

> In such a fluid world we should by all rights be building boats not houses. But this essay is a sort of ark, or dwelling for the mind, designed to float and navigate. . . . For a very profound inundation is at hand. After *us* comes the deluge: more probably than not, however, before that and out of its epigrammatic sequence.[154]

Lewis's rephrasing of a situation of powerlessness as choice anticipates the many contemporary self-help manuals that take attributes largely outside of one's control—talent, charisma, race, gender, being human—and reformulate them as instructions (*How to Be a Person in the World*; *How to Be Black*; *How to Be a Woman*, etcetera).[155] In so doing, they bring to the fore self-help's tendency to rebrand determinism as strategy, precisely what Adorno abhorred.

Yet Adorno's advocacy of modernist negation over self-help's false agency elides the extent to which the two discourses overlap; for example, both estrange habit by making a problem of the mundane. What *New Yorker* journalist Dwight Macdonald derided as howtoism's making a problem of the "supererogatory" or superfluous and Wharton disliked as the "slice of life" is, in modernism, called the "everyday."[156] This making a topic of the taken-for-granted finds expression in self-help's and modernism's joint transvaluation of the clichéd and mundane. And just as self-help is accused of privileging technique above wisdom, Lewis complained of Joyce, "What stimulates him is *ways of doing things,* and technical processes, and not *things to be done.*"[157] This seems to be a tendency that carried through to Beat writers like Jack Kerouac, for whom Joyce was a significant influence. As Gilbert Millstein wrote in the original *New York Times* review of *On the Road* (1957), one way to define the new generation was to say that "the absence of personal and social values . . . is not a revelation shaking the ground beneath them, but a problem demanding a day-to-day solution. *How* to live seems to them much more crucial than *why.*"[158]

But beyond their investment in the technical, everyday, and transhistorical, other affinities can be found between modernism and self-help. For instance, the prevalence of the micro-units of the fragment and cliché is related to the centrality of cultural appropriation to both self-help and modernist practice, a tendency particularly visible in their combining of Eastern and Western philosophical traditions (recall the link between Benjamin Franklin's and Ezra Pound's translations of Confucius).[159]

This same muddying of opposition occurs at almost every level of the attempt to cleanly distinguish self-help from modernist reading protocols. Such examples suggest that the appeal of modernism to contemporary self-help is due not only to the way it counters or opposes that ideology— not merely for its irony in regard to the project of self-cultivation, in other words—but also to those places where it crosses over and takes up the problem of life management. Despite the modernist championing of "impersonality," for Lionel Trilling, "no literature has ever been so shockingly personal—it asks us if we are content with our marriages, with our professional lives, with our friends. . . . It asks us if we are content with ourselves."[160] It would be worth exploring how the misprision of modernism as antiadvice has contributed, via the legacy of the New Critics, who also tend to be misread as amoral, to what some perceive as a bias in literary studies against self-cultivation, presentism, and practical use. Some of our most engrained disciplinary practices may be founded on a series of chain reactions to a version of modernism that never was. That is to say, our understanding of modernism's utility to our contemporary social and disciplinary moment depends on our recognition of its earnest efforts not just to negate but also to rewrite popular advice.

If once, perhaps during the heyday of Horatio Alger, the value of literature appeared to lie in its fund of motivational upward mobility stories, today its appeal is often linked to the "negative visualization" scenarios it furnishes. Robert Musil, who once described literature as "teaching of living in examples,"[161] strove in his writings to capture "a new morality capable of fitting more closely to the mobility of facts."[162] If we are being generous, we can read contemporary self-help as being engaged in a similar project. It is turning to difficult, serious literature for support in its shift away from the ideals of perfection and success and toward the more measured values of perseverance and resilience. We may need a catastrophizing imagination to counteract the reflexive and compulsory optimism that has facilitated the mass denials of our present age. In this view, negative thinking is not just an anxious tic but a strategy to prepare for the alarming mobility of facts in our uncertain circumstances.

4

JOYCE FOR LIFE

In 2009, Declan Kiberd caused a little stir among Joyceans with his new guide to James Joyce for the "common reader," *Ulysses and Us: The Art of Everyday Life in Joyce's Masterpiece.* In his latest work, the respected author of *Inventing Ireland* aimed to pry Joyce's masterpiece from the grip of the "corporate university," which "praised Joyce as the supreme technician and ignored *Ulysses* as a modern example of wisdom literature." Kiberd declared that "it is time to reconnect *Ulysses* to the lives of everyday people." Instead of tracing Homeric parallels or poring over skeleton keys, he suggests that we approach Joyce's text as nothing other than a "'self-help' manual." *Ulysses,* he explains, "is a book with much to teach us about the world—advice on how to cope with grief; how to be frank about death in the age of its denial; how women have their own sexual desires and so also do men; how to walk and think at the same time."[1]

Kiberd's book was received favorably in the popular press, and, perhaps unsurprisingly, more critically in the academic journals. Scholars appreciated his lucid, jargon-free prose but recoiled at his brash claims, his reliance on "anecdotal" evidence, and the text's "gossipy biographical flourish."[2] If Joyce's goal was really to reach the common reader, reviewers wondered why he did not write in simpler terms. The self-help manual is defined by plain speech, direct address, and an appeal to common sense, and these are qualities that Joyce's avant-garde experiment gleefully abdicates. Kiberd deftly isolates moments of universality, of quotidian intimacy and domestic wisdom, in Joyce's text, all the while brushing off its infamous difficulty:

> Is Joyce therefore in bad faith, writing a book which celebrates the common man in such forbiddingly complex ways? Not really. The book was written to be enjoyed by ordinary men and women, but it is also an account of how the intellectual can return to the actual, an account of the complex path which such persons can take back to the ordinary.[3]

"Not really," Kiberd says, betraying his own uncertainty, as he describes ordinariness as the telos of Joyce's radically innovative text. The ire of the academic reviewers is not directed at Kiberd per se but at the genre to which his latest book belongs. For them, these simplifying guides are works of "iconoclastic arrogance." "Proclaiming their fealty to the ordinary," Steven Kellman cuttingly observes, "they are driven by impatience with—even contempt for—the actual experience of reading extraordinary works."[4] Yet literature is always vulnerable to abridgment, and a text's cultural portability is also a great predictor of longevity.

In this chapter I use "self-help" guides to Joyce as an occasion to illuminate the buried history of modernism's engagement with popular morality. I suggest that the birth of Joyce's aesthetic—and, by extension, modernism more broadly—is attributable to early twentieth-century debates over the education of common readers, debates that had far-reaching political and national connotations.[5] As a corollary, I undermine the idealized portraits of "oracular" Joyce, showing *Ulysses* to be firmly a product of the contentions of its day. Just as the cases of Wharton, James, Woolf, and O'Brien undermine the facile opposition between serious literature and self-help (see chapter 3), applications like Kiberd's reveal that didacticism is not so inimical to modernism as has been supposed.

Given the ardor of Kiberd's project, and the passionate antipathy it inspired, one might think that he was the first reader of *Ulysses* to point out its everyday appeal. In reality, however, Kiberd's text is the latest in a long tradition of common reader interpretations of Joyce, including Charles Duff's *James Joyce and the Plain Reader*, William Powell Jones's *James Joyce and the Common Reader*, and Anthony Burgess's *Here Comes Everybody*, to name a few.[6] As early as 1934, *Time* magazine had declared: "For readers to whom books are an important means of learning about life, [*Ulysses*] stands preeminent above modern rivals."[7] Other contemporary authors with a related approach to Kiberd's include Philip Kitcher, Jefferson Hunter, and Arnold Weinstein, who similarly dubs *Ulysses* "nothing less than a self-help manual."[8] Such texts evince the continuance of what Julie Sloan Brannon calls the "Joyce wars," divided between specialized readers and those who read Joyce for his practical advice.[9] Although neither position is very convincing alone, together they testify to *Ulysses*'s continued status as a *locus classicus* for questioning literature's real-world value; the deterrent complexity of Joyce's narrative forces readers to articulate, perhaps even reconsider, the expectations they bring to literary texts.

Joyce's popular interpreters are quick to point out those moments when he appears to encourage their moralizing approach. For instance, the narrator of "Ithaca" informs us that Leopold Bloom "himself had applied to the works of William Shakespeare more than once for the solution of difficult problems in imaginary or real life."[10] Lest we take Bloom's method as model, however, Joyce offers the following addendum, namely, that "in spite of careful and repeated reading of certain classical passages, aided by a glossary, he had derived imperfect conviction from the text, the answers not bearing in all points."[11] Joyce's punctilious terminology, which likens literary wisdom to a failed formula or sum, also emerges in reference to Stephen Dedalus's reading of Hamlet; as Buck Mulligan puts it: "He proves by algebra that Hamlet's grandson is Shakespeare's grandfather and that he himself is the ghost of his own father."[12] Stephen's tongue-in-cheek approach to the literary masterpiece as an algebraic equation, like Bloom's quest for Shakespearean "solutions," parodies the pedagogical expectations we bring to texts.

Bloom's practice of reading for life-wisdom has a long history, one coincident with the history of reading itself. Medievalist Nicholas Howe explicates that in its Anglo Saxon roots, the verb for "reading" (*raedan*) originally also meant "giving advice or counsel," a connotation modern English gradually lost as it gravitated toward the Latin term *legere*.[13] Thus contemporary self-help interpretations are only the latest manifestation of a didactic impetus that has recurred throughout Western literary history: from Renaissance poetry's commitment to merging pleasure and utility, to the eighteenth-century argument that literature should improve and instruct, and through to the utilitarian moralism that motivates so many Victorian texts. Yet, as we've seen in previous chapters, the emergence of modernism coincides with a heightened antagonism between practicality and aesthetics. This shift reflects the modernists' resistance to Victorian moral imperatives, as well as the influence of Kantian disinterestedness upon their embrace of "*l'art pour l'art*." In the popular sphere, the rise of the best-seller list in the early twentieth century created a newly agonistic relation between the novel and the handbook, which vied for space on the same general list until 1918.[14]

For some time, and with some notable exceptions, literary critics largely followed suit in questioning literature's ethical use. Richard Posner's response to the ethical criticism of Martha Nussbaum seemed to speak for a whole generation of critics who had witnessed the well-read commit atrocities: "immersion in literature does not make us better citizens or better people," he asserted, adding that ethical readings tend to be "reductive" and "digressive."[15] Nussbaum could be describing some self-help guides to modernism when she regretfully concedes that "some writing about literature" has "given ethical writing about literature a bad name, by its neglect of literary form and its reductive moralizing manner."[16] Of course, for every action there is a reaction, and the "ethical turn" in literary studies strives to redress precisely this sublimation of the moral in literary-critical practice.[17]

Ulysses's reputation as the very paradigm of modernist inutility makes it an ideal case study of modernism's complex engagement with the pragmatism of the popular realm. Identifying the need for such a critical intervention, Julie Brannon aptly observes:

> Lawrence Rainey, Mark Morrison, Joyce Wexler, and Allison Pease, among many others, have studied how the publishing culture of the early twentieth century shaped Modernism. Yet little attention has been paid to how present day audiences, for whom Modernism is already codified, reified, and ossified as canonical, receive texts like *Ulysses*.[18]

Practical readings of *Ulysses* can bolster the scholarly effort to dismantle the ossified "great divide" narrative of modernism's antipathy to real-world use.[19] To shrug off such self-help guides to Joyce as trivial epiphenomena is to neglect their ability to illuminate the enduring sources of modernism's appeal. To that end, in this chapter I treat contemporary applications of *Ulysses* as an occasion to reassess the influence of the "average reader" on the very constitution of the modernist aesthetic.

Rather than subverting Joyce's avant-garde aims, the popular championing of *Ulysses*'s everyday use is made possible by Joyce's own attunement to the common readers of his time, people wary of authority but eager for useful advice. As we shall see, the puzzling ubiquity of practical readers in *Ulysses* reflects the demand for moralizing texts that Joyce witnessed in the reading public of his youth. It is important to remember that a "veritable revolution in literacy and education" took place in mid-nineteenth-century Ireland,[20] providing the common reader with an unprecedented influence over the literary market. These changes provide a crucial context for understanding the representation of reading in Joyce's work.

THE IDEAL READER *IN ABSENTIA*

Nobody in *Ulysses* reads like a modernist. Joyce's characters read personally, emotionally, practically, prophetically, but they do not read in the disinterested manner the modernists are conventionally thought to have promoted.

Molly reads for romantic escapism, Bloom is relentlessly mining for advice. Although Jeffrey Segall identifies Joyce's ideal audience as the New Critics,[21] even Stephen Dedalus's infamous "Hamlet theory" wouldn't pass muster in Cleanth Brooks's class, with Stephen's projecting of paternity issues, professional frustrations, and biographical background onto Shakespeare's text.[22] Joyce theorizes an "ideal" reader as one who has a purely "static" and aesthetic appreciation of the text, who doesn't seek a message or a moral, but who stays up all night reveling in the jouissance of the Joycean word.[23] But as the characters in *Ulysses* remind us, ideal readers don't buy books.

André Lefevere and Itamar Even-Zohar observe that the greatest amount of activity in literary transmission usually occurs in the lowest strata of the "polysystem," that is, in "texts that are being reconstituted in children's literature, literary guidebooks, and other popular and paraliterary genres."[24] *Ulysses* confirms this view in its depiction of self-help as a primary vector of literary transmission. In Joyce's narrative, the activity and perpetuity of the literary are persistently tied to the practical application of texts, from Dilly's French primer to Stephen's guide to seduction, to Gerty MacDowell with her tips from women's magazines. As Jennifer Wicke writes, such eminently consumable popular books "dot the text like candy."[25] Of the twenty-three texts populating Bloom's bookshelf, only four are discernibly fiction, the rest are biographies, histories, and practical guides, including *The Useful Ready Reckoner*, *The Child's Guide*, *A Handbook of Astronomy*, *Short but Yet Plain Elements of Geometry*, and last but not least, Eugen Sandow's *Physical Strength and How to Obtain It*.[26]

Although Bloom enjoys flipping through his volumes of Shakespeare for "wisdom while you wait,"[27] Joyce condemned the same approach in a 1903 review of a guide to the Bard for the "general reader," precisely like those now published on Joyce's own work. The review, facetiously titled "Shakespeare Explained," synthesizes Joyce's contempt for the reductive quality of such populist approaches:

> There is nowhere an attempt at criticism, and the interpretations are meagre, obvious, and commonplace. The passages "quoted" fill up perhaps a third

of the book, and it must be confessed that the writer's method of treating Shakespeare is (or seems to be) remarkably irreverent. . . . It will be seen that the substance of this book is after the manner of ancient playbills. Here is no psychological complexity, no cross-purpose, no interweaving of motives such as might perplex the base multitude. . . . There is something very naif about this book, but (alas!) the general public will hardly pay sixteen shillings for such naivete. . . . And even the pages are wrongly numbered.[28]

Joyce thought that even the "general reader" would see through the book and refuse to purchase it. Unlike Joyce, however, Leopold Bloom might have appreciated "Shakespeare explained." Bloom fantasizes about submitting a story to the local paper, "something quick and neat" that "begins and ends morally,"[29] a description that seems to perfectly fit this "ancient playbill" mold. Modernism likes to play with this gap between quotidian character and radical form. In speaking of *Madame Bovary*, for example, Rita Felski notes that "Emma does not read as Flaubert wishes his own novel to be read." Discussing Joyce, John Carey makes an identical point: "Bloom himself would never and could never have read *Ulysses*."[30]

Bloom prefers practical reading material such as Eugen Sandow's exercise manual. Sandow's special section on "Physical Culture for the Middle-Aged," and his article on "Physical Culture Among the Jews," would have appealed to Bloom's sensibilities.[31] W. B. Yeats was apparently also a Sandow devotee, commenting in a letter from July 19, 1905, that to his regimen "I have added Sandow exercises twice daily."[32] Perhaps Sandow appealed to literary types because, as Brandon Kershner explains, his handbook had a strong narrative element, combining autobiography with prescription much like Samuel Smiles's *Self-Help* and *Lives of Engineers*.[33] Yet Joyce's invocation of Sandow makes no allusions to these aesthetic aspects of his text, nor to *Physical Strength*'s merging of narrative and prescription. The only nugget Bloom appears to have gleaned from the text is one of Sandow's instructions for physical positioning, "On the hands down," which Bloom repeats to himself at various points in *Ulysses*. Sandow's prescriptive motto circulates in Bloom's imagination as this one

unmoored, reified prescription, to be pocketed and deployed as consolation or reminder, much like his potato or piece of soap, at key moments
throughout the day.

Sandow's text frequently arises amid Bloom's thoughts of death, aging,
and physical deterioration, as in "Calypso:"

> Grey horror seared his flesh. Folding the page into his pocket he turned into
> Eccles Street, hurrying homeward. Cold oils slid along his veins, chilling his
> blood: age crusting him with a salt cloak. Well, I am here now. Yes, I am here
> now. Morning mouth bad images. Got up wrong side of the bed. Must begin
> again those Sandow's exercises. On the hands down.[34]

The self-help devotee prefers to invent superstitious antidotes ("wrong
side of the bed"/"Sandow's exercises") rather than concede to the limitations of human agency in the face of human mortality. For Bloom, Sandow
offers much the same consolation as Molly's warm flesh: an affirmation
of immediacy, the present and life. Bloom frequently turns to the practical as an escape from negativity, a tendency that sometimes verges upon
flippancy, as when he jumps from thoughts of people drowning to wondering, "Do fish ever get seasick?" in "Nausicaa."[35] This consolation of the
material is, in some sense, what Stephen lacks, along with the discipline to
resist morbid thoughts. Above all, the self-help text for Bloom represents
will: "It is the brain which develops the muscles," as Sandow notes.[36] In
light of Sandow's emphasis on mental discipline, Bloom's choice of "equanimity" above violence in "Ithaca" suggests that, despite his disappointing
muscular developments, perhaps Bloom does succeed at following some
of Sandow's principles after all.

Sandow's text emerges again in "Circe's" surrealist phantasmagoria,
which takes place in a brothel in nighttown, to expose the potential sadomasochism of the self-help mode of textual engagement. The brothel's
Madam Bella (now transformed into the male Bello) repeats Sandow's prescription to Bloom, who has metamorphosed in this dreamlike sequence
into a groveling sow. The Homeric parallel aside, Sandow's orientation

toward the "obese" may help to explain why Bloom is transformed into a plump greedy pig, and why it is the Sandow text that facilitates this transformation. The sniveling pig that Bloom becomes dramatizes self-help's debasement of its reader:

BELLO

Down! *(he taps her on the shoulder with his fan)* Incline feet forward! Slide left foot one pace back! You will fall. You are falling. On the hands down!

BLOOM

(her eyes upturned in the sign of admiration, closing, yaps) Truffles! *(With a piercing epileptic cry she sinks on all fours, grunting, snuffling, rooting at his feet: then lies, shamming dead, with eyes shut tight, trembling eyelids, bowed upon the ground in the attitude of most excellent master.)* . . .

BLOOM

(enthralled, bleats) I promise never to disobey.[37]

To be enthralled by the experience of one's own abasement is the peculiar premise not only of modernist narratives like *Ulysses* but also of self-help. Bello exploits the supplicatory posture of the Sandow exercise, turning the degrading experience of the self-improvement regime to her domineering advantage. Joyce's insomniac reader may well empathize with Bloom in this scene, who must perpetually adapt to the whim of Bello's irrational authority. Amid Bello's onslaught of commands, Bloom rolls around on the floor in an "enthralled" revelry, begging to be given directives.

But "Circe" is not the only time that Joyce aligns the erotic and didactic modes; the first articulation of this relation is voiced by Stephen Dedalus in *A Portrait of the Artist as a Young Man*. In this earlier text, Stephen theorizes the association between eros and didacticism that "Circe" will later burlesque, in a diatribe taken from Joyce's own personal notes on aesthetics:

The feelings excited by improper art are kinetic, desire or loathing. Desire urges us to possess, to go to something; loathing urges us to abandon, to go from something. The arts which excite them, pornographical or didactic, are therefore improper arts. The esthetic emotion (I use the general term) is therefore static. The mind is arrested and raised above desire and loathing.[38]

Pointedly, in "Ithaca" Bloom is described as nothing less than a "*kinetic poet.*"[39] At the other extreme, Stephen offers a typical modernist articulation of the merits of aesthetic disinterestedness. According to him, "pornographical" and "didactic" arts are "improper" because they focus on provoking the reader rather than on the formal integrity of the work.

It might seem counterintuitive to pair the didactic, that most soporific of styles, with the pornographic mode, yet as Sarah Raff argues, the two are frequently intertwined.[40] In the eighteenth century, novelists claimed to entertain readers only to better instruct them; the narrative example, they assured, was merely the sugar for smuggling the pedagogical message through. As it turns out, though, scenes of instruction in these eighteenth-century narratives were intensely erotically charged. Associating self-help with sadomasochism in "Circe," morality tales with sexual excitation in "Nausicaa,"[41] and tutoring with seduction in "Penelope," *Ulysses* corroborates Raff's point. Such scenes rekindle the Horatian merging of utility and pleasure with a bawdy, modern twist. Molly imagines seducing Stephen as he tutors her in Italian, "Ill read and study all I can find or learn a bit off by heart if I knew who he likes so he wont think me stupid if he thinks all women are the same and I can teach him the other part Ill make him feel all over him till he half faints under me." Conversely, Bloom's fondness for Molly is often couched in imagining strategies for her instruction. Evaluating different approaches to Molly's edification, Bloom determines the most effective method to be "indirect suggestion implicating selfinterest,"[42] a fitting description of Joyce's own authorial technique.

Despite his eagerness to distance himself from the "improper" responses of less educated readers, Stephen himself registers the pleasures of "kinetic" readings. Surrounded by a group of older librarians and scholars in "Scylla and Charybdis," Stephen performs an elaborate biographical reading of *Hamlet*, invoking a quotation from Maurice Maeterlinck to support his interpretation of the play as Shakespeare's enactment of his distress over his wife's alleged infidelities. Stephen quotes Maeterlinck's poetic observation:

> If Socrates leave his house today he will find the sage seated on his doorstep. If Judas go forth tonight it is to Judas his steps will tend. Every life is many days, day after day. We walk through ourselves, meeting robbers, ghosts, giants, old men, young men, wives, widows, brothers-in-love, but always meeting ourselves.[43]

Stephen uses Maeterlinck's insight to support the idea that all of the characters in Shakespeare's plays are enacting different problems in the author's life. Patrick A. McCarthy reads the passage as asserting that "all readings— of the book and of the world—are inevitably personal readings."[44] But Stephen tellingly leaves out the full version of Maeterlinck's sentence, which reads: "If Judas go forth to-night, it is towards Judas his steps will tend, nor will chance for betrayal be lacking; but let Socrates open his door, he shall find Socrates asleep on the threshold before him, and there will be occasion for wisdom."[45] Indeed, "there will be occasion for wisdom," not only because Socrates is the "wise sage" but also because experience must always lead back to the self in order to be meaningful. In its original form, Maeterlinck's statement is not a deterministic critique of readerly projection but an observation about the crucial role of identification in the acquisition of wisdom, indicating Stephen's own susceptibility to the "kinetic" readings he critiques. Throughout *Ulysses*, Joyce depicts characters who see themselves in what they read, from Molly hating any book with a "Molly" in it, to Bloom seeing Molly's infidelity in *Sweets of Sin* ("*For him! For Raoul!*"), to Stephen projecting his loneliness onto Shakespeare's text ("And my turn? When?").[46] These scenes suggest that without projection, identification, and the prospect of personal relevance there is no textual relation.

At heart, both Stephen's and Bloom's readings are motivated by self-interest, intimating the buried affinities between intellectual and popular approaches to the literary text. The two characters put their readerly self-interest to very different uses, however. Nevertheless, their literary applications belie the view of reading as a passive, merely consumptive process, showing how each reader invents his own relation to the text. "Whether it is a question of newspapers or of Proust," says Michel de Certeau, "readers are travellers; they move across lands belonging to someone else, like nomads poaching their way across fields they did not write, despoiling the wealth of Egypt to enjoy it themselves." In de Certeau's view, this readerly "poaching" is not merely instrumental but adopts a romantic, subversive hue; it is akin to "dances between readers and texts in a place where, on a depressing stage, an orthodox doctrine had erected the statue of 'the work.' "[47] However "orthodox" in appearance, Joyce's pronouncements about his "ideal reader" strategically encourage such readerly "poaching." As the nighttown scene suggests, the textual "dance" between the desire for self-improvement and a recalcitrant aesthetic defines the taunting pleasure of the modernist text.

The popular commentators are right to protest that too much critical weight has been placed on the ideal reader who stays up all night mapping Homeric parallels and memorizing skeleton keys and not enough on *Ulysses*'s strange courtship of the common reader. Joyce came of age during a divisive period for Irish letters, marked by "utilitarian" and "romantic" political extremes.[48] The transition from parochial Irish culture to the rise of Irish modernism was not seamless. It was an ugly and protracted scuffle over the nation's literary future, culminating in a very public dispute between Charles Gavan Duffy and W. B. Yeats, out of which "battles lines formed for the contention that continues to this day."[49] These debates fostered Joyce's attunement to popular readers as gatekeepers for even the most radical aesthetic. Only by attending to the national significance of self-help to the Irish can we fully appreciate the stakes of the different reading methods represented in Joyce's text.

"THAT OLD DELUSION, DIDACTICISM": MODERNISM AND THE IRISH COMMON READER

Common reader wars are nothing new to Irish culture. In fact, twenty-first-century common reader wars in Joyce criticism are reenacting the disputes that gave rise to Irish modernism in the first place. Books by Kiberd, Weinstein, and Alain de Botton are present-day manifestations of modernism's constitutional entanglement with the popular, pragmatic, and didactic, a side of the movement that has been obscured by the received history of its disdain for the masses but that has recently received some important critical attention.[50] Tracing the branch back to the rhizome, it becomes clear that Joyce's indirect didacticism developed in response to the political hothouse that was the Dublin of his youth. The coy moralism of *Ulysses* reflects Joyce's attunement to the pleasure of the homiletic text.

It is impossible to discuss *Ulysses* and self-help without addressing the colonial connotation of "self-help" in Ireland, a nation marked by bloody fights over the rights of "Sinn Féin" (ourselves) and Home rule.[51] Rather than pure agonism, there is an "unacknowledged overlap between [Joyce's] fiction and the self-help movement of the Revivalist period."[52] Joyce published his early stories in the *Irish Homestead*, a journal that P. J. Matthews explains was primarily for farmers and was founded by the Irish Agricultural Organization Society. Joyce once disdainfully referred to the *Homestead* as "the pigs' paper," and he was apparently so ashamed to have his avant-garde art appear alongside columns about how to make your own butter that he used the pseudonym "Stephen Daedalus."[53] But in addition to being a source of income and publication for young Irish writers, the *Homestead* was instrumental in establishing village libraries across Ireland and in encouraging the spread of literacy far from urban centers.

In publishing young Irish writers, the *Homestead* was exercising the new power wielded by the rural classes in shaping the intellectual sphere. Yeats, who felt threatened by this increased literary influence of the working classes, exhorted the Irish public to resist the influence of British utilitarianism.

> On all sides men are studying things that are to get them bodily food, but no man among them is searching for the imaginative and spiritual food to be got out of great literature. Nobody, with the exception of a few ladies, perhaps, ever seems to do any disinterested reading in this library, or indeed anywhere else in Ireland. Every man here is grinding at the mill wherein he grinds all things into pounds and shillings, and but few of them will he get when all is done.[54]

Yeats felt that two grave consequences of colonial oppression—a dearth of time and money—had led to the stifling of that most essential superfluity, aesthetics. When the National Education system was founded in Ireland in 1831, the subjects taught in the schools "had little appeal to parents or their children. To them, education was synonymous with 'book learning' and left no room for activities redolent of their everyday lives."[55] Yet by the 1850s people had become more receptive to the benefits of book-learning for acquiring high-status jobs, and parents pressed the commissioners to add modern and classical languages to the curriculum. Writing in 1892, the year the Irish Education Act introduced compulsory education, Yeats was less troubled by working-class illiteracy than by the people's encroachment on the hallowed field of poetics.

Yeats also believed that the political compulsion to put a green shamrock on the cover of every Irish book was stunting the development of the nation.[56] The green "shamrock stamper" Yeats had in mind was Sir Charles Gavan Duffy, a founder of the Young Ireland movement and the *Nation* magazine. In 1892, when the precocious Joyce was already writing poems and prose, Yeats and Duffy engaged in a fierce battle over editorial control of a series called the New Irish Library, a volume of inexpensive books intended to revitalize the Irish literary scene. The scheme was initially Yeats's project to educate the Irish about their own literature, for back then, as he said, "no educated man ever bought an Irish book." But when the older and more respected Duffy returned to Ireland after years abroad, like "Odysseus returning to Ithaca," as the press said,[57] the shareholders granted him control and pushed Yeats out. All of Ireland was party to the volley of accusations in the press between Yeats and the old guard of Dublin.

Much like common reader disputes today, the New Irish Library debate centered on the uses of the literary: Is it the function of books to expand the imagination or to discipline the mind? Should language work to complicate or simplify life? The intense political climate made the New Irish Library a hothouse for competing arguments about the relation of literature to everyday practice. Both Duffy and Yeats were consumed by their insistence that there could be only one anthology—it was *The* New Irish Library, after all—and so the stakes of the project were high. Because the literary identity of Ireland appeared to depend on it, the library engendered a polarized approach to literature's social use. Ireland's revered orator John F. Taylor, whom Joyce quotes in "Aeolus" in the only passage from *Ulysses* he ever recorded, was Duffy's strident ally, and Taylor used his rhetorical skills to take up his friend's cause in the national press.[58]

No author who came of age in Ireland during these years (or after) could have escaped the New Irish Library dispute's divisive influence. The debate, which P. J. Matthews calls "a dogfight over the establishment of a canon of Irish literature,"[59] was not confined to the Emerald Isle but garnered bemused onlookers in the British press as well. As William Patrick Ryan noted in 1894, "few were to remember a time when either the press of England or Ireland had given itself so much concern about Irish books and writers."[60] Matthews describes the controversy as "an early manifestation of a sea change taking place in Ireland which was, in many ways, a generational revolution."[61] A pivotal episode "in the continuous fight of the younger writers against the literary ideals of the old school,"[62] it created a rift in Ireland's intellectual culture that continued well into the rise of Irish modernism.

Yeats believed that the literature in the library should aspire to a "mystic truth" and a "mysterious ideal" rather than to a political message.[63]

In contrast, the volumes Duffy eventually produced included a *History of Parliament* by Thomas Davis, an Irish songbook, Standish O'Grady's *Bog of Stars*, Dr. Hyde's *Short History of Gaelic Literature*, and most egregiously, a story by Balzac, the *Médecin de Campagne*, rewritten for an Irish audience as *A Parish Providence*.[64] This latter is a good example of Yeats's fear that the originality of the Irish imagination would be denationalized by the desire to keep up with British progress. Yeats lambasted the Balzac adaptation when it appeared: "Duffy has made a book out of one of the poorest of Balzac's novels, not improved by having the French names turned into English ones; an introduction on agriculture and local industry forty pages long, made up mostly out of a fifty year old article of his own, and an appendix full of quotations from a blue book."[65] In a funny turn, the obligation to be Irish leads to a poor imitation of the French. Such a volume offered proof, if any was needed, that Duffy's priority was producing not quality literature but propagandist tracts. Yet despite their polemical differences, Duffy and Yeats had more in common than they were willing to admit: Yeats was both didactic and nationalist in his own way, and Duffy evidently had some appreciation for aesthetics.

Joyce credits Duffy with publishing James Clarence Mangan, whom Joyce admired and wrote about on two separate occasions (1902 and 1907). He also references Duffy's patriotic ballads in *Ulysses*, and elsewhere laments the exportation of Duffy's "practical talent" during his years abroad.[66] Tantalizingly, however, a page from Joyce's Mangan manuscript has been lost, and his essay is suddenly cut off just where he begins to speak about Duffy.[67] In another incomplete piece from 1907, Joyce writes that the current nationalist crisis incited by the youth of the Celtic revival or Celtic twilight (derided in the *Wake* as the "cultic twalette") represents the culmination of "no less than three decisive clashes" that have recurred in Irish nationalist history, beginning with the Thomas Davis/Daniel O'Connell dispute, reemerging with the rise of Fenianism in 1867, and erupting once more with the Yeats-led revival's "boycott" of "moral and material" concerns, a boycott originating in the New Irish Library dispute.[68]

The conflict between Duffy and Yeats is echoed in the opposition between Bloom's pragmatic and Stephen's aesthetic approach to the literary. In the same way that Yeats opposes his "mystic truth" to Duffy's parochial plans, "Stephen dissented openly from Bloom's views on the importance of dietary and civic selfhelp while Bloom dissented tacitly from Stephen's views on the eternal affirmation of the spirit of man in literature." But just as Duffy and Yeats had more in common than they were willing to admit, Stephen's reworking of the Maeterlinck quotation suggests that he has a hidden kinship with Bloom's position. Joyce indicates the buried affinities between his protagonists: "there's a touch of the artist about old Bloom," as Lenehan notes, and Stephen is shown to be capable of his share of materialism as well, inquiring "Would I make any money by it?" when Haines proposes to package his Irish thoughts.[69]

Yet their ideological differences come to the fore when Bloom alights upon the idea for a series of moral publications based on Stephen's stories in "Ithaca." Conversing over cocoa, Stephen tells Bloom his enigmatic "Parable of the Plums," and the narrator describes Bloom's opportunistic, Duffy-like reaction:

Did he see only a second coincidence in the second scene narrated to him, described by the narrator as *A Pisgah Sight of Palestine* or *The Parable of the Plums*?

It, with the preceding scene and with others unnarrated but existent by implication, to which add essays on various subjects or moral apothegms (e.g. *My Favourite Hero* or *Procrastination is the Thief of Time*) composed during schoolyears, seemed to him to contain in itself and in conjunction with the personal equation certain possibilities of financial, social, personal and sexual success, whether specially collected and selected as model pedagogic themes (of cent per cent merit) for the use of preparatory and junior grade students or contributed in printed form, following the precedent of Philip Beaufoy or Doctor Dick or Heblon's *Studies in Blue*, to a publication of certified circulation and solvency or employed verbally as intellectual stimulation for sympathetic auditors, tacitly appreciative of successful narrative

and confidently augurative of successful achievement, during the increasingly longer nights gradually following the summer solstice on the day but
three following, videlicet, Tuesday, 21 June (S. Aloysius Gonzaga), sunrise
3.33 A.M., sunset 8.29 P.M.

After "repressing" his "didactic counsels" throughout the episode, Bloom
finally lets "that old delusion, didacticism, get the better of his judgment,"
to borrow Yeats's characterization of Duffy.[70] Bloom's entrepreneurial alert-
ness sees opportunity in Stephen's creative inventions. Bloom attempts to
sell the scheme by pointing out to Stephen that "originality, though producing its own reward, does not invariably conduce to success."[71] Bloom's
pragmatic urgings adopt a more antagonistic valence when read against
the background of the New Irish Library dispute, complicating the pater-
nalist paradigm through which "Ithaca" is typically read. Approaching
Bloom's didacticism through Duffy's precedent emphasizes the political stakes of his enterprise and exposes Bloom's stuffy instrumentalism,
while also underscoring Stephen's youthful insolence and irreverence.[72]
Read through the contentions of the Celtic revival, the anti-Semitic song
Stephen sings following this exchange, a point that has long troubled
readers of the episode, appears to be a juvenile defiance of Bloom's appropriating gesture, a misguided assertion of artistic autonomy. Yeats made
similar gestures of defiance throughout his inconsistent career, suddenly
turning the vehement nationalist in an 1895 fight with Unionist Edward
Dowden. "Strife is better than loneliness," as his favorite proverb said.[73]
Bloom's publication scheme is ironic because a "moral pedagogic theme"
is precisely what Stephen's Parable of the Plums resists. Stephen's parable
describes two "vestal virgins" who mount Nelson's pillar, only to get dizzy
from the view, and settle back to eat their plums and spit out the pits below.
With its inconclusive account of the women's disappointment, the story
thematizes frustrated expectations. Stephen makes a similar point with
the riddle he tells his students in "Nestor," whose answer elicits groans
because they could not possibly have foretold it. Throughout *Ulysses* Joyce
pokes fun at readers' expectations, whether for instruction ("Nestor"),

love ("Nausicaa"), erudition ("Oxen"), commonplaces ("Eumaeus"), information ("Ithaca"),[74] or arousal ("Penelope"). Bloom's deliberate denial of the ironic framework of Stephen's parable enacts the concerted elision of Joyce's obscurity that is typical of common reader interpretations of his work. At the same time, this dynamic tension between the didactic and aesthetic defines the pleasure of the Joycean text.

In the differences between Stephen's and Bloom's approaches to literature and Irish self-improvement, *Ulysses* contains its own little common reader dispute, one inextricable from generational debates over the identity of Ireland's national literature. The much-anticipated encounter between the two characters resembles a thought experiment in what would happen if the two poles of Irish letters could be induced to contemplate collaboration. Of course, it is nothing new to say that Stephen and Bloom represent two extremes of Irish society, and critics have extensively explored the racial, paternal, religious, and mythic symbolism of their meeting. But approaching this tenuous union through the lens of the library dispute suggests that Stephen and Bloom's ideological convergence enacts the birth of the modernist aesthetic. Yeats implied as much in his self-congratulatory way when he observed that if he had not resisted Duffy in 1892, "it might have silenced in 1907 John Synge, the greatest dramatic genius of Ireland."[75] Helen O'Connell concurs, arguing that "the persistent questioning of the orthodoxies of modernization and nationalism . . . produced the literature of the Revival period, culminating in the modernism of writers as diverse as W. B. Yeats, J. M. Synge, James Joyce, Samuel Beckett, and Elizabeth Bowen."[76] Yet the identity of modernism was just as dependent upon questioning the real-world import of revivalism as it was upon critiquing old-school didacticism, and this practical impetus of modernism is something that Joyce's popular readers help to expose. If the competing voices of Irish culture could share a cup of cocoa, it would not be a perfect union; there would likely be conversational misfires, inadvertent insults, ulterior motives, and irrepressible antipathies. But "Ithaca" imagines a situation in which these very different ways of reading might be admissible in the same kitchen.

164 \ JOYCE FOR LIFE

If the future of Stephen and Bloom's friendship seems dubious, the blend of the esoteric and pragmatic they represent is more promising. In *Ulysses*, the alternation between aesthetic and pragmatic extremes is both thematic and stylistic. Every grand display of linguistic experimentation in *Ulysses* is buttressed by the comfort of the proverbial. The abstruse musings of "Proteus" are offset by the homely domesticity of "Calypso"; following "Circe's" dizzying surrealism come the journalistic platitudes of "Eumaeus"; and after the disorienting narration of "Cyclops," Gerty MacDowell's magazine vernacular offers some reprieve. Like Yeats, Joyce was wary of the multitude, writing that "the artist, though he may employ the crowd, is very careful to isolate himself,"[77] and his oscillating aesthetic enacts this strategic populism. Joyce's blending of popular vernacular and heady intellectualism does not make him a martyr to the popular cause, as Kiberd would have it, nor does it make him an irascible snob, as John Carey might wish. Instead, it shows that Joyce learned from the controversies of his time to blend the people's aversion to oppressive authority with their desire for relevant texts. Joyce saw that only an oblique didacticism could register the needs of Ireland's burgeoning popular readership.

In the end, the New Library project fizzled out without a clear victor. It may be that Duffy won the battle but lost the war,[78] given the eventual success of the Abbey Theatre and the influence of the revival more generally. Yeats seems alone in declaring the library a failure ("ten thousand copies had been sold before anybody had time to read it," he said, "and then the sale came to a dead stop"),[79] whereas the press deemed it a success. Helen O'Connell observes, "It is quite possible that 'the people' of Ireland did not really want to indulge in imaginative literature, but found fulfillment instead in 'rhetoric,' didacticism, and fact."[80] The early sales were probably due to the library dispute's publicity, and Duffy had to abort the enterprise when his publications proved too tedious to sustain demand. But had Yeats been in control of the venture, he may have been too "out of touch with the Irish people," as Joyce remarked in a letter from 1907, to have attracted wide sales.[81]

It would be misguided to regard Joyce as a "solution" to the problem set up by Duffy and Yeats; this is precisely the kind of mathematical approach to the literary he mocks. Critics too often fall prey to the hagiographic tendency to imagine Joyce as somehow prophetically anticipating and resolving the paradoxes of his own reception, a position that finds its corollary in Derrida's famous description of the "hypermnesiac machine" that is Joyce's writing.[82] One way to resist this idealization is to recognize how Joyce learned the dangers of ignoring popular demand from local precedent. Indeed, "Joyce's international and cult status has concealed the ways in which his work is part of an articulate and broad debate within the Irish literary revival."[83] The historical context undermines the hagiographic fantasy by showing how Joyce's unique blend of obscurity and common sense was not, as Richard Ellmann famously said, a sign of his being so far ahead of his contemporaries that we are still struggling to catch up;[84] rather, it was Joyce's effort to catch up to the contradictory demands of his contemporaries. As the entrepreneurial Joyce knew well, didacticism was not just an atavistic impulse of old fogies like Bloom and Duffy; it was also a key to the future of the literary. At the same time, the moral capacity of *Ulysses* is about more than just sales. In his personal copy of Leo Tolstoy's *Essays*, Joyce underlined, pencil-marked, and put an exclamation point beside the following claim: "this knowledge of how men should live has from the days of Moses, Solon, and Confucius been always considered a science—the very essence of science."[85] Joyce's self-help commentators would surely agree.

Today's popular readings expose Joyce's attunement to the reading public of his time: a people characterized by both "defiance" and "impotence,"[86] who shunned authoritarianism but yearned for advice. The political stakes of literature's attunement to the popular were particularly tangible to Joyce, who had witnessed the role of nonprofessional readers in determining the identity of Ireland's literary culture. Lawrence Rainey defines the avant-garde as the "uneasy synthesis" of "the opposition between elite and popular culture, or between art and commodity."[87] Ireland's sheltering of both Duffy's and Yeats's literary extremes, its simultaneous harboring of the most vehement propagandists and impassioned aesthetes, offers a clue as to how the provincial town of Dublin became the unlikely proving ground of the movement known as high modernism.

LETTING BYGONES BE BYGONES

Learning, perhaps, from Yeats's library failure, and giving the lie to Martin Amis's view of *Ulysses* as a "war against cliché,"[88] Joyce strategically employs proverbial wisdom throughout his texts as an anchor for his more experimental, esoteric formulations. As a case in point, the simple proverb "let bygones be bygones" is woven throughout each of Joyce's major works, first as the sentimental uttering of an Irish nationalist in *Dubliners*, then amid Bloom's rumination upon the subjects of adultery and forgiveness in *Ulysses*. Finally, in *Finnegans Wake*, the bygones proverb goes viral, weaving throughout the minds of different characters, becoming part of the very texture of the book.

In one story from *Dubliners*, "Ivy Day in the Committee Room," local supporters of the nationalist party gather around a fireplace in a dingy room, drinking and eulogizing Ireland's past. Joyce uses cliché in *Dubliners* to ridicule the nationalists, who equate a history of exploitation, and the political and personal tragedy of Parnell, with something as trivial as "bygones." The men discuss King Edward's impending visit to Ireland:

> But look here, John, said Mr O'Conner. Why should we welcome the King of England? Didn't Parnell himself . . .
>
> Parnell, said Mr Henchy, is dead. Now, here's the way I look at it. Here's this chap come to the throne after his old mother keeping him out of it till the man was grey. He's a man of the world, and he means well by us. He's a jolly fine decent fellow, if you ask me, and no damn nonsense about him. He just says to himself: The old one never went to see these wild Irish. By Christ, I'll go myself and see what they're like. And are we going to insult the man when he comes over here on a friendly visit, Eh? Isn't that right, Croften?
>
> Mr Croften nodded his head.
>
> But after all now, said Mr Lyons argumentatively, King Edward's life, you know, is not very . . .

Let bygones be bygones, said Mr Henchy. I admire the man personally. He's just an ordinary knockabout like you and me. He's fond of his glass of grog and he's a bit of a rake, perhaps, and he's a good sportsman. Damn it, can't we Irish play fair?[89]

The empty futility of the proverb embodies the problem of Irish paralysis upon which *Dubliners* is premised. If nationalism is, in part, founded upon a sense of Ireland's responsibility *not* to let bygones be, the problem of Henchy, Croften, et al. is precisely their failure to judge when to seek retribution and when to let things go. In "Ivy Day" Joyce implies that the Dublin environment of suspicion, betrayal, and surveillance makes letting go of bygones practically impossible. Further, if the necessity of keeping bygones alive is part of the impetus of nationalism, the committee men are all too willing to forget the injuries of the past when it means possible economic benefits for the Irish, such as the visit of King Edward would entail. As early as *Dubliners*, the question of whether or not to let bygones be is largely circumstantial, often linked to greed and self-interest.

In "Ivy Day" it is discussion of Parnell and his legacy that inspires the emergence of the "bygones" phrase, the colonial context pointing to the worst kind of interpretation of the proverb to mean resigning oneself to a bad or unjust situation. In *Dubliners*, letting "bygones be bygones" encapsulates what Joyce viewed as the unimaginativeness of the colonial consciousness, or the failure of the oppressed to envision alternate historical possibilities from those that came to pass. Throughout Joyce's writings, the figure of Charles Parnell practically comes to stand for the instrumentalism of the distinction between bygone and pressing concern, for it was the politically motivated refusal of the Irish people to let bygones be that caused them to create a scandal out of an affair that was already public knowledge.

When the bygones proverb resurfaces in *Ulysses*, it is once again accompanied by attention to how a piece of information that is public knowledge suddenly becomes mobilized for private gain. The narrator describes

Bloom's meditation upon Parnell's tragic love affair with Katherine O'Shea in the cabman's shelter of "Eumaeus":

> On the other hand what incensed him more inwardly was the blatant jokes of the cabman and so on who passed it all off as a jest, laughing immoderately, pretending to understand everything, the why and the wherefore, and in reality not knowing their own minds, it being a case for the two parties themselves unless it ensued that the legitimate husband happened to be a party to it owing to some anonymous letter from the usual boy Jones, who happened to come across them at the crucial moment in a loving position locked in one another's arms, drawing attention to their illicit proceedings and leading up to a domestic rumpus and the erring fair one begging forgiveness of her lord and master upon her knees and promising to sever the connection and not receive his visits any more if only the aggrieved husband would overlook the matter and *let bygones be bygones* with tears in her eyes though possibly with her tongue in her fair cheek at the same time as quite possibly there were several others.[90]

The proverb emerges here as a plea of the guilty; it seems like something Bloom himself might proffer in his defense during his trial in "Circe." Bloom imagines the same instrumental use of bygones that the "Ivy Day" story conveys in his reference to Kitty O'Shea uttering the phrase "with her tongue in her fair cheek." Whether the analogy is between Parnell and King Edward, or between Captain O'Shea and Bloom, the figure of Parnell links the bygones proverb to both nationalism and adultery through dramatizing the problem of coping with betrayal.

The evocation of the bygones cliché amid Bloom's meditation upon the famously adulterous relation between O'Shea and Parnell also promotes a reading of Bloom's "equanimity" at the end of the novel as a way of letting bygones be. Although Joyce repeatedly associates bygones with economic opportunism, the occurrence of this phrase in reference to the matrimonial suggests a more positive reading of "letting bygones be bygones," entailing forgiveness. However, if bygones were really bygones, there would be no need for forgiveness (for "letting them be") in the first place. Although accepting bygones as past could be an antidote for jealousy, the question remains of what to make of the fact that throughout *Ulysses* Bloom treats as bygone something that is still to come. Bloom's letting "bygones be bygones" seems to stand at the polar extreme from Stephen's "agenbit of inwit" (prick of conscience), his morose dwelling upon specters from the past.[91] The consolation of the proverbial is something that Bloom has learned to exploit to get through the day. More broadly, though, in showing the work that proverbs do, *Ulysses* dramatizes not just the need for the bygones proverb but also its limits, or the need for "inwit" too.

The let bygones be bygones proverb undergoes several mutations throughout the course of *Finnegans Wake*, picking up the resonances of other, related clichés along the way. Tracing the evolution of the bygones proverb throughout the *Wake* reveals its essential interchangeability; one proverb could easily be replaced by another without any real damage to the integrity of the text. This linguistic interchangeability also reflects how in everyday life individuals get proverbs wrong; clichés are garbled and reinvented as they circulate in a community. What is important for Joyce is not just the moral content but the structural role of the proverbial idiom both as an axis for a character's psychological ruminations and for the text's narrative structure. For Joyce, the proverb acts as a kind of pivot from which a more nuanced reflection on experience can develop.

The prominence of the bygones proverb in the *Wake* links, through the subject of regret, the two principal themes of Joyce's writing: how to move on after marital and politico-historical transgressions. "Forget, remember!" admonishes ALP in the final pages of *Finnegans Wake*, and the question is raised of the utility of letting go of bygones within this Vichian scheme of eternal recurrence of the same, where "themes have thimes and habit reburns."[92] Although part of Joyce's project is to preserve the possibilities history has ousted, the bygones saying advises consigning such casualties to oblivion and runs counter to the modernist investment in the imaginative potential of regret, anxiety, and history. The agonistic connotation of the bygones saying highlights Joyce's vexed relation to historical violence as both generative of identity and morally oppressive; "Ireland is what she is . . . and therefore I am what I am because of the relations that have existed between England and Ireland,"[93] he wrote.

In short, just because Joyce deploys the bygones proverb does not mean his oeuvre endorses its morality. The bygones saying is first alluded to in the *Wake*'s opening chapter, where a "gnarlybird" who is also identified as a hen and as ALP rummages through the corpses and debris of battle, collecting "all spoiled goods" and putting them into her "nabsack," including the all-important letter to HCE.

> Fe fo fom! She jist does hopes till *byes will be byes*. Here, and it goes on to appear now, she comes, a peacefugel, a parody's bird, a peri potmother, a pringlpik in the ilandiskippy, with peewee, and powwows in beggybaggy, on her bickybacky, and a flick flask flecklinging its pixylighting pacts' huemeramybows, picking here, pecking there, pussypussy plunderpussy.[94]

The proverb offers a life raft of common sense amid a sea of narrative anomie, much like the maternal figure herself, who must tolerate the violence of men (boys will be boys), hoping it will come to an end (bye). Ironically, the first allusion to "letting bygones be" occurs amid the seemingly very contrary act of accumulating and salvaging the debris of the past.

The phrase "she jist does hopes till byes will be byes" also refers to ALP's maternal role, and brings together the "let bygones be" cliché with the platitude "boys will be boys," a version of which is repeated again at the end of the text. ALP sighs, "Let besoms be bosuns," during her final monologue. ALP is thinking about her family and remembering HCE's desire to have a girl after the fights between Shem and Shaun. Compared to HCE, ALP is reconciled to her fate: "I'll wait. And I'll wait. And then if all goes. What will be is. Is. is."[95] What will be will be, let bygones be bygones; these sayings tread the fine line between equanimity and resignation, much like Bloom in "Ithaca," snuggling into "the imprint of a human form, male, not his."[96] The problem of when to let bygones be has significant implications for how we read Bloom's resolution of the dilemma he faces with regard to

Molly at the end of *Ulysses*, before deciding upon "equanimity" as the best available choice.

As Joyce's works progress, such proverbial nuggets as the bygones saying accumulate significance that is detached from a particular character's consciousness and becomes woven into the very texture of the book. Taking the bygones proverb as an object lesson of Joyce's privileging of formal above thematic pedagogy suggests that Joyce's relation to common reader didacticism is not merely antagonistic. Rather, he is interested in developing a contrapuntal heuristic, one that is not hermetic but associative, oscillating between platitude and estrangement. The proverb, for Joyce, is not something to be blindly adopted but is something to be poked, prodded, and turned inside out, an orbit of linguistic play.

THE SWEETNESS OF USE

Amid a cultural surfeit of more accessible advisors, readers today are turning to modernist texts for lessons about how to live. The case study of *Ulysses* helps us understand this phenomenon by illuminating the surprising centrality of common reader didacticism to the formation of the modernist aesthetic. Instead of imitating a particular character, each reader must produce the wisdom of *Ulysses* by navigating the text's demotic and rarified extremes. Max Eastman once asked Joyce why he did not offer the reader more hints as to the meaning of his text, to which Joyce apparently replied, "You know people never value anything unless they have to steal it. Even an alley cat would rather snake an old bone out o' the garbage than come up and eat a nicely prepared chop from your saucer."[97] Implicit in self-help guides to Joyce's work is the conviction that the reward or "bone" for working through his texts is the life-wisdom to be painstakingly mined from his pages. Such de Certeau-like "poachings" support Kenneth Burke's comment that even the most difficult work may contain "proverbs writ large."[98] They evince the persistence of the impulse to mine literary texts for advice, an impulse that even the most forbidding avant-garde complexity cannot fully deter.

Accounts of modernity's antipathy to moral instruction do not hold up when one takes into account the literature's popular use. Although Michael McKeon identifies "the relative unimportance of the moral in the modern evaluation of literature,"[99] in the reception of Joyce didacticism becomes a means of reclaiming modern literature for the common folk. Even Bloom, before retiring, "reflected on the pleasures derived from literature of instruction rather than of amusement."[100] Whereas age-old Horatian precept mixes the utile with the dulce, the modern readers represented by Bloom find the useful to be sweet in its own right. In a realist novel, a precept may appear to be an unwelcome diversion from the action of the story, but the same precept will be embraced as an oasis of common sense if inserted into a plotless modernist pastiche. For Joyce's readers, the precept becomes the guilty pleasure, the taboo indulgence or reward, an association already latent in eighteenth-century works.

Understanding literature's widespread appeal today is a pressing task, and one for which modernism's popular interpreters are uniquely positioned to offer assistance. One such interpreter, Arnold Weinstein, inquires:

> So what is the case for Joyce, for the literate, interested, yet unprofessional reader? What will you get from the many hours needed to read *Ulysses*? (We'll leave *Finnegans Wake* out of the picture entirely.) I sometimes feel that this—what's in it for me?—is the most ducked question in academic and intellectual culture. Partly, no doubt, because it is so hard to answer. But doesn't this no-nonsense principle lurk in all readers' hearts, even if one is loath to articulate it? Highbrow utterances about "edification" are customarily invoked as the rationale for reading; but I have written this book for the general reader, and I am obeying the principle that all reading—whatever the professors say to the contrary—is an affair of gains and losses, or usable or discardable insights, of equipment that does or does not add to one's repertory, one's life. *Ulysses* pays off on precisely this front.[101]

Weinstein's readerly empiricism sounds troublingly close to the "grinding all things into pounds and shillings," including art and ideas, that

Yeats had woefully described. Despite Joyce's celebration of his "usylessly unreadable Blue Book of Eccles,"[102] Weinstein asserts that Joyce's practical advice is precisely what makes his narratives worthwhile; he suggests that reading can never be fully divorced from the economy of advice, "whatever the professors say."

For professional literary critics, learning from self-help means turning away from what the genre says and looking instead to what it does, outlining the alternative reading space to the school and academy that self-help represents. As practical applications of modernism unwittingly suggest, self-help's agency is not necessarily where it says it is—in exaggerated promises of secrets to happiness or keys to success. Its agency lies in its potential as aesthetic or hermeneutic provocation. In this respect, self-help readings of literature can be compared to the provocations of conceptual poetry. What, after all, makes Kiberd's reading of *Ulysses* as a self-help manual a less radical retooling of authorial intention than John Cage's mesocrostic approach to *Finnegans Wake*, which rewrites the text looking for repetitions of Joyce's name, or David Melnick's homophonic translation of Homer's *Iliad*?[103] Self-help's method, however, is not some arbitrary linguistic imposition or rule but the process of extracting portable insights for personal use. Meaning and ethics still matter to self-help, and this may be where the comparison to conceptual poetry has its limits. Though it bears affinities with these irreverent literary experiments, self-help also reanimates the rather old-fashioned view of the textual encounter as a collaborative, co-creative process of making sense of things.

5

MODERNISM WITHOUT TEARS

THE PAIN OF PROUST

Aside from Flaubert and Woolf, one would be hard pressed to find a more emphatic defender of modernist autonomy than the Frankfurt school theorist Theodor Adorno. Writing amid the mid-twentieth-century growth of social activism, Adorno contends that art is most resistant when it is most remote, that modernist form itself mounts a challenge against the instrumentalism of the capitalist economy, and, further, that any overt message in art is acquiescing to the demand for use-value justification instead of, shall we say, giving ideology the "silent treatment." Forty years later, Alain de Botton strove to reinsert modernism precisely into this use-value economy of practical yields and personal gains. In *How Proust Can Change Your Life*, de Botton sets the stage for future applications like Declan Kiberd's *Ulysses and Us* by taking a novel that had become "almost a byword for obscurity and irrelevance" and performing what journalist Dwight Macdonald calls the "alchemy" of transmuting avant-garde complexity into palatable advice. Adorno observes that "where [Proust] is correct there is pain,"[1] but de Botton's Proust is practically painless.

A precedent for de Botton's book can be found in Julian Barnes's mock memoir *Flaubert's Parrot*, which also merges life writing and self-help discourse, but in a more fictional vein. In the past decade, numerous other self-help readings of modernism have emerged: *A Guide to Better Living Through the Work and Wisdom of Virginia Woolf*; *Why You Should Read Kafka Before You Waste Your Life*; *Ulysses and Us*; *The Heming Way*; *What W. H. Auden Can Do for You*; and *What Would Virginia Woolf Do?* These applications signal a paradigm shift in what can be considered self-helpful, and so are revealing of our cultural needs and predilections today.[2]

As with all self-help, titles are important, and in the aforementioned works they operate not just as attention-grabbing gimmicks but also almost as performative contradictions. These titles maintain that the experience of reading an author like Auden or Kafka is vital and irreplaceable but then offer the text to follow as a proxy for that reading experience. The fact that the answers to these guides' titular provocations are never totally convincing or satisfying (and sometimes completely abandoned after the front matter) proves their thesis about modernism's necessity. In true modernist fashion, these guides have to fail in order to succeed. If James Hawes's guide could neatly summarize why reading Kafka will save your life, we wouldn't need Kafka in the first place. Modernism continues to have currency because guides like this will never completely answer or resolve the ontological problems they raise.

Previous chapters uncovered the buried influence of early self-help on the difficult literature of authors including Flaubert, Wharton, James, Woolf, O'Brien, and Joyce. In this chapter, I explore some unlikely cases of modernist literature influencing recent self-help in turn. I compare the analyses of Marcel Proust offered by Alain de Botton and Theodor Adorno; the interpretations of Nathanael West's surrealist story *Miss Lonelyhearts* advanced by twin sisters Dear Abby and Ann Landers, and the sisters' own diagnoses of Miss Lonelyhearts's ills; and examine appeals to Samuel Beckett as a model for corporate resilience. These case studies also present an opportunity to more fully address a presence linking the preceding chapters and an important influence on the intellectual reception of self-help: Adorno and his arguments against the culture industry's deceptions. Adorno's warnings are a thread uniting these literary cases: "The concoctions of the culture industry are neither guides for a blissful life, nor a new art of moral responsibility, but rather exhortations to toe the line, behind which stand the most powerful interests."[3]

Adorno has contributed significantly to the version of critique we have inherited (and that some are currently challenging), which is premised on the ruthless demystification of the joys and pleasures of popular culture, a position that underwrites the intellectual tradition of deriding self-help. As Adorno (and Foucault) helps us to see, the tradition of critique being contested today is premised, in ways that have not been fully reckoned with, on a fierce opposition to self-help and everything it represents: escapism, wish fulfillment, identification, and instrumentalism. In addition, as we shall see, the opposition between critical theory and self-help hinges on their divergent understanding of the value of pain as a truth portal or an encumbrance, respectively. As Wharton's *Twilight Sleep* made clear (chapter 3), self-help's shortcut culture is viewed by some authors as a product of modern society's impulse to anesthetize discomfort.[4] This makes self-help applications of avant-garde writers all the more disconcerting because discomfort is the currency of the modernist aesthetic.

To be sure, there is also an element of nostalgia at play in self-help applications of modernist works. The dissonance they stage between desire and contemporary circumstance—the feeling that one must turn to another era to find compatible advice—is another version of Freud's foundling fantasy or Marthe Robert's foundling plot.[5] They reflect what Ernst Bloch described as the "nonsynchronicity" of one who "does not fit into a very modern organization" and "stands on a bad footing with Today but nevertheless belongs to it."[6]

In addition, these books exemplify what Macdonald viewed as the midcult's particular offense: "The special threat of midcult is that it exploits the discoveries of the avant-garde."[7] Macdonald's own invectives against the self-help spirit were inspired by what he saw as Adorno and Horkheimer's "brilliant" denunciations of mass culture.[8] Although Macdonald admires the fancy footwork of guides like *A Skeleton Key to Finnegans Wake*, which manages to popularize such an "impenetrably avant-garde work," his polemic is directed against those "lapsed avant-gardists who know how to use the modern idiom in the service of the banal." Macdonald sneers that "in London one meets stockbrokers who go to concerts, politicians who have read Proust."[9]

In contrast, de Botton believes that all the London stockbrokers and politicians should read Proust. He wants to counteract the way that academics have blinded readers to the moments in Proust that invite a therapeutic and personal approach. He recounts how Proust enjoyed comparing his acquaintances to famous portraits from the Louvre; for example, Proust was delighted to spot the resemblance between his friend the Marquis de Lau and a figure in a Ghirlandaio painting. Turning the Marquis de Lau incident into a reading method, de Botton coins the phrase the "MLP Phenomenon" to describe the tendency to relate the subjects of an artwork to the people in one's life, which he reproduces by inserting a picture of his girlfriend "Kate" into a discussion of Proust's Albertine.[10] Reports that Proust looked to thinkers like Ruskin as guides encourage de Botton to approach the modernist with similar intentions.

But behind the mountain of evidence de Botton compiles to suggest that Proust would have approved of his method lies the more complex and interesting suggestion that the best reader of Proust might not in fact be Proustian (in the sense of longwinded, inactive, and removed from the exigencies of everyday life), or that insights can be gained from being translated into a paradigm different from one's own. These self-help readings of modernism are most generative not when they defer to the "intentional fallacy," as they can appear to do, but for the way they thumb their nose at the authority of original intention.[11] It is in these moments that self-help approaches the status of interpretive provocation.

One might assume that as rarified a reader as Adorno would repudiate the kind of therapeutic identification endorsed by de Botton, but Adorno's reading of Proust engages in its own version of these tendencies: "Everyone who brings to the reading of Proust the necessary prerequisites for it will feel at many points that this is what it was like for him too, exactly what it was like." For Adorno, too, the problem Proust raises is the problem of happiness. He is careful to clarify, "But this happiness achieved through the rescue of experience, a happiness that will not let anything be taken from it, represents an unconditional renunciation of consolation."[12] Such comments intimate that the real problem for Adorno would not be the midcult's investment in happiness or aesthetic identification but the fact that these do not go far enough, stopping at content rather than assimilating and identifying with the author's method. For him, the synthesizing approach to modernism elides the experiences of searching, sorting, and reckoning with the inconclusive that are integral to the Proustian method. Where Adorno and de Botton diverge is not that Proust *can* change your life but *how*, to what end, and also about how best to explicate Proust's relevance to readers. Where they differ is not solely, or even primarily, ideological, but more pronouncedly on the matter of pedagogy.

Adorno outlines his method:

> I do not want merely to point out the ostensible high points of his work, nor to advance an interpretation of the whole that would at best simply repeat the statements of intention which the author himself inserted into his work. Instead, I hope, through immersion in fragments to illuminate something of the work's substance, which derives its unforgettable quality from the coloring of the here and now. I believe I will be more faithful to Proust's own intention by proceeding in this way than by trying to distill it and present it in abstract form.[13]

Adorno does not want to simply repeat Proust's "statements of intention," but he is guided by the lodestar of intention; he believes his fragmentary method is "more faithful" to Proust's intention. On a granular level, Adorno's method is differentiated from de Botton's by a narrower scale and smaller units of discussion, which corresponds to opposing views of whether it is in the fragmentary or the synthetic that the work's meaning resides.

The underlying contention is that the best way to read, understand, and explain an author is to emulate his or her method rather than to translate the author's utterances. Adorno's approach here is in the spirit of what C. S. Lewis described in 1939 as "The Personal Heresy," which argued that one "must make of [the poet] not a spectacle but a pair of spectacles."[14] At the same time, Adorno's reading is still guided by the fantasy that the modernist author would sanction his approach. This is where de Botton's approach is generative. Whatever his expressed self-conception, it is clear that de Botton does not necessarily believe that the best way to understand modernism is to be a modernist, in the reified sense of detached, disinterested, and reluctant to offer transparent advice. In short, he is not going to get his glasses "Proust corrected" any time soon.

The popular tendency to interpret modernism through a realist or pragmatist paradigm is often condescendingly read by scholars simply as a failure of irony and critical thinking among nonacademics. But the contrast between these two versions of Proust raises the possibility that, just as the best therapist is not necessarily someone suffering from depression, the most effective interpreter of modernism is not necessarily an aesthete or New Critic; and that, rather than a blindness, this negation of the modernist hermeneutic among popular readers can be a deliberate choice. The inheritance of this debate underlies the recent scholarly turn against the hermeneutical values of detachment, superiority, and suspicion that are associated with the modernists and the deconstructive theorists they influenced.[15]

In this respect, self-help readers of modernism should not be approached as the losers of the Bourdieusian game of aesthetic or intellectual taste but for their refusal to play by the "rules of art" in the first place.[16] One of the most useful models for approaching these kinds of popular cultural expressions is not a work of literary criticism—although reader-response analyses like Janice Radway's *Reading the Romance* also offer useful precedents— but Robert Venturi's classic architectural study *Learning from Las Vegas*.[17] Venturi's investment in learning from the so-called low—in the pedagogy of unlikely spaces—is an orientation this project shares. As Venturi explains, Las Vegas was built to be experienced from the highway; its billboards are meant to be absorbed at high velocities through the frame of a car window. Everything about Vegas, from the proliferation of parking lots to the garish signs, privileges the communicative over the architectural. Similarly, self-help applications of difficult modernist works are geared toward the busy and unsatisfied masses; they are for people who do not have the leisure to plod through the entirety of *À la Recherche du Temps Perdu*. Like the Las Vegas billboard, self-help's modernism is meant to be viewed while in motion, ideally from a distance, and this may be why academics are so vexed by it, because their careers have traditionally involved examining literature slowly and close up. In self-help, modernism becomes a sign. This is drive-thru modernism at its most audacious.

De Botton and Adorno are both right. Both sides of Proust—the soul searcher and the social critic—are present and deserving of attention. Where their positions become irreconcilable is in their opposing views of the pedagogical value of pain. "*Minima Moralia* hurts," Jakob Norberg observes in his compelling discussion of Adorno's own use of advice conventions, "to stimulate not readers' self-confidence but rather their lucid understanding of their utter helplessness." In the tradition of Flaubert's book of anti-advice the *Dictionary of Clichés*, Adorno wrote his own "advice to intellectuals," "a book of disempowerment"[18] that was envisioned as a riposte to the "can-do spirit of the achievement expert" in the growing self-improvement and self-help literature for careerists.[19] "Smart self-help" before its time.[20] Through such initiatives and his own literary interpretations, Adorno aims to reproduce the "shock of the unintelligible" that reading Proust engenders. For him, the wisdom of modernism is precisely the disappointments and limits of knowledge, use, and understanding, a lesson that, in his view, offers the best possible preparation for life in a totally administered society.[21]

This issue of life preparation is key to these divergent Proustian pedagogies. As a foil, self-help allows us to see the extent to which the modernist investment in difficulty, boredom, and pain internalizes and reanimates the classical educational view of difficulty being crucial preparation for life. This perspective, articulated by the ancient Greeks, was taken up by the curricular principle of "mental discipline," also sometimes called "faculty psychology," which dominated university training right up to the end of the nineteenth century. Mental discipline advocated training the mind as a muscle through difficult, often unpleasant intellectual exercises and grammatical drills. Its proponents—such as Harvard president Charles Eliot and the faculty of Yale—argued that "the more difficult, the more abstract, indeed the more useless the subject, the greater its value as a trainer for the mind."[22]

Although the modernists are widely viewed as protesting the dogmatism of rote and authoritarian learning, mental discipline's curricular ideology has some intriguing affinities with modernist practice. For Adorno, the use of art is its uselessness, which functions as protest against the utilitarian imperatives of capitalist society; similarly, for mental discipline advocates, "the immediate practical value of a subject and its disciplinary value are usually in an inverse relation to each other."[23] In addition to its transvaluation of impracticality and inutility, the ethos of mental discipline, like that of modernism, led to a depersonalized pedagogic style with an emphasis on form above content, because the precise object of study was less important than the kind of training afforded by the experience of its form.[24] The premise was that learning to tolerate seemingly futile classroom tasks offers necessary preparation for the drudgery of the real world: It is "the old humdrum monotony, the ceaseless drill," that provides "the best preparation for the business of life."[25] As president of Yale College Noah Porter observed, "The student who has acquired the habit of never letting go a puzzling problem—say a rare Greek verb—until he has analyzed its every element, and understands every point in its etymology, has the habit of mind which will allow him to follow a legal subtlety with the same accuracy."[26] Predictably, this practice led to complaints of mental discipline's "absurdity," "cruelty," "torture" and "fetich worship," all critiques that were, during the same decades, being waged against literary modernism (see, for example, Arnold Bennett's complaint that *Ulysses* turns reading into "penal servitude").[27] Mental disciplinarians believed that educational reformists were "taking the backbone out of education by making it interesting," and it is widely perceived that the modern university is still "recovering from this mistake."[28] The twentieth century ushered in a backlash against this ideology, with the progressive educational philosophy of John Dewey and the behaviorist arguments of E. L. Thorndike largely discrediting the mental discipline model.

With its anti-institutional pedagogy of shock and novelty, the literary avant-garde might be assumed to have participated in the protest against such conservative disciplinary traditions, as exemplified by reformist antitextbooks such as Ezra Pound's *ABC of Reading* and Louis Zukofsky's *A Test of Poetry*.[29] However, mental discipline's fundamentally absurdist view of professional life as demanding the skills of concentration and perseverance in the face of repetitive tasks with no obvious purpose has provocative correspondences to the outlooks of Beckett, Camus, Kafka, and Adorno. It was precisely modernism's new classicist dogmatism that rankled critics of the movement such as Laura Riding and Wyndham Lewis. In addition, the valuation of pain that Adorno finds in Proust's work has affinities with mental discipline's classicist pedagogy: Adorno and de Botton diverge in their willingness to enact the old adage that, at least when it comes to reading, difficulty builds character. Adorno approvingly quotes Paul Valéry: "The truly *strong* man in any sphere is the one who most clearly realizes that nothing is *given*, that all must be made and paid for; who is uneasy when he fails to find obstacles, and so invents them."[30]

In addition to bringing into relief modernism's unlikely affinities with classical, conservative pedagogy, the joint history of modernism and self-help makes visible the astonishing steadfastness of the self-help interpretive prism. This prism has survived the contempt of intellectuals throughout the decades and will not be deterred by even the most radical gesture of modernist negation. Existing in seemingly limitless supply, if one way is barred, the self-help hermeneutic will find another path.

This persistence of the self-help paradigm is not wholly negative, at least not for those committed to culture and the future of literary influence and exchange. The fact that readerly appeals to modernism for counsel persist amid such a cultural surfeit of more willing advisors indicates a popular desire for knowledge that resists being easily absorbed into an economy of practical use. At the same time, of course, such appeals are paradoxically attempting to apply the modernist aesthetic to practical ends. With its mandate of aesthetic autonomy, embodied by the slogan "art for art's sake," modernism is a litmus test of the utility of oblique advice. It is for this reason that rhetorical studies of the role of "indirect communication" in facilitating persuasion and imaginative transportation routinely cite modernism for corroboration and case studies.[31] Modernism may be the "rhetoric" of the literary—what Paul de Man understood as the literariness of language—at its most extreme and provocative form.[32]

As a radical version of literary and pedagogic indirectness, modernism offers readers an occasion to contemplate and question the (in)utility of the aesthetic. Although scholars and self-help readers entertain utterly different approaches to literature, they share a view of the modernist artwork as an occasion for questioning literature's place in the world and for contemplating its necessity. Is there a reader of Joyce who has never once wondered, upon sitting down to *Finnegans Wake*, "what is it all for?" What makes modernism unique is that every engagement with it is like encountering the foreignness and artificiality of all literature for the first time. Every self-help reading of modernism is a very intimate, subjective replaying of this question of literature's right to exist.

NATHANAEL WEST'S FAILED MESSAGES

In 1955 Eppie Lederer (née Eppie Friedman) won a contest to become the next Ann Landers, and her editor gave her a copy of *Miss Lonelyhearts*, Nathanael West's 1933 story of a disillusioned advice columnist. Landers read West's story as a handbook for rookie counselors, a lovelorn columnist's cautionary tale. "I have to separate myself from the readers and realize that what is happening to them is not happening to me," she said. "Too close an identification could put me in the same boat with Miss Lonelyhearts."[33] Never one to be outdone, Landers's twin sister Dear Abby also got hold of West's novella and offered her own lengthy discussion of it in her column. She summarily concluded that "a couple chuckles a day, which is the least you can expect of a lovelorn column, would have saved Miss Lonelyhearts and ruined Mr. West's novel."[34] With such statements, the columnists appear to be the quintessential "bad readers" that Merve Emre describes as "individuals socialized into the practices of readerly identification, emotion, action, and interaction."[35] Their readings of West lay bare the paradoxes inherent in self-help's attempt to insert modernist negation into an affirmative program.[36]

Historically, the advice column purported to dispense with the novel's cumbersome narrative digressions, instead cutting straight to the practical message.[37] The popular appeal of the advice column had to do with its offering a participatory reading space free of the orthodoxies of the writers' salon or academy, and one oriented toward real-world use. The alternate interpretive community of the advice column, with its insistence on the pragmatic use of West's tale, valorizes the very moral decisiveness that West's novella condemns. *Miss Lonelyhearts* depicts the violence of the decision, and in so doing corroborates Derrida's pronouncement that the instant of the decision must be mad.[38] In contrast, the columnists' glib diagnoses of West's story undermine the poststructuralist "distaste for the definitive," as Terry Eagleton puts it, or what Franco Moretti calls modernism's "spell of indecision."[39] In this respect, like de Botton's usage of Proust, their pragmatic applications carry a critical charge.

West's fate in becoming grist for the advice industry seems ironic given that *Miss Lonelyhearts* originated as a critique of Susan Chester's 1920s "heart-to-heart" column for the *Brooklyn Daily Times*. Critics have long believed that West's friend S. J. Perelman (humorist and screenwriter for many of the Marx Brothers' films) introduced him one evening over dinner to an advice columnist named "Susan Chester." The story goes that West saw Chester's letters and immediately recognized their literary potential, and he combined his experiences as clerk for the down-and-out patrons of the Sutton Hotel in New York with almost verbatim passages from Chester's column to construct *Miss Lonelyhearts*. In his biography of West, Jay Martin notes, "If any one moment could be regarded as absolutely crucial in West's discovery that he was an artist, it occurred during this night of 1929" when he was shown the Chester letters.[40] More recently, however, biographer Marion Meade has unearthed strong evidence suggesting that Susan Chester never existed and that the true author of the "heart-to-heart" column was West's old schoolmate Quentin Reynolds. Reynolds probably used the Chester byline because he feared that his stint as an advice columnist would tarnish his reputation for more serious journalism.[41] Although it was common for advice columns to be collaborative undertakings, Meade's discovery about the female column's male authorship is significant in light of the import of gender passing to West's novella, a theme that Jane Goldman has explored.[42]

Nestled next to a column titled "We Women," a place for the exchange of tips, recipes, and advice, and the comic strip "Modish Mitzi," which kept women up to date on the latest trends, the Susan Chester column advertised itself as a forum for female "heart-to-hearts." Readers looked to "Dearest Sue" as a role model for their own behavior. Chester's columns corroborate T. J. Jackson Lears's point that "tendencies inherent in the therapeutic ethos helped to defuse demands for female equality" by promoting inner fulfillment above social change, self-realization instead of group liberation, accommodation instead of indignation.[43] "Know your place and stay in it," Sue advises a secretary who is unhappy with her job and yearns for more.[44] Like therapists, advice columnists can serve as society's "cooling out" agents.[45] They provide a secular, relatively innocuous forum for frustrations that might otherwise seek a more inconvenient social outlet.

Miss Lonelyhearts's editor Shrike proclaimed that "the Susan Chesters, the Beatrice Fairfaxes and Miss Lonelyhearts are the priests of twentieth-century America."[46] Chester's letters alerted West to the advice column's authoritarian tendencies, its dependence on masquerade and deception, and its willingness to belittle readers for the sake of a breezy riposte. In his analysis of the *Los Angeles Times* astrology column, Adorno asked "What drives people into the arms of the various kinds of 'prophets of deceit'?",[47] and both he and West saw the advice column as a window into this question. Both writers also recognized this susceptibility at play in the totalitarian state.[48] In *Twilight Sleep*, Edith Wharton associates self-help's virulent optimism with war propaganda. For her, self-help represents the dangers of propaganda and the monomania of present aspirations, a phenomenon the war emphasized in a particularly dramatic and consequential way. Her sentiment is echoed by John Dewey, who noted that "There is literally no difference between the methods by which Couéism has been exploited and the methods of propaganda used in the war."[49] In a similar vein, Virginia Woolf referred to Mussolini as the "Coué of Italy."[50] Concerned with the possibility of an emergent American fascism, West and Adorno regarded the advice column as a troubling symptom of the public's propensity to heed the irrational dictates of charismatic moral authorities. This trajectory is laid out once again in West's *A Cool Million*, a story pieced together from verbatim passages in Horatio Alger that shows the path from the American dream to the fascist mob mentality.[51]

Indeed, the advice column's readers seem all too eager to be mocked and berated by spurious authorities like Susan Chester. One of Chester's readers, "Chubby Milly," writes in because she hates school and wants to leave it: "I know you're going to call me a silly kid," she writes, "but this means a lot to me, and what you say goes." Chester responds:

My Dear Milly:

In other words, you just want to sit on a sofa and have the world brought to your feet. You lazy, foolish, fat girl. Throwing away what you will be so anxious to regain in later years. . . . What you need is a good spanking, and a strong hand. I only hope your parents will see where you're drifting and put their individual feet down.[52]

It is worth noting that "Chubby Milly" anticipates Chester's abrasive reaction, and this expectation of a harsh response even appears to motivate her appeal for help.[53] But at least one reader was appalled by Chester's comments. She wrote in and admonished:

> *Dear Susan Chester:*
>
> *I never thought you, of all the nice folks I know, would ever say to a girl who was tired of school that she deserved a nice sound spanking. I was amazed and disappointed that lovable, wholehearted Susan, would suggest an old fashioned treatment for a girl simply because she dislikes school.*[54]

That the subscriber feels she "knows" Chester reflects the intimacy of the column's rapport with its readership. In response, Chester attempts to explain her strong reaction to Chubby Milly's letter: "That attitude makes me boil and a girl of that particular caliber needs something to show her where AUTHORITY is as far as she is concerned."[55] Adorno could almost have been describing Chester's advice column, with its frustrated appeal to a capitalized "AUTHORITY," when he noted, "the astrological ideology resembles, in all its major characteristics, the mentality of the 'high scorers' of the 'Authoritarian Personality,' " confessing that "it was, in fact, this similarity which induced us to undertake the present study." For Adorno, the success of the astrology column indicates "a most sinister social potential: the transition of an emasculated liberal ideology to a totalitarian one." He explains, "Just as those who can read the phony signs of the stars believe that they are in the know, the followers of totalitarian parties believe that their special panaceas are universally valid and feel justified in imposing them as a general rule."[56] It is precisely this transition from emasculated liberalism to authoritarianism that West's narrative depicts, with its account of the coercive potential of universalizing prescriptions.

As if enacting the dangers of the "emasculated liberalism" Adorno describes, an inebriated Miss Lonelyhearts and his acquaintance dub themselves "Havelock Ellis" and "Krafft-Ebing," and they proceed to interrogate an older man from the bar:

> "Your age, please, and the nature of your quest?"
> "By what right do you ask?"
> "Science gives me the right."

"Let's drop it," Gates said. "The old fag is going to cry."

"No, Krafft-Ebing, sentiment must never be permitted to interfere with the probings of science."

Miss Lonelyhearts put his arm around the old man. "Tell us the story of your life," he said, loading his voice with sympathy.

"I have no story."

"You must have. Every one has a life story."

The old man began to sob.

"Yes, I know, your tale is a sad one. Tell it, damn you, tell it."

When the old man still remained silent, he took his arm and twisted it. Gates tried to tear him away, but he refused to let go. He was twisting the arm of all the sick and miserable, broken and betrayed, inarticulate and impotent. He was twisting the arm of Desperate, Broken-hearted, Sick-of-it-all, Disillusioned-with tubercular husband.[57]

Miss Lonelyhearts's abusive behavior toward the man is a transparent displacement of his own, blatant sexual anxiety, which he attributes to the influence of the lovelorn column and hopes might be corrected through a stint in the sports department. If the old man is a "fag," it is Miss Lonelyhearts who crosses genders, switching from the man of science to the sympathetic confidant without missing a beat. Such a tactical combination of sympathy and clinical detachment was essential to the success of the advice column, which exploited both the soft voice of compassion and the hard logic of common sense. The popularization of psychology fostered by figures like Ellis and Krafft-Ebing contributed to the advice column's ascendency in the 1930s, with columnists frequently borrowing their terminology from this field. Even Karl Menninger, the respected American psychiatrist, ran an advice column for eighteen months in the *Ladies Home Journal*. But unlike Menninger, the Miss Lonelyhearts of the world needed no training or accreditation to dispense their advice. In this sense, the encounter between Miss Lonelyhearts and the "pervert" parodies not just the violence of science but also what happens when these amateur authorities have free rein on the street. The vulgarization of psychoanalysis in the popular press spawned a legion of counselors who could go around twisting people's arms in the name of Ellis and Krafft-Ebing.

On one hand, as David Gudelunas suggests, the advice column offered an interactive forum for public dialogue, and so at best it can be viewed as a popular extension of democracy.[58] On the other, however, the assertive, judgmental approach of the early columnists acted to critique liberalism's communitarian ethos of tolerance, free speech, and equality. The high demand for such columns reflected people's yearning for an advisor untethered by the constraints of political correctness or public consensus, for someone who will "tell it like it is," a desire I unpack more extensively in chapter 6.

THE SOB SISTERS WRITE BACK

Decades after West's exposé of the advice racket was published, sisters Dear Abby and Ann Landers offered their own interpretations of Miss Lonelyhearts's ills. Born Esther (Eppie) and Pauline (Popo) Friedman, Ann Landers and Abigail Van Buren (Dear Abby) were identical twin sisters born in Sioux City, Iowa, in 1918. The twins were always together; they dressed alike throughout their high school years and married in a dual ceremony in 1939 (Eppie married Jules Lederer, who would go on to become a founder of Budget Rent-a-Car). After a decade of volunteer political work and childrearing, in 1955 Eppie applied for a job to replace the original Ann Landers as advice columnist for the Chicago *Sun Times*. When Popo learned of her twin's new gig, she got herself a job as an advice columnist too, but without consulting her sister, a move that caused a rift in their relationship and led to decades of estrangement.

Nathanael West's novella pops up in almost every interview Landers gave, becoming a part of her professional mythology. As Rick Kogan relates, "Eppie read the novel and once described it succinctly to a TV interviewer 'This is a story about a man who was an advice columnist, and he let the problems get to him to the point where he couldn't function himself'. "[59] In an interview for the Canadian Broadcasting Corporation with Adrienne Clarkson (who received a master's in English literature from the University of Toronto and was Governor General of Canada from 1999 to 2005), Eppie/Landers further discusses West's novella:

> Clarkson: It used to be that your kind of column was called a "Miss Lonely-hearts" column. I don't know if you know the novel by Nathanael West?
> Landers: Yes, yes I do, it was called *Miss Lonelyhearts.*
> Clarkson: Yes. That was really a column which broke your heart, I mean, that novel showed you how the person became so involved that they weren't able to keep apart from it and gradually got a Christ complex and ended up killing themselves.[60] Do you ever get so involved that you feel this?
> Landers: Well it's very hard to be callous and cold when you read some of these tragic sad letters. . . . But I learned early in this work that if I'm going to be effective and useful I cannot sit down and cry with these people. I must be the strong one, I must be the wise one, and I must show them where they must go.[61]

In the video, Landers's repetition of the imperative "must" is reinforced by a cutting hand gesture. Similar to Susan Chester's insistence upon "AUTHORITY," Landers sees herself as compensating for the weaknesses of others; she is a martyr of the hard line. Like Susan Chester, she is enabled by what West calls "that sureness that comes from the power to limit experience arbitrarily."[62] One of her techniques for evading Miss Lonelyhearts's fate was reading her letters in the bathtub, a practice that kept her relaxed while she read and offered a healthier substitute for the booze in which West's protagonist seeks relief. Having sex with his readers, drinking and fighting with them, Miss Lonelyhearts personifies failed professionalism. In contrast, despite prodding from interviewers, Landers rarely betrayed any inkling of self-doubt, declaring that for every unwitting mistake she

Ann Landers press shot.
Credit: © Eliott Erwitt/Magnum Photos.

has provided one thousand good answers. "Do you worry about being 'for real'?", asked interviewer John Day. Landers replied, "Never. No. Because I know who I am and this has never been a problem. For *other* people it is a problem."[63] Eager to consult her elite network of professional contacts for input about readers' dilemmas, Landers viewed herself as an altruistic mediator between lower-class readers without access to expert counsel and the top specialists of American society.[64]

In keeping with their competitive dynamic, Landers's twin Abigail Van Buren (Dear Abby) offered a detailed assessment of *Miss Lonelyhearts* in her column too. Despite West's dramatic negation of "the joke" of the advice column, Abby prescribes the tonic of laughter for his protagonist. She writes:

> Miss Lonelyhearts is a literary masterpiece. Or so the critics seem to agree. But as a representation of how a "lovelorn" column goes, the picture is not without its flaws. . . . [A] tougher minded Miss Lonelyhearts, one who could laugh and bring healing laughter to his sorry clients, might have accomplished something useful with his life. But he didn't, and alas, the poor guy gloomed along and came to grief.[65]

Abby reads West as if modernism never occurred. Referencing "the late Mr. West, who saw the world dark and dealt in despair as a matter of practice,"[66] she troubles the facile dichotomy between the nobility of art and mass-cultural commodification, pointing out that modernism too exploits agony and negativity, and that perhaps the novel has a vested interest in leaving readers' problems unsolved. After all, West was not averse to pitching his stories as screenplays, or to profiting from the "business of dreams" himself.[67]

Reading Miss Lonelyhearts's moral crisis as a temperamental flaw, Abby and Landers elide West's trenchant critique of the violence of advice. Of course, West did not "forget the saving grace of humor," as Abby claims,[68] but he feared its anesthetizing effects. Humor is disturbing, not palliative, in his world. Indeed, West's ambivalence toward the comedic is integral to his literary treatment of commercial advice. Speaking of Horatio Alger, West is reported to have observed, "Only fools laugh at Horatio Alger, and his poor boys who make good. The wiser man who thinks twice about that sterling author will realize that Alger is to America what Homer was to the Greeks."[69] Likewise, from the story of Miss Lonelyhearts's inception, when Perelman supposedly gave him the "Susan Chester" letters thinking they would make a great comedy, West was wary of imposing the comedic paradigm on his tale. Dear Abby, on the other hand, would have written the story Perelman wanted. In this way, West's story perhaps confronts most trenchantly of all in this monograph the problem of the joke of self-help raised in my introduction. It is the joke of self-help that initially attracts its narrative satirists to the subject, who eventually come to feel the flimsiness of imposing a parodic perspective on an advice discourse that means so much to some of society's most earnest and desperate members.

Nevertheless, Abby's reading raises the possibility that perhaps the systemic violence of the culture industry is not the whole story. Perhaps there is some dispositional accountability in *Miss Lonelyhearts* too. West may have even agreed with Abby's view of pragmatism and the artistic temperament as being opposed. As Max Eastman declared just two years after *Miss Lonelyhearts* was written, "there is no clearer demarcation among human types than that between the artist and the man of action."[70] Describing his life in California as he was writing *The Day of the Locust*, West confided to Malcolm Cowley:

> Out here we have a strong progressive movement and I devote a great deal of time to it. Yet, although this new novel is about Hollywood, I found it impossible to include any of those activities in it. I made a desperate attempt before giving up. I tried to describe a meeting of the Anti-Nazi League, but it didn't fit and I had to substitute a whore house and a dirty film. The terrible sincere struggle of the League came out comic when I touched it and even libelous.[71]

A King Midas of cliché, everything West touches turns to irony or commonplaces. He wrote in a letter to Malcolm Cowley on May 11, 1939, "The ancient bugaboo of my kind—'why write novels'—is always before me. I have no particular message for a troubled world. . . . The art compulsion of ten years ago is all but vanished."[72] In contrast to West's failure to promote the anti-Nazi league, Landers had no qualms about enlisting people to support her cause of cancer research or her petition for nuclear disarmament.

At the same time, the columnists would have done well to more carefully heed West's warnings about moral complacency. In 1982 an attentive reader of Ann Landers noticed that some of her columns seemed familiar, and it was discovered that both Landers and Abby had been recycling old letters for years rather than printing new material. Some people brushed off the deception, likening it to reruns on television, but admonishing that the reused material should have been labeled as such. Others were less forgiving and wrote in expressing their outrage. They charged that the recycling evinced that Landers was not motivated by an earnest desire to help, and in addition to laziness, that her actions revealed a sense that all problems are the same and all sufferers interchangeable. The column was almost canceled as a result. Landers received more than three hundred thousand letters a year, and not a single appeal had a hope of response because she was no longer even bothering to pull out her letter opener. It turns out that the reprints were an act of deliberate deception, for "not only were the letters reprinted, but the ages of the writers were changed and different signatures attached, apparently to make the letters look fresher."[73] The disillusionment among loyal fans was severe; they regarded the incident as a sign of "the general decline of scrupulous, to-the-last-drop honesty."[74] "Another ikon shattered, another illusion wiped away," another subscriber sighed.[75]

The professionalism that began as a defense against internalizing the problems of readers ultimately produced a perfunctory indifference to the singularity of readers' crises. Like Miss Lonelyhearts, whose moral crisis she blithely dismissed, Landers "had given her readers many stones."[76] The scandal brought home the poignant repetitiousness of existence to readers in a way that West's modernist novella never could. The episode implied that Landers was bored by her subscribers' problems, regarding them, West says, as all "stamped from the dough of suffering with a heart-shaped cookie knife."[77] "There is little about the banalities of the human condition that is new," sighed one reader in the *Kansas City Star*.[78] "In the end, Ms. Landers has shown, we're all on our own," and she "proves that nothing's sacred."[79]

With the recycled letter scandal, the fiction of the advice column's speciation from the novel was exposed. It revealed that the advice column was always deeply novelistic and more invested in fiction than cures, despite its resistance to sentimentalizing narratives. In a defense that evokes Renaissance disputes over whether literature should delight or instruct, Landers retaliated that her column was read for entertainment more than real advice. "In her initial response to the discovery, Miss Landers defended herself by saying people read her column for entertainment and that 'the technique doesn't matter'. "[80] Downplaying the moral offense as a technical one, Landers selectively disavows any allegiance to the standards of "high-brow" aesthetics. The published responses to the scandal document a society attempting to parse the difference between art and advice. At least one subscriber countered, "There are many works of literature and journalism worth repeating, phrases and quotes worth hearing again and again. But Dear Ann columns somehow don't qualify."[81] Or, as Cyril Connolly put it, "Literature is the art of writing something that will be read twice; journalism what will be grasped at once."[82] Further, the scandal brought to light the social confusion over this rising figure of the commercial, syndicated advice columnist, raising the question of whether the column should aim to help the individual reader or the thousands of readers with a similar problem whom the individual reader represents.

Vancouver's *The Sun* pleaded with subscribers to continue writing letters to Ann: "Don't let Miss Lonelyhearts live up to her name."[83] And the *Virginian-Pilot*, perhaps unwittingly, alluded to the plot of Nathanael West's novella:

> Advice columnists have come a long way since a bygone editor invented Miss Lonelyhearts and invited readers to tell her their troubles. Considering the bind that our Ann Landers got herself into last week by using fictitious names and rehashing old material, we blush to recall that the original Miss Lonelyhearts column was secretly written by a mister, not a miss.[84]

The allusion to West's novella is apt, given that West's story is an extended meditation on what happens when the advising relation becomes perfunctory. Although Miss Lonelyhearts yearns to develop a meaningful response to the letters piled high on his desk, he ends up sounding "like a conductor calling stations."[85]

Thankfully, the contemporary advice column appears to have learned from the mistakes of its plucky midwestern forebears, without succumbing to Westian paralysis in the process. Randy Cohen, author of the *New York Times* column "The Ethicist," confesses, "I admired Lederer's jaunty self-assurance, but I understand Miss Lonelyhearts's crisis."[86] An interview with Cheryl Strayed for *The Oregonian* similarly relates, "She's read *Miss Lonelyhearts*, Nathanael West's classic 1933 novel about a nameless advice columnist overwhelmed by the misery and meanness in the world. It's [a] big responsibility, trying to solve people's problems, and Strayed has attacked it by playing to her strengths, telling stories and putting her nurturing nature on full display."[87]

Far from disappearing in modernity, as Walter Benjamin claimed, advice has become a "growth industry," as Rita Barnard puts it.[88] And instead of heralding a counsel-free art, as many understand modernism's mandate, *Miss Lonelyhearts* initiated a new breed of popular, self-negating advice. Contemporary columnists synthesize advice column pragmatism and Westian irony to produce more trustworthy guides. For instance, Dan Savage's column resembles a "blank parody" of the advice column genre; it is "anti-advice" for those "who are sick of advice."[89] Another well-known columnist, Carolyn Hax, is equally self-reflexive about the clichés of her trade; "weary of the stock answers of advice columnists," Hax "constantly winks and nods at the tradition she is taking part in while simultaneously distancing herself from being simply another sob sister."[90] Likewise, the immensely popular Strayed "is unlikely to tell you what to do." Aware that "giving advice is often futile," she offers compassionate, personalized responses instead.[91] West's self-reflexive moralism and his ironic engagement with cliché are conceits that the modern advice column has been learning to exploit.

Table 5.1 plots out these epistemological shifts in the advice genre over time. In 1950, 91 percent of readers wrote to Ann Landers to "ask a question," but by the 1990s only 34 percent of people wrote in with personal questions, the other incentives being to share information and to comment on a columnist's or a writer's remark. This shift from an instructional to a participatory mode has found its ideal forum on the internet, where every reader is also a writer, every sufferer also a self-appointed guide.

TABLE 5.1 Letter-Writers' Purpose in Writing Ann Landers, 1955–2002 (in percent)

Decade	Ask a question	Settle a dispute	Comment on columnist remark	Comment on writer remark	Share information with other readers	Thank/praise columnist or request a favorite column reprint
1955–1960	91	5	2	2	0	0
1960s	56	16	7	9	12	1
1970s	43	8	13	14	20	2
1980s	40	6	14	14	20	6
1990s	34	3	12	17	23	11

Source: David Gudelunas, *Confidential to America: Newspaper Advice Columns and Sexual Education* (New Brunswick, N. J.: Transaction, 2008), 23.

The enduring appeal of the advice column, it would seem, is not its reliance on hierarchical directives but its capacity to incite textual exchange.

Instead of sure-footedness, it is the ambivalence of the contemporary advice columnist that makes her persuasive; the idea being that a salesman or propagandist wouldn't need to be coaxed into offering insights. This new self-consciousness about the columnist's limits assumes different guises in contemporary columns: in some cases, as an embrace of the role of listener and confidant, in others as a shift to a more raucous, comedic approach. But in all cases it reflects an embrace among advice columnists of what has long remained buried and implicit: the overlap between the industries of literature and advice. Whereas Dear Sugar eschews explicit counsel in favor of digressive personal essays inspired by the letters she receives, both Savage and Hax underplay their function as dispensers of advice ("problem solving isn't really the point" says the *New York Times*[92]). These writers are aware that the desire for advice is no longer the primary reason that people turn to their columns, the stronger incentive being the occasion for public exchange, the airing of opinions, and the opportunity to follow another person's intimate dramas—desires similarly exploited by fiction. Because of the time lag between letter composition and columnist's response, and the poor odds of having one's letter selected, it is unlikely that the advice columnist will be able to offer the individual letter writer any useful aid. When the possibility of solving the particular problem of an individual reader is eliminated, the column's generalist advice and fabricated scenarios are increasingly difficult to distinguish from the universalizing precepts of fiction. Today the crossover between the two fields is only increasing; as *The New Yorker*'s Katy Waldman notes, "a field of advice columns that lob texts at people's troubles has flowered recently, from the Times's 'Match Book' to Lit Hub's 'Dear Book Therapist' to the Paris Review Daily's 'Poetry Rx.' " She observes that "the books we choose to spend time with, the voices we want in our heads, are windows into who we are and who we long to be—which also happens to be the domain of the advice-giver."[93] Literature wears its imaginary qualities on its sleeve, whereas its surreptitious exploitation of irrationality and fantasy is what makes commercial advice so troubling for Adorno and other like-minded critics.

BECKETT FOR BUSINESSMEN

Adorno's suspicion of authoritarian persuasion and culture industry consolations was grounded not only in his engagements with popular advice forms such as the astrology column but also in his readings of literary modernism.[94] This is especially apparent in his discussions of Samuel Beckett, which provided the basis for his celebration of uncompromising, radical negativity in the face of the delusions of both popular culture and the engaged art of existentialism.[95] Yet, in a turn that could only have made Adorno apoplectic, Beckett's wisdom has had a striking appeal for all manner of corporate business types, a trend that journalists from *New Inquiry* and *Slate* have observed.[96] As these journalists note, this appeal is epitomized by Timothy Ferriss (whom we met as the self-experimenter or self-proclaimed "human guinea pig" in chapter 2), whose self-help guide *The 4-Hour Workweek* explains: "I deal with rejection by persisting, not by taking my business elsewhere. My maxim comes from Samuel Beckett, a personal hero of mine: 'Ever tried. Ever failed. No matter. Try again. Fail again. Fail better.' You won't believe what you can accomplish by attempting the impossible with the courage to repeatedly fail better."[97] Ferriss's appropriation garnered media attention because of the way Beckett relentlessly rejects the affirmative, utilitarian imperative in his own writing. One of his collections is called "Texts for Nothing," and the name of a late work, "How It Is," is very pointedly not "How It *Should Be*." There is a persistent negation of the prescriptive throughout Beckett's career, in which—in contrast to self-help books stressing the power of "yes"[98]—the word "no" is the "leitmotif," as Richard Seaver observes.[99] As with Marcel Proust and Nathanael West, Beckett's resistance to explicit didacticism has only enhanced his moral appeal in the twenty-first century. Like an itch that demands to be scratched, negation exercises a kind of irresistible irritation in the positive thinking era; corporate culture simply cannot leave Beckett's "no" alone.

The puzzle that emerges is how Beckett's writing could at once provide the impetus for Adorno's *Aesthetic Theory*, a defense of art's right to resist the intractable utilitarianism of consumer culture, and which was going to be dedicated to the modernist author, and Ferriss's self-help "manifesto for the mobile lifestyle," a guide to outmaneuvering the entrepreneurial culture of anxiety and overwork.[100] One potential conclusion to be drawn from this juxtaposition is that readers will simply impute anything they want to a literary text as long as it confirms their own self-image or commitments. But both applications also raise fundamental questions about art's place in contemporary culture and about its value in modern life. Adorno opens his work with these words: "Today it goes without saying that nothing concerning art goes without saying, much less without thinking. Everything about art has become problematic: its inner life, its relation to society, even its right to exist."[101] Although less concertedly engaging with such issues than Adorno, Ferriss's invocation of Beckett is symptomatic of the continuance of these same questions: it indirectly asks what the purpose is of experiences like reading Beckett that do not directly contribute to the metrics of use or productivity, how we can adapt the temporality of reading to the "mobile lifestyle," and how we should reconcile modernism's defense of "failure" with the omnipresent valorization of impact, efficiency, and success.

Beckett's "fail better" piece of antiadvice is originally from *Worstward Ho* (1983); the title is a play on *Westward Ho!*, an adventure tale by Charles Kingsley (1855). For writers like Joyce and Beckett, the success ethos conjured associations with the late-Victorian discourses of masculinist self-discipline embodied by Kingsley's works.[102] *Westward Ho!*, as James Eli Adams explains, "one of the most popular of all Victorian novels, is exemplary in transferring the burden of manhood from martial courage to inner struggle: 'The prerogative of a man is to be bold against himself.' "[103] Beckett's parody of Kingsley's adventure tale of "muscular Christianity"[104] reads:

All of old. Nothing else ever. Ever
tried. Ever failed. No matter. Try again.
Fail again. Fail better.[105]

But Ferriss reassigns a triumphalist context to Beckett's guttural lament. He turns Beckett's descriptive statement about "failing better" into a prescription in a way that illustrates the tenuousness of the distinction. (Is true, neutral description even possible? Or is all description implicitly advancing an argument about how to live?) For Ferriss, to fail better means to resist the fantasy of perfection, to allow oneself a margin for error and growth. And yet, even if Beckett is in fact being prescriptive, the point of the quotation is unclear. Does Beckett mean that one should become a more extreme kind of loser, or that one should become less of a failure, i.e., a success? This ambiguity did not escape Beckett's attention, of course, but is built into the text. "Fail again. Better again. Or better worse," he writes, highlighting the many gradations between the poles of inadequacy and accomplishment. Evidently, what Ferriss's extraction of Beckett elides is the text's formal enactment of the painfulness of the journey it represents—the "worstward ho" of language itself. In the same way that Beckett said of Joyce, "his writing [is] not just *about* something; it *is* that something itself,"[106] Beckett's writings reproduce the thwarted resolution they describe.

The remarkable popularity of Beckett's "fail better" motto tells us two things. First, self-help readings of modernism have to undertake some fairly extreme contortions to fit an author like Beckett into their agendas. This suggests that authors like Beckett must offer these readers something that a more obviously affirmative, inspirational author—such as, for instance, Ralph Waldo Emerson—does not. Far from being a deterrent, Beckett's moral recalcitrance operates as an advertisement of his authenticity for contemporary readers negotiating our advice-saturated, "loser-wins" marketplace of cultural production.[107] In addition, this reluctance leaves an opening for the agency of the advisee to fill in the prescriptive blanks, thereby offsetting the potential authoritarianism of the conventional self-help relation with an opportunity for reader participation. Second, it tells us that hundreds of Kindle readers are first encountering Beckett through *The 4-Hour Workweek*. The second fact confirms once again the work of knowledge transfer that self-help accomplishes. It is not always as crude a form of knowledge transfer as is recounted here. As we have seen, self-help texts have historically acted as significant vectors of international literary exchange, with writers like Smiles importing key Western texts to nations across the globe.

Ever alert to the buried self-improvement subtext underlying Irish modernist works, Declan Kiberd points out that Beckett's works "are filled with ferocious assaults on the Protestant ethic of effort, work, and inevitable reward."[108] In his early writing, Beckett was fascinated with the character of Dante's Belacqua—the archetype of the lazy man—who defers repenting in favor of lying around in the shade of a rock. When asked by Dante to explain his apathy, Belacqua complains, "O Brother, what's the use of climbing?"[109] *The Unnamable* laments,

All this business of a labor to accomplish . . . I invented it all, in the hope that it would console me, help me to go on, allow myself to think of myself as somewhere on a road, moving, between a beginning and an end.[110]

The tropes of the road and quest figure prominently in Beckett's corpus. His pared down tableaus bring the pathos of ambition and expectation that much more starkly into view. As Celia in *Murphy* concludes, she "cannot go where livings are made without feeling they were being made away."[111] For Beckett, self-help is merely one facet of the mirage of productivity that all worldly goals sustain.

In addition, as suggested in chapter 4, there is a specifically Irish context for Beckett's interest in failure and paralysis. There is a saying that although they are a nation of famous talkers, "the Irish have no vocabulary for success."[112] Oscar Wilde made a similar point when he described his birthplace as a "nation of brilliant failures."[113] As early as 1854, the Irish nationalist rebel John Mitchel set down the terms of this Irish antisuccess philosophy in his *Jail Journal*:

> Success confers every right in this enlightened age; wherein, for the first time, it has come to be admitted and proclaimed in set terms, that Success is Right, and Defeat is Wrong. If I profess myself a disbeliever in that gospel, the enlightened age will only smiles and say, "the defeated always are." Britain being in possession of the floor, any hostile comment on her way if telling our story is an unmannerly interruption; nay, is nothing short of an *Irish howl*.[114]

Irish political history brings home the point that a degree of failure—in the sense of damage, wounds, loss of life—attends all representation, even the most seemingly neutral or official. This point comes across in Brian Friel's *Translations* and Eavan Boland's "That the Science of Cartography Is Limited," which both depict the losses and biases not only of triumphalist historical accounts but also of mundane objects like street names.[115] Events such as the 1921 Anglo-Irish treaty revealed that a "successful" campaign was simply an oxymoron in such a violent and divisive political climate. As in the case of Mr. Biswas, with his "Samuel Smiles depression" (recounted in chapter 1), the exclusion of the colonial histories embodied by Biswas or John Mitchel from triumphalist historical accounts imbues them with a new authority for contemporary readers, most of whom, whether within or outside of the West, see themselves as casualties of the gospel of success.

The status of Celticity as a resource for counterintuitive success strategies is detailed in Stephen Brown's corporate manifesto "Fail Better! Samuel Beckett's Secrets of Business and Branding Success" (the exclamation point says it all).[116]

Brown writes that Beckett's "secrets of branding success" constitute

a characteristically Celtic worldview which is antithetical to the essentially Anglo-Saxon ethos that dominates contemporary management thought. Whereas the Saxon perspective foregrounds facts, figures, order, rigor, and incredible attention to detail (all laudable and necessary traits), Celticity relies on imaginative leaps, compelling storytelling, irreverent iconoclasm . . . and the crock of good fortune at the end of commercial rainbows. Both are needed in business.[117]

Instead of simply opposing capitalist culture, Beckett challenges corporate operators to be more creative and reflexive. What is latent in Brown's text, of course, is an argument for the value of Beckett apart from his corporate applicability, for certainly we do not *need* Beckett to learn techniques that can as easily be gleaned from Microsoft or Tide themselves. Yet in citing Celticity as a model of less predictable business practice, Brown is not alone in attributing a productive potential to Irish modernism's resistance of the business ethic. The literary critic Gregory Dobbins similarly argues that the stereotype of "Irish idleness" offers a form of productive colonial dissent. Dobbins argues, "If Irish modernism is indeed distinct from other national modernisms, then I want to suggest that the specific function idleness had within it is one of the primary indicators of that difference."[118] Brown's preference for Beckettian "idleness" above Anglo-Saxon productivity discourse has precedents in the revival tradition of celebrating Ireland's rural antimodernism as an alternative to British industrialization.

Brown's and Ferriss's applications incite us to read Beckett's writings not as existing outside of the Puritan work ethic but in its heart of darkness. *Waiting for Godot* and self-help literature deal with many of the same themes: habit, codependency, ambition, and happiness. In a perverse way, Vladimir and Estragon are the very picture of Protestant ethic perseverance. The tramps do not suffer from apathy—as many critics claim—but from a diligence verging on the ridiculous. They wait, desperate for the slightest hint of upper-level encouragement, ever rationing their meager resources and deferring their rewards. As Vladimir observes, "We are not saints but we kept our appointment. How many people can boast as much?" ("Billions," Estragon rejoins.) Yet Vladimir is somewhat right. Vladimir and Estragon suffer from an automatism of counsel; they are trying to implement instructions and not getting them quite right. ("He said to wait by the tree." . . . "You're sure it was here?") Their frequent garbling of familiar proverbs suggests that their assimilation of cultural knowledge is slightly askew: "hope deferred maketh the something sick," they fumble, "strike the iron before it freezes."[119] Their discourse is sprinkled with half remembered precepts that have outlived their usefulness.

In addition, the tramps are constantly scrutinizing the state of their happiness—wondering whether they are more happy now than before, more happy together or apart. Vladimir intones: "Say, I am happy." Estragon: "I am happy." Vladimir: "So am I." Estragon: "So am I." Vladimir: "We are happy." Estragon: "We are happy. [*Silence.*] What do we do now, now that we are happy?"[120] This repetition of positive precepts is a technique we have already seen advanced by positive thinking gurus like Coué, with his "every day in every way I keep getting better and better." Likewise, it is not a stretch to say that a character like Winnie in Beckett's *Happy Days* offers a retort to the rise of positive thinking culture.

"So much to be thankful for," she insists—"great mercies" "that is what I find so wonderful"—endlessly repeating her "survival kit" of clichés.[121] Beckett establishes a grotesque contrast between her affirmative words and her decaying body trapped in the sand.

In *Godot*, the characters of Pozzo and Lucky further confound the Western ideal of self-fashioning. No one better embodies the reality of the self-made man than Pozzo, the landowner who is not really self-made at all but needs a slave in order to succeed. Like the self-made man, Pozzo has a very strict "schedule" that he observes. He entirely approves of the tramps' commitment to their rendezvous: "I myself in your situation, if I had an appointment with Godin . . . Godet . . . Godot . . . anyhow you see who I mean, why I'd wait till it was black night before I gave up."[122]

Pozzo lives by the monosyllabic commands that he hurls at Lucky, his "slave," and most critics agree that the pair embodies the impulse toward worldly domination. Pozzo's grand monologue toward the end of the First Act of *Godot* can be read as a lesson in the importance of time management. "Behind this veil of gentleness and peace night is charging (*vibrantly*) and will burst upon us (*snaps his fingers*) pop! Like that! (*his inspiration leaves him*) just when we least expect it. (*Silence, Gloomily.*) That's how it is on this bitch of an earth." As self-improvement discourse knows well, an awareness of one's finitude offers the best incentive for productivity. "Do not squander Time," warns Benjamin Franklin, "for it is the stuff life is made of." Pozzo embodies both the instrumentalism and the maudlin sentimentality of self-improvement discourse: "From the meanest creature one departs wiser, richer, more conscious of one's blessings," he pontificates.[123] In contrast, the pathos of the tramps stems from their inability to metabolize prescription into action. Unlike with the authors of self-help, however, this failure is not for Beckett something that can be overcome through a mere temperamental adjustment. For him, all of culture represents a heap of unusable counsel, and life itself is nothing but an overly literalized obeisance to an expression meant to be taken figuratively.

This Beckettian perspective is extended by contemporary dystopian fiction, in which self-help often emerges as a nostalgic artifact from another time. Margaret Atwood's dystopian satire *Oryx and Crake* centers on a protagonist who writes his dissertation on "Self-Help Books of the Twentieth Century." He recites passages from the cultural relics of his research to peers for laughs at the local pub.[124] The escapist appeal of the apocalypse is partly in the way it replaces the burden of self-betterment with the urgency of brute survival; the paradox of late-capitalist choice is erased in one cataclysmic sweep. In the recently televised adaptation of Atwood's *The Handmaid's Tale*, Commander Fred smuggles Offred a women's magazine whose advice on topics such as "10 ways to tell how he feels about you" adopts a twisted irony in a world where consensual dating rituals have been replaced by state-sponsored reproductive servitude.[125] Similarly, the new mother in Megan Hunter's apocalyptic novel *The End We Start From*, who is on the run from a giant flood with her newborn, remembers with a melancholy pang: "sleep when they sleep, went the old advice in a book far away and underwater." Self-help seems as out of place in such worlds as the "optimistic colors of nappy packaging" in the backseat of the getaway vehicle.[126] As Walker Percy wrote in *Lost in the Cosmos: The Last Self-Help Book*, "In the face of the deracination of Western Culture, all talk of self-enrichment through this or that psychological technique is cosmetic, like rearranging the deck chairs of the *Titanic*."[127]

Although *Godot* is sprinkled with epigrammatic insights, it withholds a literary message in the crucial places. Throughout Beckett's works, the maxim operates more as a linguistic tic than as a culminating flourish. In Act Two, for instance, curtains rise to Vladimir, singing this:

A dog came in the kitchen
And stole a crust of bread.
Then cook up with a ladle
And beat him till he was dead.

Then all the dogs came running
And dug the dog a tomb—
. . .

And wrote upon the tombstone
For the eyes of dogs to come:

A dog came in the kitchen
And stole a crust of bread.
Then cook up with a ladle
And beat him till he was dead.[128]

Vladimir's song makes the extraction of a portable lesson impossible—the only moral to the song is its repetition. Similarly, Krapp, of *Krapp's Last Tape*, fast-forwards in disgust all of his youthful "revelations;" his epiphanies and insights about life. The recorded voice excitedly exclaims, "What I suddenly saw then was this, that the belief I had been going on all my life, namely—(Krapp switches off impatiently, winds tape forward, switches off again)."[129] Beckettian form is characterized by this cycle of promised and thwarted moral summation.

The pieces of life insight that Beckett does offer are presented not as the directed didacticism of his Victorian precursors but as the unavoidable by-product or detritus of cultural memory. As Beckett sighs in *Molloy*, "you think you are inventing, you think you are escaping, and all you do is stammer out your lesson, the remnants of a pensum one day got by heart and long forgotten."[130] Indeed, the "fail better" quote ("Ever tried. Ever failed. No matter. Try again. Fail again. Fail better.") is reminiscent of the popular children's rhyme from the nineteenth-century William McGuffey reader, whose logic is already entirely circular, and which Beckett probably heard in his youth: "Try, try again / If you find your task is hard / Try, try again."[131] For Beckett, the literary maxim signifies the irresistibility of communication and the fundamentally social, borrowed quality of all language and thought. In this way, self-help operates in modernism less as a celebration of individual agency than as a humbling reminder of the determinism of the social and natural order. There is no escaping death or prescription.

RELUCTANT ORACLES

Ever since the Renaissance era of courtiers and monarchs, counselors have struggled with the problem of how to make their wisdom heard. The need to persuade advisees of one's authority without challenging their autonomy does not go away in a modern democracy, but one's ruler shifts from the monarch to the greater reading public. The problem for contemporary advisors is how to offer meaningful reflections on life that readers will not resent or mistrust as a sign of ulterior motives or pedantry. The anonymity of advertising represents one solution. The reluctant oracle is another.

As the popular applications of these recalcitrant authors make clear, the desire for textual advice never disappears; rather, society develops changing standards for what counts as acceptable, persuasive moral authority. The commercialization of counsel undermined the integrity of the narrative moral, and the rise of political propaganda during the First World War made the public increasingly wary of rhetorical manipulation of all kinds. It is under these conditions that modernism established its famed resistance to the moralizing mode.

In modernity, the reluctance to advise becomes a marker of sincerity in a way that is parodied by works such as Jerzy Kosinski's 1970 *Being There* and Robert Zemeckis's 1994 film *Forrest Gump*, which depict wisdom as a relational construct born of the fortuitous meeting of circumstance and projection.[132] With parables increasingly incorporated into self-help and advertising copy, it suddenly appears vulgar and suspicious for writers to broadcast their moral insights. Modernism exploits this fascination with moral detachment. This dynamic also informs the high-cultural realm of literary theory and pedagogy; consider, for instance, the students of Paul de Man, who enthused in a special issue devoted to their teacher:

> The last thing he probably would have wanted to be was a moral and pedagogical—rather than merely intellectual—example for generations of students and colleagues, yet it was precisely his way of not seeking those roles

that made him so irreplaceably an exception, and such an inspiration. He never sought followers; people followed him in droves.[133]

The bias against moralizing associated with the modernists came to inform the approach of their scholarly commentators and to infiltrate their pedagogy. What Lionel Trilling says of narration applies to many other discursive spheres as well, from literary pedagogy to prestige television: "A chief part of the inauthenticity of narration would seem to be its assumption that life is susceptible of comprehension and thus of management."[134]

Self-help is not simply a decontextualization but a pragmatic *translation*—to return to a key term from chapter 1—of ironic modernist diction. This translation is not literally revelatory in the way that it fancies itself to be, by reducing the modernist text to a proverbial lesson, or, as is often the case, using the modernist author's biography as a way of illuminating his or her narrative's practical applicability. Rather, it is revelatory in the way that it stages the clash between reticence and use, intention and legacy. Despite their claims, what popular self-help readers show is not that modernism secretly *is* self-help, or can be reduced to it but the extent to which modernism is engaging in a critique and rewriting of self-help. Of course, all critique is, in a sense, prescriptive, entailing an alternate sense of how to live. It is chiefly in this respect, with regard to the prescriptive impetus of all critique, to the normative impulse of all description, that we can say that modernism is secretly also self-help, or that it is anti-self-help, as the case may be.

Although the conventional model of the authoritative, confident self-help guru retains a great deal of force, the tides of moral persuasion are shifting in modernism's more oblique direction. Chapter 6 addresses what the neo-modernism of the new self-help presages for the newest wave of fiction and popular advice.

6

PRACTICALITY HUNGER

HOW-TO FICTIONS

Self-help has gone from being a dark horse of the Victorian print market in Samuel Smiles's time to a $10 billion industry in our own time.[1] This is due, in part, to the fact that self-help flourishes amid periods of political unrest; sales have risen 11 percent in the Trump era, and Brexit is leading record numbers of Britons to reach for how-to guides.[2] But self-help's contemporary popularity also reflects the fact that the industry's intellectual disrepute has waned: "Self-help books used to be something to smirk about," said Paul Sweetman, a London bookstore owner. "Now they're a badge of honour and 'as good to read as any novel.'"[3] The rising prestige of self-help is manifest in the increasingly popular genre of the how-to narrative, which includes titles such as Sheila Heti's *How Should a Person Be?* (2010), Charles Yu's *How to Live Safely in a Science Fictional Universe* (2010), Mohsin Hamid's *How to Get Filthy Rich in Rising Asia* (2013), Tash Aw's *Five Star Billionaire* (2013), Eleanor Davis's *How to Be Happy* (2014), Jesse Ball's *How to Set a Fire and Why* (2016), Paula Cocozza's *How to Be Human* (2017), and many more. These how-to fictions turn self-help's steamroller didacticism into a compositional method. As it turns out, Mr. Biswas confusing Smiles's *Self-Help* manual for a novel in V. S. Naipaul's *A House for Mr Biswas* (1961) was less an error than a foreshadowing.

Self-help guides like Smiles's borrowed dramatic conventions from novels, but today novels are increasingly acting like handbooks. When Stendhal described beauty as "a promise of happiness" in 1822, he probably could not have imagined the extent to which future novelists would exploit this promise by collapsing the distinction between life guide and aesthetics.[4] Contemporary author Mohsin Hamid has developed the most sustained account of the overlap between literature and self-help in the era of global capitalism. Hamid states that self-help has become necessary because of the "huge dislocation" wrought by the decline of the rural economy and the rise of globalization. He notes that "people are looking for guidance, and their immediate circle of friends may not be able to offer it."[5] In *How to Get Filthy Rich in Rising Asia*, Hamid suggests that "all books, each and every book ever written, could be said to be offered to the reader as a form of self-help." The second-person narration asks the reader:

> Why, for example, do you persist in reading that much-praised, breathtakingly boring foreign novel, logging through page after page after please-make-it-stop page of tar-slow prose and blush-inducing formal conceit, if not out of an impulse to understand distant lands that because of globalization are increasingly affecting life in your own? What is this impulse of yours, at its core, if not a desire for self-help?[6]

Hamid destigmatizes the self-help compulsion, first by aligning it with the motives of educated readers of the global novel, such as, presumably, his own, and second by placing Western self-help discourse in dialogue with the tradition of counsel found in Sufi love poetry. Hamid has recounted the story of how the self-help premise of his narrative began as a "joke" and then developed into something more serious.[7] Given Hamid's account of his attempts to adapt the "incredibly narcissistic genre" of self-help to "render the self less central,"[8] it is tempting to read his novel as a simple satire of the "solipsistic self of the self-help book."[9] However, Hamid has explained his changing perspective of the genre, which he grew to read as the symptom of a hunger for moral discussion in an era when religion has become perilously politicized. To read *How to Get Filthy Rich* as a mere parody of self-help's neoliberal bent is to miss its central point about literature's complicity in the mimetic desire for identification, emulation, and cross-cultural connection that keeps the self-help industry in business.

As I explained in chapter 1, Onitsha pamphleteers were titling works of fiction with how-to imperatives long before the appearance of the best-selling novels this chapter explores. In addition, as should now be clear, contemporary rewritings of the how-to manual have antecedents in modernist texts such as Gustave Flaubert's *Dictionary of Clichés* (1881), Henry James's "The Jolly Corner" (1908), Virginia Woolf's "How Should One Read a Book?" (1925), Ezra Pound's "How to Read" (1929), Gertrude Stein's *How to Write* (1931), and Nathanael West's *Miss Lonelyhearts* (1933), among others. But the contemporary authors are less tormented by the threat of utilitarianism than their modernist forebears, who were anxious to elevate themselves above the didacticism of the Victorians on one hand, and the perceived instrumentalism of the increasingly literate masses on the other. The modernist repudiation of self-help reading protocols is advanced nowhere as vehemently as in the character of Emma Bovary, who "reads literally, and out of pure self-interest, searching for only specular images with which she can identify."[10] However, as we've seen, with its cautionary impetus, the narrative practice of Flaubert—the grandfather of modernist autonomy—has more in common with self-help's prescriptive motives than he was ready to admit. In contrast, authors of how-to fictions are more self-aware and forthcoming about their own complicity in the market for textual advice (or counteradvice). After encountering a summary of Flaubert's aesthetic principles of objectivity, neutrality, and anonymity in James Wood's review of *Madame Bovary*, Canadian author Sheila Heti decided that her book *How Should a Person Be?* "is going to be the opposite of all of those things."[11] For Heti, high modernism's pretense of impersonality has itself become the negative exemplar.

Heti's narrative entwines Western self-help with the Hebrew Bible's parabolic wisdom, whose style it increasingly adopts as it advances, just as Hamid's book merges the conventions of the Western success manual with Sufi love poetry, which, he points out, is also written in second-person address and also offers life counsel.[12] Like Hamid, Heti describes literature as self-help for both reader and author. This collaborative orientation is not erected in opposition to the self-help ethic but as an extension of it. Hamid's narrator in *How to Get Filthy Rich* relates how, "like all books, this self-help book is a co-creative project," insisting that, contrary to their reputed individualism, "self-help books are two-way streets . . . Relationships."[13] In her turn, Heti aims to develop a "relational aesthetics": "not a book understood by the author and given to you, but undergone by the author and undergone by the reader."[14]

Critics have attempted to nudge these novelists toward confessing the facetiousness of their self-help narrative prisms, but they have resisted this positioning of their work as sheer parody or renunciation. Just as Hamid finds the self-help compulsion to be universal, and Eleanor Davis sees self-help as part of the "noble" struggle for meaning and happiness, when prodded by an interviewer to censure those readers expecting to find an answer to her novel's titular question, Heti replies, "I disagree when people say the book doesn't answer the question. There are useful answers or half-answers, throughout it."[15]

Heti read "lots of self-help books" as preparation for her novel, and she singles out Smiles's book in particular.

I had this book called *Self Help* by Samuel Smiles, it's the earliest self-help book, it's where the term was coined—it's from the late 1800s. And the way it's written is that every chapter is a different great man and his habits. You're just supposed to emulate them.[16]

As she elaborates elsewhere, Smiles's emulative practice aligns his approach with the methods of fiction: "to a certain extent, it's a bit more like a novel in the format, and the idea that you can be better by imitation."[17] Like the Onitsha pamphleteers, Heti finds opportunity in her exclusion from self-help's conservative canon: "One good thing about being a woman is we haven't too many examples yet of what a genius looks like. It could be me." Smiles is undoubtedly a card-carrying member of that class of "just another man trying to teach me something," whose values Sheila, as Heti's protagonist is called, has internalized and, as the novel develops, struggles to escape.[18] Though she finds creative potential in his omissions, Heti's narrative also shows that the "Samuel Smiles depression" (SSD) has become the status quo.

How Should a Person Be? depicts both the gendered and the geographic bias of self-help's emulation compulsion. At the height of her professional crisis, Sheila sits at the Toronto Greyhound bus station, on the margins of the Western halo of success, trying to decide where to go. She opens the only book she brought for the journey, a thick tome called *Important Artists*, scouring it for advice on how to be great, "moving carefully through the pages with a pink highlighting pen and a yellow one, like a beautiful, anxious, pregnant young mother studying for her medical school exams."[19]

As Sheila combs through the book's biographies, taking notes, she remarks, "I learned that the artists originated in a hundred and eleven cities, but by the Important phase of their careers, they populated thirty-nine." She tabulates:

Glasgow	4
Dusseldorf	5
Mexico City	6
Paris	7
Amsterdam	8
Los Angeles	9
London	15
Berlin	19
New York	30

Converting the book's anecdotes into an algorithm of success, Sheila decides to enact the quintessential trajectory of cosmopolitan ambition— she decides to move to Manhattan: "There, the odds of meeting someone Important, and thus becoming Important myself, were best."[20] Sheila's approach to *Important Artists*—which superstitiously treats contingent details as clues to life management—is not that different from the Gilded Age success manuals that analyzed youthful portraits of famous men such as Cornelius Vanderbilt and Henry Clay for clues to their prosperity.[21] The scene reinforces the point that self-help's cultural intervention is its implementation of an alternative way of reading. Historically, as we have seen, self-help readers undermine the generic distinction between the novel and the handbook, poring over manuals with an aesthetic reverence, sifting out the practical advice in works of fiction. These taxonomic agitators are presentist in the boldest sense; they subordinate the history and intention of the text to the reader's current ambitions. Shakespeare is read together with Henrik Ibsen for insights into modernization, the opening sequences of soap operas are a stimulus to entrepreneurial achievement, and the biographies of *Important Artists* become a guide to relocation.

How Should a Person Be? began as a self-help book. It grew out of a collaboration between Heti and the "leadership speaker" and Toronto event coordinator Misha Glouberman, who also appears as a character in Heti's novel, and whose practical life advice the friends eventually turned into the nonfictional life philosophy compendium, *The Chairs Are Where the People Go*.[22] From her novel's conception, the discourses of self-help and narrative fiction were entangled, a relationship whose traces remain visible in the novel's final form.

Describing the influence of the practical how-to ethos on the literature of Ernest Hemingway and other American authors in a 1985 review, Edward Said suggested that "a useful way of understanding this peculiar structure of perception is to see it as a substitute for the feeling of historical depth and continuity." Discussing the how-to ethos's privileging of technique above wisdom, Said disapprovingly observes that "experience of the here-and-now—the relevant—is given priority,"[23] an ahistorical tendency underlying the reading of Polonius in Meiji Japan as an authority on modern capitalism. Complaining of this same presentist impulse, Christopher Lasch argues that, in self-help's "narcissistic" culture, "to live for the moment is the prevailing passion—to live for yourself, not for your predecessors or posterity."[24] However, as philosopher Pierre Hadot makes clear, far from a product of narcissistic modernity, to embrace the pure present is the goal uniting virtually all of the schools of ancient philosophy, including Platonism, Stoicism, and Epicureanism.[25] As self-help's curatorial tradition suggests, the how-to is not so much an erasure of the historical as it is a reshuffling of the archive of cultural wisdom under the mantle of present uses.

Hamid's book upholds romantic love as the ideal of ego-transcendence, whereas Heti's affirms the love between Sheila and her best friend Margaux. By her novel's conclusion, Sheila has formulated a more proactive, authentic relation to self-help, and to novel writing, a change documented by her evolving relation to the self-help catchphrase "who cares?" This phrase, reminiscent of the title *Don't Sweat the Small Stuff*, a popular guide by Richard Carlson, is one of Margaux's first childhood verbalizations. Margaux hears it spouted by her mother's self-help-obsessed friend, but by the end of the narrative it stimulates Sheila's aesthetic departure from convention: "*Who cares?* . . . Who am I to hold myself aloof from the terrible fates of the world? My life need be no less ugly than the rest."[26] In Hamid's narrative, a parallel appropriation of self-help lingo takes place when Hamid labels his penultimate chapter "Focus on the Fundamentals," an entrepreneurial metaphor common in corporate self-help culture that also harks back to Hamid's *The Reluctant Fundamentalist*, and here carries the double connotations of cost-reduction measures and deathbed moral reckoning.[27]

Both *How Should a Person Be?* and *How to Get Filthy Rich* conclude with the injunction to isolate and cherish the essentials of life, leading Wood to regret the "earnestness" of Heti's novel[28] and Pankaj Mishra to regret the "wistful" and "maudlin tone" of Hamid's.[29] But Heti's and Hamid's commitment to a new didacticism is proved by their willingness to risk such sentimentalism in the service of their moral visions. These authors believe that the job of the artwork is to communicate the artist's reverence for existence. In contrast to Edward Said's claim, for Heti, Aw, and Hamid, self-help is not a strategy for evading existential wisdom but a vehicle for posing meaningful questions about how to most fully inhabit and savor the present.

GETTING REAL

Contemporary novelists and self-help authors meet in their eagerness to sift out the superfluities and to cut more quickly to the heart of life. Of course, self-help has been urging both art and individuals to "get real" since it began over a hundred years ago (it is from Dr. Phil that I borrow the phrase). In the field of self-help, this getting real imperative has a practical, therapeutic benefit. Self-help writing *has* to get real so that it can help people change. Ostensibly, this therapeutic realism proceeds by stripping the individual's self-talk of its delusions and self-justifications. Such escalating rhetorical appeals to realism in self-help can help us understand parallel appeals to realism taking place in literature. Together they allow us to see the pursuit of practical wisdom as an engine of genre innovation.

Self-help does not just love to tell *people* to "get real," it loves to say this to literature as well. Self-help has always been committed to corralling the excesses of the romantic imagination. As explained in chapter 5, people wrote to advice columnists such as Dear Abby for their no-nonsense guidance, which took the form of a rhetorical reality slap intended as an antidote to the implausible expectations learned from reading fiction. This is especially striking in the realm of relationship advice. As Beatrice Fairfax, the early advice columnist, complained in 1899:

> The lady novelists of the last generation have much to answer for; they sent their heroes sighing through twenty chapters, madly in love, yet keeping away from their inamoratas through fear, doubt, delicacy and numbers of other foolish feminine reasons that never enter into a man's philosophy.

When a man wants to see a woman he manages it. When he wants to stay away he is indifferent, all of the lady novelists with their little pernickety manikin heroes to the contrary.[30]

Self-help has historically been driven by an almost maniacal compulsion to negate the delusions of the imagination, to "recognize only realist representation," as Pierre Bourdieu says.[31] This is nowhere more apparent than in the realm of relationship manuals, which offer a glimpse into self-help's general method. This method involves disassembling those ideals that threaten to captivate and control: whether love, popularity, charisma, or acclaim. The how-to manual breaks up these passions into strategic units, stripping them of their power to intimidate and overwhelm. It does this partly by presenting itself as a corrective to the romantic imaginary. For Fairfax, the irresponsible "lady novelists" are to blame for the delusions of an entire generation of lovelorn female readers. If she were to meet Elizabeth Bennet from Austen's *Pride and Prejudice*, she would probably tell her to stop moping and get over it. "Listen honey," she would say, "Mr. Darcy is just not that into you." This desire for blunt, mean speech— for a figure who "tells it like it is,"—is, of course, also a motif of contemporary political rhetoric.

As in the case of Fairfax, for self-help, the therapeutic injunction to "get real" used to be tied to the repudiation of novels. For the early self-help of Samuel Smiles and William Robinson, getting real meant purging oneself of the delusions of the imaginary through the strategic use of nonfiction. They administered a healthy dose of straight talk as antidote to the false hopes and consolations generated by literature. The problem is that readers have grown inured to self-help's blunt exhortations; Dear Abby's cheeky jibes no longer have the same sting. As a result, contemporary advice has to resort to increasingly extreme measures to achieve the same effect of provoking readers into self-change. But how to administer the shock of the real today? How to shake readers up enough that they will heed your advice? This is the problem faced by self-help and, to a degree, by the novel as well.

Contemporary self-help has two solutions to this problem of how to shock readers into action. The first solution is profanity. Self-help manuals today advertise themselves as "truth bombs"; they use crass language to restage old interventions and jolt readers into change. In these new manuals, expletives are the shock treatment of choice.[32] Recent guidebooks by Mark Manson, Sarah Knight, and Michael and Sarah Bennett make even the no-nonsense Dr. Phils and Dear Abbys of the past seem quaint. Self-help guru Tony Robbins describes this practice as employing "the science of taboo language" in order "to provoke people back to the reality of the moment."[33]

Self-help is in the midst of a generational change; industry stalwarts such as Stephen Covey, Dear Abby (a.k.a. Abigail van Buren), and Wayne Dyer have recently passed, and a new generation of youthful self-help has emerged to take their place. The new manuals incorporate autocritique of the industry (they are like anti-self-help self-help guides) and describe themselves as "life advice that doesn't suck."[34] Written for those suspicious of "traditional aspirational systems,"[35] this self-help is writing back to the Dale Carnegie tradition, with its emphasis on people-pleasing, happiness, and conformity. This new genre of "self-help books for the rest of us"[36] teaches readers to purge themselves of the false values and anxieties inherited from the traditional success ethic. In a popular example, Mark Manson, author of the antihandbook *The Subtle Art of Not Giving a Fuck*, articulates his riposte to "all the positive and happy self-help stuff," whose "fixation on the positive—on what's better, what's superior—only serves to remind us over and over of what we are not, of what we lack."[37] Manson's book urges readers to become more judicious about how they distribute their care, a sentiment Harvard graduate Sarah Knight echoes in advising readers to draw up a "fuck budget"—a breakdown of those items worth worrying about and those not worthy of their time.[38] There are different gendered valences to these male and female repudiations of perfectionism, which tend to target professional and domestic ideals, respectively. But for both authors, "maturity" means learning to "become more selective about the fucks we're willing to give."[39]

Illustration from Mark Manson, "The Subtle Art of Not Giving a Fuck,"
January 8, 2015, https://markmanson.net/not-giving-a-fuck.
Credit: Meme originally created by Susannah ("MollyBlue").

The bar of rhetorical extremity in self-help has gotten so very high that there is almost nowhere else to go to get real—this brinkmanship of blunt speech seems to have reached its emphatic limit. However, self-help might have *one* last place to turn to shock and surprise, a place it has traditionally dismissed and repudiated. Self-help's final recourse is fiction.

In contrast to William Robinson, who, in 1845 reluctantly conceded that perhaps every one in two hundred novels *might* be worthwhile, Svend Brinkmann's 2017 guide *Stand Firm: Resisting the Self-Improvement Craze* prescribes readers "one novel a month."[40] The new self-help authors are paradoxically appealing to fiction for better, more realistic advice. Notably, the advice of the manuals and the how-to novels is the same. Sheila Heti's eventual embrace of the "Who cares?" mantra presents a literary counterpart to the realignment of priorities advocated in the manuals of Manson, Knight, and their peers.[41] In place of the Protestant ethic of industrious activity, self-help now bears witness to a new apathy prestige. Tiffany Dufu's *Drop the Ball* and Stephen Marche's *The Unmade Bed* abide by the principle that "caring less is the hope of the future."[42] Both self-help and the contemporary novel recommend detaching from the anxieties and aspirations that drove the market for traditional self-help.

Like most other popular forms, self-help is growing more ironic, which Christy Wampole claims is "the most self-defensive mode." She describes how irony "pre-emptively acknowledges its own failure to accomplish anything meaningful. No attack can be set against it, as it has already conquered itself."[43] Benjamin Schreier's *The Power of Negative Thinking* writes back to Norman Vincent Peale's positivity gospel, while Simon Critchley's *How to Stop Living and Start Worrying* offers a titular reversal of Carnegie's "action manual."[44] The most obvious reading of this trend is that it is capitalism learning to circumvent public skepticism; it is self-help adapting to survive. At the same time, the old self-help is already more complex, ironic, and ambivalent than most recognize. Such ambivalence manifested itself in Carnegie's stumbling over the paradoxes of performing sincerity in *How to Win Friends and Influence People*, and in Smiles's protestations against readings of his work as advancing a "gospel of selfishness."[45] But if once this ambivalence erupted in passing contradictions or betrayals of self-doubt, it has now become the occasion for the genre's renewal. As in the novel genre, self-help's neo-realist imperative is tied to its project of generic reappraisal.

This discussion of the reality imperative in self-help or fiction today calls to mind David Shields and his popular manifesto *Reality Hunger*, first published in 2010, the same year as Heti's novel.[46] According to Shields, what reality TV, hip-hop sampling, and the latest novels have in common is that "they express or fulfill a need for reality, a need that is not being met by the old and crumbling models of literature."[47] But Shields's next book after *Reality Hunger* has the pseudo-self-help title *How Literature Saved My Life*; this is a work that describes the consolation and guidance literature provides.[48] Taken together, these texts do not herald a turn to realism for its own sake but for the sake of better life management: not reality hunger but something like practicality hunger.

In short, the rhetorical escalations in contemporary manuals (their turn to profanity and fiction) are tied to their project of redressing the failures of the self-help tradition. These guides are writing back to self-help while also, of course, reproducing and continuing self-help. This is where contemporary fiction and self-help strikingly converge. Manson is not the only one flipping off Dale Carnegie to carve a space for his own, better kind of advice. A parallel project of undercutting and rewriting the self-help tradition informs the whole subgenre of contemporary how-to fiction. Invoking the how-to form in their titles, such works often hinge on the irony of presenting themselves as a guide to something undesirable, such as losing a lover or being a mistress. In other cases, the title's promise is undermined by the actual text, which either dispenses with or destabilizes the instruction manual premise.

Hamid's novel *How to Get Filthy Rich* best exemplifies the genre. The story reads at once as a novel and as a get-rich-quick book, and each chapter of the narrative is structured according to a different rule for success. Hamid's reader and character are jointly addressed in the second person as "you," which lends the book the flavor of a choose-your-own adventure novel. As the story develops, reader and protagonist together discover the costs of a life spent chasing material success. Hamid's novel does not just aim to invalidate self-help but to appropriate and refine its strategies of life management. It is as if his novel is ingesting the self-help genre, metabolizing its nutritive bits, and expelling the rest as so much neoliberal waste.

One of the potentially beneficial aspects of self-help that Hamid's novel seeks to preserve is its technique of what is sometimes called "personal inventory-taking." Like so many of self-help's "technologies" of self-management, this is a practice that has roots in the spiritual exercises of the Stoics. The practicality hunger of recent fiction is a product of the same urges that have led to the revival of a stoic philosophy among life hackers and podcast gurus. It is not hard to see the lineage from the Stoical practice of "get[ting] at things" and "go[ing] right into them,"[49] to Beatrice Fairfax's deflation of romantic expectations and to Dr. Phil's slogan "get real." Describing his nightly "examination of conscience," during the middle of the first century AD, Seneca recounted how, "Every evening I extinguish the lamp, and when my wife has become silent, I withdraw into myself and take stock of my day."[50] Such rituals instructed the individual to take a step back from present concerns in order to arrive at the "correct appreciation of the value of things." This detached perspective was not so much meant to negate worldly concerns, as Stoicism is often understood, but rather to reintegrate each concern into its larger "cosmic context."[51]

For the Stoics, this project of ethical realignment took place through the practice of "reductive description," or "description that aims to discredit."[52] The Stoics emphasized the role of perception in shaping experience: nothing is inherently good or bad but thinking makes it so. Related to this is the fact that language and description play a crucial role in shaping our moral impressions: "a single action can have many different descriptions";[53] it is through the act of describing that individuals assert their agency and reason. Epictetus explains the practice: "His ship was lost. What happened? His ship was lost. He was hauled off to prison. What happened? He was hauled off to prison. But the comment, 'He has fared ill' is an addition that each man makes on his own responsibility."[54] Self-help is usually associated with callous and sweeping generalizations, but it can also operate as an extension of the Stoic's quest for greater emotional precision.

As I briefly mentioned in chapter 3, like modernism, stoicism is currently enjoying a revival in self-help. The modernist and stoical impulses of the new wave of self-help are linked through their shared emphasis on adapting to loss rather than chasing after achievement. "Nothing to be done" is a phrase from Beckett, but it could be from Epictetus. More broadly, though, this association helps us to see that self-help enacts a pick-and-choose, bricolage approach to ideology rather than the hegemonic worldview it is often assigned. As Burkeman observes, "Anyone can become somewhat Stoic, or a bit more Buddhist, or practice *memento mori* a little more frequently . . . the negative path to happiness isn't an all or nothing affair."[55] Nevertheless, when compared to other philosophical systems, Stoicism does hold a privileged place in self-help's history because of its practical interest in how to live (which for the Stoics is, of course, really about learning how to die).

It is telling that the very same authors quoting lines from Beckett can be found promoting Stoicism as a "life hack." Timothy Ferriss, who popularized the "fail better" quotation as a lifestyle mantra, gave a TED talk on Stoicism in which he describes it as "an operating system for thriving in high stress environments."[56] Numerous handbooks are updating Aurelius, Epictetus, and other Stoics for contemporary life; there is even an annual conference called "Stoicon." The affinities between Stoical and modernist positions have not been lost on literary critics; Hugh Kenner, for instance, chose to title his study of Flaubert, Joyce, and Beckett *The Stoic Comedians*, which he defined as "one who considers, with neither panic or indifference, that the field of possibilities available to him, however large or small, is closed."[57] Modernism's neo-classicism and self-help's neostoicism are linked celebrations of the fragmentary wisdom of cultural memory. The appeal of Stoicism in both spheres has to do with the way it represents a more measured or "realistic" version of self-care that involves coping with limited agency and the mess of human experience rather than spouting hyperbolic promises of mastery or containment. At the same time, Theodor Adorno qualifies Kenner's alignment of the two movements; he maintains that what "seems Stoical" in the work of Samuel Beckett is "full of inaudible cries that things should be different."[58]

Classical scholars have noted that interest in the Stoics declined dramatically in the early nineteenth century but experienced a revival in the early twentieth century, just as modernism was coalescing, in a way that points to the surprising affinities between the two ethics. One sign of the mounting interest in Stoicism at the end of the nineteenth century was publication of a new volume of the works of the teachings of the philosopher and former slave Epictetus in 1868, which sought to argue for the Stoic's relevance to modern life. The volume was reviewed by Henry James, whose account of Epictetus anticipates contemporary critiques of self-help's accomodationist politics. James censures Stoicism's philosophy of submission for being inconsistent with the modern ideas of progress and rights. Just as many today argue that self-help privileges self-transformation above political reform, James maintains that "Epictetus never once intimates the existence of an idea of rights." He goes on to observe that Stoicism's entire philosophy of submitting to that which is outside our power is inconsistent with the ideas of rights and social progress. To explain the anachronistic resignation that Stoicism expresses, James advises us to imagine Epictetus's philosophy being embraced by a southern slave: "imagine a negro slave . . . keenly conscious of all of the indignities of his position, dogmatically making the best of them, preaching indifference to them, and concluding, in fact, that weariness and blows and plantation fare are rather good things." Yet he also notes that Epictetus was one of the favorite authors of the Haitian revolutionary and former slave Toussaint L'Ouverture. There is a good and a bad Stoicism, says James, and we moderns must learn to "apply Epictetus." He concludes, sounding a great deal like Burkeman with his bricolage method, "Let us take Epictetus as we take all things in these critical days, eclectically. Let us take what suits us, and leave what does not suit us. There is no doubt but we shall find much to our purpose."[59]

A Stoical practice that has endured is the tradition of *memento mori*: the Stoics believed that by meditating dispassionately on death we can strip it of its power. Instead of an abstract source of bewitchment and fear, they urged us to conceive of death as a prosaic and natural process. The idea is that representing death as a natural case of material decomposition facilitates a productive realignment of present concerns. This is better living by being more literal about the representations that govern our lives.

Both contemporary novels and manuals are internalizing the practical value of such death meditations. This personal inventory-taking, this death meditation, is a technique Hamid employs in his conclusion, which bears remarkable similarities to the conclusion of Mark Manson's self-help manual:

Last paragraph of Mark Manson's	Last paragraph of Mohsin Hamid's
The Subtle Art of Not Giving a Fuck (2015)	*How to Get Filthy Rich in Rising Asia* (2013)
"Then one day, on our deathbed, (hopefully) surrounded by the people we gave the majority of our fucks to throughout our life, and those few who still give a fuck about us, with a silent gasp we will gently let our last fuck go. Through the tears and the gently fading beeps of the heart monitor and the ever-dimming fluorescence encapsulating us in its divine hospital halo, we drift into some unknowable and unfuckable place."[60]	"Until one day you wake up in a hospital bed, attached to inter- faces electric, gaseous, and liquid. Your ex-wife and son are there . . . and you are ready, ready to die well, ready to die like a man, like a woman, like a human, for despite all else you have loved, you have loved your father and your mother and your brother and your sister and your son and, yes, your ex-wife, and you have loved the pretty girl, you have been beyond yourself . . . and so may you, may I, may we, so may all of us confront the end."[61]

These texts revive the ancient *ars moriendi* (art of dying), which extends through the Middle Ages and back to antiquity and aimed "to induce conversion from false worldly comforts toward an ascetic mode of self-knowledge."[62] Despite considerable differences in language and style, the similarities are striking. Both depict the hospitalized deathbed as a web of overlapping technological and familial attachments. Both invoke the scene of death as a way to authorize their advice. Hamid's second-person focalization enacts the unsettling pedagogy of the memento mori on a formal, as well as a thematic, register. It imbues the reading experience with a feeling of spectrality, forcing the reader to hover in the liminal space between actor and observer. As the scholar Alice Bennett observes, the second person is "a technique which takes hold of us and forces us into consciousness of our own death, with a view to shaping behaviour in the present."[63]

Foucault explains the role of the deathbed meditation as a stock-taking exercise:

> What gives the meditation on death its particular value is not just that it anticipates what opinion generally represents as the greatest misfortune; it is not just that it enables one to convince oneself that death is not evil; rather, it offers the possibility of looking back, in advance so to speak, on one's life. By considering oneself as at the point of death, one can judge the proper value of every action one is performing.[64]

The second person thus mobilizes Walter Benjamin's point in "The Story-teller" that the value of counsel is tied to the authority that the dying man possesses over the living. This was what he worried was disappearing in modernity, with the sequestering of death from public view.[65] (On this note, Hamid has said that part of the inspiration for his novel was his experience of death's matter-of-factness in intergenerational Pakistani households, with grandparents dying next to children being born, which inspired his interest in the domestic panorama of the individual lifespan.) Also preoccupied with mortality, Heti concludes her novel with a parable about a gravedigger. An awareness of death is what impels these projects of personal and aesthetic regrouping.

Of course, it is also in "The Storyteller" that Benjamin laments the supplanting of the storyteller's old-fashioned counsel with technical information, whose new prestige is for him embodied by the rise of the novel genre, which, he argues, antedating Said, is less interested in meaning than in practical expertise.[66] In Hamid, however, far from being opposed, the desire for practical information and spiritual meaning are part of the same utilitarian continuum: "as the emerging-market equity trader does, and as the rapid-fire TV remote user and the multiple-computer-window opener do, all of us learning to combine this information, to find patterns in it, inevitably to look for ourselves in it, to reassemble out of the present-time stories of numerous others the lifelong story of a plausible unitary self."[67] For Hamid, information mining is not a negation of the search for wisdom but a natural extension of the desire to find the logic and pattern to human experience.

In place of the social web of the Victorian novel, Hamid inserts the invisible interfaces and infrastructures in which he shows the individual's agency to be embedded. In his novel, like in Flaubert's *Dictionary of Clichés* (see chapter 2), the epigrammatic voice of Victorian moral authority is replaced by the more sinister generalizations of the self-help manual. But like his contemporaries, Hamid is less exercised by pointing out self-help's manipulations and more deeply absorbed by the collaborative longing it expresses for a productive model of textual influence unsullied by propaganda, religious divisions, and commercial manipulation. Thus, while the how-to manual proper is scrambling to dissociate itself from self-help's negative associations, novelists are becoming less dismissive, using self-help as an opportunity to modernize a potentially maudlin textual ethics.

The how-to conceit first gained real traction in a spate of 1980s and 1990s fiction that took up this formal premise (see chapter 2), including Junot Díaz's "How to Date a Browngirl, Blackgirl, Whitegirl, or Halfie," Dany Laferrière's *How to Make Love to a Negro Without Getting Tired*, Pam Houston's "How to Talk to a Hunter," Lorrie Moore's *Self-Help*, and Jay McInerney's *Bright Lights, Big City*.[68] Before Hamid, for instance, Díaz's writings had depicted how impersonal self-help directives have come to take the place of the more organic or familial advice networks. Whereas that great classic of American success and self-making, *The Great Gatsby*, begins with the exchange of advice between a father and his son,[69] the presence of paternal advice is conspicuously absent from both Hamid's and Díaz's fictions. Instead, through the temporal sleight of hand enabled by the second-person narration, the protagonist seems to be recursively advising himself. Their fictions appear to enact Nietzsche's observation that "if one hasn't had a good father, then it is necessary to invent one."[70]

Like Moore, whom I discussed in chapter 2, and who uses second-person narration in "How to Be Another Woman" to reflect on the amorous naiveté of her youthful alter ego, Díaz uses the how-to frame to depict the incongruity between romantic passion and the calculated impression management stratagems of the relationship manual. The narrator reassures Díaz's adolescent seducer: "You have choices. If the girl's from around the way, take her to El Cibao for dinner. Order everything in your busted-up Spanish. Let her correct you if she's Latina and amaze her if she's black. If she's not from around the way, Wendy's will do." By the end of the text, however, the narration has shifted from this plethora of possibilities to a tone of resignation conveyed through a cascade of negative imperatives: "During the next hour the phone will ring. You will be tempted to pick it up. Don't. Watch the shows you want to watch, without a family around to debate you. Don't go downstairs. Don't fall asleep. It won't help."[71] The story concludes with a negation of the very possibility of self-help.

Read as a commentary on the self-help tradition, the second person of such narratives has some interesting effects. It documents the double consciousness of social role and emphasizes the surplus impression management demanded of the disenfranchised. It brings to the fore those groups and identities excluded from the tacit universalism of the genre's second-person address. And it also undermines the illusion of individual agency—the *sine qua non* of self-help—by turning characters into automatons who appear to be acting out scripts of internalized commands. Incidentally, the feeling the second-person narration engenders—that we are watching living things behave like machines—is for philosopher Henri Bergson the very essence of the comedic.[72]

The ability of the second person to capture the automatism of social convention makes it an ideal form for depicting the internalization of the American dream that second-generation immigrant authors such as Díaz describe having inherited from their parents. This may account for the how-to conceit's rising popularity among recent works by Asian American authors who have grown up inculcated with the myth of the model minority and the promise of "upward mobility on the strength of self-help."[73] "In the last decade," as Eleanor Ty observes, "a number of literary and filmic works" have emerged by Asian Americans and Asian Canadians that challenge their parents' values and "have queried the means to and the type of happiness by chronicling the unhappy or failed life."[74] This is a project for which the self-help conceit is particularly suited, as deployed in such recent works as Alexander Chee's *How to Write an Autobiographical Novel: Essays*, Anelise Chen's self-help, fiction, memoir hybrid, *So Many Olympic Exertions*, and Charles Yu's *How to Live Safely in a Science Fictional Universe*. Yu's novel describes the protagonist's father's feverish search for "systems of thought, for patterns, rules, even instructions. Fake religions, real religions. How-to books. *Turn Three Thousand into Half a Million*. Turn half a million into ten. *Conquer Yourself. Inventory of Your Soul*."[75] His father's reading is explained by his son as part of the immigrant strategy for adapting to the combination of opportunity and constraint that defines the new environment. But the real-life authors of these how-to narratives, the children who grew up with the anxieties and the aspirations of their dislocated parents, develop a much more measured perspective of self-help's combined function as coping mechanism and source of disappointment. This may help to explain why some of the most rigorous second-person how-to experiments are today being undertaken in the service of documenting the psychology of disenfranchised and minority experience.

Yu wryly notes, "Life is, to some extent, an extended dialogue with your future self about how exactly you are going to let yourself down over the coming years."[76] Staged as an encounter between the narrator's immature, aspirational self and future, wizened perspective, how-to fictions seem to literalize Dale Carnegie's fantasy of writing back to his younger self, which he records in the opening pages of *How to Win Friends and Influence People*. He writes, "As I look back now across the years, I am appalled at my own frequent lack of finesse and understanding. How I wish a book such as this had been placed in my hands twenty years ago! What a priceless boon it would have been!"[77]

In Carnegie, as in Yu, Díaz, and Moore, advice strives to compensate for the shortsightedness of the present. And with its heady second-person collapse of reader, narrator, and character, the how-to fiction represents the counterfactual space where one's mature and naïve selves can converse. With their doubling back on past decisions, such narratives model the recursive temporality of Stoical reflection. As Foucault writes, for the Stoics, "Even if we are hardened, there are means by which we can recover, correct ourselves, and become again what we should have been but never were."[78]

The counterfactual fantasy underwriting the advice relation, already present in Benjamin Franklin's never-written "The Art of Virtue," is literalized in Yu's *How to Live Safely in a Science Fictional Universe*. The title, we are informed by the narrator, refers to "This book, this autobiography, this self-instruction manual (self-coercion manual), self-creation manual" which, in a heady twist, the protagonist Yu is at once reading and writing and transcribing at the same time. If in Hamid, Moore, and Díaz the second-person voice enables the narrator to figuratively toggle between their naïve and worldly self, the time-traveling narrator of Yu's sci-fi tale is able to physically inhabit this conditional grammatical tense: "I have traveled, chronogrammatically, out of the ordinary tense axes and into this place, into the subjunctive mode."[79]

In "How to Be an Other Woman," Lorrie Moore's second-person narrator figuratively hovers before her younger self, who is "spread out like a ridiculous cake on the bed," in order to offer her pointers about how to behave; whereas Yu watches his younger self "through the glass case of memory-proof material along this corridor of the aquarium of the past."[80] During one of his parent's agonizing fights he sees himself

pretending to work on the [computer] program . . . pretending in my room alone, pretending to myself, as if someone was watching me from above, some semi-omniscient, bird's eye view observer was watching over me, and what I didn't realize then was that there was an observer and in fact, it was me, it's me now, looking back at myself from inside this time machine.[81]

Yu's alter ego writes the how-to manual Carnegie dreams of and uses time travel to go into the past and hand it to his younger self. The cover of the book we read is supposed to be the cover of this manual. In what begins to approach a definition of advice, Yu describes "time [as] a machine: it will convert your pain into experience. Raw data will be compiled, will be translated into a more comprehensible language."[82]

At the same time as the advice-giver is impelled by a wish to process and redress the irreversibility of her own experience, it is this same temporal irreversibility that brings advisee and adviser together, that is the condition of possibility for advice. "Imagine," says Yu's father in the novel, "If we could just stop at any moment in time and change our lives. Rearrange them. . . . Instead of the ordinary problems of life, the problem of what to do next, of what to do first, of what to do ever, at all, even the smallest step, we would also have the problem of what to do yesterday, of what to do last year, of how to justify anything, ever."[83] Yu's time travel conceit caricatures self-help's prosaic efforts to master time through inventories and to-do lists. If we could fully control time, as self-help attempts on a minor scale, this would not solve our problems but turn problem solving into something limitless and interminable.

This is why the problems of death and advice are inextricable. We need the wisdom of others to compensate for our enforced sequentiality, which is a product of our mortality. A response to these constraints, advice, like literature, is an outsourcing of experience. The final pages of Yu's novel erupt in a second-person crescendo of direct advice. In sparing the reader the time and pain of sifting and mining for a portable lesson, such moments participate in the urge to economize the reader/text communication underlying the contemporary novel's practicality hunger, its impatience with plot, contrivance, and convention.

THE RACIALIZED IMPERATIVE

Just as the growing Asian American literature of failure uses the self-help paradigm to document the traumas and disenchantments of the upward-mobility ethic,[84] the revival of the second-person instructional mode also informs new directions in African American memoir, comedy, poetry, and fiction. As such works make clear, the second-person mock how-to manual is a useful vehicle for depicting the invisible labor foisted on minority groups and identities and also for undermining the rhetoric of assimilation and adjustment.[85] This potential of self-help to underscore and satirize overlooked aspects of racial experience comes across strikingly in recent literary how-to riffs such as Terrance Hayes's book of poetry *How to Be Drawn*, and Baratunde Thurston's memoir *How to Be Black*, both of which use the second-person imperative mode to advance their social commentaries on the bad faith of neoliberal choice in the context of racial inequities.[86]

Together these works invoke the twinned energies of self-help, beginning with Booker T. Washington's argument that African Americans should persevere by learning to please the dominant group and to cater to that group's expectations. This spirit is encapsulated in the hefty 1895 tome *The College of Life or Practical Self-Educator: A Manual of Improvement for the Colored Race*. This 700-page encyclopedic guide to Afro-American success includes the typical inspirational biographies and motivational lessons found in the mainstream advice literature of the period, but with an African American slant.[87] It is to this tradition of individualized improvement at the expense of social reform that Henry A. Giroux refers when he discusses how self-help historically pathologized problems of race as "issues of character, individual pathology, or genetic inferiority" and "displaces responsibility for social welfare from government to individual citizens." He argues that "the discourses of self-help and demonization, while appearing to serve different purposes, end up complementing each other" by enabling the persistence of social inequality while simultaneously "blaming African American youth for their plight."[88]

But contemporary how-to spinoffs like Thurston's and Hayes's are also tapping into the other, more politically productive tradition of African American self-help, which advocates a version of self-help as autonomy, racial unity, and self-sufficiency. This can be seen in Marcus Garvey's "Universal Negro Improvement Association" in the 1920s, Gwendolyn Brooks's 1980 *Primer for Blacks*, and perhaps even in the growing genre of hip-hop self-help exemplified by *The 50th Law*, cowritten by rapper 50 Cent and self-help guru Robert Greene, and DJ Khaled's *The Keys*, whose guidebook offers readers step-by step guides on how to deal with the neo-Heideggerian figure of the "They"—all those who are trying to stand in the way of your success.[89]

Like for Díaz, the mock-self-help frame offers Thurston a useful means of describing the way that race heightens the stakes of self-presentation. In his chapter on "How to Be the Black Employee," which includes instructions on topics such as "whether or not to eat the watermelon" at the holiday party, Thurston warns: "While everyone around you may decide to let it all hang out, you have a responsibility to maintain a bit more control. Don't drink too much. Don't end up alone with someone else's date. And when anyone asks you how you like working at the company, you tell that person that you fucking love it here and can't imagine working with a better group of people." His use of a pile-up of negative imperatives to depict the burden of internalized white expectation is reminiscent of the conclusion of Díaz's story, which uses the same anaphoric structure. Thurston elsewhere cautions: "Your job doesn't stop when you leave the [office] building."[90] In fact, as *How to Be Black* explains, when "you" got your new job, you were not only hired for the job of "research associate" but "you were also hired for another job: your blackness." This Job #2 will require you to:

- Part A: represent the black community
- Part B: defend the company against charges of racism or lack of diversity.
- Part C: increase the coolness of the office environment by enthusiastically participating in company events.[91]

Thurston sees his comedy as serving a political purpose and remarks of his satire that "while I definitely intend for it to be funny, there is a message in it." This message is summed up in his exhortation, "So, black people, let's repeatedly put out information about our own images of blackness, be it fighting for justice or making videos on a green screen or hosting TV shows on Al Jazeera or camping or writing books about the infinite possibilities for how to be black."[92]

Although written in a more serious tone, and using a vastly different form, Hayes's *How to Be Drawn* is framed with a similar concession to the burden and determinism of external perception. In Hayes's book, the how-to conceit dons the various guises of a nineteenth-century parenting manual, séance-hosting instructions, and a drawing handbook. Like Thurston's, Hayes's contemporary take is a far cry from the unbounded celebrations of uplift and self-determination found in the writings of Booker T. Washington or in the *Manual for the Improvement of the Colored Race*. In place of irresponsible promises of material transcendence, these works are concerned with the much more complex problem of how to cope with the reality of limited agency in a way that does not lead to political resignation. "There are theories about freedom, and there is a song that says / None of us are free," Hayes writes, and it is not easy to say where exactly his poems fall on this divide.[93] Both he and Thurston are concerned with the problem of how to exist in a world where one is always being represented—and representative—whether in politics, art, or a police report. Far from enacting the naïve voluntarism of self-help's early iterations, these authors share a view of personal and social reckoning as coextensive rather than antipodal projects. In addition, comedic works like Thurston's or D. L. Hughley and Doug Moe's more recent *How Not to Get Shot: And Other Advice from White People* put the "joke" of self-help to a very different use from that found in Gustave Flaubert or Nathanael West, deploying it as a means of satirizing the pretense of legal order, justice, or individual responsibility when it comes to racial confrontations.[94] In such texts, the stakes of the clash between the individual's limited agency and self-help's rhetoric of transcendent power come that much more starkly into view.

ON ADJUSTMENT

Thurston, Hughley, and Moe use comedy to subvert the values and assumptions of the discourse of self-determination, whereas Ali Smith's recent how-to novel adopts a different tactic. *How to Be Both* resists offering explicit directives and chooses instead to defend the acts of guesswork and approximation. Smith's narrative reminds us of the value of the work of reaching, sifting, and adapting an author's sentences to suit our purposes. For her, narrative indirection is not a time-wasting diversion from relevance but a pedagogic lesson. Given this position, it is revealing that Smith wrote her PhD on modernism and that she was interested precisely in modernism's celebration of the ordinary and everyday, despite its reputation for impersonal and disinterested thinking.[95] *How to Be Both* is not an attack on the self-help industry but a critique of the dualistic and teleological intellectual impulses underpinning the thirst for self-help's clear-cut answers. In a passage on the art of looking, Smith offers the anti-argument to self-help's advocacy of aesthetic identification and presentism. Describing her character George's changing relationship to a painting of a monk looking off to the side in an art gallery, Smith notes how "it's like she is meeting an old friend, albeit one who won't look her in the eye because the saint is always looking off to the side. But that's good too. It's good, to be seen past, as if you're not the only one, as if everything isn't happening just to you. Because you're not. And it isn't."[96] Indeed, this decentering of the self and the ego is precisely how Philip Weinstein describes the value of modernist unknowing.[97] Contemporary how-to novels would agree with Weinstein and modernism that the ego needs to be unsettled and transcended, but this is a point that their second-person narration threatens to counterproductively undermine by accommodating the reader's desire for direct validation and address.

Aside from its indifference to the value of this work of relation and adjustment, a limit of the "reality hunger" argument is its failure to account for the enormous popularity of genre fiction and science fiction. It is for this reason that "reality hunger" is more accurately described as "practicality hunger," or what I elsewhere discuss as "therapeutic redescription."[98] The urge to strip away the inessential *can* lead to heightened realism—but it can also lead to doubling down on fantasy—it can produce both Sheila Heti's pseudo-memoir and Charles Yu's science fiction. Likewise, "When you read genre fiction," argues Lev Grossman, "you leave behind the problems of reality—but only to re-encounter those problems in transfigured form, in an unfamiliar guise, one that helps you understand them more completely, and feel them more deeply."[99] The same point has been made about memoir. Wendy Simonds describes how one of her interviewees "considered biography to be self-help books because they enabled her to reflect on her own life."[100] Likewise, G. Thomas Couser maintains that memoir appeals to readers' desires for "wisdom and self-knowledge," and "for what the main character, who is always the author, has learned."[101] If one looks at the art and entertainment consumed today, it is evident that there is still a strong demand for fantasy and fiction. This is no mere "reality hunger"; a moral, prescriptive, and spiritual hunger compels these generic experiments.

In *The Self-Help Compulsion*, I have contended that self-help is inextricable from the history and future of literature's production and reception around the globe. In his essay "Literature as Equipment for Living," Kenneth Burke identified self-help's literary import when he argued that readings of manuals are more often motivated by fantasy than by empirical outcomes.[102] Burke's statement is often taken to mean that self-help books are useless, but it could alternatively suggest that that their appeal exceeds sheer instrumentalism. The pleasure of self-help might not be that different from the *jouissance* (pleasure) of fiction.

Both self-help and fiction experiment with scenarios of life management; both entice with the prospect of advice. Self-help's advice may not be substantiated by results, as Burke points out, but it is predicated on the possibility of future action (a temporality underscored by the how-to fiction's second-person narrative tense). Unlike the related speech acts of "judgments" and "assessments," advice is defined by its prospective orientation.

It offers directives as to "what should or could be done,"[103] and herein lies a clue to self-help's "prepolitical" potential. Not only does such counsel keep alive the endangered idea that the other's experience is valuable and worthy of communication (discussed in Benjamin's "The Storyteller"), it also presupposes that this experience can be converted into useful knowledge. The novelists I have discussed cast longing glances at self-help's tacit assurance of the ongoing relevance of textual wisdom and of the intimacy of the genre's discursive situation. This is not to say that they are indifferent to the industry's nefarious consequences. To the contrary, these authors are committed to documenting the success ethic's pernicious, even tragic, effects. But they also recognize self-help as one of the few communities clinging to the conviction that a book can change the present.

CODA

THE SHADOW UNIVERSITY OF SELF-HELP

I n 1912, a twenty-four-year-old Dale Carnegie offered his services as an extension-school teacher to both NYU and Columbia. After these universities rebuffed him, he settled on the Harlem YMCA as the venue for his public-speaking course; this course contained the nucleus of his 1936 best-seller, *How to Win Friends and Influence People*, which was initially intended as a take-home souvenir for class participants. Carnegie's incredulity at academia's indifference to his skill set made its way into his best-seller's opening pages. The "ability to deal with people," it states, is a valuable commodity just like "sugar or coffee." But despite the scouring of his research team, Carnegie claims to have been unable to find a single "practical textbook" on the subject.[1] *How to Win Friends* was intended to fill that gap in a way that renders explicit self-help's status as a form of "cultural pedagogy."[2]

Self-help's use of the university as a foil for its alternate pedagogy has a long history that can be traced back to some of the very earliest uses of the term. In Thomas Carlyle's novel *Sartor Resartus* (1833–1834), the phrase "self-help" makes one of its first appearances, tellingly, in a chapter titled "Pedagogy," which presents an invective against the pieties of the "rational university." After the main character has "expectorated his antipedagogic spleen," he forges "the highest of all possessions, that of Self-help."[3] Samuel Smiles likewise expressed deep suspicion of institutional education, hailing working-class groups, or what he called "People's Colleges," as the greatest hope for social progress. In *Self-Help* Smiles rails against the ill effects of excessive study and competitive examinations, and he elsewhere declared: "It is not governments, then, but THE PEOPLE who must educate the people."[4]

Since the late nineteenth century, self-help has continued to offer an alternative to the academy. Its cultural classifications and reading methods unsettle the specialization promoted by the modern research university. As folklorist Sandra Dolby observes, "Readers of self-help books are *active* learners" who "create their own curricula and course designs."[5] The conceit informs manuals like Og Mandino's 1980 *The University of Success*, which approvingly cites Carlyle's description of books as "the true university" as the inspiration for its title and method. The chapters of Mandino's guide present themselves as "semesters" and "lessons" on topics such as "how to separate the possible from the impossible" and "how to use life's options wisely." The appendix lists "faculty" and "source material."[6] The idea for the "curriculum" behind Helen Schucman's *A Course in Miracles*, for another example, originated when the author's department chair at Columbia University's College of Physicians and Surgeons grew exasperated with the "angry" and "stressful" departmental dynamics and appealed to Schucman to come up with an alternative.[7]

Self-help has changed a great deal since its early associations with Victorian autodidacts and mutual improvement associations. Its emphasis has shifted from morality to morale, from collective uplift to competitive individualism. Perhaps most significant, it is no longer confined to the printed book, having undergone a product diversification so enormous that it infiltrates almost all facets of contemporary experience. Acacia Parks's observations about positive psychology's growing campus presence apply to self-help: "In no area of application has positive psychology flourished more . . . than in higher education," she enthuses. She continues:

> More departments than ever are offering courses in positive psychology, and demand for these courses is consistently high. . . . Educational institutions

have expressed interests in using principles of positive psychology to inform institutional structure, faculty development, and pedagogy. [8]

Self-help's campus presence is not confined to those highly visible happiness courses on "The Science of Happiness" or "The Meaning of Life" but is also operative at an infrastructural level. It can be found not only in predictable campus outlets like the Center for Wellness, the Business School, or the Department of Psychology, but also in unlikely and informal spaces: creative writing workshops, course catalogs, seminars in expository writing and religious studies, office hours, well-being newsletters, and new faculty training and development. In short, a great deal has changed since Dale Carnegie was booted off of the Columbia campus.

But is it fair to group a happiness course, the success ethic of the business school, and the new figure of the campus well-being officer, together under the banner of self-help? Self-help is notoriously difficult to define because it encompasses both utilitarian and therapeutic ideals—the aspirational mentality of the professional managerial culture and the softer discourses of well-being and self-care. In reality, as Micki McGee has argued, these two sides of self-help are mutually reinforcing. Therapeutic self-realization exercises offer temporary compensation for the pressures of hypercompetition.[9] Such therapeutic measures are better than nothing, perhaps, but they also allow the more competitive form of self-help to persist by patching over its most pernicious effects.

The university's turn to self-help can be attributed to a convergence of factors, and chief among these is what Henry Giroux has described as "the transformation of the university into an adjunct of corporate power."[10] Supplanting the university's civic mission with for-profit interests has not only led to an obsession with efficiency and outcomes, performance and competitive achievement, but also to absorption of the corporate sphere's strategies for managing liability and diffusing dissent.

But the situation is a little more complex. Although so much of scholarly, intellectual practice is premised on exposing the illusion of neoliberal choice, academia's elaborate informal advising networks remain deeply invested in the liberal-humanist construct of the agentic, self-determining individual, and that is not an entirely bad thing. The absorption of self-help by the academy has been facilitated by its resemblance to the tradition of Arnoldian self-culture that defined the university in the years leading up to the First World War. As the president of Colorado College put it in 1891, "A college training aims to develop man's self-making power . . . which, other things being equal, is the key to success." "At its most inspired," Laurence Veysey says in *The Emergence of the American University*, "the quest for personal fulfillment might be the high-minded struggle of a William James; at the opposite extreme it could already assume a tone not unlike that of Dale Carnegie."[11] In some respects, self-help has always been part of American higher education, and its resurgence represents a counterfactual university in which the generalizing tendencies of the liberal arts never went out of style.

Self-help has always been at once para-academic and counteracademic; tendencies that persist to this day, for instance, in the polemics of Alain de Botton, whose School of Life in London offers courses on "How to Be Confident" and "How to Find Love." De Botton asserts that "the modern university . . . remains wholly uninterested in training students to use culture as a repertoire of wisdom."[12] The School of Life is meant to redress this lack; its location just next door to University College London dramatizes the contrast with academe that has informed self-help from Carlyle onward.

In de Botton's latest venture, written with John Armstrong, this antiacademicism is rendered even more explicit. *Art as Therapy* argues that we need to reorganize museums according to therapeutic, rather than historical, categories. It goes so far as to reprint the course description for "Italian Renaissance Art" from Yale's art history department catalog and offer a disapproving appraisal: "The course is deliberately impersonal. It carefully avoids asking 'what do these works mean to me?' Or, 'what problems and issues might I have in common with a painter or sculptor from 1300 to 1500?'"[13] Self-help has long been questioning the dominance of impersonal historicism as a curatorial and academic organizing framework.

In fact, the polemical opposition between self-help and academia elides the extent to which self-help has started to migrate to the center of the official academic curriculum. A watershed moment was the emergence of Harvard's most popular course of all time, Tal Ben-Shahar's 2006 "Positive Psychology" course, which was based on his best-selling self-help manual, *Happier: Learn the Secrets to Daily Joy and Lasting Fulfillment*. The book's introduction proposes "to bridge the ivory tower and Main Street, the rigor of academe and the fun of the self-help movement."[14] The exchange between Ben-Shahar's self-help and classroom practice flowed both ways. His follow-up book, *Even Happier*, incorporates activities tested in the classroom.[15]

The popularity of Ben-Shahar's course has spawned many emulators: Yale's most popular course in its 316-year history was Laurie Santos's "Psychology and the Good Life," offered just last year, the final assignment of which, "The Hack Yo'Self Project," is an exercise in personal improvement.[16] Nor is this phenomenon confined to the Ivy League; in 2007, a *New York Times* article noted the ironic fact that George Mason University, once considered by the *Princeton Review* to be one of the unhappiest campuses in America, was home to a tremendously popular course on happiness and well-being.[17] At Alamo College, a controversy erupted when a dean attempted to replace a humanities general education requirement with a course based entirely on Stephen Covey's *The Seven Habits of Highly Effective People*. When the public caught on and complained, the district was forced to unload the 2,500 copies of Covey's guide it had purchased and to defend its accreditation, which came under attack.[18]

To be sure, the vocational bent of Alamo's Covey course differs from the therapeutic orientation of Yale's Santos sensation in a way that reflects the different circumstances of the respective student populations. But taken together, these examples suggest the broad spectrum of pedagogic experience that has attended the rise of the "neoliberal university," premised on the belief that well-being and entrepreneurialism can happily coexist. Meanwhile, the ubiquity among all kinds of universities of an economic emphasis on productivity and "deliverables," to use an unfortunate corporate neologism that has migrated into university life, has led to a resurgence of academic counter-self-help that strives to mitigate the effects of the efficiency ethic.

Consider Maggie Berg and Barbara Seeber's *The Slow Professor: Challenging the Culture of Speed in the Academy*, which offers itself as "a self-help book for academics."[19] Seeber and Berg align themselves with the self-help industry's softer, therapeutic investments and against the managerial culture of the modern university. Likewise, some universities are taking steps to offset an ascendant entrepreneurialism; Harvard's Transcript Project, for instance, is a creative initiative that urges students to use their transcripts to reflect on the value of their college experience beyond grades and preprofessionalization—a kind of Arnoldian self-culture shored against rampant competitive self-improvement. Such initiatives cannot in themselves solve the problem of the university's corporatization, but they do strive to offset the commodification of value and wisdom.

An important mediating term in the self-help/university dialectic is adult education. Self-help and adult education were always entwined discourses; in the Victorian Great Britain of Samuel Smiles, the education of the adult working classes was promoted under the banner of self-help. In the United States, for the early part of the twentieth century, adult education was largely an extramural activity, but today adults twenty-five and older comprise almost half of the U.S. undergraduate population, a trend coextensive with the increased campus presence of self-help.[20]

Despite these strides, access to adult education remains limited at best. Higher education remains out of reach for the vast majority, and here is where self-help's status as a cheaper and more accessible alternative comes in, thrice removed, you might say, from the experience of educational privilege. In its reified fashion, self-help, like adult education, challenges the relegation of learning to a brief period of youthful preparation and advances a belief in the buildable self, in personality as a fluid, unfinished construct. The appeal of self-help, in other words, has partly to do with its reorganization of the educational teleology of the individual life.

Self-help and adult education are both also invested in the more modest reorganization of the individual's bookshelf. They share the view that a curriculum should revolve around the individual's daily problems and interests. The rallying cry of early adult education was that learning should be organized around "situations, not subjects."[21] This perspective antici-pates not only de Botton's disruption of the chronology of the syllabus and art museum but also the arguments against periodization advanced by scholars such as Rita Felksi and Eric Hayot. If, according to Hayot, in his essay "Against Periodization," "the near-total dominance of the concept of periodization in literary studies . . . amounts to a collective failure of imagination and will," self-help is a field where the "value of the period" as ideological construct has long been willfully, and even imaginatively, con-tested.[22] It is in this respect that the self-help reader can resemble Edward

Mortimer Adler with his "Sytopicon."

Credit: George Skadding / The LIFE Picture Collection/Getty Images.

Said's idealization of the "amateur" as one who questions professional routine, who "instead of asking what one is supposed to do" asks "why one does it, who benefits from it, how it can reconnect with a personal project and original thoughts."[23]

In the 1940s, Mortimer Adler, the "great books" popularizer, put the tenet of "situations, not subjects" into practice. Like Smiles and Carnegie, Adler also got his start in adult education. When Adler, an associate professor of philosophy at the University of Chicago, published his two-volume Encyclopedia Britannica set *Great Books of the Western World*, he accompanied it with an invention he called the Syntopicon. This was a massive index that attempted to recatalog Western intellectual history according to 102 ideas or themes contained therein. Through such initiatives, Adler helped to place books and reading methods at the center of conversations about lifelong learning and the endlessly revisable self.

LITERARY CRITICISM AND THE HIDDEN CURRICULUM OF SELF-HELP

Four years after *How to Win Friends* took over the best-seller lists, Mortimer Adler published the tremendously successful *How to Read a Book*, whose title, he conceded, implied "a Dale Carnegie contribution to the how-to genre." The book grew out of a course Adler designed to introduce pre-law students to the liberal arts.[24] Adler's book attracted the ire of the intelligentsia for the way it "canned Western culture, put a lid on it, and belted it into the supermarket," as Dwight Macdonald quipped.[25] In its efforts to redress the "deplorable failure" of American education, the book concludes with its own counter-syllabus: a "guide to intelligent reading" that lists over one hundred recommended texts, from Homer to Kafka. It is interspersed with reading "tests" that look a great deal like those a student might encounter in the final examination of a course on English literature.

But the affinities between Adler's method and those of the midcentury English department begin to unravel in his chapter on "How to Read Imaginative Literature," which begins by negating three axioms of the mid-century English department. Adler instructs: "Don't try to resist the effect that a work of imaginative literature has on you." "Don't look for terms, propositions, and arguments in imaginative literature." And finally, "Don't criticize fiction by the standards of truth and consistency that properly apply to the communication of knowledge."[26] These three tenets—disinterestedness, argumentation, and what might be described as political or historicist criticism—have largely defined the discipline of English since Adler's time. Above all, and anticipating recent shifts in the field, Adler argues for the merits of "appreciation" before critique: "before you express your likes and dislikes, you must first be sure that you have made an honest effort to appreciate the work. By appreciation, we mean having the experience that the author tried to produce for you by working on your emotions and imagination." Only then, he states, antedating "surface reading," are you in a position to "judge."[27]

Self-help's embroilment in questions of upward mobility and individual psychology might make it seem like a natural problem for the social sciences, but, as I've argued, its investment in the question of what to read and how to read it has special relevance for literary critics. This point was not lost on I. A. Richards, who is often credited as the inventor of the close-reading method that has come to largely shape literary scholarship for the past century. Joining the chorus of resistance to Adler's *How to Read a Book*, in 1942 Richards published *How to Read a Page*, which incorporated one hundred of the most important *words* everyone should know ("Amount, Argument, Art, Be, Belief, Cause . . ."), the point being that what distinguishes serious reading from a how-to guide is patience, decorum, and modesty of expectation.[28]

The book, which has become a kind of "icon for the close-reading Richards pioneered,"[29] was envisioned as what Richards called a "counterblast" to Adler's method.[30]

Cover of Mortimer Adler, *How to Read a Book* (1940).

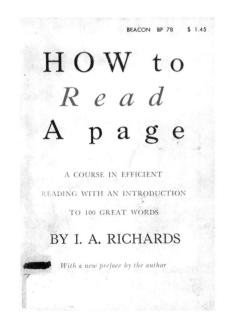

Cover of I. A. Richards, *How to Read a Page* (1942).

Richards explained why we need to understand the one hundred words he enumerates:

> We do not read Shakespeare, or Plato, or Lao Tzu, or Homer, or the Bible, to discover what their authors—about whom otherwise we know so little—were thinking. We read them for the sake of the things their words—if we understand them—can do for us. But understanding them, of course, is not making them mean something we know of and approve of already, nor is it detecting their ignorance and limitations. It is using them to stretch our minds as they have stretched the minds of so many different readers through the centuries.[31]

Far from advocating disinterestedness, Richards seems to agree with Adler's argument for art's instrumental relevance. Much like Adorno and de Botton with their different methods for reading Proust, where Richards and Adler diverge is not that literature can change your life but *how* and to what purpose.

Richards plays a key role in Joseph North's revisionary history of literary criticism, which maintains that the discipline has suffered from its elision of the moral and practical aims of first-generation New Criticism North argues, invoking the argument of Gerald Graff in *Professing Literature*, that "the work of literature, for Richards, was therefore to be a kind of therapeutic technology, and the critic was to be something like a doctor of applied psychology."[32]

When literary criticism at least nominally embraced Richards's formalism but expelled his therapeutic orientation, it may have surrendered to self-help one of its most promising demographics. At the same time, the commercial efforts of figures like Adler went a long way toward galvanizing the defenses of technical expertise articulated by Richards and eventually by the New Critics. Identifying a first mover in this dynamic is probably a losing endeavor, but it is clear that a history of reciprocal influence, rivalry, and critique contributed to the consolidation of both fields.

Self-help made the liberal discourse of self-cultivation banal, even taboo, among literary theorists. The discipline's present trajectory has been shaped by a two-pronged recoil from self-help, which was manifest, on one hand, as New Critical technical specialization and, on the other, as the poststructuralist denigration of the delusion of the unified and agentic self. There is an inverse relation between the rise in self-help titles celebrating "will-power" as the twentieth century progressed and the depreciation of this concept in literary theory. Lisa Ruddick notices a deep-seated resistance to the categories of selfhood and identity in the field and maintains that "the most suspect of all the ideas connected with selfhood is that of 'self-cultivation.'"[33] David Wayne Thomas concurs: "A generalized sense that cultivation is reducible to hegemony has come to permeate scholarly readings."[34] Added to this is what Rita Felski identifies as the discipline's "deep reservoir of mistrust toward the idea of use."[35] The suspicion of self-cultivation and use coincides with what historian David Armitage has observed in the humanities as an overarching rejection of reading for "guides to life" in favor of "short-termism," the "micro-history," and the archival.[36]

Of course, this embrace of the archival and the decentering of the self is related to the tremendous influence of Michel Foucault on literary criticism in the second half of the twentieth century. It was Foucault who so persuasively outlined the "technologies of self-management" that the prevalent view of self-help as another form of governmentality reproduces, a view that my monograph has devoted considerable energy to nuancing and expanding.[37] Despite his early reputation for a kind of ruthlessly deterministic political worldview, in his late writings Foucault directed his last energy toward the problem of how to build the self, how to construct a good and soulful life. The shift is striking on several registers. In these last, profound meditations, Foucault explained his surprising "return to the self after a career dedicated to its extinction," as one perplexed commentator put it,[38] with the comment that "there is no first or final point of resistance to political power other than in the relation one has to oneself."[39] Although Foucault was certainly no fan of self-help, which he dismissed as part of the "Californian cult of the self,"[40] what late Foucault tells us is that the therapeutic and political agendas of literary criticism can be coextensive, rather than opposed, a thread the affect theory of later thinkers such as Eve Sedgwick has resumed.[41] And so, if the discipline has been shaped by a skewed interpretation of Richards, it has been no less defined by a selective reading of Foucault that emphasizes his writings on power above his revitalizing of the ancient art of living. Amanda Anderson has recently sought to redress this point in a short piece discussing the "Therapeutic Criticism" of Foucault, Sedgwick, and Berlant.[42]

It's possible that the disciplinary repression of its therapeutic genealogy is tied to the undervaluing of pedagogy in favor of "research" that Laura Heffernan and Rachel Buurma are uncovering in their study of literary criticism's neglected "teaching archive."[43] If we could reconstruct it, actual classroom practice would probably tell a very different story from the one Ruddick and North describe, in which questions of use and life relevance persist only in "residual, nostalgic, and discredited forms."[44] This alternate history would no doubt show reputed literary critics exploiting all vestiges of "life relevance" for the sake of student engagement.

Despite the usefulness of North's corrective, the repression of self-help as a context for the disciplinary ambivalence toward the therapeutic persists in his monograph. He muses in his introduction:

> Very few people, it seems to me, start reading a novel by Virginia Woolf with the primary aim of learning more about British cultural life in the 1920s. Most of those who do are scholars. What nonspecialist readers are looking for in literature is rather less easy to define: perhaps the best we can do at the moment is to say that they are looking for something to go on with, something that will help them live their lives.[45]

What North almost says, but does not, is that nonspecialist readers are looking for self-help. His difficulty in defining what nonspecialists want, which will be familiar to any who have attempted the task, is what creates an opening for self-help. It is telling, then, that North situates his book in the Leavisian tradition, for, as mentioned in chapter 3, it was F. R. Leavis who notoriously coined the idea of the "Life spirit" of a literary work. Leavis claimed that the best authors "are all distinguished by a vital capacity for experience, a kind of reverent openness before life, and a marked moral intensity."[46] To which René Wellek countered, voicing the skepticism of many in the field, "I am, I fear, too much of a theorist not to feel strongly the ambiguity, shiftiness, and vagueness of Leavis's ultimate value criterion, Life."[47]

Self-help is thus symptomatic of the problem the discipline confronts of the nebulousness of literary knowledge, and of our impoverished vocabulary for articulating its life value in autonomous disciplinary terms. Too often scholars who attempt to explain why literature matters find themselves flailing around in what Bourdieu derided as "verbal generalities" about "essence."[48] Self-help, full of passionate intensity, is not hampered by such misgivings. The fear of sounding like self-help has impeded the discipline from articulating its use value as a necessary and explicit alternative to commercialized advice.[49]

North's choice of Virginia Woolf as an illustrative example of literature's elusive life relevance is important. The repression of the instrumental that North attributes to the New Critics found authorization not just in their selective appropriations of Richards but also in the autonomy doctrine of the high modernists. Discussing the "modernist genealogy of the contemporary literature department," Andrew Goldstone maintains that modernism "provided both the principles and the occasions for the new discipline of academic literary criticism that came to dominate English and other departments in North American and British universities over the course of the century." As a "decisive moment" for the "crystallization" of "aesthetic autonomy," modernism initiated a bias against self-cultivation that continues to inform contemporary academic departments[50] (think of E. M. Forster's Leonard Bast, crushed by his own self-improvement initiative, or of Bouvard and Pécuchet's pathetic experiments with self-reinvention). A significant occasion for disciplinary autonomy, we might say, was the heteronomy of self-help.

Though self-help handbooks positioned themselves as alternatives to the failings of official literary education, this does not mean that self-help's version of the literary was always reactionary or belated. Before Bourdieu described aesthetic discrimination as a product not of nature but of upbringing, Arnold Bennett was breaking down for readers how to identify and assimilate literary taste. Before Barthes referred to the text as a "tissue of quotations," Samuel Smiles unapologetically announced in his *Self-Help* that "there was nothing in the slightest degree new in this counsel, which was as old as the Proverbs of Solomon, and possibly quite as familiar."[51] Rather than merely fantasizing about returning to ancient practices of self-care, as Foucault does in his late lectures, self-help authors have long been repurposing the insights of the ancients for use by modern individuals.

The discipline lags behind self-help, too, in its ability to slough off an absence of empirical validation. A *New York Times* article on the rise of happiness courses marvels at how the students enrolled in the University of Pennsylvania's master's program in applied positive psychology "were a self-selected group, willing to pay almost $40,000 for a degree with no clear career track."[52] Despite self-help's bombastic rhetoric of outcomes and payoffs, as Steve Salerno writes, "in any meaningful sense, there is almost no evidence—at all—for the utility of self-help, either in theory or in practice," a genre of complaint with which humanities professors are well familiar.[53] According to psychology professor John C. Narcross, "more than 95 percent of self-help books and programs have never been subjected to scientific scrutiny."[54] As for those self-help precepts that have undergone scientific review, the results are indeterminate. For instance, according to a recent study by University of Waterloo researchers, positive affirmations can have a deleterious effect when uttered by those with low self-esteem (for those who are already confident, conversely, the positive statements seemed to work).[55] This is not to recommend hucksterism as a model for humanities recruitment but to point out that compelling arguments for a curriculum's life relevance can be as persuasive to prospective students as evidence of job placement or economic benefits.

The discipline of English's sublimation of use and self-cultivation is beginning to change, alongside a wholesale reappraisal of amateurism and professionally maligned reading practices being undertaken by current scholars.[56] To be sure, a skeptic could regard the newfound fashionableness among literary critics of those very reading practices Adler once advocated—for affect, use, therapy, presentism, and appreciation—in contradistinction to those of formalist or ideological criticism, as yet another facet of the incursion of corporatization into the university sphere. To detractors, the "postcritique" movement in literary studies might sound troublingly close to Carnegie's famous injunction: "never criticize."[57] A more sympathetic reading could counter that the discipline has been harmed by suppressing the therapeutic and utilitarian impulses that could serve as a bridge between academics and popular aspirants. In this view, the interest in utility is less a selling out than a new honesty regarding the long-sublimated motives of university research and pedagogy. Of course, even formalist and ideology criticism contain an implicit argument about how to live, a belief in the value of experiential exchange, a residual hope in the persistence of some measure of individual agency. From this perspective, the renewed disciplinary interest in the therapeutic is not a concession to the university's corporatization but an attempt to regain control over the discourse of advice.

Despite the incursion of self-help into so many corners of contemporary academic life, the antipathy between academic and self-help cultures persists. For example, on the summer stipend page of its website, the National Endowment for the Humanities includes the stipulation that such grants may not be used for "the writing of guide books, how-to books, and self-help books."[58] In reality, however, with the rise of academic trade books and crossover publishing, it is more difficult than ever to tell these genres apart.[59]

The line between scholarship and self-help is becoming blurred, not just because the university is increasingly seeking recourse to self-help's inspirational, colloquial, and practical rhetoric but also because of self-help's tendency to pilfer academic research and to imitate university practice. As Elaine Scarry has noted, "While universities (and above all the humanities) appear to be greatly undervalued in the public media, there are many signs that they are instead an object of emulation and aspiration. Many tech companies are organized as 'campuses.' The TED talks are modeled on (and often draw on) faculty lectures."[60]

There are many historical examples of self-help's emulative spirit vis-à-vis academe, from Emanuel Haldeman-Julius's Little Blue Books of the 1920s, dubbed "A University in Print," to contemporary self-help guru Tony Robbins, who titles his capstone retreat "Mastery University," to Malcolm Gladwell's contentious adaptations of scholarly work.[61] Even more than emulation, though, self-help's engagement with academe may be most accurately described as caricature, another genre that has been historically maligned by academe, as Charles Baudelaire complained in his 1857 essay on the topic. Indeed, the common critique of self-help polemicists is that they present a caricature of humanist practice, using academe as a scapegoat for their populist counter-message. Caricature, says Werner Hoffman in his study of the form, "binds itself to the model it is dethroning, and is sustained by the system it attacks."[62] Defending the import of caricature against the derision of the "pedantic corpses" of the French academy, Baudelaire applauds its ability to find the element of beauty in the spectacle of human moral and physical ugliness.[63] Applying this to the subject at hand, we could say that the distorted mirror of self-help amplifies not just the university's failings but also its strengths: the belief in mentorship, in pedagogic community, in trying to determine a curriculum for survival.

This discussion of caricature brings us back to the problem of the joke, which I first raised in my introduction, and which has haunted literary engagements with the self-help industry from the modernist satires of

Gustave Flaubert and Nathanael West to the more earnest engagements of Mohsin Hamid, Sheila Heti, and Eleanor Davis. The superiority theory of humor posits that laughter is an eruption of an unforeseen feeling of superiority over others or our younger selves.[64] In contrast, Baudelaire reminds us that *"the wise man never laughs but he trembles."*[65] The potential for humility and reversal was not lost on Carl Cederström and André Spicer, two academics who experimented with different self-help systems for a lark, only to confront the widespread desperation that these systems manifest. As Cederström recounts, "Before going to the retreat, I had thought of spiritual training as a middle-class indulgence. But now, after I saw the pain that these people were suffering and how desperate they were to get better, I could no longer stand on the side and laugh."[66] What such experiences bring into relief is not the pathos of popular strategies for life management but the failure of intellectual skepticism to account for the hopes and coping mechanisms necessary to endure everyday life.

"But is self-help good or bad?" This is the question I most frequently receive, and one that is impossible to answer when faced with the pluralism of the field and the multifaceted uses to which self-help is put. Wendy Simonds, the author of *Women and Self-Help Culture*, resisted similar queries. She describes the many interlocutors who would inquire, "Well, does reading help these women or not?" or "Is self-help reading a good thing or a bad thing?" She explains, "If I would say that these are not really the questions in which I was interested, people would be disappointed." And she adds, "But if I would say that I was interested in what self-help reading had to show about our culture . . . this would please people a little more."[67] To assign a final judgment on self-help would be to fall into the cultural studies (good) / ideology critique (bad) stalemate that Patricia Neville argues has stalled the scholarly investigation into how self-help is wielded and used.[68] In pursuit of this latter question, particularly as it pertains to literary history, at various points I have entertained both of these positions, ultimately finding that neither alone sufficiently accounts for the dynamic complexity of self-help's social and cultural consequence.

It is an axiom of disability studies that everyone should care about disability because the mere act of aging will eventually bestow even the most able-bodied individual with some degree of incapacity. Similarly, we are all potentially self-help readers in the making. This is partly because self-help is everywhere, as I've said, but also because there's just no way of knowing what life holds in store, or to what kind of measures this vale of tears—and joys—might, one day, compel us.

NOTES

INTRODUCTION

1. Paula Cocozza, *How to Be Human* (New York: Viking, 2017); Heather Havrilesky, *How to Be a Person in the World* (New York: Doubleday, 2016).
2. Sheila Heti, *How Should a Person Be?* [2010] (New York: Picador, 2012); Charles Yu, *How to Live Safely in a Science Fictional Universe* (New York: Vintage, 2010); Mohsin Hamid, *How to Get Filthy Rich in Rising Asia* (New York: Riverhead, 2013); Eleanor Davis, *How to Be Happy* (Seattle, Wash.: Fantagraphics, 2014); Terrance Hayes, *How to Be Drawn* (New York: Penguin, 2015); Jesse Ball, *How to Set a Fire and Why* (New York: Vintage, 2016); Ryan North, *How to Invent Everything: A Survival Guide for the Stranded Time Traveler* (New York: Riverhead, 2018).
3. *A New Commonplace Book, in Which the Plan Recommended and Practised by J. Locke Is Enlarged and Improved* (Cambridge, 1777), 1; see also contemporary self-help celebrity Ryan Holiday, "Why to Keep a Commonplace Journal" (blog), January 24, 2014, https://ryanholiday.net/how-and-why-to-keep-a-commonplace-book/.
4. Robert Darnton, "Extraordinary Commonplaces," *New York Review of Books* 47, no. 20 (2000): 82–87.
5. Michel Foucault, *Technologies of the Self* (Amherst: University of Massachusetts Press, 1988), 19.
6. Wendy Simonds, *Women and Self-Help Culture* (New Brunswick, N.J.: Rutgers University Press, 1992), 47.
7. Alex Williams, "The Gospel According to Pinterest," *New York Times*, October 3, 2012.
8. Simonds, *Women and Self-Help Culture*, 133.

9. Boris Kachka, "The Power of Positive Publishing: How Self-Help Publishing Ate America," *New York Magazine*, January 6, 2013, http://nymag.com/health /self-help/2013/self-help-book-publishing/.

10. Dale Carnegie, *How to Win Friends and Influence People* (New York: Simon & Schuster, 1936), 17.

11. Carnegie, *How to Win Friends*, 13.

12. Quoted in Steven Watts, *Self-Help Messiah: Dale Carnegie and Success in Modern America* (New York: Other Press, 2013), 131.

13. Gail Thain Parker, "How to Win Friends and Influence People: Dale Carnegie and the Problem of Sincerity," *American Quarterly* 29, no. 5 (1977): 506.

14. A. R. Craig, *Room at the Top* (Chicago: Sumner, 1883), 3.

15. Roland Barthes, *Image-Music-Text*, trans. Stephen Heath (New York: Hill and Wang, 1977), 142.

16. J. M. O'Neill, "The True Story of $10,000 Fears," *The Quarterly Journal of Speech Education* 5, no. 2 (1919): 121–37.

17. Quoted in Watts, *Self-Help Messiah*, 178.

18. Watts, 178.

19. See Watts, 180. *All That I Have* describes a love triangle between Jean Burns, a young woman desperate to escape the stifling confines of her hometown; Forrest Croy, a wealthy Missouri businessman who impregnates Jean right before he enlists in the U.S. Army, only to die before they can marry; and Reverend Wendell Phillips Curnutt, a charismatic preacher (and Carnegie alter ego) who altruistically convinces the pregnant Jean to become engaged to him after Croy's death, until, in an awkward twist, the falsely deceased Croy returns.

20. Quoted in Watts, 185.

21. Watts, 190.

22. "Créer un poncif, c'est le génie. Je dois créer un poncif" [To Create a Cliché, This Is Genius. I Must Create a Cliché], from Charles Baudelaire, "Fusées," in *Oeuvres Complètes* (Paris: Gallimard, 1965), 23.

23. Dorothy Carnegie, preface to the 1981 edition of *How to Win Friends and Influence People*, by Dale Carnegie (New York: Pocket, 1981), xi.

24. Lenny Bruce, *How to Talk Dirty and Influence People* (New York: Fireside, 1963); Toby Young, *How to Lose Friends and Alienate People* (Boston: Da Capo Press, 2002).

25. A. Victor Segno, *The Law of Mentalism* (Los Angeles: American Institute of Mentalism, 1902), 138–39.

26. Carnegie, *How to Win Friends*, 38, 37.

27. Bruce Robbins, *Upward Mobility and the Common Good: Toward a Literary History of the Welfare State* (Princeton, N.J.: Princeton University Press, 2007), xiv.

28. Sociologist Patricia Neville explains that the study of self-help has attracted scholars "from psychology to sociology to media studies, cultural studies and feminism." Notably absent from the list is the discipline of literary criticism. Patricia Neville, "Helping Self-Help Books: Working Towards a New Research Agenda," *Interactions Studies in Communications and Culture* 3, no. 3 (2012): 363.

29. See Neville, "Helping Self-Help Books," 361; John Crace, "Eyes Wide Open by Noreena Hertz—Digested Read," *The Guardian*, September 22, 2013, https://www.theguardian.com/books/2013/sep/23/eyes-wide-open-noreena-hertz-digested-read.

30. For a sampling of these approaches, see Micki McGee, *Self-Help, Inc.: Makeover Culture in American Life* (Oxford: Oxford University Press, 2005); Steven Starker, *Oracle at the Supermarket: The American Preoccupation with Self-Help Books* (New Brunswick, N.J.: Transaction, 1989); Eva Illouz, *Saving the Modern Soul: Therapy, Emotions, and the Culture of Self-Help* (Berkeley: University of California Press, 2008); Roy M. Anker, *Self-Help and Popular Religion in Modern American Culture: An Interpretive Guide* (Westport, Conn: Greenwood Press, 1999).

31. T. J. Jackson Lears, "From Salvation to Self-Realization: Advertising and the Therapeutic Roots of the Consumer Culture, 1880–1930," *Advertising and Society Review* 1, no. 1 (2000): 2.

32. Timothy Aubry, *Reading as Therapy: What Contemporary Fiction Does for Middle Class Americans* (Iowa City: University of Iowa Press, 2011), 16.

33. Leah Price, "Bibliotherapy and Its Others," in *Literature and Human Flourishing*, ed. James English and Heather Love (Oxford: Oxford University Press, forthcoming).

34. Boethius, *The Consolation of Philosophy*, trans. Richard Green (Indianapolis: Bobbs-Merril Educational, 1962); Ovid, *The Art of Love*, trans. James Michie (New York: Random House Modern Library, 2002); Epictetus, *The Encheiridion*, trans. W. A. Oldfather (Edinburgh: Loeb Classical Library, 1928).

35. Cicero, *De Officiis* [On Obligations], trans. P. G. Walsh (Oxford: Oxford University Press, 2000); Elizabeth Joceline, *The Mothers Legacie to Her Unborn Child* (London: John Haviland, 1622); Sir Walter Raleigh, *Instructions to His Sonne and to Posteritie* (London: Printed for Benjamin Fisher, dwelling in Aldersgate-street at the Talbot, 1632); Rudolphe M. Bell, *How to Do It: Guides to Good Living for Renaissance Italians* (Chicago: University of Chicago Press, 1999).

36. Cotton Mather, *Bonifacius: Essays to Do Good* [1710]. Facs. Reprod. With an Intr. By J. K. Piercy.

37. Joseph Alleine, *A Sure Guide to Heaven* (London: 1689); Belzebub, *A Sure Guide to Hell* (London: 1751).

38. For more on conduct books, see Arthur M. Schlesinger, *Learning How to Behave: A Historical Study of American Etiquette Books* (New York: Macmillan, 1946);

Nancy Armstrong and Leonard Tennenhouse, *The Ideology of Conduct: Essays in the History of Sexuality* (New York: Routledge, 1987). Complementary conduct literature for boys most famously took the form of Horatio Alger's enormously popular tales, which described the mix of luck and wit necessary to urban prosperity. Horatio Alger, *Ragged Dick* (New York: Signet, 2014).

39. Benjamin Franklin, *The Autobiography of Benjamin Franklin* [1791]. Penn reading project ed. (Philadelphia: University of Pennsylvania Press, 2005), 72–73.

40. Carnegie, *How to Win Friends*, 38.

41. Benjamin Franklin, "From the Morals of Confucius," *Pennsylvania Gazette*, February 28–May 7, 1738, 2.

42. Quoted in Alfred Owen Aldridge, *The Dragon and the Eagle: The Presence of China in the American Enlightenment* (Detroit: Wayne State Press, 1993), 27–28.

43. David Weir, *American Orient: Imagining the East from the Colonial Era Through the Twentieth Century* (Amherst: University of Massachusetts Press, 2011), 20.

44. Starker, *Oracle at the Supermarket*, 170; Irvin Wyllie, *The Self-Made Man in America* (New Brunswick, N.J.: Rutgers University Press, 1954), xi. I do not mean to single out these texts alone; this conception is characteristic of the overwhelming majority of self-help research that has been undertaken, chiefly by scholars in American studies.

45. Eric C. Hendriks, "China's Self-Help Industry: American(ized) Life Advice in China," in *Handbook of Cultural and Creative Industries in China*, ed. Michael Keane (Cheltenham: Edward Elgar, 2016), 313.

46. Earl H. Kinmonth, "Nakamura Keiu and Samuel Smiles: A Victorian Confucian and a Confusion Victorian," *The American Historical Review* 85, no. 3 (June 1980): 535.

47. Samuel Smiles, *Self-Help: With Illustrations of Character, Conduct, and Perseverance* (New York: Harper & Brothers, 1859), 25.

48. See Jonathan Rose, *The Intellectual Life of the British Working Classes* (New Haven, Conn.: Yale University Press, 2001), 68.

49. Thomas Carlyle, *Sartor Resartus: The Life and Opinions of Herr Teufelsdröckh* (London: Chapman & Hall, 1831), 70; Ralph Waldo Emerson, "Self-Reliance," 1841; Smiles, *Self-Help*.

50. Smiles, *Self-Help*, 25.

51. J. F. C. Harrison, *Learning and Living 1790–1960: A Study in the History of the English Adult Education Movement* (Abingdon, Oxon: Routledge, 1961), 55.

52. Smiles, *Self-Help*, 366.

53. William Robinson, *Self-Education, or The Value of Mental Culture* (London: Hamilton, 1845), 92–98.

54. George Cary Eggleston, preface to *How to Make a Living: Suggestions Upon the Art of Making, Saving, and Using Money* (New York: Putnam, 1874).

55. Gertrude Stein, *How to Write* (Paris: Plain Edition, 1931); Ezra Pound, *ABC of Reading* (New York: New Directions, 1934); Virginia Woolf, "How Should One Read a Book [1925] in *The Second Common Reader*, ed. Andrew McNeillie (San Diego: Harvest, 1986), 258–70, at 258.

56. Sandra Dolby, for instance, in an interesting book, describes "the self-help book as a historical phenomenon emerging out of the 1960s and 1970s and continuing in full force into the new millennium." Sandra Dolby, *Self-Help Books: Why Americans Keep Reading Them* (Champaign: University of Illinois Press, 2005), 11.

57. Mercè Mur Effing, "US Self-Help literature and the Call of the East" (PhD dissertation, Departament de Filologia Anglesa i Germanística de la Universitat Autònoma de Barcelona, 2011), 51.

58. Horace Fletcher, *Menticulture* (Chicago: McClurg, 1895), 42.

59. Ignas K. Skrupskelis and Elizabeth M. Berkeley, eds., *William and Henry James: Selected Letters* (Charlottesville: University of Virginia Press, 1997), 517.

60. Joan Shelley Rubin, *The Making of Middlebrow Culture* (Chapel Hill, N.C.: University of North Carolina Press, 1992), 6–10.

61. Émile Coué, *Self-Mastery Through Conscious Autosuggestion*, trans. Archibald Stark Van Orden (New York: Malkan, 1922), 8. Despite his influence on the movement, Coué distinguished himself from New Thought practitioners.

62. *The Saturday Review*, quoted in Dean Rapp, "'Better and Better'—Couéism as a Psychological Craze of the Twenties in England," *Studies in Popular Culture* 10, no. 2 (1987): 24.

63. Sigmund Freud, *A General Introduction to Psychoanalysis* (New York: Horace Liveright, 1920), 374.

64. See discussion of this in Eva Illouz, *Saving the Modern Soul: Therapy, Emotions, and the Culture of Self-Help* (Berkeley: University of California Press, 2008), 153.

65. Maury Klein, *Rainbow's End: The Crash of 1929* (Oxford: Oxford University Press, 2001), 125.

66. E. J. Hardy, *How to Be Happy Though Married: Being a Handbook to Marriage*, 7th ed. (London: T. F. Unwin, 1887); Spencer Wallis, *The Scientific Elimination of Failure* (1912); Vance Thomson, *Eat and Grow Thin* (New York: Dutton, 1914); C. Franklin Leavitt, *Are You You?* (Chicago: Advanced Thought, 1921); Elsie Lincoln Benedict, *How to Analyze People on Sight: The Five Human Types* (East Aurora, N.Y.: Roycrofters, 1921); Genevieve Behrend, "How to Live Life and Love It," in *The Writings of Genevieve Behrend: Your Invisible Power; Attaining Your Desires; How to Live Life and Love It* [1929] (New York: Start Publishing, 2013); Orisen Swett Marden, *The Conquest of Worry* (London: Rider, 1924); R. H. Jarrett, *It Works* [1926] (Camarillo, Calif.: DeVorss, 2000); Joseph L. Greenbaum, *What the Hell Are You*

Living For? (New York: Mass, 1927); Ernest Dimnet, *The Art of Thinking* (New York: Simon & Schuster, 1928); Walter B. Pitkin, *Life Begins at Forty: How to Make Sure You Enjoy Middle Age* (New York: Whittlesey House, McGraw-Hill, 1932).

67. They also developed as offshoots of niche spiritual/occultist periodicals such *Self-Culture Magazine* (Chicago: Werner, 1895–1900); *New Thought: An Organ of Optimism* (Chicago and New York: Psychic Research Company; New Thought, 1901–1910); *Mental Science Magazine and Mind Cure Journal* (Chicago: Mental Science University, 1886–1889); *The New Age*, ed. A. R. Orage (London: New Age Press, 1907–1922); *The Problem of Life*, ed. W. J. Colville (San Francisco: Unity, 1890–1894); *Success Magazine*, ed. Orison Swett Marden (New York: Lowry-Marden, 1897–1912).

68. Charles Baudelaire, "Let Us Flay the Poor" [Assomons les Pauvres!], in *Baudelaire: His Prose and Poetry*, ed. T. R. Smith (New York: Boni and Liveright, 1919), 102–104.

69. Pierre Bourdieu, *Distinction* (New York: Routledge, 1984), 24.

70. Lauren Berlant, *Cruel Optimism* (Durham, N.C.: Duke University Press, 2011).

71. Marjorie Garber, *The Use and Abuse of Literature* (New York: Pantheon, 2011), 7.

72. Alain de Botton, *How Proust Can Change Your Life* (London: Picador, 1998); Ilana Simons, *A Guide to Better Living Through the Work and Wisdom of Virginia Woolf* (New York: Penguin, 2007); James Hawes, *Why You Should Read Kafka Before You Waste Your Life* (New York: St. Martin's Press, 2008); Declan Kiberd, *Ulysses and Us: The Art of Everyday Life in Joyce's Masterpiece* (New York: Norton, 2009); Marty Beckerman, *The Heming Way: How to Unleash the Booze-Inhaling, Animal Slaughtering, War-Glorifying, Hairy Chested Retro Sexual Lesson Within* (New York: St. Martin's Griffin, 2011); Alexander McCall Smith, *What W. H. Auden Can Do for You* (Princeton, N.J.: Princeton University Press, 2013); Nina Lorez Collins, *What Would Virginia Woolf Do?* (New York: Grand Central Life & Style, 2018).

73. Timothy Ferriss, *The 4-Hour Workweek* (New York: Crown, 2009), 54.

74. Paul Pearsall, *The Last Self-Book You'll Ever Need* (New York: Basic Books, 2007), 19.

75. Svend Brinkmann, *Stand Firm: Resisting the Self-Improvement Craze* (Cambridge: Polity Press, 2017), 97, 88.

76. Jennifer Fleissner, *Women, Compulsion, Modernity: The Moment of American Naturalism* (Chicago: Chicago University Press, 2004), 42.

77. See, for instance, Laurie Maguire, *Where There's a Will There's a Way, or All I Really Need to Know I Learned from Shakespeare* (New York: Penguin, 2006); Sarah Bakewell, *How to Live: Or a Life of Montaigne in One Question and Twenty Attempts at an Answer* (London: Chatto & Windus, 2010); Lori Smith, *The Jane Austen Guide to Life: Thoughtful Lessons for the Modern Woman* (Guilford, Conn.: Pequot Press, 2012).

78. Raymond Williams, "When Was Modernism?", in *The Politics of Modernism* (London: Verso, 1989), 35.

79. See Helen Booth, "How Self-Help Is Getting a Millennial Makeover," *Stylist*, May 2017, https://www.stylist.co.uk/books/best-self-help-books-anxiety-wellness-depression /130168.

80. Dwight Macdonald, "Masscult and Midcult," in *Masscult and Midcult: Essays Against the American Grain* (New York: New York Review of Books, 2011), 50.

81. Rubin, *The Making of Middlebrow Culture*, 1–33.

82. Virginia Woolf, "Middlebrow," [October 1932, unsent] in "To The Editor of the New Statesman" published in *The Death of the Moth and Other Essays* (New York: Harcourt Brace, 1942), 183.

83. Dwight Macdonald, "The Book-of-the-Millennium Club," *The New Yorker*, November 29, 1952; "Howtoism" *The New Yorker*, May 22, 1954; "Masscult and Midcult: I," *Partisan Review* 27, no. 4 (Fall 1960): 203–33; and "Masscult and Midcult: II," *Partisan Review* 27, no. 4 (Fall 1960): 589–631, at 609.

84. Starker, *Oracle at the Supermarket*, 64, 93.

85. David Riesman, *The Lonely Crowd* (New Haven, Conn.: Yale University Press, 1950).

86. Macdonald, "Howtoism," 91, 85.

87. Aubry, *Reading as Therapy*.

88. Elizabeth Gilbert, *Eat Pray Love* (New York: Viking, 2006).

89. For a useful account of the therapeutic in contemporary culture and intellectual history, see Timothy Aubry and Trish Travis, *Rethinking Therapeutic Culture* (Chicago: University of Chicago Press, 2015), at 3, 8.

89. For helpful discussions of this, see Sarah Brouillette, *Literature and the Creative Economy* (Stanford, Calif.: Stanford University Press, 2014); and John Patrick Leary, *Keywords: The New Language of Capitalism* (Chicago: Haymarket Books, 2019).

90. Alexander Linklater, "Philosophy for Life and Other Dangerous Situations by Jules Evans—Review," *The Guardian*, June 16, 2012.

91. See *New York Times* blurb on back cover of Eva Hoffman, *How to Be Bored* (London: Macmillan, 2016).

92. Mark Manson, personal website, https://markmanson.net.

93. Promotional endpapers for A. Craig, *Room at the Top, Or How to Reach Success, Happiness, Fame and Fortune* (Chicago: Henry A. Sumner, 1883).

94. Peter Kyne, *The Go-Getter: A Story That Tells You How to Be One* (New York: Rinehart, 1921).

95. See "Ulysses Lands," *Time*, January 29, 1934; see also Simonds, *Women and Self-Help Culture*, 138–39.

96. William Shinker quoted in Viv Groskop, " 'Shelf-Help' Books Set to Fill Publishers' Coffers in 2014," *The Guardian*, December 28, 2013, https://www.theguardian.com /books/2013/dec/28/self-help-books-literature-publishers-growth.

97. Jim Collins, *Bring on the Books for Everybody: How Literary Culture Became Popular Culture* (Durham, N.C.: Duke University Press, 2010), 76–77.

98. Hamid, *How to Get Filthy Rich in Rising Asia*, 20.

99. Hoffman, *How to Be Bored*; Ella Berthoud and Susan Elderkin, *The Novel Cure: From Abandonment to Zestlessness, 751 Books to Cure What Ails You* (New York: Penguin, 2014), promotional materials.

100. Seneca, *How to Keep Your Cool: An Ancient Guide to Anger Management*, trans. James Romm (Princeton, N.J.: Princeton University Press, 2019).

101. Leah Price, *What We Talk About When We Talk About Books* (New York: Basic Books, 2019), 138.

102. Brinkmann, *Stand Firm*, 13, 88.

103. Eleanor Davis, *How to be Happy*, 139.

104. Front pages for *How to Be Happy*, by Davis.

105. Eleanor Davis interview with Tim O'Shea, "Talking Comics with Tim: Eleanor Davis on How to Be Happy," *CBR.com*, June 30, 2014, https://www.cbr.com /talking-comics-with-tim-eleanor-davis-on-how-to-be-happy/.

106. Eleanor Davis interview with James Cartwright, "Eleanor Davis on the Motivations Behind Her Stunning Upcoming Book," *It's Nice That*, June 19, 2014, https://www .itsnicethat.com/articles/eleanor-davis-1.

107. Mohsin Hamid interview with Alison Cuddy, Chicago Humanities Festival, March 11, 2014, https://www.youtube.com/watch?v=0EaIkSNAsWU.

108. Nathanael West, *Miss Lonelyhearts*, in *Nathanael West: Novels and Other Writings* (New York: Library of America, 1997), 94.

109. Flaubert, *Oeuvres Complètes de Gustave Flaubert*, Vol. 10, *Correspondence II (1850– 1859)* (Paris: Club de l'honnête homme, 1974–1976), 99.

110. Jenny Offill, *Dept. of Speculation* (New York: Knopf, 2014), 114.

111. Sianne Ngai, "Theory of the Gimmick," *Critical Inquiry* 38, no. 2 (Winter 2017): 473.

112. Rita Felski, *The Uses of Literature* (Malden, Mass.: Blackwell, 2008), 8.

113. Ole Jacob Madsen, *Optimizing the Self: Social Representations of Self-help* (London: Routledge, 2015), 3.

114. McGee, *Self-Help, Inc.*, 138.

115. Theodor Adorno, "Free Time," in *The Culture Industry: Selected Essays on Mass Culture* (London: Routledge, 1991); Foucault, *Technologies of the Self*; Michel Foucault interview by Hubert L. Dreyfus and Paul Rabinow, "How We Behave: Sex, Food, and Other Ethical Matters," *Vanity Fair* 46, no. 9 (1983).

116. See Neville, "Helping Self-Help Books," for an excellent elucidation of this impasse.

117. Jackson Lears, "From Salvation to Self-Realization"; Christopher Lasch, *The Culture of Narcissism: American Life in an Age of Diminishing Expectations* (New York: Norton, 1979); Berlant, *Cruel Optimism*.

118. Janice A. Radway, *Reading the Romance: Women, Patriarchy, and Popular Literature* (Chapel Hill: University of North Carolina Press, 1984). However, as Neville notes, there is division on the subject even within feminist criticism. See Neville, "Helping Self-Help Books," 365.

119. Arlie Russell Hochschild, *The Managed Heart: Commercialization of Human Feeling* (Berkeley: University of California Press, 1983), 193; McGee, *Self-Help, Inc.*, 24.

120. Verta Taylor, *Rock-a-By Baby: Feminism, Self-Help, and Postpartum Depression* (New York: Routledge, 1996), 23.

121. Audre Lorde, *Burst of Light: Essays by Audre Lorde* (Ithaca, N.Y.: Firebrand, 1988), 131.

122. Henry A. Giroux, "From 'Manchild' to 'Baby Boy': Race and the Politics of Self-Help," *JAC* 22, no. 3 (Summer 2002): 529, 530; see also Paul Gilroy, " 'We Got to Get Over Before We Go Under': Fragments for a History of Black Vernacular Neoliberalism," *New Formations* 80–81 (Winter 2013): 23–38.

123. Gayle McKeen, "Whose Rights? Whose Responsibility? Self-Help in African American Thought," *Polity* 34, no. 3 (Summer 2002): 414, 412.

124. McKeen, "Whose Rights?", 409.

125. W. E. B. Du Bois, *Africa, Its Geography, People and Products* (Girard, Kans.: Haldeman-Julius, 1930); W. E. B. Du Bois, *Africa—Its Place in Modern History* (Girard, Kans.: Haldeman-Julius, 1930); see also Eric Schocket, "Proletarian Paperbacks: The Little Blue Books and Working-Class Culture," *College Literature* 29, no. 4 (Fall 2002): 74.

126. Richard Wright, "Self-Help in Negro Education" (Philadelphia: Committee of Twelve for the Advancement of the Interests of the Colored Race, 1909); and Richard Wright, "Psychiatry Comes to Harlem," *Free World* (September 1946): 351, where he references the "fanatic forms of violent self-help (crime)" to which Harlem youth seek recourse.

127. Chris Abani, *GraceLand* (New York: Farrar, Straus, and Giroux, 2004).

128. Todd Tiede, *Self-Help Nation: The Long Overdue, Entirely Justified, Delightfully Hostile Guide to the Snake Oil Peddlers Who Are Sapping Our Nation's Soul* (New York: Atlantic Monthly Press, 2001); Wendy Kaminer, *I'm Dysfunctional You're Dysfunctional: The Recovery Movement and Other Self-Help Fashions* (Boston: Addison-Wesley, 1992); Barbara Ehrenreich, *Bright-Sided: How Positive Thinking Ruined America* (New York: Metropolitan Books, 2009); Steve Salerno, *SHAM: The Self-Help and Actualization Movement* (New York: Crown, 2005).

129. McGee, *Self-Help, Inc.*, 16.

130. Chris Roycroft-Davis, "Did This Positive Thinker's Self-Help Book Make Donald Trump President?" *Sunday Express*, November 16, 2016, http://www.express.co.uk /life-style/life/733097/Donald-Trump-election-winning-confidence-self-help -book.

131. Richard Butler, *U Nu of Burma* (Stanford, Calif.: Stanford University Press, 1963), 31; Hammad Shahidian, "Contesting Discourses of Sexuality in Post-Revolutionary Iran," in *Deconstructing Sexuality in the Middle East*, ed. Pinar İlkkaracan (Farnham: Ashgate, 2008), 101–38, at 102.

132. Jeff Guinn, *Manson: The Life and Times of Charles Manson* (New York: Simon & Schuster, 2013), 59–62.

133. See the representation of self-help in Zadie Smith, *NW: A Novel* (New York: Penguin 2012); and Hamid, *How to Get Filthy Rich in Rising Asia*.

134. William Shinker quoted in Kachka, "The Power of Positive Publishing."

135. John T. Fenner and Audrey Fenner, "Retrospective Collection Development: Selecting a Core for Research in 'New Thought,'" in *Selecting Materials for Library Collections*, ed. Linda S. Katz (New York: Routledge, 2012), 194.

136. Amy Blair, *Reading Up: Middle Class Readers and the Culture of Success in the Twentieth Century United States* (Philadelphia: Temple University Press, 2012), 8.

137. Joan Shelley Rubin, "Making Meaning: Analysis and Affect in the Study and Practice of Reading," in *A History of the Book in America*, vol. 5 (Chapel Hill: University of North Carolina Press, 2009), 511.

138. Huang Xiaocao, "Souring Taste of Chicken Soup," *China Daily Europe*, May 15, 2015, http://www.chinadaily.com.cn/beijing/2015-05/15/content_20728010.htm.

139. Carl F. Kaestle and Janice Radway, *A History of the Book in America: Vol. 4, Print in Motion, The Expansion of Publishing and Reading in the United States 1880–1940* (Chapel Hill: University of North Carolina Press, 2009), 666, 4.

140. Darnton, "Extraordinary Commonplaces"; Mortimer Adler, *How to Read a Book: The Classic Guide to Intelligent Reading* (New York: Simon & Shuster, 1940); Michel de Certeau, "Reading as Poaching," in *The Practice of Everyday Life* (Berkeley: University of California Press, 1988); Louise Rosenblatt, *The Reader, the Text, the Poem: A Transactional Theory of the Literary Work* (Carbondale: Southern Illinois University Press, 1978); Blair, *Reading Up*.

141. Jeffrey T. Kenney, "Selling Success, Nurturing the Self," *International Journal of Middle East Studies* 47 (2005): 671.

142. Jennifer Fleissner, "Historicism Blues," *American Literary History* 25, no. 4 (Winter 2013): 699–713; V21 Collective, "Manifesto of the V21 Collective," *V21: Victorian Studies for the 21st Century*, http://v21collective.org/manifesto-of-the-v21-collective

-ten-theses; Eric Hayot, "Against Periodization, or On Institutional Time," *New Literary History* 42, no. 4 (Autumn 2011): 739–56; Joseph North, *Literary Criticism: A Concise Political History* (Cambridge, Mass.: Harvard University Press, 2017).

143. Laurence M. Porter, ed., *A Gustave Flaubert Encyclopedia* (Westport, Conn.: Greenwood Press, 2001), 73.

144. Simonds, *Women and Self-Help Culture*, 47.

1. SELF-HELP'S PORTABLE WISDOM

1. Michel Foucault, *Technologies of the Self* (Amherst: University of Massachusetts Press, 1988); Heidi Marie Rimke, "Governing Citizens Through Self-Help Literature," *Cultural Studies* 14, no. 1 (2000): 61–78.

2. Roland Barthes, "The Death of the Author," in *The Book History Reader*, ed. David Finkelstein (New York: Routledge, 2002), 277–280, at 279.

3. Samuel Smiles, *Self-Help: With Illustrations of Character, Conduct, and Perseverance* [1859] (New York: Harper & Brothers, 1877); Keiko Kockum, *Ito Sei: Self-Analysis and the Modern Japanese Novel* (Stockholm: Stockholm University, 1994), 102–3.

4. Patricia Neville, "Helping Self-Help Books: Working Towards a New Research Agenda," *Interactions Studies in Communications and Culture* 3, no. 3 (2012): 372.

5. Azadeh Moaveni, "Seeking Signs of Literary Life in Iran," *New York Times*, May 27, 2007, https://www.nytimes.com/2007/05/27/books/review/Moaveni-t.html.

6. Jeffrey T. Kenney, "Selling Success, Nurturing the Self," *International Journal of Middle East Studies*, no. 47 (2005): 665.

7. Sarah Knudson, "Crash Courses and Life Long Journeys: Modes of Reading Non-fiction Advice in a North American Audience," *Poetics* 41, no. 3 (2013): 213.

8. Paul Lichterman, "Self-Help Reading as a Thin Culture," *Media, Culture & Society* 14, no. 3 (1992): 426.

9. Lichterman, 423.

10. In transactional theory, Louise Rosenblatt employs the term *efferent reading* describes how "the reader's attention is primarily focused on what will remain as a residue *after* the reading—the information to be acquired, the logical solution to a problem, the actions to be carried out." Louise Rosenblatt, "Efferent and Aesthetic Reading," in *The Reader, the Text, the Poem: A Transactional Theory of the Literary Work* (Carbondale: Southern Illinois University Press, 1978), 23.

11. See a fascinating discussion of the rise of African do-it-yourself literacy in Karin Barber, *Africa's Hidden Histories: Everyday Literacy and Making the Self* (Bloomington: Indiana University Press, 2006); for a discussion on the effect of the Islamic revolution on the demand for self-help, see Moaveni, "Seeking Signs

of Literary Life in Iran"; to explore the complex status of Western self-help in post-Soviet Russia, see Suvi Salmenniemi and Mariya Vorona, "Reading Self-Help Literature in Russia: Governmentality, Psychology, Subjectivity," *The British Journal of Sociology* 65, no. 1 (January 2014): 44, https://doi.org/10.1111/1468-4446.12039; for more on how the work of translating important Western texts into Japanese was given urgency by Japan's 1858 signing of treaties with the United States, Holland, and other Western powers, see Douglas Howland, *Translating the West: Language and Political Reason in Nineteenth-Century Japan* (Honolulu: University of Hawai'i Press, 2002), 62; for an explanation of the economic upheavals leading to the self-help boom in China, see Daniel Nehring, Emmanuel Alvarado, Eric C. Hendriks, and Dylan Kerrigan, *Transnational Popular Psychology and the Global Self-Help Industry* (London: Palgrave Macmillan, 2016), 55.

12. I use this term in the sense employed by Bhabha when he describes Bibles as "objets trouvés of the colonial discourse." Homi Bhabha, *The Location of Culture* (New York: Routledge, 1994), 131.

13. Smiles, *Self-Help*, xi.

14. Benjamin C. Duke, *The History of Modern Japanese Education: Constructing the National School System* (New Brunswick, N.J.: Rutgers University Press, 2009), 141.

15. Samuel Smiles and Thomas Mackay. *The Autobiography of Samuel Smiles* [1905] (Cambridge: Cambridge University Press, 2013), 229.

16. Smiles, *Self-Help*, 28.

17. R. H. Jarrett, *It Works* [1926] (Camarillo, Calif.: DeVorss, 2000).

18. Jonathan Rose, *The Intellectual Life of the British Working Classes* (New Haven, Conn.: Yale University Press, 2001), 68.

19. Vladimir Trendafilov, "The Origins of Self-Help: Samuel Smiles and the Formative Influences on an Ex-Seminal Work," *The Victorian* 3, no. 1 (2015): 4.

20. John Hunter, *The Spirit of Self-Help: A Life of Samuel Smiles* (London: Shepheard-Walwyn, 2017), 37.

21. Trendafilov, "The Origins of Self-Help," 11.

22. See Jerome Meckier, "'*Great Expectations*' and '*Self-Help*': Dickens Frowns on Smiles," *The Journal of English and Germanic Philology*, vol. 100, no.4 (October 2001): 537.

23. Smiles, *Self-Help*, vi, vii.

24. Meckier, "'*Great Expectations*'" and '*Self-Help*'. 538, 541.

25. Asa Briggs, *Victorian People: A Reassessment of Persons and Themes, 1851–67* (Chicago: The University of Chicago Press, 1955), 118.

26. H. G. Wells, "The Jilting of Jane," *Pall Mall Budge*, July 12, 1894.

27. Hunter, *The Spirit of Self-Help*, 3–4.

28. Smiles, quoted in Hunter, 38.

29. David Brooks, *The Road to Character* (New York: Random House, 2015); Daniel Pink, *Drive: The Surprising Truth About What Motivates Us* (New York: Riverhead Books, 2009); Malcolm Gladwell, *Outliers: The Story of Success* (New York: Little, Brown, 2008).

30. Warren Susman, *Culture as History: the Transformation of American Society in the Twentieth Century* (New York: Pantheon, 1973), 273–74.

31. Alison Booth, "Neo-Victorian Self-Help, or Cider House Rules," *American Literary History* 14, no. 2 (Summer 2002): 284–285.

32. Lauren M. E. Goodlad, *Victorian Literature and the Victorian State: Character and Governance in a Liberal Society* (Baltimore, Md.: Johns Hopkins University Press, 2003), 123.

33. Samuel Smiles, *The Autobiography of Samuel Smiles* (New York: Dutton, 1905), 29.

34. Hunter, *The Spirit of Self-Help*, 38–40, 176.

35. Smiles, *Self-Help*, 121–22.

36. *Critical Writings of Ford Madox Ford*, ed. Frank MacShane, (Lincoln: University of Nebraska Press, 1964), 23.

37. Smiles, *Self-Help*, 40.

38. Keith Joseph, introduction to *Self-Help*, by Samuel Smiles, rev. ed. (London: Sidgwick & Jackson, 1986).

39. Rose, *The Intellectual Life of the British Working Classes*, 69.

40. Rose, 70.

41. Quoted in John Dunn, "Nnamdi Azikiwe's *My Odyssey: An Autobiography*" (review), *The Spectator* 226 (May 8, 1971): 634.

42. Quoted in Cyrus Schayegh, *Who Is Knowledgeable, Is Strong: Science, Class, and the Formation of Modern Iranian Society, 1900–1950* (Berkeley: University of California Press, 2009), 186.

43. Sukehiro Hirakawa, *Japan's Love-Hate Relation with the West* (Leiden, NL: Global Oriental, Brill, 2004), 43.

44. Jirjī Zaydān and Thomas Philipp, *The Autobiography of Jurji Zaidan: Including Four Letters to His Son* (Washington, D.C.: Three Continents Press, 1990), 45.

45. Matti Mooosa, *The Origins of Modern Arabic Fiction* (Boulder, Colo.: Lynne Rienner, 1997), 198.

46. Marwa Elshakry, *Reading Darwin in Arabic, 1860–1950* (Chicago: University of Chicago Press, 2013), 338.

47. Zaydān and Philipp, *The Autobiography of Jurji Zaidan*, 45.

48. Donald M. Reid, "Syrian Christians, the Rags-to-Riches Story, and Free Enterprise," *International Journal of Middle East Studies* 1, no. 4 (October 1970): 358–67, at 359, 363.

49. Zaydān and Philipp, *The Autobiography of Jurji Zaidan*, 12.

50. Stephanie Newell, *Literary Culture in Colonial Ghana: "How to Play the Game of Life"* (Manchester: Manchester University Press, 2002), 90–91, 43.

51. Smiles, *Self-Help*, 366.

52. Newell, *Literary Culture in Colonial Ghana*, 90.

53. Leah Price, "When Doctors Prescribe Books to Heal the Mind," *Boston Globe*, December 22, 2013.

54. V. S. Naipaul, *A House for Mr Biswas*, 3rd ed. (London: A. Deutsch, 1984), 153, 71.

55. Landeg White, *V. S. Naipaul: A Critical Introduction* (London: Macmillan, 1975), 30.

56. Nehring, Alvarado, Hendriks, and Kerrigan, *Transnational Popular Psychology*, 143.

57. Newell, *Literary Culture in Colonial Ghana*, 90.

58. Earl H. Kinmonth, "Nakamura Keiu and Samuel Smiles: A Victorian Confucian and a Confusion Victorian," *The American Historical Review* 85, no. 3 (June 1980): 554; Houra Yavari, "The Persian Novel," *Iran Chamber Society*, 2002, http://www.iranchamber.com/literature/articles/persian_novel.php.

59. Orison Swett Marden, *Pushing to the Front or Success Under Difficulties* (New York: The Success Company, 1911); Orison Swett Marden, *The Conquest of Worry* (New York: Crowell, 1924).

60. Jeffrey Gitomar, "Orison Swett Marden an Original Thinker," *Success*, July 7, 2001, https://www.success.com/article/orison-swett-marden-an-original-thinker.

61. Steven Watts, *Self-Help Messiah: Dale Carnegie and Success in Modern America* (New York: Other Press, 2013), 131, 142.

62. Dwight Macdonald, "Howtoism," *The New Yorker*, May 22, 1954, 85.

63. Nehring Alvarado, Hendriks, and Kerrigan, *Transnational Popular Psychology*, 5.

64. Chinua Achebe, "The Novelist as Teacher," *Hopes and Impediments: Selected Essays, 1965–1987* (London: Heinemann, 1988), 69.

65. Stephanie Newell, ed., introduction to *Readings in African Popular Fiction* (Bloomington: Indiana University Press, 2002), 2.

66. Chinua Achebe, "The Novelist as Teacher," 73.

67. Ngũgĩ wa Thiong'o, *In the House of the Interpreter: A Memoir* (New York: Pantheon, 2012), 171.

68. Jed Esty, "The Colonial Bildungsroman: The Story of an African Farm and the Ghost of Goethe," *Victorian Studies* 49, no. 3 (Spring 2007): 407–30; Tsitsi Jaji, "Cassava Westerns: Theorizing the Pleasures of Playing the Outlaw in Africa," *The Western in the Global South*, ed. MaryEllen Higgins, Rita Keresztesi, and Dayna Oscherwitz (New York: Routledge, 2015), 24–41.

69. Dipesh Chakrabarty, foreword to *The Ambiguous Allure of the West: The Colonial in Thailand*, ed. Rachel V. Harrison and Peter A. Jackson (Ithaca, N.Y.: Cornell University Press, 2010), xv.

70. Barber, *Africa's Hidden Histories*, 7, 5.

71. Homi Bhabha, *The Location of Culture* (New York: Routledge, 1994); Helen Tiffin, "Post-Colonial Literatures and Counter-Discourse," *Kunapipi* 9, no. 3 (1987): 17–34.

72. Chinua Achebe, *Conversations with Chinua Achebe*, ed. Bernth Lindfors (Jackson: University Press of Mississippi, 1997), 85.

73. The term *brochure masterpiece* is from a description of the pamphlets in Ryszard Kapuscinsk, *The Shadow in the Sun*, trans. Klara Gloweczewska (Toronto, Canada: Vintage Canada, 2002), 300.

74. Ulli Beier, quoted in Kurtz Thometz, introduction to *Life Turns Man Up and Down: Highlife, Useful Advice, and Mad English* (New York: Pantheon, 2001), xix.

75. Sunday Okenwa Olisah, "No Condition Is Permanent by the Master of Life." (Fegge-Onitsha: Njoku & Sone, Umeh Brothers Press, 1964) in *Life Turns Man Up and Down: Highlife, Useful Advice, and Mad English*, ed. Kurtz Thomez (New York: Pantheon, 2001), 81, 100.

76. Frank E. Odili, "What Is Life?" (Onitsha: N. Njoku & Sons, 1961) in *Life Turns Man Up and Down: High Life, Useful Advice, and Mad English: African Market Literature*, ed. Kurt Thometz (New York: Pantheon, 2001), 321.

77. Wole Soyinka, *Art, Dialogue and Outrage: Essays on Literature and Culture*, rev. ed. (London: Methuen, 1993), 267.

78. Emmanuel N. Obiechina, *An African Popular Literature: A Study of Onitsha Market Pamphlets* (Cambridge: Cambridge University Press, 1973), 21–22.

79. Sunday Okenwa Olisah, "Money Hard to Get but Easy to Spend," (Onitsha, Nigeria: J.O. Nnadozie, New Era Press, 1965), in *Life Turns Man Up and Down: High Life, Useful Advice, and Mad English: African Market Literature*, ed. Kurt Thometz (New York: Pantheon, 2001), 107–130, at 110; Olisah, "No Condition is Permanent," 77–103, at 92.

80. Donatus Nwoga, "Onitsha Market Literature," in *Readings in African Popular Fiction*, ed. Stephanie Newell (Bloomington: Indiana University Press, 2002), 42.

81. Chris Abani, *GraceLand* (New York: Farrar, Straus, and Giroux, 2004), 112.

82. Abani, *GraceLand*, 112.

83. Abani, acknowledgments in *GraceLand*, endpapers.

84. For an example of this Joycean flair, Strausbaugh cites the opening of the pulp romance *Rosemary and the Taxi Driver*: "The sun flickered over her canonball head, with the hairs on her forehead, heightened like onboard type of shaving. She resoluted to follow the train at the earliest declining hour of the day." John

Strausbaugh, "High Life and Mad English" (review), *New Yorker Press*, November 24–December 4, 2001, 14, 48.

85. As Thometz suggestively notes, it is particularly remarkable that both pieces were produced in the same year, 1962. Kurt Thometz, ed., introduction to *Life Turns Man Up and Down*, xxxv.

86. Édouard Glissant, *L'Imaginaire des Langues: Entretiens avec Lise Gauvin* (Paris: Gallimard, 2010), 16.

87. Michel de Certeau, "Reading as Poaching," in *The Practice of Everyday Life* (Berkeley: University of California Press, 1988); Wendy Simonds, *Women and Self-Help Culture* (New Brunswick, N.J.: Rutgers, 1992), 47.

88. Suvi Salmenniemi and Mariya Vorona, "Reading Self-Help Literature in Russia: Governmentality, Psychology and Subjectivity," *The British Journal of Sociology* 65, no. 1 (2014): 46, 53.

89. Fariba Adelkhah, *Being Modern in Iran* (New York: Columbia University Press, 2000), 155.

90. Laura Miller, "There's More Than *Manga*: Popular Nonfiction Books and Magazines," in *A Companion to the Anthropology of Japan*, ed. Jennifer Robertson (Malden, Mass.: Blackwell, 2005), 316, 323, 317.

91. Earl H. Kinmonth, "Nakamura Keiu and Samuel Smiles: A Victorian Confucian and a Confucian Victorian," *The American Historical Review* 85, no. 3 (June 1980): 535–556, at 541.

92. Hirakawa, *Japan's Love-Hate Relation with the West*, 103, 102.

93. Hirakawa, *Japan's Love-Hate Relation with the West*, 107.

94. Kinmonth, "Nakamura Keiu and Samuel Smiles," 543.

95. See Arthur Versluis, *American Transcendentalism and Asian Religions* (New York: Oxford University Press, 1993).

96. Meech-Pekarik, *The World of the Meiji Print: Impressions of a New Civilization* (Weatherhill, 1987), 120, as cited in Brooklyn Museum search catalog.

97. Kinmonth, "Nakamura Keiu and Samuel Smiles," 552,

98. Kinmonth, 536.

99. Kinmonth, 546–547, 544; Hirakawa, *Japan's Love-Hate Relation with the West*, 108.

100. See Toyoda Minoru, *Shakespeare in Japan: An Historical Survey* (Shakespeare Association of Japan by the Iwanami Shoten, 1940), 32; Friederike von Schwerin, *High Shakespeare, Reception and Translation: Germany and Japan* (New York: Continuum Press, 2004), 60.

101. Kishi and Bradshaw, *Shakespeare in Japan*, 2–3.

102. As Kockum writes, "a close examination of the works translated into Japanese . . . shows that the writers mentioned by Smiles predominate. Furthermore, popular

and important contemporary writers who were not mentioned by Smiles remained untranslated into Japanese, even if their books were to be found in Japan." Kockum, *Ito Sei: Self-Analysis and the Modern Japanese Novel*, 103.

103. Kinmonth, "Nakamura Keiu and Samuel Smiles," 556.

104. Hirakawa, *Japan's Love-Hate Relation with the West*, 112–13.

105. Kiri Paramore, *Japanese Confucianism: A Spiritual History* (Cambridge: Cambridge University Press, 2016), 134–35.

106. Eric Hayot, "Chinese Modernism, Mimetic Desire, and European Time," in *The Oxford Handbook of Global Modernisms*, ed. Mark Wollaeger and Matthew Eatough (Oxford: Oxford University Press, 2012), 153.

107. Michael Korda, *Making the List: A Cultural History of the American Bestseller, 1900–1999: As Seen Through the Annual Bestseller Lists of* Publishers Weekly (New York: Barnes & Noble, 2001), 71–72.

108. Qian Suoqiao, "Liberal Cosmopolitanism: Lin Yu Tang and Middling Chinese Modernity," in *Ideas, History, and Modern China*, vol. 3, ed. Ban Wang, Wang Hui, and Geremie Barmé (Boston: Brill, 2011), 161.

109. Quoted in Suoqiao, "Liberal Cosmopolitan," 176.

110. Quoted in Suoqiao, 176.

111. Quoted in Suoqiao, 178.

112. See Eric C. Hendriks, "China's Self-Help Industry: American(ized) Life Advice in China," chap. 22 in *Handbook of Cultural and Creative Industries in China*, ed. Michael Keane (Northampton, Mass.: Edward Elgar, 2016), 311–328; Nehring, Alvarado, Hendriks, and Kerrigan, *Transnational Popular Psychology*; Yuebai Liu, "When Self-Help Becomes a Group Activity," *Slate*, April 1, 2016, http://www.slate .com/articles/news_and_politics/roads/2016/04/one_woman_s_foray_into_china _s_self_help_culture.html.

113. Nehring, Alvarado, Hendriks, and Kerrigan, *Transnational Popular Psychology*, 64.

114. Hendriks, "China's Self-Help Industry," 312.

115. David Weir, *American Orient: Imagining the East from the Colonial Era Through the Twentieth Century* (Amherst: University of Massachusetts Press, 2011), 21, 22.

116. Quoted in Weir, *American Orient*, 21.

117. Weir, 20.

118. Feng Lan, quoted in Weir, 134.

119. D. H. Lawrence, "Benjamin Franklin," in *Studies in Classic American Literature* (London: Penguin, 1923). In a literal instance of modernism rewriting self-help, Lawrence transcribed Franklin's list of virtues and then inserted his own definitions underneath as rebuttals. On page 23, under "Industry," Franklin originally writes, "Lose no time; be always employed in something useful; cut off all unnecessary

actions." Lawrence changes it to "Lose no time with ideals; serve the Holy Ghost, never serve mankind."

120. Weir, *American Orient*, 135, 256.

121. Gregory K. Ornatowski, "On the Boundary Between 'Religious' and 'Secular': The Ideal and Practice of Neo-Confucian Self-Cultivation in Modern Japanese Economic Life, "*Japanese Journal of Religious Studies* 25, nos. 3–4 (Fall 1998): 371.

122. Neha Thirani Bagri, "A Conversation With: Novelist Tash Aw," India Ink, *The New York Times*, November 18, 2013, https://india.blogs.nytimes.com/2013/11/18/a -conversation-with-novelist-tash-aw/.

123. Nehring, Alvarado, Hendriks, and Kerrigan, *Transnational Popular Psychology*, 13.

124. I am indebted to my former student and research assistant Siqi Liu for translations of Aw's work and her brilliant analysis of the phenomenon in her two-part final paper for my seminar. Liu translated the sentences from Aw for me and researched their provenance. Siqi Liu, "The Phenomenon of Western Advice in Modern-Day China" and "Translation and Self-Help in Five Star Billionaire," Harvard 90HL seminar, "How to Live: When Literature Meets Self-Help" (Fall 2016). Thanks also to Han Zhang for her additional research into the translations.

125. Qian Suoqiao refers to "recycled Orientalism" in describing the strange process by which Yutang's American translations of Chinese folk wisdom were, after their American popularity had waned in the 1950s, retranslated literally back into Chinese. Suoqiao, "Liberal Cosmopolitanism," 196.

126. Tash Aw, *Five Star Billionaire* (New York: Speigel & Grau, 2013), xii.

127. Aw, *Five Star Billionaire*, 61.

128. Aw, 227.

129. Aw, 72, 196, 139, 97.

130. Aw, 135.

131. Aw, 4, 5.

132. Aw, xii.

133. Hunter, *The Spirit of Self-Help*, 178.

134. Neville, "Helping Self-Help Books," 370.

135. Shunsuke Ozaki, "American and Japanese Self-Help Literature," *Oxford Research Encyclopedia of Literature*, October 2017, 3, http://literature.oxfordre.com/view /10.1093/acrefore/9780190201098.001.0001/acrefore-9780190201098-e-164.

136. Dale Carnegie, *The Illustrated New Translation: How to Stop Worrying and Start Living* [*Japanese title*]: *The Road Will Open Up Before You* (*Michi wa hirakeru*), trans. Shimon Tauchi, ed. Foreign Masterpieces Research Group [*Kaigai meicho kenkyūkai*] (Tokyo: Kadokawa Books, 2015). My thanks to Kimberlee Sanders for her assistance with translations of the book's captions.

137. Marie Kondo and Yuka Uramoto, *The Life Changing Manga of Tidying Up*, trans. Cathy Hirano (Berkeley, Calif.: Ten Speed Press, 2017).

138. Perhaps it is due to this homology between visual and emotional containment that Nathanael West initially envisioned his story about the commercial advice industry, *Miss Lonelyhearts* (the subject of chapter 5), as a comic strip: "The chapters to be squares in which many things happen through one action. The speeches contained in conventional balloons. I abandoned this idea but retained some of the comic strip technique . . ". Nathanael West, "Some Notes on Miss L.," in *Nathaniel West: A Collection of Critical Essays*, ed. Jay Martin (Upper Saddle River, N.J.: Prentice Hall Spectrum, 1971), 66.

139. Uday Singh Mehta, *Liberalism and Empire: A Study in Nineteenth-Century British Liberal Thought* (Chicago: University of Chicago Press, 1999), 4.

140. Carol Pateman, *The Patriarchal State in Feminism, the Public and the Private* (Oxford: Oxford University Press, 1998); for more on this see David Wayne Thomas, *Cultivating Victorians: Liberal Culture and the Aesthetic* (Philadelphia: University of Pennsylvania Press, 2004), 6.

141. Goodlad, *Victorian Literature and the Victorian State*; Amanda Anderson, "The Liberal Aesthetic," in *Theory After 'Theory'*, ed. Jane Elliott and Derek Attridge (New York: Routledge, 2011), 249–62; Thomas, *Cultivating Victorians*, x.

2. *BOUVARD AND PÉCUCHET*: FLAUBERT'S DIY DYSTOPIA

1. John Hunter, *The Spirit of Self-Help: A Life of Samuel Smiles* (London: Shepheard-Walwyn, 2017), 107.

2. Samuel Smiles, *Self-Help: With Illustrations of Character and Conduct* (London: Ward Lock, 1850), x.

3. J. F. C. Harrison, *Learning and Living 1790–1960: A Study in the History of the English Adult Education Movement* (New York: Taylor & Francis, 2013), 10–11, 55.

4. Harrison, *Learning and Living 1790–1960*, 54.

5. Theodor Adorno, "Free Time," in *The Culture Industry: Selected Essays on Mass Culture*, ed. Jay M. Bernstein (London: Routledge, 1991), 187–97, at 194.

6. Frances Ferguson, "Too Much Information: Flaubert's *Bouvard and Pécuchet*," *Modern Language Notes* 125 (2010): 783.

7. Laurence M. Porter, ed., *A Gustave Flaubert Encyclopedia* (Westport, Conn.: Greenwood Press, 2001), 73; Rita Felski, *The Gender of Modernity* (Cambridge, Mass.: Harvard University Press, 1995), 81; Leo Bersani, *The Culture of Redemption* (Cambridge, Mass.: Harvard University Press, 2000), 130.

8. Gustave Flaubert, *Correspondence*, ed. Louis Conard (Paris, 1923), III: 67.

9. One exception to the critical reticence is Mary Orr, who notes that "BP is the ironic fictional version of a potted self-help series (encyclopedia or compendium) on every topic known to man." Mary Orr, *Flaubert: Writing the Masculine* (Oxford: Oxford University Press, 2000), 119. Orr's aside notwithstanding, self-help's status as a target of Flaubert's prescient wrath has not been fully addressed.

10. Alison Booth, *How to Make It as a Woman: Collective Biographical History from Victoria to the Present* (Chicago: University of Chicago Press, 2004), 79. See Booth, 77–80, for an excellent discussion of the role of biography and "role models" in Smiles's self-help.

11. Quoted in Harrison, *Learning and Living 1790–1960*, 56.

12. Gustave Flaubert, *Bouvard and Pécuchet*, trans. Mark Polizzotti (Normal, Ill.: Dalkey Archive Press, 2005), 14, 37.

13. For a detailed account of the specific manuals Flaubert consulted, see Stéphanie Dord Crouslé, "Flaubert et les Manuels Roret ou le paradoxe de la vulgarization: L'art des jardins dans Bouvard et Pécuchet," *Le partage des savoirs* (18th–19th siècles), ed. Lise Andries (Lyon: Presses Universitaires de Lyon, 2003), 93–118.

14. Bersani, *The Culture of Redemption*, 132.

15. Harrison, *Learning and Living 1790–1960: A Study in the History of the English Adult Education Movement*, 51.

16. Although Smiles was inspired in his lectures by local Scottish improvement clubs, remember that he modeled much of his written handbook on French precedents.

17. Charles Louandré, "De l'Association littéraire et scientifique en France: Les societies savants et littéraires de la province," *Revue des deux mondes* (1846): 528, 521. (Translations of this text are my own.)

18. M. A. Kirchner, archiviste, "Table Générale Récapitulative," in *Mémoires de la Société D'Émulation du Doubs, 1841–1905* (Besancon: Typographie et Lithographie Dodivers, 1907) 2, 41, 39, 12, 12. (Translations are my own.)

19. Robert Fox, "The Savant Confronts His Peers: Scientific Societies in France, 1815–1914" in *The Organization of Science and Technology in France 1808–1914*, ed. Robert Fox and George Weisz (Cambridge: Cambridge University Press, 1980), 257; Carol Harrison, *The Bourgeois Citizen in Nineteenth-Century France: Gender, Sociability, and the Uses of Emulation* (Oxford: Oxford University Press, 1999), 79.

20. Fox, "The Savant Confronts His Peers," 243.

21. Flaubert, *Bouvard and Pécuchet*, 250.

22. Gustave Flaubert, *Madame Bovary: Provincial Lives*, trans. Alan Russell (Harmondsworth: Penguin, 1950), 186, 358, 357.

23. Fox, "The Savant Confronts His Peers," 244.

24. Gustave Flaubert, "On doit toujours faire partie d'un cercle." See *The Dictionary of Accepted Ideas*, trans. Jacques Barzun (New York: New Directions, 1968), 24.

25. Robert Fox, "The Savant Confronts His Peers," 241.

26. Carol Harrison, *The Bourgeois Citizen in Nineteenth-Century France*, 2–3.

27. Flaubert, *Madame Bovary*, 355–356.

28. Flaubert, *Madame Bovary* 225.

29. Gustave Flaubert, *Sentimental Education* (Mineola, N.Y.: Dover, 2006), 17.

30. Jonathan Culler, *Flaubert: The Uses of Uncertainty* (Ithaca, N.Y.: Cornell University Press, 1974), 197.

31. There is no direct record of Flaubert having said this phrase, only third-hand reporting of his having said it. See Rene Descharmes, *Flaubert. Sa vie, son caractère et ses idées avant 1857* (Ferroud, 1909), 103.

32. "Combien je regrette souvent de nètre pas un savant, et comme jènvie ces calmes existences passées à étudier des pattes de mouche, des étoiles ou des fleurs!" Gustave Flaubert, Lettre à Mademoiselle Leroyer de Chantepie, March 1, 1858, in *Oeuvres Complètes de Gustave Flaubert*, Vol. 10, *Correspondence II (1850–1859)* (Paris: Club de l'honnête homme, 1974–1976).

33. Flaubert, *Madame Bovary*, 137–138.

34. Flaubert, *Bouvard and Pécuchet*, 106, 118.

35. Micki McGee, *Self-Help, Inc.: Makeover Culture in American Life* (New York: Oxford University Press, 2005), 18; Steve Salerno, *SHAM: How the Self-Help Movement Made America Helpless* (New York: Crown, 2005), 6.

36. Theodor Adorno, *The Culture Industry: Selected Essays on Mass Culture*, ed. Jay M. Bernstein (London: Routledge, 1991), 194.

37. Pericles Lewis, *The Cambridge Introduction to Modernism* (Cambridge: Cambridge University Press, 2007), xx.

38. Karl Marx and Friedrich Engels, *The German Ideology* [1932] (New York: International Publishers, 2004), 105.

39. Flaubert, *Bouvard and Pécuchet*, 48.

40. Flaubert, 205.

41. Flaubert, 50.

42. Marx and Engels, *The German Ideology*, 118.

43. Rebecca Mead, "Better, Faster, Stronger," *The New Yorker*, September 11, 2011, https://www.newyorker.com/magazine/2011/09/05/better-faster-stronger.

44. Stephen J. Dubner, "How to Be Tim Ferriss," *Freakonomics*, http://freakonomics.com/podcast/tim-ferriss/.

45. This episode is described and quoted in Harrison, *The Bourgeois Citizen in Nineteenth-Century France*, 49–50.

46. Flaubert, *Bouvard and Pécuchet*, 55, 59.

47. Flaubert, *Bouvard and Pécuchet* 61.

48. Flaubert, *Bouvard and Pécuchet* 65.

49. Flaubert, *Madame Bovary*, 355.

50. Pierre Bourdieu, *The Rules of Art, Genesis and Structure of the Literary Field*, trans. Susan Emanuel (Stanford, Calif.: Stanford University Press, 1995), 21.

51. In *Sentimental Education*, Frédéric "thought of the plot of a play and of subjects for paintings," "dreamt of symphonies," "wanted to paint," and attempts "to write a novel called *Sylvio, A Fisherman's Son*, etc." Assembled in Bourdieu, *The Rules of Art*, 5.

52. Claudine Cohen, "Bouvard et Pécuchet réécrivent les sciences," *Alliage* 37–38 (1998): 2. (My translation).

53. Flaubert, quoted in Mark Polizzotti "Introduction," *Bouvard and Pécuchet*, xxxi–xxxii.

54. Mark Polizzotti, "Introduction" to *Bouvard and Pecuchet*, ix–x.

55. Charles Louandre, "De l'association littéraire et scientifique en france. I. Les Sociétéssavantes et littéraires de Paris," *Revue des deux mondes*, vol. 16 (Paris: 1846), 522.

56. Cohen, "Bouvard et Pécuchet réécrivent les sciences," 3.

57. Larry Duffy, *Flaubert, Zola, and the Incorporation of Disciplinary Knowledge* (New York: Palgrave Macmillan, 2015), 218.

58. Flaubert, *Bouvard and Pécuchet*, 37, 38.

59. Flaubert, 39.

60. Pierre Boitard, *Manuel de L'Architecte des Jardins: L'art de les composer et de les décorer*, 2nd ed. (Paris: Chez Leonce Laget, 1846), 35. (My translations). On Flaubert's use of Boitard, see Stéphanie Dord Crouslé, "Flaubert et les Manuels Roret ou le paradoxe de la vulgarization" 101.

61. Boitard, *Manuel de L'Architecte des Jardins*, 38.

62. Flaubert, *Bouvard and Pécuchet*, 44, 45–47.

63. Boitard, *Manuel de L'Architecte des Jardins*, 36.

64. Boitard, 38.

65. Flaubert had largely completed the *Dictionary* by 1850, prior to beginning *Bouvard and Pécuchet*. From his letters and notes, it seems he may have planned for the *Dictionary* to compose an entire second volume to *Bouvard and Pécuchet*, "consisting almost entirely of quotations" (Flaubert, *The Letters of Gustave Flaubert: 1830–1857*, 263). He died, however, before the volume was complete, leaving the much shorter appendix that is often published with *Bouvard and Pécuchet* today.

66. Gustave Flaubert, *The Dictionary of Accepted Ideas*, trans. Jacques Barzun (New York: New Directions, 1968), 68, 66–67.

67. Flaubert, *The Dictionary of Accepted Ideas*, 64, 80, 92.

68. Jacques Barzun, "Introduction," Flaubert, *The Dictionary of Accepted Ideas*, 8.

69. Flaubert, *The Dictionary of Accepted Ideas*, 17.

70. Émile Coué, *Self Mastery Through Conscious Autosuggestion* (New York: American Library Service, 1922); Project Gutenberg eBook, accessed September 26, 2014, http://www.gutenberg.org/files/27203/27203-h/27203-h.htm.

71. Gustave Flaubert, quoted in Albert Thibaudet, *Gustave Flaubert* (Paris: Plon-Nourrit et cie, 1922), 136.

72. Flaubert, *Oeuvres Complètes de Gustave Flaubert*, 99.

73. We know from his letters that Flaubert read Kant. See Aimee L. McKenzie, trans., *The George Sand-Gustave Flaubert Letters* (New York: Boni & Liveright, 1921), 248; see also Francis Steegmuller, ed., *The Letters of Gustave Flaubert: 1857–1880* (Cambridge, Mass.: Belknap Press, 1982), 248.

74. "Of all these three kinds of satisfaction [the pleasant, the good, the beautiful], that of taste in the beautiful is alone a disinterested and free satisfaction; for no interest, either of interest or reason, here forces our assent." Immanuel Kant, *Critique of Judgment* (New York: Hafner, 1951), 44.

75. Ralph Ellison, *Invisible Man* (New York: Random House, 1952), 6.

76. Lorrie Moore, "How to Be an Other Woman," in *Self-Help: Stories* (New York: Knopf, 1985), 4.

77. Jonathan Holden, "The Abuse of the Second Person Pronoun," in *The Rhetoric of the Contemporary Lyric* (Bloomington: Indiana University Press, 1980), 38–56.

78. David Gates, "English Lessons," *The New Yorker*, September 29, 1996, https://www.nytimes.com/1996/09/29/books/english-lessons.html.

79. Brian Richardson, "The Poetics and Politics of Second-Person Narration," *Genre* 24 (Fall 1991): 327.

80. Richardson, "The Poetics and Politics of Second-Person Narration," 319.

81. Matt Del Conte, "Why You Can't Speak: Second-Person Narration, Voice, and a New Model for Understanding Narrative," *Style* 37, no. 2 (Summer 2003): 216, n4.

82. Richardson, "The Poetics and Politics of Second-Person Narration," 313.

83. James Phelan, *Narrative as Rhetoric: Technique, Audiences, Ethics, Ideology* (Columbus: Ohio State University Press, 1996), 153, 148.

84. Jessica Anne, *A Manual for Nothing* (Noemi Press, 2017).

85. Mark McGurl, *The Program Era* (Cambridge, Mass.: Harvard University Press, 2011).

3. NEGATIVE VISUALIZATION

1. Marshall McLuhan, "Dale Carnegie: America's Machiavelli" ("Dale Carnegie's Moral Arithmetic"), 1939, manuscripts, vol. 128, file 2, Marshall McLuhan Archives, National Archives of Canada, 1, 13–14, 2.

2. Dale Carnegie, *How to Win Friends and Influence People*, rev. ed. (New York: Pocket Books, 1982), 37 (*in original*).

3. Brundtland Commission, *Our Common Future: Report of the World Commission on Environment and Development* (New York: United Nations, 1987), 37.

4. Lauren Berlant, *Cruel Optimism* (Durham, N.C.: Duke University Press, 2011), 2.

5. "Kludge," Wikipedia, 2018, https://en.wikipedia.org/wiki/Kludge.

6. The phrase "sustainable self-help" is a riff on Elizabeth Lasch-Quinn's wonderful discussion of "sustainable self-making." Elizabeth Lasch-Quinn, "The New Old Ways of Self-Help," *The Hedgehog Review* 19, no. 1 (Spring 2017), https://iasculture.org/THR/THR_article_2017_Spring_LaschQuinnEXC.php.

7. Theodor Adorno, *Minima Moralia: Reflections from Damaged Life*, trans. E. F. N. Jephcott (London: Verso, 1978); Jakob Norberg, "Adorno's Advice: *Minima Moralia* and the Critique of Liberalism," *PMLA*, 126, no. 2 (March 2011): 404.

8. Norberg, "Adorno's Advice," 408, 400.

9. Michel Foucault, *Hermeneutics of the Subject: Lectures at the Collège de France 1981–82*, ed. Frédéric Gros, trans. Graham Burchell (New York: Palgrave Macmillan, 2005).

10. Peter Sloterdijk, *You Must Change Your Life*, trans. Wieland Hoban (Malden, Mass.: Polity, 2013), 452. For more on this, see Quinn, 79–80.

11. Oliver Burkeman, *Antidote: Happiness for People Who Can't Stand Positive Thinking* (New York: Farrar, Straus, and Giroux, 2012), 207.

12. Svend Brinkmann, *Stand Firm: Resisting the Self-Improvement Craze* (Malden, Mass.: Polity, 2017), 407.

13. Marie Kondo, *The Life Changing Magic of Tidying Up* (Berkeley, Calif.: Ten Speed Press, 2014).

14. Flann O'Brien, *The Third Policeman: A Novel* (Normal, Ill.: Dalkey Archive Press, 1999), 29, 30.

15. O'Brien, *The Third Policeman*, 29.

16. Harold Bloom, *The Anxiety of Influence: A Theory of Poetry* (New York: Oxford University Press, 1973).

17. Flann O'Brien, epigraph to *The Hard Life: An Exegesis of Squalor* (New York: Simon & Schuster, 2003).

18. Émile Coué, *Self Mastery Through Conscious Autosuggestion* (New York: Malkan, 1922), 18.

19. Coué, *Self Mastery*, 25 (italics in original).
20. O'Brien, *The Hard Life*, 127–28.
21. O'Brien, 101.
22. Stephanie Rains, " 'Do You Ring? Or Are You Rung For?': Mass Media, Class, and Social Aspiration in Edwardian Ireland," *New Hibernian Review* 18, no. 4 (Winter 2014): 26. Rains offers a fascinating discussion of the ambitions and anxieties of the Irish clerkly classes at this time.
23. Sidney Flower, *The Mail-Order Business: A Series of Lessons* (Chicago: S. Flower, 1902), 40–41.
24. "The International Association for the Preservation of Spiritualist and Occult Periodicals on Sydney Flower," *The Hypnotic Magazine*, vol. 2 (January 1897), http://www.iapsop.com/archive/materials/hypnotic_magazine/.
25. O'Brien, *The Hard Life*, 125–26.
26. H. G. Wells, *Tono-Bungay* (New York: Penguin, 2005), 148.
27. O'Brien, *The Hard Life*, 166.
28. Robert Musil, *The Man Without Qualities*, trans. Sophie Wilkins and Burton Pike (New York: Vintage International, 1996), 353.
29. Flann O'Brien, *The Third Policeman* (Chicago: Dalkey Archive Press, 2007), 15.
30. O'Brien, *The Third Policeman*, 93, 144, 146.
31. O'Brien, 93.
32. Charles Baxter interview by Chris Lehmann, "The Funniest, and Scariest, Book Ever Written," August 22, 2006, *NPR.org*, https://www.npr.org/templates/story/story.php?storyId=5684946.
33. Leo Tolstoy, "Modern Science" (1898), in *Essays and Letters by Count Leo Tolstoy*, trans. Aylmer Maude (New York: Funk and Wagnalls, 1904), 223.
34. O'Brien, *The Third Policeman*, 3.
35. James Joyce, *Ulysses, The Corrected Text*, ed. Hans Walter Gabler, Wolfhard Steppe, and Claus Melchior (New York: Random House, 1986), 2:239.
36. Philip Coulter, "A Critical Study of Flann O'Brien's Early Novels" (master of arts thesis, McGill University, Montreal, Canada, July 28, 1971), 83.
37. O'Brien, *The Third Policeman*, 159.
38. Hugh Kenner, "The Fourth Policeman," in *Conjuring Complexities: Essays on Flann O'Brien*, ed. Anne Clune and Tess Hurson (Belfast: Institute of Irish Studies, 1997), 71.
39. O'Brien, *The Third Policeman*, 162.
40. O'Brien, 159, 74–77.
41. See Seneca, "On the Happy Life," in *Dialogues and Essays*, ed. John Davie (Oxford: Oxford University Press, 2007), 87.
42. O'Brien, 84.

43. Edith Wharton, *Twilight Sleep* [1927] (New York: Simon & Schuster, 1997).

44. Robin Peel, *Apart from Modernism: Edith Wharton, Politics, Fiction* (New York: Rosemont, 2005).

45. Wharton, *Twilight Sleep*, 119.

46. F. Scott Fitzgerald, *The Great Gatsby* [1925] (New York: Scribner, 2004), 173.

47. Wharton, 9–10, 45, 14.

48. Aldous Huxley, "Hocus Pocus," in *Aldous Huxley's Hearst Essays*, ed. James Sexton (New York: Garland, 1994), 78,

49. Aldous Huxley, "Hocus Pocus," 78.

50. For example, see Walter Benjamin, "The Storyteller," in *Illuminations* (New York: Schocken, 1969), 83–110.

51. Pericles Lewis, *Religious Experience and the Modernist Novel* (Cambridge: Cambridge University Press, 2010).

52. William James, "The Varieties of Religious Experience," in *Writings 1902–1910* (New York: Library of America, 1987).

53. Aaron Jaffe, *Modernism and the Culture of Celebrity* (Cambridge: Cambridge University Press, 2005); Jonathan Goldman, *Modernism Is the Literature of Celebrity* (Austin University of Texas Press, 2011).

54. See Hugh Kenner, "In Defense of a Guru" (review of James Moore's *Gurdjieff and Mansfield*), *New York Times*, January 25, 1981.

55. Virginia Woolf writes of the incident in *Roger Fry: A Biography* (Orlando, Fla.: Harcourt Brace Jovanovich, 1940), where Fry describes Coué as "a kind of secular Jesus Christ." Woolf notes that his time with Coué inspired Fry's aesthetic interest in primitivism:

> At first it seemed impossible for Fry to be anything but a detached and sympathetic spectator. "It's terribly difficult for people with so external and analytic a mind as I have to submit," he wrote. For six hours a day he sat on a camp stool repeating "Ca passé" [Coué's motto] and tried to realize that his skepticism was merely "instinctive and irrational." At last the charm began to work. His pain left him, and he went on to develop a theory of the unconscious, and that theory was, of course, brought to bear upon art. The séances at Nancy had their share in developing his growing interest in uncivilized races.

56. For example, see Janet Beer and Avril Horner, "Wharton the 'Renovator': *Twilight Sleep* as Gothic Satire," *The Yearbook of English Studies* 37, no. 1 (2007): 177–92.

57. Quoted in Rebecca Rauve, "An Intersection of Interests: Gurdjieff's Rope Group as a Site of Literary Production," in "American Writers and France," special issue, *Twentieth Century Literature* 49, no. 1 (2003): 46–81, at 59.

58. The name "Rope Group" referred to Gurdjieff's allegory that a work group must be "like climbing a high mountain. For safety, each must be roped together, each one thinking of the others, all helping one another 'as hand washes hand.'" William Patrick Patterson, *Ladies of the Rope: Gurdjieff's Special Left Bank Women's Group* (Berkeley, Calif.: Arete Communications, 1999), 96.

59. John Bennet, *Gurdjieff: Making a New World* (London: Turnstone, 1973), 273.

60. Margaret Anderson, *The Unknowable Gurdjieff* (New York: Samuel Weiser, 1962), 53.

61. Wharton, on Woolfian stream of consciousness, is quoted in Dale M. Bauer, *Edith Wharton's Brave New Politics* (Madison: University of Wisconsin Press, 1994), 44; Wharton on Joyce in a letter to Bernard Berenson, January 6, 1923, in *The Letters of Edith Wharton*, ed. R. W. B. Lewis and Nancy Lewis (New York: Scribners, 1989), 461.

62. Edith Wharton, "Tendencies in Modern Fiction," *The Saturday Review of Literature* 10, no. 28 (January 27, 1934): 434.

63. Wharton "confessed to liking James the individual more than his later books." Quoted in Peel, *Apart from Modernism*, 17.

64. Wharton, "Tendencies in Modern Fiction," 434.

65. Rauve, "An Intersection of Interests," 49.

66. Wharton quoted in Peel, *Apart from Modernism*, 89.

67. Kathryn Hulme, *Undiscovered Country: A Spiritual Adventure* (Boston: Little, Brown, 1966), 1.

68. For a lengthy discussion of the Rope Group output, see Rauve, "An Intersection of Interests," 46.

69. Pound preferred Gurdjieff's soup to his philosophy, joking that "if he had more of that sort of thing in his [culinary] repertoire he could . . . have worked on towards at least one further conversation." Lewis described the guru as a "Levantine psychic shark," and Yeats advised his friend, "I have had a lot of experience of that sort of thing in my time, and my advice to you is—leave it alone." Quoted in Rauve, "An Intersection of Interests," 57.

70. Quoted in Tobin Siebers, *Cold War Criticism and the Politics of Skepticism* (New York: Oxford University Press, 1993), 53.

71. Siebers, *Cold War Criticism*, 53, 52–53, 53.

72. Stephen Best and Sharon Marcus, "Surface Reading: An Introduction," *Representations* 108, no. 1 (2009): 1–21; Rita Feslki, *The Limits of Critique* (Chicago: University of Chicago Press, 2015).

73. Siebers, *Cold War Criticism*, 5.

74. Frank Channing Haddock, *The Power of Will* (Auburndale: Power-Book Library, 1909); Annie Payson Call, *Nerves and Common Sense* (Boston: Little, Brown, 1925);

Dale Carnegie, *How to Win Friends and Influence People* (New York: Simon & Schuster, 1936). Richardson relates that "[Annie Payson Call's] popular self-help books would be based on James's views about the power of habit. James, in turn, learned much about the importance of relaxation—muscular relaxation—from Call's work." Robert D. Richardson, *William James: In the Maelstrom of American Modernism* (New York: First Mariner Books, 2007), 283.

75. Oliver Burkeman, *The Antidote: Happiness for People Who Can't Stand Positive Thinking* (New York: Farrar, Straus, and Giroux, 2012); Neel Burton, *The Art of Failure: The Anti-Self-Help Guide* (Chatham: Acheron Press, 2010).

76. William James, *Principles of Psychology* (New York: Henry Holt, 1918), 125. Speaking of this passage, Posnock notes that "it is difficult not to detect in this description a caricature of Henry." Ross Posnock, *The Trial of Curiosity: Henry, William James, and the Challenge of Modernity* (New York: Oxford University Press, 1991), 64.

77. William James letter to Henry James, October 22, 1905; Henry James to William James, November 23, 1905, in *William and Henry James Selected Letters*, ed. Ignas K. Skrupskelis and Elizabeth M. Berkeley (Charlottesville: University of Virginia Press, 1997), 463, 467.

78. Henry James letter to Grace Norton, July 28, 1883, in *Henry James Letters*, vol. 2, ed. Leon Edel (Cambridge, Mass.: Harvard University Press, 1975), 424.

79. Steven Starker, *Oracle at the Supermarket: The American Preoccupation with Self-Help Books* (New Brunswick, N.J.: Transaction, 1989), 34.

80. Henry James, "The Jolly Corner," in *The New York Stories of Henry James* (New York: New York Review Books, 2006), 463–500, at 473.

81. William James, *The Energies of Men* (New York: Moffat, Yard, 1914), 8. *Energies* was originally delivered as a Presidential Address at Columbia University in 1906 and was first published in 1907 under the title "The Powers of Men."

82. W. James, *The Energies of Men*, 14–15.

83. Carnegie, *How to Win Friends and Influence People*, 17.

84. W. James, *The Energies of Men*, 15, 5.

85. W. James, *Varieties of Religious Experience*, 92.

86. Michel Foucault, "How We Behave: Sex, Food, and Other Ethical Matters," Hubert L. Dreyfus and Paul Rabinow (interview), *Vanity Fair* 46, no. 9 (1983): 61–69; Theodor Adorno, *The Stars Down to Earth* (London: Routledge, 1994).

87. W. James, *Varieties of Religious Experience*, 104–5.

88. Orison Swett Marden, *How to Get What You Want* (New York: Thomas Y. Crowell, 1917), 10–11.

89. H. James, "The Jolly Corner," 474.

90. Micki McGee, *Self-Help, Inc.: Makeover Culture in American Life* (New York: Oxford University Press, 2005), 34.

91. H. James, "The Jolly Corner," 473, 467.

92. Bruce MacLelland, *Prosperity Through Thought Force* [1907] (New York: Cosimo, 2007), 31, 25.

93. Frank Channing Haddock, *Power of Will: A Practical Companion Book for Unfoldment of the Powers of Mind* (New York: J. F. Tapley, 1907), 9.

94. Henry James read *Varieties* in 1902, six years before "The Jolly Corner" was published. F. O. Mattheissen, *The James Family* (New York: Knopf, 1947), 338.

95. Henry Wood, *Ideal Suggestion Through Mental Photography: A Restorative System for Home and Private Use* (Boston: Lee and Shepard, 1893), 108–9.

96. Steven Starker, *Oracle at the Supermarket: The American Preoccupation with Self-Help Books* (New Brunswick, N.J.: Transaction, 1989), 29.

97. H. James, "The Jolly Corner," 486, 493.

98. Prentice Mulford, *Thought Is a Thing* (Radford: Wilder, 2008). Another important precedent for this scene within the context of self-help's prehistory is the philosophy of Swedenborgism to which Henry James Senior subscribed. See R. W. B. Lewis, introduction to *The Turn of the Screw and Other Short Fiction* (New York: Bantam Books, 2008), xx.

99. Sigmund Freud, "The Relation of the Poet to Day Dreaming" (1908), in *Character and Culture* (Springfield: Crowell-Collier, 1963), 37, 43.

100. In a suggestive essay, Cohen describes "talk" in late James as a form of "performative self-help." Paula Marantz Cohen, "Henry James and Self-Help," in *Henry James and the Poetics of Duplicity* (Newcastle: Cambridge Scholars, 2013), 145–52, at 149.

101. Eve Sedgwick, *Epistemology of the Closet* (Berkeley: University of California Press, 2008), 188; Eric Savoy, "The Queer Subject of 'The Jolly Corner,'" *Henry James Review* 20, no. 1 (1999): 1–21, at 1, 3. An alternate approach to the self-help capacities of James's writing is found in Carroll's "evolutionary criticism," which argues that James inherits the Arnoldian view of the literary as "a heroic pursuit leading ultimately to 'perfection.'" Joseph Carroll, *Evolution and Literary Theory* (Columbia: University of Missouri Press, 1995), 196.

102. Philip Weinstein, *Unknowing: The Work of Modernist Fiction* (Ithaca, N.Y.: Cornell University Press, 2005).

103. The New Thought Alliance was established in London in 1914. See Horatio W. Dresser, *A History of the New Thought Movement* (New York: Thomas Y. Crowell, 1919), 263; Rhonda Byrne, *The Secret* (Luxembourg: Atria Books, 2006).

104. Quoted in Matthew Peters, "Henry James, American Social Change, and Literary Revision," *The Cambridge Quarterly* 34, no. 4 (2005): 323–31, at 323.

105. Henry James, *The American Scene*, in *Collected Travel Writings: Great Britain and America* (New York: Library of America, 1993), 734.

106. H. James, "The Jolly Corner," 475.

107. Squillace offers a fascinating assessment of Bennett's self-help and its often conflicted relation to his fiction. Robert Squillace, "Arnold Bennett's Other Selves," in *Marketing the Author: Authorial Personae, Narrative Selves and Self-Fashioning, 1880–1930* (Basingstoke: Palgrave Macmillan, 2004), 156–183, at 157.

108. Arnold Bennett, *How to Live on Twenty-Four Hours a Day* (New York: Bookman, 1910); Arnold Bennett, *Literary Taste: How to Form It* (New York: George H. Doran, 1909); Arnold Bennett, *Mental Efficiency* (New York: George H. Doran, 1911); Arnold Bennett, *The Human Machine* (London: New Age Press, 1908); Arnold Bennett, *Self and Self-Management* (New York: W. M. H. Wise, 1918); Arnold Bennett, *How to Make the Best of Life* (New York: George H. Doran, 1923).

109. Endpapers promotional blurb for *How to Live on Twenty-Four Hours a Day*, *The Bristol Daily Mercury*, repr. in Arnold Bennett, *The Human Machine* (London: New Age Press, 1908).

110. William James's readings of Stoic philosophers Epictetus and Marcus Aurelius is described in Richardson, *William James*, 53.

111. Arnold Bennett, quoted in James Hepburn, *Arnold Bennett: The Critical Heritage* (1971; repr. London: Routledge, 1997), 43.

112. Arnold Bennett, *The Author's Craft and Other Critical Writings of Arnold Bennett*, ed. Samuel Hynes (Lincoln: University of Nebraska Press, 1968), 264.

113. James Hepburn, ed., *Arnold Bennett* (New York: Routledge, 2013), 43.

114. Bennett, *How to Live on Twenty-Four Hours a Day*, 16.

115. Bennett, 14.

116. W. Whitten, endpapers promotional blurb for *How to Live on Twenty-Four Hours a Day*, *The Tattler*, repr. in Bennett, *The Human Machine*; William James, *The Energies of Men* (New York: Dodd, Mead, 1926), 8–9.

117. Max Weber, *The Protestant Ethic and the Spirit of Capitalism* (New York: Scribner, 1930), 181.

118. Arnold Bennett, "Young Authors," in *The Author's Craft and Other Critical Writings of Arnold Bennett*, 218–220, at 219; Arnold Bennett, "James Joyce's *Ulysses*," in *The Author's Craft and Other Critical Writings of Arnold Bennett*, 211–217, at 215.

119. Arnold Bennett, "Translating Literature into Life," *Things That Have Interested Me* (London: Chatto and Windus, 1921), 42–45, at 42.

120. Virginia Woolf, "Mr. Bennett and Mrs. Brown," [1924] in *The Virginia Woolf Reader*, ed. Mitchell A. Leaska (Orlando, Fla.: Harcourt, 1984), 192–212, at 194.

121. Samuel Smiles, *Character* (New York: Harper, 1876); William James, *Habit* (New York: Henry Holt, 1890), 61; Bennett, *The Human Machine*, 34.

122. Woolf, "Mr. Bennett and Mrs. Brown," 195.

123. Melba Cuddy-Keane, "Virginia Woolf and the Public Sphere," in *Cambridge Companion to Virginia Woolf*, 2nd ed., ed. Susan Sellers (Cambridge: Cambridge University Press, 2010), 231–49, at 199, 203. Keane further writes that "modeling discourse is, for Woolf, intervention in the public sphere," 238.

124. Virginia Woolf, "How Should One Read a Book?", [1926] in *The Second Common Reader*, ed. Andrew McNeillie (San Diego: Harvest Books, 1986), 258–70, at 258.

125. The dialogic possibilities afforded Woolf by the essay form, in contrast to the novel, are even more marked when considering the opposition between the essay and the self-help tract. On Woolf's essayistic style, see Randi Saloman, *Virginia Woolf's Essayism* (Edinburgh: Edinburgh University Press, 2012).

126. Virginia Woolf, "A Sketch of the Past," in *Moments of Being: A Collection of Autobiographical Writing*, 2nd ed., ed. Jeanne Schulkind (New York: Harcourt Brace, 1985), 61–160, at 77.

127. Virginia Woolf, *Mrs. Dalloway* (Orlando: Harvest Books, 1981), 21–22.

128. Woolf, *Mrs. Dalloway*, 84.

129. E. F. Garasché, quoted in William K. Beatty, "A Historical Review of Bibliotherapy," *Library Trends* 11, no. 2 (1962): 106–117, at 107.

130. The Woolf quotes are from Mrs. Dalloway, 67, 24, and 66. William James, *The Meaning of Truth: A Sequel to Pragmatism* (New York: Longmans, Green, 1909). Similarly, in *Nightwood*, the sole moral voice is the schizophrenic doctor Matthew O'Connor, who sputters out his insights like a record on a loop. Djuna Barnes, *Nightwood* (New York: New Directions, 2006), 35.

131. Lionel Trilling, *Sincerity and Authenticity* (Cambridge, Mass.: Harvard University Press, 1972), 170.

132. Virginia Woolf, *The Diary of Virginia Woolf*, vol. 4, ed. Anne Olivier Bell (London: Hogarth, 1977), 126.

133. Virginia Woolf, "Craftsmanship," in *The Death of the Moth and Other Essays* (Orlando, Fla.: Harcourt, 1970), 198–207, at 206.

134. Pierre Bourdieu, *Distinction: A Social Critique of the Judgment of Taste* (Cambridge, Mass.: Harvard University Press, 1984). Bennett is the working-class "hero" of John Carey, *The Intellectuals and the Masses* (London: Faber and Faber, 1992); whereas "class-conscious disapproval" is implicit in Woolf's critique of him. Samuel Hynes, "The Whole Contention Between Mr. Bennett and Mrs. Woolf," *Novel: A Forum on Fiction* 1, no. 1 (1967): 34–44, at 37. For an example of a feminist reading, see Beth

Rigel Daugherty, "The Whole Contention Between Mr. Bennett and Mrs. Woolf, Revisited," in *Virginia Woolf: Centennial Essays*, ed. Elaine K. Ginsberg and Laura Moss Gottlieb (Troy, N.Y.: Whitson, 1983), 269–94.

135. F. R. Leavis notoriously relied upon the rather elusive notion of an author's "life-impulsion" in his literary criticism. See, for example, F. R. Leavis, *D. H. Lawrence: Novelist* (New York: Knopf, 1956), 298.

136. Edwin J. Kenney Jr., "The Moment, 1910: Virginia Woolf, Arnold Bennett, and Turn of the Century Consciousness," *Colby Library Quarterly* 13, no. 1 (1977): 42.

137. Arnold Bennett, "Another Criticism of the New School," in *Arnold Bennett: The Evening Standard Years, "Books and Persons" 1921–1931*, ed. Andrew Mylett (London: Chatto and Windus, 1974), 4–6, at 5.

138. Virginia Woolf, "Modern Fiction," in *The Virginia Woolf Reader*, ed. Mitchell A. Leaska (Orlando, Fla.: Harcourt, 1984), 283–92, at 286–87.

139. Jackson Lears and Richard Wightman Fox, *The Culture of Consumption: Critical Essays in American History, 1880–1980* (New York: Pantheon Books, 1983), 10.

140. Arnold Bennett: *The Savour of Life: Essays in Gusto* (London: Cassell, 1928). As the *Times Literary Supplement* commented in a review on September 15, 1910, "Towards the end of 'Clayhanger' a phrase occurs that seems to reveal as with a flashlight the whole impulse and motive of Mr. Arnold Bennett's prodigious novel—'a terrific zest for life'. "Quoted in Hepburn, *Arnold Bennett*, 244.

141. Arnold Bennett, *Clayhanger* (London: Eyre Methuen, 1910), 530.

142. Abraham Myerson, *When Life Loses Its Zest* (Boston: Little, Brown, 1925).

143. Myerson, *When Life Loses Its Zest*, xiv. Myerson quotes and cites William James approvingly throughout his book.

144. Myerson recommended Benzedrine for anhedonic depressives as well as "normal people with morning hangovers and low moods." Nicolas Rasmussen, "Making the First Anti-Depressant: Amphetamine in American Medicine, 1929–1950," *Journal of the History of Medicine and Allied Sciences* 61, no. 3 (2006): 288–323, at 309.

145. For an engaging analysis of the overlap between American modern poetry and self-help, see Matt Sandler, "A Poetics of Self-Help in America" (PhD dissertation Columbia University, 2009).

146. Victor A. Segno, *The Law of Mentalism: A Practical, Scientific Explanation of Thought or Mind Force: The Law Which Governs All Mental and Physical Action and Phenomena: The Cause of Life and Death* (Los Angeles: American Institute of Mentalism, 1902), 23. According to the International Association for the Preservation of Spiritualist and Occult Periodicals, Segno was born in Ontario, Canada, as William Albert Hall. He ran a lucrative operation as the founder of the "Segno School of Success" in Los Angeles until he was forced to flee the

persecution of the U.S. Postal Service Inspection Division, which was investigating him for mail-order fraud. Segno published volumes such as *How to Live 100 Years* (1903) and *The Secret of Memory* (1906), only to disappear from the public record in 1915. See http://www.iapsop.com/archive/materials/segnogram/; see also http://ehbritten.blogspot.com/2016/02/out-of-nowhere-some-notes-on-victor .html.

147. Prentice Mulford, "How Thoughts Are Born," *Your Forces, and How to Use Them* (New York: F. J. Needham, 1888), 1.

148. Woolf, *Mrs. Dalloway*, 30, 39, 139.

149. Alex Zwerdling, *Virginia Woolf and the Real World* (Berkeley: University of California Press, 1986), 279.

150. See John S. Rickard, *Joyce's Book of Memory: The Mnemotechnic of Ulysses* (Durham, N.C.: Duke University Press, 1998), 22–23; Marcel Proust, *In the Shadow of Young Girls in Flower*, trans. James Grieve (London: Penguin, 2002), 51.

151. Georg Lukács, *The Theory of the Novel*, trans. Anna Bostock (Cambridge, Mass.: MIT Press, 1999), 116.

152. Wyndham Lewis, *Time and Western Man* (London: Chatto & Windus, 1927), 11.

153. Toby Avard Foshay, *Wyndham Lewis and the Avant-Garde: The Politics of the Intellect* (Montreal: McGill-Queen's University Press, 1992), 91.

154. Wyndham Lewis, *The Art of Being Ruled* (London: Chatto & Windus, 1926), 16.

155. Heather Havrilesky, *How to Be a Person in the World* (New York: Doubleday, 2016); Baratunde Thurston, *How to Be Black* (New York: HarperCollins, 2012); Caitlin Moran, *How to Be a Woman* (London: Ebury, 2011).

156. When Macdonald wrote about the spread of "howto" books in 1954, he argued that such works are, "to say the least, supererogatory." "Do we really need, for instance, Dorothea Biddle's and Dorothea Bom's 'Christmas Idea Book?'—two hundred and twenty-one pages about Christmas decorations," or Dorothea F. Sullivan's "How to Attend a Conference"? Dwight Macdonald, "Howtoism," *The New Yorker*, May 22, 1954, 85.

157. Wyndham Lewis, "The Revolutionary Simpleton," in *The Enemy: A Review of Art and Literature: January 1927–First Quarter 1929*, 3 vols. (London: Frank Cass, 1927–1929, 1968), 109.

158. Ann Charters and Samuel Charters, *Brother-Souls: John Clellon Holmes, Jack Kerouac, and the Beat Generation* (repr. Jackson: University Press of Mississippi, 2010), 256.

159. Although too large and tangential a subject for the present monograph, this invocation of Eastern and New Age philosophy carries through to mid-century with the Beats. Victor Segno is even mentioned by the character Cody Pomeray in Kerouac's

Visions of Cody, which describes how when he was in the "joint" the assistant war-
den gave him "books like *The Law of Mentalism*, by Sechnal [*sic*]." Jack Kerouac,
Visions of Cody (New York: McGraw Hill, 1972), 228.

160. Lionel Trilling, *Sincerity and Authenticity* (Cambridge, Mass.: Harvard University
Press, 1972), 7.

161. Quoted in and trans. Mette Blok, "Robert Musil's Literary Ethics: The Man Without
Qualities Reconsidered," *New German Review* 26, no. 1 (2014): 4.

162. Musil, *The Man Without Qualities*, 272.

4. JOYCE FOR LIFE

1. Declan Kiberd, *Ulysses and Us: The Art of Everyday Life in Joyce's Masterpiece* (New
York: Norton, 2009), 31, 11, 245, 31.

2. Joseph Kelly, "Saving Joyce from the Professors," *South Carolina Review* 43, no. 1
(2010): 264.

3. Kiberd, *Ulysses and Us*, 258.

4. Steven G. Kellman, "James Joyce for Ordinary Blokes?", *The Chronicle of Higher
Education*, September 21, 2009, 6, http://chronicle.com/article/James-Joyce-for
-Ordinary/48427/.

5. I use the term "common reader" because it is the phrase used by the modernists
and their early critics, but I realize that it fails to adequately capture the diversity—
or indeed the originality—of popular approaches to the literary text.

6. Charles Duff, *James Joyce and the Plain Reader* (London: Hammersworth, 1932);
William Powell Jones, *James Joyce and the Common Reader* (Norman: University of
Oklahoma Press, 1955); Anthony Burgess, *Here Comes Everybody* (London: Faber
and Faber, 1965).

7. "Ulysses Lands," *Time*, January 29, 1934.

8. Philip Kitcher, *Joyce's Kaleidoscope: An Invitation to Finnegans Wake* (Oxford:
Oxford University Press, 2007); see also Jefferson Hunter, *How to Read Ulysses
and Why* (New York: Peter Lang, 2002); Arnold Weinstein, *Recovering Your Story,
Understanding the Self Through Five Great Modern Writers: Proust, Joyce, Woolf,
Faulkner, Morrison* (New York: Random House, 2006), 101.

9. Julie Sloan Brannon, *Who Reads Ulysses?: The Rhetoric of the Joyce Wars and the
Common Reader* (New York: Routledge, 2003), 2.

10. James Joyce, *Ulysses: The Corrected Text* (1922), ed. Hans Walter Gabler, Wolfhard
Steppe, and Claus Melchior (New York: Random House, 1986), 17.385–87.

11. Joyce, *Ulysses*, 17.389–91.

12. Joyce, *Ulysses*, 1.555–57.

13. Nicholas Howe, "The Cultural Construction of Reading in Anglo-Saxon England," in *The Ethnography of Reading*, ed. Jonathan Boyarin (Berkeley: University of California Press, 1992), 58–79, at 63.

14. In 1918, the nonfiction list was permanently established. See Frank Luther Mott, *Golden Multitudes: The Story of Best Sellers in the United States* (New York: Bowker, 1946), 205.

15. Richard Posner, "Against Ethical Criticism," *Philosophy and Literature* 21, no. 1 (1997): 2, 12.

16. Martha Craven Nussbaum, *Love's Knowledge: Essays on Philosophy and Literature* (Oxford: Oxford University Press, 1990), 172.

17. See, for example, Marjorie Garber, Beatrice Hanssen, and Rebecca L. Walkowitz, eds., *The Turn to Ethics* (New York: Routledge, 2000); "Ethics and Literary Study," special issue, *PMLA* 114, no. 1 (January 1999). In fact, a great deal of recent scholarship enacts an ethical approach, from the Victorian studies scholarship of Amanda Anderson's *Psyche and Ethos: Moral Life After Psychology* (Clarendon Lectures in English Literture (Oxford, 2018) to the modernist and contemporary criticism of Jessica Berman's *Modernist Commitments* (New York: Columbia University Press, 2012) and Robert Chodat's *The Matter of High Words: Naturalism, Normativity, and the Postwar Sage* (Oxford: Oxford University Press, 2017).

18. Brannon, *Who Reads Ulysses?*, xiii.

19. The argument for a "great divide" between modernism and mass culture was most famously advanced by Andreas Huyssen, *After the Great Divide: Modernism, Mass Culture, Postmoderism* (Bloomington: Indiana University Press, 1986).

20. Terry Eagleton, *Heathcliff and the Great Hunger: Studies in Irish Culture* (London: Verso, 1995), 146.

21. Jeffrey Segall, *Joyce in America: Cultural Politics and the Trials of Ulysses* (Berkeley: University of California Press,1993), 135.

22. Nash notes, "Nowhere in Joyce's work is there a model of an 'ideal reader.'" John Nash, *James Joyce and the Act of Reception: Reading, Ireland, Modernism* (Cambridge: Cambridge University Press, 2006), 6.

23. Joyce complained, "The pity is the public will demand and find a moral in my book— or worse they may take it in some more serious way, and on the honor of a gentleman, there is not one single serious line in it." Djuna Barnes, "A Portrait of the Man Who Is, at Present, One of the More Significant Figures in Literature," *Vanity Fair*, April 1922, https://www.vanityfair.com/news/1922/03/james-joyce-djuna-barnes-ulysses. Joyce describes his "ideal reader [as] suffering from an ideal insomnia." James Joyce, *Finnegans Wake* (1939; repr. New York: Penguin Classics, 1999), 120.13.

24. Friederike Von Schwerin-High, *Shakespeare, Reception and Translation: Germany and Japan* (New York: Continuum, 2004), 64. Even-Zohar describes the literary

system as coexisting with other social systems, whether religious, legal, etc., which taken together constitute the polysystem.

25. Jennifer Wicke, " 'Who's She When She's at Home?': Molly Bloom and the Work of Consumption," in *Molly Blooms: A Polylogue on "Penelope,"* ed. Richard Pearce (Madison: University of Wisconsin Press 1994), 174–95, at 179.

26. Joyce, *Ulysses*, 17.1361–98. For discussions of the role of Sandow's self-help text in *Ulysses*, see Brandon Kershner, "The World's Strongest Man: Joyce or Sandow?", in *Images of Joyce*, vol. 1, ed. Clive Hart, George C. Sandulescu, Bonnie Kime Scott, and Fritz Senn (Gerrards Cross, UK: Colin Smythe, 1998), 237–52; Vike Martina Plock, "A Feast of Strength in Ithaca," *Journal of Modern Literature* 30, no. 1 (2006): 129–36.

27. Joyce, *Ulysses*, 11.906.

28. James Joyce, *Occasional Critical and Politics Writings*, ed. Kevin Barry (Oxford: Oxford University Press, 2009), 97–98.

29. Joyce, *Ulysses*, 4.511–515.

30. Rita Felski, *The Gender of Modernity* (Cambridge, Mass.: Harvard University Press, 1995), 83; John Carey, *The Intellectuals and the Masses* (London: Faber and Faber, 1992), 20.

31. Plock, "A Feast of Strength in Ithaca," 135.

32. W. B. Yeats, "Letter to Florence Farr, July 19, 1905," in *Collected Letters of W. B. Yeats*, Vol. 4, *1905–1907*, ed. John Kelly (New York: Oxford, 2005), 134.

33. Kershner, "The World's Strongest Man," 246.

34. Joyce, *Ulysses*, 4.230–34.

35. Joyce, 13.1162.

36. Eugen Sandow, *Strength and How to Obtain It* (London: Gale & Polden, 1897), 9.

37. Joyce, *Ulysses*, 15.2846–64.

38. James Joyce, *A Portrait of the Artist as a Young Man* (1916; repr. Harmondsworth: Penguin, 1967), 205.

39. Joyce, *Ulysses*, 17.410.

40. Sarah Raff, "Quixotes, Precepts, and Galateas: The Didactic Novel in Eighteenth-Century Britain," *Comparative Literature Studies* 43, no. 4 (2006): 466–81.

41. For a discussion of the morality tale *The Lamplighter*, which informs this episode, see Thomas Karr Richards, "Gerty MacDowell and the Irish Common Reader," *English Literary History* 52, no. 3 (Autumn 1985): 755–76.

42. Joyce, *Ulysses*, 18.1362–64, 16.1653, 17.672, 17.704.

43. Joyce, 9.1042.

44. Patrick A. McCarthy, "Reading in Ulysses," in *Joycean Occasions: Essays from the Milwaukee James Joyce Conference*, ed. Janet E. Dunleavy, Melvin J. Friedman, and Michael Patrick Gillespie (Newark: University of Delaware Press, 1991), 19.

45. Maurice Maeterlinck, *Wisdom and Destiny*, trans. Alfred Suto (New York: Dodd, Mead, 1918), 32.

46. Joyce, *Ulysses*, 19.657, 10.609, 9.261.

47. Michel de Certeau, *The Practice of Everyday Life* (Berkeley: University of California Press, 1998), 174, 175.

48. Seamus Heaney, "A Tale of Two Islands: Reflections on the Irish Literary Revival," in *Irish Studies*, vol. 1, ed. P. J. Drudy (Cambridge: Cambridge University Press, 1980), 72–87, at 72.

49. Malcolm Brown, *The Politics of Irish Literature* (Seattle: University of Washington Press, 1972), 370.

50. See, for instance, Lisi Schoenbach, *Pragmatic Modernism* (Oxford: Oxford University Press, 2012); Liesl Olsen, *Modernism and the Ordinary* (Oxford: Oxford University Press, 2009).

51. For a discussion of the political significance of "self-help" to the Irish, see Kiberd, *Ulysses and Us*, 33.

52. Vike Martina Plock, "Modernism's Feast on Science: Nutrition and Diet in Joyce's *Ulysses*," *Literature & History* 16, no. 2 (2007): 34.

53. P. J. Matthews, " 'A.E.I.O.U': Joyce and the Irish Homestead," in *Joyce on the Threshold*, ed. Anne Fogarty and Timothy Martin (Gainesville: University of Florida Press, 2005), 151–168, at 153.

54. W. B. Yeats, "Dublin, Nov. 6, 1892," in *Letters to the New Island*, ed. George Bornstein and Hugh Witemeyer (New York: Macmillan, 1989), 65.

55. John Logan, "Sufficient to Their Needs: Literary and Elementary Schooling in the Nineteenth Century," in *The Origins of Popular Literacy in Ireland: Language Change and Educational Development, 1700–1920*, ed. Mary Daly and David Dickson (Dublin: Trinity College Press, 1990), 113–38, at 129.

56. W. B. Yeats, "Ireland After Parnell," in *The Collected Works of W. B. Yeats*, Vol. 3, *"Autobiographies,"* ed. William H. O'Donnel and Douglas N. Archibald (1922; repr. New York: Scribner, 1999), 172.

57. Yeats, "Ireland After Parnell," 170, 186.

58. On Joyce's use of the Taylor speech in *Ulysses*, see Damien Keane, "Quotation Marks, the Gramophone Record, and the Language of the Outlaw," *Texas Studies in Literature and Language* 51, no. 4 (2009): 400–415.

59. P. J. Matthews, *Revival: The Abbey Theatre, Sinn Féin, the Gaelic League, and the Cooperative Movement* (Notre Dame, Ind.: University of Notre Dame Press, 2003), 15.

60. William Patrick Ryan, *The Irish Literary Revival; Its History, Pioneers and Possibilities* (London: Ward & Downey, 1894), 67.

61. Matthews, *Revival*, 16.

62. Ernest Augustus Boyd, *Ireland's Literary Renaissance* (New York: John Lane, 1916), 91.

63. W. B. Yeats, "Young Ireland," in *Uncollected Prose by W. B. Yeats*, ed. John P. Frayne and Colton Johnson (1880–1883; repr. New York: Columbia University Press, 1976), 34.

64. The full chronological list of New Irish Library publications includes Thomas Davis, *The Patriot Parliament of 1689*, ed. Charles Gavan Duffy (1893); Standish O'Grady, *The Bog of Stars and Other Stories and Sketches of Elizabethan Ireland* (1893); *The New Spirit of the Nation*, ed. Martin MacDermott (1894); E. M. Lynch, *A Parish Providence: A Country Tale*, with an introduction by Charles Gavan Duffy (1894); *The Irish Song Book*, ed. Alfred Perceval Graves (1894); Douglas Hyde, *The Story of Early Gaelic Literature* (1895); John Todhunter, *Life of Patrick Sarsfield, Earl of Lucan* (1895); J. F. Taylor, *Owen Roe O'Neill* (1896); Michael MacDonagh, *Bishop Doyle: A Biographical and Historical Study* (1896); Sir Samuel Ferguson, *Lays of the Red Branch*, with an introduction by Mary Ferguson (1897).

65. W. B. Yeats, "Some Irish National Books," in *The Collected Works of W. B. Yeats*, Vol. 9, *"Early Articles and Reviews,"* ed. John Frayne and Madeleine Marchaterre (1894; repr. New York: Scribner, 2004), 247.

66. Mangan praise articles are reprinted in Joyce, *Occasional Critical and Politics Writings*, 53–60, 127–136. Joyce, *Ulysses*, 12.134, 13.1149; Joyce, *Occasional Critical and Politics Writings*, 124.

67. Joyce, *Occasional Critical and Politics Writings*, 128. The extant manuscript ends with "the foundation of the separatist journal, *The Nation*, founded by three leaders, Thomas Davis, John Blake Dillon (father of the ex-leader of the Irish Parliamentary Party)"; Duffy, the third founder, would have begun the lost page.

68. Joyce, *Finnegans Wake*, 344.12. Joyce, *Occasional Critical and Politics Writings*, 137. Yeats's first publication after the Duffy dispute was *The Celtic Twilight* (1893).

69. Joyce, *Ulysses*, 17.28, 10.582, 1.490.

70. Joyce, *Ulysses*, 17.639–56, 17.248; Yeats, "Some Irish National Books," 247.

71. Joyce, *Ulysses*, 17.606.

72. Bloom is not the only character in *Ulysses* with plans to capitalize on Stephen's wit. "I intend to make a collection of your sayings if you will let me," the Englishman Haines says to Stephen at the beginning of the text, "That one about the cracked lookingglass of a servant being the symbol of Irish art is deuced good." Joyce, *Ulysses*, 1.480.

73. Brown, *The Politics of Irish Literature*, 13.

74. The catechism form of the episode lampoons this mode of instruction.

75. W. B. Yeats, *The Trembling of the Veil* (London: Laurie, 1922), 90.

76. Helen O'Connell, *Ireland and the Fiction of Improvement* (Oxford: Oxford University Press, 2006), 204. O'Connell's book offers a tremendously thorough and generative account of the New Irish Library dispute.

77. Joyce, *Occasional Critical and Politics Writings*, 50.

78. Malcolm Brown makes this suggestion in Brown, *The Politics of Irish Literature*, 359.

79. Yeats, "Ireland After Parnell," 188.

80. O'Connell, *Ireland and the Fiction of Improvement*, 198–99.

81. James Joyce, "Letter to Stanislaus Joyce, February 11, 1907," in *Selected Letters of James Joyce*, ed. Richard Ellmann (New York: Viking, 1927), 147. Conflictingly, Joyce also chastised Yeats for his "floating esthete's will" and "treacherous instinct of adaptability" in pandering to the masses. Joyce, *Occasional Critical and Politics Writings*, 51. But Brown similarly identifies Yeats's "laughable alienation from the Irish nation, past or present." Brown, *The Politics of Irish Literature*, 370. Joyce's contradictory relation to Yeats is a very complex affair, informed by their different religious backgrounds, among other factors, as explored by Alistair Cormack, *Yeats and Joyce: Cyclical History and Reprobate Tradition* (Aldershot: Ashgate, 2008).

82. Jacques Derrida, "Two Words for Joyce," in *Post-Structuralist Joyce: Essays from the French*, ed. Derek Attridge and Daniel Ferrer (Cambridge: Cambridge University Press, 1984), 145–61, at 147.

83. Kevin Barry, introduction to *James Joyce: Occasional, Critical, and Political Writings*, ed. Kevin Barry (Oxford: Oxford University Press, 2000), xxix.

84. Richard Ellmann, *James Joyce: New and Revised Edition* (Oxford: Oxford University Press, 1983), 3.

85. Thomas E Connolly, "Personal Library of James Joyce: A Descriptive Bibliography," *University of Buffalo Studies* 22, no. 1 (April 1955): 38.

86. Brown, *The Politics of Irish Literature*, 4.

87. Lawrence Rainey, *Institutions of Modernism: Literary Elites and Public Culture* (New Haven, Conn.: Yale University Press, 1983), 13.

88. Martin Amis, *The War Against Cliché: Essays and Reviews 1971–2000* (Los Angeles: Miramax, 2001), 441.

89. James Joyce, *Dubliners* (1914; repr. New York: Signet, 1991), 134.

90. Joyce, *Ulysses*, 16.535 (italics added).

91. Joyce, 10.879.

92. Joyce, *Finnegans Wake*, 614.22, 614.8.

93. Quoted in Jon Hegglund, "Ulysses and the Rhetoric of Cartography," *Twentieth Century Literature* 49, no. 2 (Summer 2003): 164–92, at 178.

94. Joyce, *Finnegans Wake*, 11.07-11.13 (italics added).

95. Joyce, *Ulysses*, 621.01, 620.31–32.

96. Joyce, *Ulysses*, 17.2124.

97. James Joyce, quoted in Max Eastman, *The Literary Mind: Its Place in an Age of Science* (New York: Scribner, 1935), 104.

98. Kenneth Burke, "Literature as Equipment for Living," in *Perspectives by Incongruity*, ed. Stanley Edgar Hyman (Bloomington: Indiana University Press, 1964), 296.

99. Michael McKeon, "Prose Fiction: Great Britain," in *Theory of the Novel: A Historical Approach*, ed. Michael McKeon (Baltimore: Johns Hopkins University Press, 2000), 610.

100. Joyce, *Ulysses*, 17.384.

101. Weinstein, *Recovering Your Story*, 102.

102. Joyce, *Finnegans Wake*, 179.26–27.

103. John Cage, *Writing Through Finnegans Wake* (Tulsa, Okla.: University of Tulsa Monograph Series, 1978); David Melnick, *Men in Aida* (Berkeley, Calif.: Tuumba, 1983).

5. MODERNISM WITHOUT TEARS

1. Promotional blurb for Alain de Botton, *How Proust Can Change Your Life* (London: Picador, 1998); Dwight Macdonald, "Masscult and Midcult," in *Masscult and Midcult: Essays Against the American Grain* (New York: New York Review of Books, 2011), 50; Theodor Adorno, "Short Commentaries on Proust," *Notes to Literature*, vol. 1 (New York: Columbia University Press, 1991), 182.

2. Julian Barnes, *Flaubert's Parrot* (New York: Vintage Reissue, 1990); Ilana Simons, *A Guide to Better Living Through the Work and Wisdom of Virginia Woolf* (New York: Penguin, 2007); James Hawes, *Why You Should Read Kafka Before You Waste Your Life* (New York: St. Martin's, 2008); Declan Kiberd, *Ulysses and Us: The Art of Everyday Life in Joyce's Masterpiece* (New York: Norton, 2009); Marty Beckerman, *The Hemingway: How to Unleash the Booze-Inhaling, Animal Slaughtering, War-Glorifying, Hairy Chested Retro Sexual Lesson Within* (New York: St. Martin's Griffin, 2011); Alexander McCall Smith, *What W. H. Auden Can Do for You* (Princeton, N.J.: Princeton University Press, 2013) Nina Lorez Collins, *What Would Virginia Woolf Do?* (New York: Grand Central Life & Style, 2018).

3. Theodor Adorno, "Culture Industry Reconsidered," in *The Culture Industry: Selected Essays on Mass Culture*, ed. Jay M. Bernstein (London: Routledge, 1991), 98–107, at 105.

4. Edith Wharton, *Twilight Sleep* (New York: Simon & Schuster, 1997).

5. Sigmund Freud, "Family Romances" [Der Familienroman der Neurotiker], in *The Standard Edition of the Complete Words of Sigmund Freud*, ed. James Strachey

[1908] (London: Hogarth, 1925), 9:237–41; Marthe Roberts, *Origins of the Novel*, trans. Sacha Rabinowitch (Bloomington: Indiana University Press, 1980), 138.

6. Ernst Bloch, "Nonsynchronism and the Obligation to Its Dialectics," trans. Mark Ritter, *New German Critique* 11 (Spring 1977): 22, 27.

7. Macdonald, "Masscult and Midcult." *Masscult and Midcult*, 47.

8. Quoted in Louis Menand, "Browbeaten: Dwight Macdonald's War on Midcult," *The New Yorker*, September 5, 2011, https://www.newyorker.com/magazine/2011/09/05/browbeaten.

9. Macdonald, "Masscult and Midcult," 50, 48, 61.

10. De Botton, *How Proust Can Change Your Life*, 24–25.

11. William K. Wimsatt and Monroe C. Beardsley, "The Intentional Fallacy," *The Verbal Icon: Studies in the Meaning of Poetry* (Lexington: University of Kentucky Press, 1954).

12. Theodor Adorno, "Short Commentaries on Proust," 181; Adorno, "On Proust," *Notes to Literature* 2 (New York: Columbia, 1974): 317.

13. Adorno, "Short Commentaries on Proust," 175.

14. C. S. Lewis and E. M. W. Tillyard, *The Personal Heresy: A Controversy* [1939] (New York: HaperCollins, 2017), 14.

15. Stephen Best and Sharon Marcus, "Surface Reading: An Introduction," *Representations* 108, no. 1 (Fall 2009): 1–21.

16. Pierre Bourdieu, *The Rules of Art, Genesis and Structure of the Literary Field*, trans. Susan Emanuel (Stanford, Calif.: Stanford University Press, 1995).

17. Janice A. Radway, *Reading the Romance: Women, Patriarchy, and Popular Literature* (Chapel Hill: University of North Carolina Press, 1984); Robert Venturi, *Learning from Las Vegas* (Cambridge, Mass.: MIT Press, 1972).

18. Jakob Norberg, "Adorno's Advice: *Minima Moralia* and the Critique of Liberalism," *PMLA* 126, no. 2 (March 2011): 398–411, at 406, 407.

19. Ryan Lizza, quoted in Norberg, "Adorno's Advice," 407.

20. Linsday Baker, "Textual Healing: Self-Help Books Get Smart," *BBC Culture*, October 21, 2014, http://www.bbc.com/culture/story/20140122-self-help-books-textual-healing.

21. Theodor Adorno, "Commitment," in *Notes to Literature*, vol. 2, trans. Shierry Weber Nicholsen (New York: Columbia University Press, 1991), 79.

22. Charles Eliot quoted in Walter B. Kolesnik, *Mental Discipline in Modern Education* (Madison: University of Wisconsin Press, 1958), 20.

23. William Payne quoted in Kolesnik, *Mental Discipline in Modern Education*, 20.

24. Gerald Graff, *Professing Literature: An Institutional History* (Chicago: University of Chicago Press, 1987), 33; Kolesnik, *Mental Discipline in Modern Education*, 4.

25. Kolesnik, *Mental Discipline in Modern Education*, 19.

26. Noah Porter quoted in Graff, *Professing Literature*, 31.

27. Graff, *Professing Literature*, 31, 34; Arnold Bennett, "James Joyce's *Ulysses*," in *The Author's Craft and Other Critical Writings of Arnold Bennett*, ed. Samuel Hynes (Lincoln: University of Nebraska Press, 1968), 211–17, at 215.

28. Kolesnik, *Mental Discipline in Modern Education*, 15, 5.

29. For an interesting discussion of these, see Alan Golding, "Louis Zukofsky and the Avant-Garde Textbook," *Chicago Review* 55, nos. 3–4 (Autumn 2010): 27–36.

30. Paul Valéry quoted in Theodor Adorno, "The Artist as Deputy," in *Notes to Literature*, 1958, vol. 1, 105.

31. See, for example, Maja Djikic and Keith Oatley, "The Art in Fiction: From Indirect Communication to Changes of the Self," *Psychology of Aesthetics, Creativity, and the Arts* 8, no. 4 (2014): 498–505; see also the discussion of *The Great Gatsby* in Melanie C. Green and Timothy C. Brock, "The Role of Transportation in the Persuasiveness of Public Narratives," *Journal of Personality and Social Psychology* 79, no. 5 (2000): 701–21.

32. John Guillory, *Cultural Capital: The Problem of Literary Canon Formation* (Chicago: University of Chicago Press, 1993), 210.

33. Anne Landers, *Daily News*, October 16, 1985.

34. Abigail Van Buren, *The Best of Dear Abby* (Kansas City, Mo.: Andrews McMeel, 1981), 165–166.

35. Merve Emre, *Paraliterary* (Chicago: University of Chicago Press, 2017), 3.

36. For me, "modernist negation" designates the movement's formal and thematic repudiation of paradigms of progress, participation, and integration.

37. One of the first advice columns was John Dunton's *Athenian Mercury* in 1690. In 1704 Daniel Defoe came across Dunton's publication and started an advice column of his own, which eventually became so popular he was forced to make it a separate publication, *The Little Review*. Soon thereafter the advice column crossed the Atlantic, where Benjamin Franklin offered counsel under the guise of different characters in his *Pennsylvania Gazette* (1729). In the early twentieth century, the advice column found an eager audience among Jewish immigrants to the United States, most notably in novelist Abraham Cahan's *Bintel Brief* (1906), which tackled problems pertaining to cultural integration in Manhattan's Lower East Side. But it was chiefly in the writings of Beatrice Fairfax and Dorothy Dix (1802–1887) that the advice column would emerge in the form we recognize today, with its specialization in social and domestic quandaries. These women's columns borrowed some of their popularity from the success of Victorian serialized, epistolary narratives. And the influence went both ways: the Edwardian novelist Arnold Bennett got his start penning a women's advice column under the pseudonym "Gwendolyn." For

more on the origins of the advice column, see W. Clark Hendley, "Dear Abby, *Miss Lonelyhearts*, and the Eighteenth Century: The Origins of the Newspaper Advice Column," *The Journal of Popular Culture* (Fall 1977), https://doi.org/10.1111/j.0022 -3840.1977.00345.x. Despite its title, Hendley's piece does not discuss Abby's references to West's novella.

38. Jacques Derrida, "Force of Law: The 'Mystical Foundation of Authority'," in *Deconstruction and the Possibility of Justice*, ed. Drucilla Cornell, Michel Rosenfeld, and David Gray Carlson (New York: Routledge, 1992), 26.

39. Terry Eagleton, *The Function of Criticism* (London: Verso Press, 1984), 98; Franco Moretti, "The Spell of Indecision," *New Left Review* 1, no. 164 (July–August 1987): 27–33.

40. Jay Martin, *Nathanael West: The Art of His Life* (New York: Farrar, Straus and Giroux, 1970), 110.

41. Marion Meade, *Lonelyhearts: The Screwball World of Nathanael West and Eileen McKenney* (New York: Mariner, 2010), 145.

42. As Goldman notes, with every reference to Miss Lonelyhearts in the third person masculine, a "crisis in gender categorization" comes to the fore. Jane Goldman, '*Miss Lonelyhearts* and the Party Dress': Cross-Dressing and Collage in the Satires of Nathanael West," *Glasgow Review* 2 (1993): 40–54.

   The jarring fact of the female advice column's male authorship is something West exploits from the very first line of *Miss Lonelyhearts*, which reads: "The Miss Lonelyhearts of the New York Post Dispatch (Are-you-in-trouble?—Do-you-need-advice?—Write-to-Miss-Lonelyhearts-and-she-will-help-you) sat at his desk and stared at a piece of white cardboard." Nathanael West, *Miss Lonelyhearts*, in *Nathanael West: Novels and Other Writings* [1933] (New York: Library of America, 1997), 59.

43. T. J. Jackson Lears, "From Salvation to Self-Realization: Advertising and the Therapeutic Roots of the Consumer Culture, 1880–1930," *Advertising and Society Review* 1, no. 1 (2000): 13.

44. Susan Chester, "Never Too Busy," *Brooklyn Daily Times*, February 6, 1929.

45. Erving Goffman, "On Cooling the Mark Out: Some Aspects of Adaptation to Failure," *Psychiatry* 15 (1952): 451–63.

46. West, *Miss Lonelyhearts*, 62.

47. Theodor Adorno, *The Stars Down to Earth* (London: Routledge, 1994), 155.

48. As David Galloway explains, *A Cool Million* shows "that the inevitable outcome of the frustration of the success dream was the growth of Fascism." Nathanael West, *A Cool Million* (London: Neville Spearman, 1954), 119. *A Cool Million* follows the travails of Lemuel Pitkin as he becomes embroiled in an American fascist organization inspired by the self-help philosophy of Benjamin Franklin.

49. John Dewey, "A Sick World," *New Republic* 33 (1923): 217–18.

50. Virginia Woolf, *The Diary of Virginia Woolf*, ed. Anne Olivier Bell (New York: Harcourt Brace Jovanovich, 1977), 263.

51. See Douglas Shepard, "Nathanael West Rewrites Horatio Alger Jr.," *Satire Newsletter* 3 (Fall 1965): 13–28.

52. Susan Chester, "School for You," *Brooklyn Daily Times*, January 17, 1929.

53. Recall the masochism of the Sandow scene in Joyce's "Circe" that I discussed in chapter 4.

54. Susan Chester, "Not a Smarty Type," *Brooklyn Daily Times*, January 31, 1929.

55. Susan Chester, "Response to 'Not a Smarty Type,' " *Brooklyn Daily Times*, January 31, 1929.

56. Adorno, *The Stars Down to Earth*, 163, 164.

57. West, *Miss Lonelyhearts*, 77–78.

58. David Gudelunas, *Confidential to America: Newspaper Advice Columns and Sexual Education* (New Brunswick, N.J.: Transaction, 2008), 23, 206.

59. Rick Kogan, *America's Mom: The Life, Legacy, and Letters of Ann Landers* (New York: Harper Collins, 2003), 73.

60. Evidently, Clarkson also misreads the end of West's story, unless she was misinformed by Landers's written comments about the story during her interview prep.

61. Ann Landers interview with Adrienne Clarkson, "Ann Landers on Take 30," February 14, 1968, CBC digital archives, http://www.cbc.ca/archives/discover/programs/t/take-30/dear-ann-landers.html.

62. West, *Miss Lonelyhearts*, 71.

63. John Day interview with Ann Landers, "Day at Night," February 12, 1974, Paley Center for Media, New York.

64. Gudelunas, *Confidential to America*, 96. However, critics charged that rather than offering access to experts Landers merely supplanted their accredited advice with her own unfounded opinions. Nevertheless, according to her, it was this willingness to consult her many contacts from her political years, including a Supreme Court Justice and the president of Notre Dame University, for their input on readers' problems that landed her the job. According to other accounts, however, it was simply her physical resemblance to the previous Ann Landers, a nurse from Chicago named Ruth Crowley, that got her hired. Although she downplayed the work of her predecessor, the column had already been successful for seven years when Landers took over the Dear Ann mantle in 1955.

65. Van Buren, *The Best of Dear Abby*, 166.

66. Van Buren, *The Best of Dear Abby*, 166.

67. West, *Miss Lonelyhearts*, 84.

68. Van Buren, *The Best of Dear Abby*, 166.

69. Nathanael West, with Boris Ingster, "A Cool Million: A Screen Story," in *Novels and Other Writings*, ed. Sacvan Bercovitch (New York: Library of America, 1997), 745.

70. Max Eastman, *Art and the Life of Action* (London: George Allan & Unwin, 1935), 66.

71. Nathanael West, *Novels and Other Writings* (New York: Library of America, 1997), 794–95.

72. Nathanael West, "Letter to Malcolm Cowley, May 11, 1939," in *Nathanael West: Novels and Other Writings*, 794.

73. Editorial, *Nevada State Journal* [Reno], May 7, 1982, in *Editorials on File* 13, no. 9, 540.

74. Editorial, *The Kansas City Star,* May 6, 1982, in *Editorials on File* 13, no. 9, 540.

75. Editorial, *The Kansas City Star*, May 6, 1982, in *Editorials on File* 13, no. 9, 538.

76. West, *Miss Lonelyhearts*, 63.

77. West, 59.

78. Editorial, *The Kansas City Star*, May 6, 1982, in *Editorials on File* 13, no. 9, 538.

79. Eitorial, *The Sun* [Vancouver, B.C.], May 7, 1982, in *Editorials on File* 13, no. 9, 539.

80. James Litke, Associated Press, "Ann Landers Recycles Old Letters In Advice Column." *The Associated Press*, May 3, 1982, Monday, AM cycle, https://advance-lexis-com .ezp-prod1.hul.harvard.edu/api/document?collection=news&id=urn:contentItem :3SJ4-HH70-0011-53H8-00000-00&context=1516831.

81. Editorial, *The Hartford Courant*, May 6, 1982, in *Editorials on File* 13, no. 9, 540.

81. Cyril Connolly, *Enemies of Promise* (Chicago: University of Chicago Press, 1983), 19.

83. Editorial, *The Sun* [Vancouver, B.C.], May 7, 1982, in *Editorials on File* 13, no. 9, 539.

84. Editorial, *The Virginian-Pilot* [Norfolk, Va.], May 10, 1982, in *Editorials on File* 13, no. 9, 541.

85. West, *Miss Lonelyhearts*, 689.

86. Randy Cohen, "The Ethicist: Stealth Progressive," *New York Times*, December 29, 2002.

87. Cheryl Strayed interview with Jeff Baker, "Portland Author Cheryl Strayed, also Known as Dear Sugar, Writes Personal Stories That Bond with Her Devoted Readers," *The Oregonian*, February 18, 2012.

88. Rita Barnard, "The Storyteller, the Novelist, and the Advice Columnist: Narrative and Mass Culture in 'Miss Lonelyhearts'," *NOVEL: A Forum on Fiction* 27, no. 1 (Autumn 1993): 44.

89. Gudelunas, *Confidential to America*, 158.

90. Gudelunas, 158.

91. Jessica Weisberg, "The Advice Columnist We Deserve," *The New Yorker*, October 9, 2012. https://www.newyorker.com/books/page-turner/the-advice-columnist-we-deserve.

92. William Grimes, "Dear Abby Doesn't Live Here Anymore," *New York Times*, March 30, 1997.

93. Katy Waldman, "The Advice Columnists Who Prescribe Literature as Medicine," *The New Yorker*, March 21, 2018, https://www.newyorker.com/books/page-turner /the-advice-columnists-who-prescribe-literature-as-medicine.

94. For a generative defense of literary consolation that emerged during the late stages of this book's production, see David James, *Discrepant Solace: Contemporary Literature and the Work of Consolation* (Oxford: Oxford University Press, 2019).

95. Theodor Adorno, "Trying to Understand Endgame," *New German Critique* 26 (Spring–Summer 1982): 119–50.

96. Ned Beauman, "Fail Worse," *The New Inquiry*, February 9, 2012, http://thenewinquiry .com/essays/fail-worse/; Mark O'Connel, "The Stunning Success of Fail Better," *Slate*, January 29, 2014, http://www.slate.com/articles/arts/culturebox/2014/01 /samuel_beckett_s_quote_fail_better_becomes_the_mantra_of_silicon_valley .html.

97. Timothy Ferriss, *The 4-Hour Workweek* (New York: Crown, 2009), 56.

98. See, for instance, Roger Fisher, *Getting to Yes: How to Negotiate Agreement Without Giving In* (New York: Penguin Press, 1981).

99. Richard Seaver, introduction to *I Can't Go On, I'll Go On: A Samuel Beckett Reader*, ed. Richard W. Seaver (New York: Grove, 1976), 352.

100. Blurb on Ferriss, *The 4-Hour Workweek*.

101. Theodor Adorno, *Aesthetic Theory* (London: Routledge & Kegen Paul, 1984), 1.

102. James Joyce, *Dubliners* (New York: Signet Classic, 1991).

103. Charles Kingsley, *Westword Ho!* (London: Macmillan, 1894), 16; quoted in James Eli Adams, *Dandies and Desert Saints: Styles of Victorian Masculinity* (Ithaca, N.Y.: Cornell University Press, 1995),7.

104. Joseph Valente, *The Myth of Manliness in Irish National Culture, 1880–1922* (Chicago: University of Illinois Press, 2011), 1.

105. Samuel Beckett, *Worstward Ho* (London: John Calder, 1983), 45.

106. Samuel Beckett, "Dante . . . Bruno. Vico. Joyce," in *A Samuel Beckett Reader* (New York: Grove, 1976), 117.

107. Pierre Bourdieu, *The Field of Cultural Production* (New York: Columbia University Press, 1993), 169.

108. Declan Kiberd, "Samuel Beckett and the Protestant Ethic," in *The Genius of Irish Prose*, ed. Augustine Martin (Dublin and Cork: Mercier, 1984), 123.

109. Dante, *Purgatorio*, trans. Allen Mandlebaum (Toronto: Bantam, 1982), Canto IV, 123.

110. Samuel Beckett, *The Unnamable* (New York: Grove, 1958), 314.

111. Samuel Beckett, *Murphy* (New York: Grove, 1957), 67.

112. Lawrence O'Donnel quoted in Francis Mulraney, "Lawrence O'Donnell Comments on Irish Culture's Failure to Accept Success," *Irish Times*, November 23, 2017, www .irishcentral.com/culture/entertainment/lawrence-odonnell-marc-maron-boston -irish.

113. Oscar Wilde, quoted in *The Life of Oscar Wilde* (Boston: Aldine, 1910), 181.

114. John Mitchel, *Jail Journal, or Five Years in British Prisons* (New York: Office of the "Citizen," 1854).

115. Brian Friel, *Translations* (New York: Farrar, Straus and Giroux, 1995); Eavan Boland, "That the Science of Cartography Is Limited," *In a Time of Violence* (New York/London: Norton & Company, 1994), 7.

116. Stephen Brown, "Fail Better! Samuel Beckett's Secrets of Business and Branding Success," *Business Horizons* 49, no. 2 (2006): 161–69.

117. Brown, "Fail Better!," 168.

118. Gregory Dobbins, *Lazy Idle Schemers: Irish Modernism and the Cultural Politics of Idleness* (Dublin: Field Day, 2010), 5.

119. Samuel Beckett, *Waiting for Godot* (Grove: New York, 1954), 51, 10, 8, 12.

120. Beckett, *Waiting for Godot*, 39.

121. Émile Coué, *Self-Mastery Through Conscious Autosuggestion*, trans. Archibald Stark Van Orden (New York: Malkan, 1922), 8; Samuel Beckett, *Happy Days* (New York: Grove, 1961), 11, 52, 24.

122. Beckett, *Waiting for Godot*, 25, 24.

123. Beckett, *Waiting for Godot*, 25; Benjamin Franklin, The Works of Benjamin Franklin, vol. 2, ed. John Bigelow (New York & London: G.P. Putnam's Sons, 1904) 29; Beckett, *Waiting for Godot*, 20.

124. Margaret Atwood, *Oryx and Crake* (New York: Anchor, 2004), 245.

125. *The Handmaid's Tale*, season, 1, episode 5, "Faithful," Hulu, May 10, 2017.

126. Megan Hunter, *The End We Start From* (New York: Grove, 2017), 84, 36.

127. Walker Percy, *Lost in the Cosmos: The Last Self-Help Book Ever Written* (New York: Noonday, 1983), 87.

128. Beckett, *Waiting for Godot*, 37–38.

129. Samuel Beckett, *Krapp's Last Tape and Other Dramatic Pieces* (New York: Grove, 1957), 21.

130. Samuel Beckett, *Molloy* (New York: Grove, 1955), 41.

131. William H. McGuffey, "Try, Try Again," in *McGuffey's New Fourth Eclectic Reader: Instructive Lessons for the Young* (New York: Wilson, Hinkle, 1856), 95.

132. Jerzy Kosinski, *Being There* (New York: Grove, 1970); *Forrest Gump*, directed by Robert Zemeckis (Paramount Pictures, 1994).

133. Quoted in John Guillory, *Cultural Capital: The Problem of Literary Canon Formation* (Chicago: University of Chicago Press, 1993), 185.

134. Lionel Trilling, *Sincerity and Authenticity* (Cambridge: Harvard University Press, 1972), 135.

6. PRACTICALITY HUNGER

1. "The Market for Self-Improvement Products & Services," 12th ed., Marketdata Enterprises, 2018, https://www.marketdataenterprises.com/studies/#SELFIMPROVEMENT.

2. See Gerry Smith, "Trump Turmoil Gives Much-Needed Jolt to Book Publishing Business," *Bloomberg News*, September 27, 2018, https://www.bloomberg.com/news/articles/2018-09-27/trump-turmoil-gives-much-needed-jolt-to-book-publishing-business; Robert Walker, "Stressed Britons Buy Record Number of Self-Help Books," *The Guardian*, March 9, 2019, https://www.theguardian.com/books/2019/mar/09/self-help-books-sstressed-brits-buy-record-number.

3. Paul Sweetman quoted in Walker, "Stressed Britons Buy Record Number of Self-Help Books."

4. Stendhal, *De L'Amour* (Paris: Classiques Garnier, 1959), 41.

5. Mohsin Hamid quoted in Bryan Appleyard, "He's Seen Our Future," *The Sunday Times*, March 17, 2013.

6. Mohsin Hamid, *How to Get Filthy Rich in Rising Asia* (New York: Riverhead, 2013), 20, 19.

7. Mohsin Hamid, interview by Alison Cuddy, Chicago Humanities Festival, March 11, 2014, https://www.youtube.com/watch?v=0EaIkSNAsWU.

8. Mohsin Hamid, "Mohsin Hamid: 'I Think the Personal Is Political and the Political Is Personal,'" interview by Sophie Elmhirst, *New Statesman*, April 12, 2013, https://www.newstatesman.com/culture/culture/2013/04/mohsin-hamid-i-think-personal-political-and-political-personal.

9. Angelia Poon, "Helping the Novel: Neoliberalism, Self-Help, and the Narrating of the Self in Mohsin Hamid's *How to Get Filthy Rich in Rising Asia*," *The Journal of Commonwealth Literature* 52, no. 1 (2015): 2.

10. Rita Felski, *The Gender of Modernity* (Cambridge, Mass.: Harvard University Press, 1995), 83.

11. Sheila Heti, "How Should a Novel Be? Don't Ask Sheila Heti," interview by John Barber, *Globe and Mail*, April 13, 2013, https://www.theglobeandmail.com/arts/books-and-media/book-reviews/how-should-a-novel-be-dont-ask-sheila-heti/article11134050/.

12. Mohsin Hamid, "Mohsin Hamid Comes Home to Roost in Pakistan," interview by Reed Johnson, *Los Angeles Times*, March 14, 2013, http://articles.latimes.com/2013/mar/14/entertainment/la-et-jc-mohsin-hamid-20130314.

13. Hamid, *How to Get Filthy Rich*, 97, 77.

14. Sheila Heti, "How Should a Person Be? Talking to Sheila Heti," interview by Adam Robinson, *BOMB*, June 11, 2012, https://bombmagazine.org/articles/how-should-a-person-be-talking-to-sheila-heti/.

15. Eleanor Davis, "Talking Comics With Tim: Eleanor Davis on How to Be Happy," interview by Tim O'Shea, *CBR.com*, June 30, 2014, https://www.cbr.com/talking-comics-with-tim-eleanor-davis-on-how-to-be-happy/; Sheila Heti, "Sheila Heti on *Girls*, Self-Help Books, and Why We Do Drugs," interview by Shona Sanzgirl, *San Francisco Weekly*, June 22, 2012, https://archives.sfweekly.com/exhibitionist/2012/06/22/interview-sheila-heti-on-girls-self-help-books-and-why-we-do-drugs.

16. Sheila Heti, "Sheila Heti on Her Novel, *How Should a Person Be?*", interview by Henry Giardina, *Bullett*, June 20, 2012, http://bullettmedia.com/article/sheila-heti/.

17. Sheila Heti, "Interview with Sheila Heti," interview by Madeleine Schwartz, *The Harvard Advocate* (Spring 2011), http://theharvardadvocate.com/article/205/interview-with-sheila-heti/.

18. Sheila Heti, *How Should a Person Be?* (New York: Picador, 2012), 4, 17, 228.

19. Heti, *How Should a Person Be?*, 189.

20. Heti, *How Should a Person Be?*, 190, 190–91.

21. Judith Hilkey, *Character Is Capital: Success Manuals and Manhood in Gilded Age America* (Chapel Hill: University of North Carolina Press, 1997), 34–38.

22. Chris Waddington, "Rule-Breaking Novelist Sheila Heti Will Discuss 'How Should a Person Be?' in New Orleans," *The Times Picayune*, June 25, 2013, http://www.nola.com/books/index.ssf/2013/06/rule-breaking_novelist_sheila.html.

23. Edward Said, "How Not to Get Gored," review of *The Dangerous Summer*, by Ernest Hemingway, *The London Review of Books*, November 21, 1985, https://www.lrb.co.uk/v07/n20/edward-said/how-not-to-get-gored.

24. Christopher Lasch, *The Culture of Narcissism* (New York: Norton, 1991), 5.

25. Pierre Hadot, *Philosophy as a Way of Life* (Malden, Mass.: Blackwell, 1995), 69.

26. Heti, *How Should a Person Be?*, 274.

27. Hamid, *How to Get Filthy Rich*, 195; Mohsin Hamid, *The Reluctant Fundamentalist* (San Diego, Calif.: Harcourt, 2007).

28. James Wood, "True Lives: Sheila Heti's 'How Should a Person Be?' " review of *How Should a Person Be?*, by Sheila Heti, *The New Yorker*, June 25, 2012, https://www.newyorker.com/magazine/2012/06/25/true-lives-2.

29. Pankaj Mishra, "Asia: 'The Explosive Transformation,'" review of *How to Get Filthy Rich in Rising Asia*, by Mohsin Hamid, *The New York Review of Books*, April 25, 2013, http://www.nybooks.com/articles/2013/04/25/asia-explosive-transformation/.

30. Beatrice Fairfax quoted in David Gudelunas, *Confidential to America: Newspaper Advice Columns and Sexual Education* (Piscataway, N.J.: Transaction, 2008), 40.

31. Pierre Bourdieu, *Distinction: A Social Critique of the Judgment of Taste* (Cambridge, Mass: Harvard University Press, 1984), 44.

32. Mark Manson, *The Subtle Art of Not Giving a Fuck* (New York: HarperOne, 2016); Sarah Knight, *Get Your Shit Together: How to Stop Worrying About What You Should Do So You Can Finish What You Need to Do and Start Doing What You Want to Do* (New York: Little, Brown, 2016); Luvvie Ajayi, *I'm Judging You: the Do-Better Manual* (New York: Henry Holt, 2016); Sarah Knight, *The Life-Changing Magic of Not Giving a Fuck: How to Stop Spending Time You Don't Have with People You Don't Like Doing Things You Don't Want to Do* (New York: Little, Brown, 2015); Michael Bennett and Sarah Bennett, *Fuck Feelings: One Shrink's Practical Advice for Managing All Life's Impossible Problems* (New York: Simon & Schuster, 2015); Derek Doepker, *Break Through Your BS: Uncover Your Brain's Blind Spots and Unleash Your Inner Greatness* (self-pub., ExcuseProof.com, 2015); Jen Sincero, *You Are a Badass: How to Stop Doubting Your Greatness and Start Living an Awesome Life* (Philadelphia: Running Press, 2013); Gary John Bishop, *Unfuck Yourself: Get Out of Your Head and Into Your Life* (New York: HarperOne, 2017). Some of these books even have their own imprint, advertised as "A No F*cks given guide."

33. *Tony Robbins: I Am Not Your Guru*, directed by Joe Berlinger, July 15, 2016, Netflix, https://www.netflix.com/title/80102204.

34. Mark Manson, "Mark Marson: Author. Thinker. Life Enthusiast," accessed July 20, 2018, Infinity Squared Media LLC, markmanson.net.

35. Promotional blurb for Rachel Hoffman, *Unf*ck Your Habitat: You're Better Than Your Mess*, https://www.amazon.com/Unf-Your-Habitat-Youre-Better/dp/1250102952.

36. Blurb for Eva Hoffman, *How to Be Bored (The School of Life)* (London: Macmillan, 2016).

37. Manson, *The Subtle Art of Not Giving a Fuck*, 4.

38. Knight, *The Life-Changing Magic of Not Giving a Fuck*, 35.

39. Manson, *The Subtle Art of Not Giving a Fuck*, 19.

40. Svend Brinkmann, *Stand Firm: Resisting the Self-Improvement Craze* (Cambridge: Polity, 2017), 86.

41. Compare with John Parkin, *Fuck It Therapy: The Profane Way to Profound Happiness* (London: Hay House, 2015); Jen Sincero, *You Are a Badass: How to Stop Doubting Your Greatness and Start Living an Awesome Life* (Philadelphia: Running Press,

2013); Carl Alasko, *Beyond Blame: Freeing Yourself from the Most Toxic Emotional Bullsh*t* (New York: Jeremy P. Tarcher/Penguin, 2011).

42. Quoted in Sandra Tsing Loh, "Don't Do It: The Simple Solution to Clearing the To-Do List," *New York Times*, March 28, 2017.

43. Christy Wampole, "How to Live Without Irony," *New York Times* (blog), November 17, 2012, opinionator.blogs.nytimes.com/2012/11/17/how-to-live-without-irony/?mcubz =1&_r=0.

44. Benjamin Schreier, *The Power of Negative Thinking: Cynicism and the History of American Literature* (Charlottesville: University of Virginia Press, 2009); Simon Critchley, *How to Stop Living and Start Worrying* (Boston: Polity, 2010).

45. Samuel Smiles, "Preface," *Self-Help: With Illustrations of Character, Conduct, and Perseverance* (New York: Harper & Brothers, 1877), v–vi.; Carnegie, *How to Win Friends*, 37.

46. David Shields, *Reality Hunger: A Manifesto* (New York: Vintage, 2010).

47. As described by Luc Sante, "The Fiction of Memory," review of *Reality Hunger: A Manifesto*, by David Shields, *New York Times*, March 14, 2010, https://www.nytimes .com/2010/03/14/books/review/Sante-t.html.

48. David Shields, *How Literature Saved My Life* (New York: Random House, 2013).

49. R. Kamtekar, "Marcus Aurelius," in *Stanford Encyclopedia of Philosophy*, last modi-fied December 22, 2017, https://plato.stanford.edu/entries/marcus-aurelius/.

50. Seneca, quoted in Michel Foucault, *The Hermeneutics of the Subject: Lectures at the Collège de France 1981-1982*, trans. Graham Burchell (New York: Picador, 2005), 162.

51. Kamtekar, "Marcus Aurelius."

52. Foucault, *The Hermeneutics of the Subject*, 305.

53. Gertrude E. M. Anscombe, *Intention*, 2nd ed. (Ithaca, N.Y.: Cornell University Press, 1969), 11.

54. Epictetus *Discourses*, trans. W. A. Oldfather (Edinburgh: Loeb Classical Library, 1928), 3.8.1–5.

55. Oliver Burkeman, *The Antidote: Happiness for People Who Can't Stand Positive Thinking* (New York: Farrar, Straus and Giroux, 2012), 208.

56. Tim Ferriss, "Why You Should Define Your Fears Instead of Your Goals," TED Talk, April 2017, https://www.ted.com/talks/tim_ferriss_why_you_should_define _your_fears_instead_of_your_goals.

57. Hugh Kenner, *Flaubert, Joyce, and Beckett: The Stoic Comedians* (Normal, Ill.: Dalkey Archive, 2005), xii.

58. Theodor Adorno, *Negative Dialectics* (New York: Seabury, 1979). 381.

59. Henry James, "The Works of Epictetus," *Literary Criticism: Essays on Literature, American Writers, English Writers* (New York: Library of America, 1984), 10, 13.

60. Manson, *The Subtle Art of Not Giving a Fuck*.

61. Hamid, *How to Get Filthy Rich*, 222.

62. Amy Appleford, *Learning to Die in London, 1380–1540* (Philadelphia: University of Pennsylvania Press, 2015), 105.

63. Alice Bennett, *Afterlife and Narrative in Contemporary Fiction* (Basingstoke, UK: Palgrave Macmillan, 2012), 31.

64. Foucault, *The Hermeneutics of the Subject*, 504.

65. Walter Benjamin, "The Storyteller," in *Illuminations* (New York: Schocken Books, 1969), 83–107.

66. Benjamin, "The Storyteller," 89.

67. Hamid, *How to Get Filthy Rich*, 160.

68. Junot Díaz, "How to Date a Browngirl, Blackgirl, Whitegirl, or Halfie," chap. 8 in *Drown* (New York: Riverhead, 1997), 139–49; Dany Laferrière, *How to Make Love to a Negro Without Getting Tired*, trans. David Homel (Vancouver, B.C.: Douglas & McIntyre, 1989); Pam Houston, "How to Talk to a Hunter," in *The Best American Short Stories 1990*, ed. Richard Ford and Shannon Ravenel (Boston: Houghton Mifflin, 1990), 98–104; Lorrie Moore, *Self-Help* (New York: Vintage Contemporaries, 1985); Jay McInerney, *Bright Lights, Big City* (New York: Vintage, 1984). This American fiction followed the European second-person experiments of authors such as Italo Calvino and Georges Perec.

69. F. Scott Fitzgerald, *The Great Gatsby* [1925] (New York: Scribner, 2004), 1.

70. Friedrich Nietzsche quoted in Harold Bloom, *The Victorian Novel* (New York: Chelsea House, 2004), 8.

71. Diaz, "How to Date a Browngirl," 145, 149.

72. Henri Bergson, *Laughter: An Essay on the Meaning of the Comic*, trans. Cloudesly Brereton and Fred Rothwell (Mineola, N.Y.: Dover, 2005).

73. David Palumbo-Lui, *Asian/American: Historical Crossings of a Racial Frontier*. (Stanford, Calif.: Stanford University Press, 1995), 399.

74. Eleanor Ty, *Asianfail: Narratives of Disenchantment and the Model Minority* (Urbana: University of Illinois Press, 2017), 10, 16, 10.

75. Alexander Chee, *How to Write an Autobiographical Novel: Essays* (Boston: Mariner, 2018); Anelise Chen, *So Many Olympic Exertions* (Los Angeles: Kaya, 2017); Charles Yu, *How to Live Safely in a Science Fictional Universe: A Novel* (New York: Vintage, 2010), 37.

76. Yu, *How to Live Safely in a Science Fictional Universe*, 111.

77. Dale Carnegie, *How to Win Friends and Influence People* (New York: Simon & Schuster, 1936), 12.

78. Foucault, *The Hermeneutics of the Subject*, 95.

79. Charles Yu, *How to Live Safely in a Science Fictional Universe: A Novel* (New York: Vintage, 2010), 115, 125.

80. Lorrie Moore, "How to Be an Other Woman," in *Self-Help: Stories* (New York: Knopf, 1985), 17; Yu, *How to Live Safely in a Science Fictional Universe*, 144.

81. Yu, *How to Live Safely in a Science Fictional Universe*, 148.

82. Yu, 54.

83. Yu, 152–53.

84. Eleanor Ty, *Asianfail*, 16.

85. Ty, *Asianfail*, 16.

86. Terrance Hayes, *How to Be Drawn* (New York: Penguin, 2015); Baratunde Thurston, *How to Be Black* (New York: HarperCollins, 2012).

87. Henry Davenport Northrop, Joseph R. Gray, and I. Garland Penn, *The College of Life or Practical Self-Educator: A Manual of Improvement for the Colored Race* (Washington, D.C., 1895).

88. Henry A. Giroux, *The Abandoned Generation: Democracy Beyond the Culture of Fear* (New York: Palgrave MacMillan, 2003), 123; 124.

89. Gwendolyn Brooks, *Primer for Blacks* (Chicago: Black Position, 1980); 50 Cent and Robert Greene, *The 50th Law* (New York: G-Unit, 2009); DJ Khaled, *The Keys* (New York: Crown Archetype, 2016).

90. Thurston, *How to Be Black*, 166, 163.

91. Thurston, 150–51.

92. Thurston, 226, 224.

93. Hayes, *How to Be Drawn*, 8–9.

94. D. L. Hughley and Doug Moe, *How Not to Get Shot: And Other Advice from White People* (New York: Harper Collins, 2018).

95. Ali Smith, "Ali Smith: 'There Are Two Ways to Read This Novel, But You're Stuck With It—You'll End Up Reading One of Them,'" interview by Alex Clark, *The Guardian*, September 6, 2014, https://www.theguardian.com/books/2014/sep/06 /ali-smith-interview-how-to-be-both.

96. Ali Smith, *How to Be Both* (New York: Anchor, 2014), 134–35.

97. Philip Weinstein, *Unknowing: The Work of Modernist Fiction* (Ithaca, N.Y.: Cornell University Press, 2005), 2.

98. Beth Blum, "Therapeutic Redescripton," in *Literature and Human Flourishing*, ed. James English and Heather Love, forthcoming.

99. Lev Grossman, "Literary Revolution in the Supermarket Aisle: Genre Fiction Is Disruptive Technology," *Time*, May 23, 2012, http://entertainment.time.com/2012/05/23 /genre-fiction-is-disruptive-technology/; quoted in Günter Leypoldt's discussion of the rising prestige of genre fiction, "Social Dimensions of the Turn to Genre: Junot

Diaz's Oscar Wao and Kazuo Ishiguro's The Buried Giant," http://post45.research.yale.edu/2018/03/social-dimensions-of-the-turn-to-genre-junot-diazs-oscar-wao-and-kazuo-ishiguros-the-buried-giant/.

100. Wendy Simonds, *Women and Self-Help Culture*, 47.

101. G. Thomas Couser, *Memoir: An Introduction* (Oxford: Oxford University Press, 2012); quoted in Stephanie Burt, "Literary Style and the Lessons of Memoir," *The New Yorker*, July 26, 2017, https://www.newyorker.com/books/page-turner/literary-style-and-the-lessons-of-memoir.

102. Kenneth Burke, "Literature as Equipment for Living," in *The Philosophy of Literary Form: Studies in Symbolic Action* (Berkeley: University of California Press, 1941), 293–304, at 299.

103. *O.E.D.* definition of "advice," quoted in Miriam Locher, *Advice Online: Advice Giving in an American Internet Health Column* (Amsterdam: John Benjamins, 2006), 3.

CODA: THE SHADOW UNIVERSITY OF SELF-HELP

1. Dale Carnegie, *How to Win Friends and Influence People*, (New York: Simon & Schuster, 1936), 13, 14.

2. Douglas Kellner, introduction to *Media/Cultural Studies: Critical Approaches*, ed. Rhonda Hammer and Douglas Kellner (New York: Peter Lang, 2009), 6.

3. Thomas Carlyle, *Sartor Resartus* (1833–1834; repr. New York: Oxford University Press, 2008), 85–88.

4. Samuel Smiles, "The Education of the Working Classes" reprinted in *The Northern Star*, 8, no. 404 (August 9, 1845), 3.

5. Sandra K. Dolby, *Self-Help Books: Why Americans Keep Reading Them* (Urbana: University of Illinois Press, 2005), 26.

6. Og Mandino, *University of Success* [1980] (New York: Bantam, 1983).

7. Helen Schucman, "How it Came Into Being," *A Course in Miracles* (1977), accessed July 31, 2019, https://acim.org/acim/how-it-came-into-being/.

8. Acacia C. Parks, "The State of Positive Psychology in Higher Education: Introduction to the Special Issue," *The Journal of Positive Psychology* 6, no. 6 (November 2011): 429.

9. Micki McGee, *Self-Help, Inc.: Makeover Culture in American Life* (New York: Oxford University Press, 2005), 29.

10. Henry A. Giroux, "Higher Education Under Attack: An Interview with Henry A. Giroux," interview by C. Cryn Johannsen, *Truthout*, April 22, 2011, http://www.truth-out.org/news/item/633:higher-education-under-attack-an-interview-with-henry-a-giroux.

11. Laurence Veysey, *The Emergence of the American University* (Chicago: University of Chicago Press, 2007), 66.

12. Alain de Botton, "Can Tolstoy Save Your Marriage?" *Wall Street Journal*, December 18, 2010, https://www.wsj.com/articles/SB10001424052748704828104576021713651690094.

13. Alain de Botton and John Armstrong, *Art as Therapy* (London: Phaidon Press, 2013), 11.

14. Tal Ben-Shahar, introduction to *Happier: Learn the Secrets to Daily Joy and Lasting Fulfillment* (New York: McGraw-Hill, 2007), x–xi.

15. Tal Ben-Shahar, *Even Happier: A Gratitude Journal for Daily Joy and Lasting Fulfillment* (New York: McGraw-Hill, 2010), xi.

16. David Shimer, "Yale's Most Popular Class Ever: Happiness," *New York Times*, January 26, 2018, https://www.nytimes.com/2018/01/26/nyregion/at-yale-class-on-happiness-draws-huge-crowd-laurie-santos.html.

17. D. T. Max, "Happiness 101," *New York Times Magazine*, January 7, 2007, https://www.nytimes.com/2007/01/07/magazine/07happiness.t.html.

18. Colleen Flaherty, "Kicking the Habits," *Inside Higher Ed*, December 19, 2016, https://www.insidehighered.com/news/2016/12/19/alamo-colleges-drop-required-7-habits-course-reaccreditation-risk.

19. Maggie Berg and Barbara Seeber, *The Slow Professor: Challenging the Culture of Speed in the Academy* (Toronto: University of Toronto Press, 2016), 13.

20. See Joseph F. Kett, *The Pursuit of Knowledge Under Difficulties: From Self-Improvement to Adult Education in America, 1750–1990* (Stanford, Calif.: Stanford University Press, 1994), xviii.

21. Eduard C. Lindeman quoted in Kett, *The Pursuit of Knowledge Under Difficulties*, 442.

22. Rita Felski, "Context Stinks!", *New Literary History* 42, no. 4 (Autumn 2011): 573–91; Eric Hayot, "Against Periodization, or On Institutional Time," *New Literary History* 42, no. 4 (Autumn 2011): 2–3.

23. Edward S. Said, *Representations of the Intellectual* (London: Vintage, 1994), 61–62.

24. Tim Lacy, *The Dream of a Democratic Culture: Mortimer J. Adler and the Great Books Idea* (New York: Palgrave MacMillan, 2013), 30, 87.

25. Dwight Macdonald quoted in Lacy, *The Dream of a Democratic Culture*, 141.

26. Mortimer Adler and Charles Van Doren, *How to Read a Book: The Classic Guide to Intelligent Reading* (New York: Simon & Schuster, 1940), 205–7.

27. Adler and Van Doren, *How to Read a Book*, 213–14.

28. Ivor A. Richards, *How to Read a Page* (Boston: Beacon, 1941), 22.

29. Paul Fry, "I. A. Richards," in *The Cambridge History of Literary Criticism*, ed. A. Walton Litz, Louis Menand, and Lawrence Rainey (Cambridge: Cambridge University Press, 2000), 179–99, at 190.

30. I. A. Richards quoted in David Bartholomae, "The Reading of Reading: I. A. Richards and M. J. Adler," in *Writing on the Margins: Essays on Composition and Teaching* (New York: Palgrave Macmillan, 2005), 218.

31. Richards, *How to Read a Page*, 15.

32. Gerald Graff, *Professing Literature: An Institutional History* (Chicago: University of Chicago Press, 1989), 150; Joseph North, *Literary Criticism: A Concise Political History* (Cambridge, Mass.: Harvard University Press, 2017), 29.

33. Lisa Ruddick, "When Nothing Is Cool," *The Point Magazine* 10 (2015), https://thepointmag.com/2015/criticism/when-nothing-is-cool.

34. David Wayne Thomas, *Cultivating Victorians: Liberal Culture and the Aesthetic* (Philadelphia: University of Pennsylvania Press, 2004), 6.

35. Rita Felski, *The Uses of Literature* (Malden, Mass.: Blackwell, 2008), 7.

36. David Armitage and Joe Guldi, "Bonfire of the Humanities," *Aeon Ideas*, October 20, 2014, https://aeon.co/essays/the-role-of-history-in-a-society-afflicted-by-short-termism.

37. Michel Foucault, *Technologies of the Self: A Seminar with Michel Foucault* (Amherst: University of Massachusetts Press, 1988).

38. Kevin Lamb, "Foucault's Aestheticism," *Diacritics* 35, no. 2 (Summer 2005): 53.

39. Michel Foucault, *Hermeneutics of the Subject: Lectures at the Collège de France 1981–82*, ed. Frédéric Gros, trans. Graham Burchell (New York: Palgrave Macmillan, 2005), 242. On this last point, it is interesting to consider Pierre Hadot's critique of the self-centeredness of Foucault's concept of ancient spiritual exercises, which Hadot reminds us were ultimately oriented toward the transcendence of the self not its affirmation. Pierre Hadot, "Reflections on the Cultivation of the Self," in *Philosophy as a Way of Life*, trans. Michael Chase (Malden, Mass.: Blackwell, 1995), 206–13.

40. Michel Foucault interview by Hubert L. Dreyfus and Paul Rabinow, "How We Behave: Sex, Food, and Other Ethical Matters," *Vanity Fair* 46, no. 9 (1983), 60–69.

41. Sedgwick describes the influence of Foucault's "care of the self" on her theory of repair in Eve Sedgwick, *Touching Feeling: Affect, Performativity, Pedagogy* (Durham, N.C.: Duke University Press, 2003), 137.

42. Amanda Anderson, "Therapeutic Criticism," *Novel* 50, no. 3 (November 2017): 321–28.

43. Rachel Buurma and Laura Heffernan, *The Teaching Archive* (Chicago: University of Chicago Press, 2019).

44. Ruddick, "When Nothing Is Cool"; North, *Literary Criticism*, 170, 7.

45. North, *Literary Criticism*, 6.

46. F. R. Leavis, *The Great Tradition* (New York: New York University Press, 1964), 9.

47. René Wellek, "The Literary Criticism of Frank Raymond Leavis," in *Literary Views: Critical and Historical* (Chicago: University of Chicago Press, 1964), 190.

48. Pierre Bourdieu, *The Rules of Art: Genesis and Structure of the Literary Field*, trans. Susan Emanuel (Stanford, Calif.: Stanford University Press, 1996), 321.

49. See Hayot's argument that the humanities need to amp up their claims about life relevance and usefulness. Eric Hayot, "The Sky Is Falling," *MLA Profession*, May 2018, https://profession.mla.hcommons.org/2018/05/21/the-sky-is-falling/.

50. Andrew Goldstone, *Fictions of Autonomy: Modernism from Wilde to de Man* (New York: Oxford University Press, 2013), 3, 6.

51. Pierre Bourdieu, *Distinction* (New York: Routledge, 1984); Arnold Bennett, *Literary Taste: How to Form It* (New York: George H. Doran, 1909); Roland Barthes, "The Death of the Author," in *The Book History Reader*, ed. David Finkelstein (New York: Routledge, 2002), 277–280; Samuel Smiles, *Self-Help: With Illustrations of Character and Conduct* (London: Ward Lock, 1850), xi.

52. D. T. Max, "Happiness 101,"*New York Times*, January 7, 2007.

53. Steve Salerno, *SHAM: How the Self-Help Movement Made America Helpless* (New York: Crown, 2005), 12.

54. Narcross quoted in Maia Szalavitz, "How to Protect Yourself Against Bad Self-Help," *Scientific American*, July 1, 2014, www.scientificamerican.com/article/how-to-protect-yourself-against-bad-self-help/.

55. See Joanne V. Wood, W. Q. Elaine Perunovic, and John W. Lee, "Positive Self-Statements: Power for Some, Peril for Others," *Psychological Science* 20, no. 7 (2009): 860–66, http://journals.sagepub.com/doi/abs/10.1111/j.1467-9280.2009.02370.x.

56. For instance, Aarthi Vadde and Melanie Micir "Obliterature: Towards an Amateur Criticism," *Modernism/Modernity* 25, no. 3 (September 2018): 517–49; Merve Emre, *Paraliterary: The Making of Bad Readers in Postwar America* (Chicago: University of Chicago Press, 2017); Rita Felski, *The Uses of Literature* (Malden, Mass.: Blackwell, 2008); Leah Price, *What We Talk About When We Talk About Books* (New York: Basic Books, 2019).

57. Rita Felski, *The Limits of Critique* (Chicago: University of Chicago Press, 2015); Carnegie, *How to Win Friends and Influence People*, 42.

58. See "Summer Stipends," National Endowment for the Humanities (webpage), accessed July 14, 2019, https://www.neh.gov/grants/research/summer-stipends.

59. For some recent examples, see Jordan Peterson, *12 Rules for Life: An Antidote to Chaos* (Toronto: Random House Canada, 2018); Steven Pinker, *Enlightenment Now* (New York: Viking, 2018); James E. Ryan, *Wait, What?: And Life's Other Essential Questions* (San Francisco: HarperOne, 2017).

60. Elaine Scarry, "The Intimate Life of Violence," interview by Brad Evans, *Los Angeles Review of Books*, December 4, 2017.

61. Tony Robbins, promotional pamphlet, accessed July 14, 2019, https://cdnwp
.tonyrobbins.com/wp-content/uploads/2018/04/29521380-MU-Brochure_NB.pdf.

62. Werner Hofmann, *Caricature: From Leonardo to Picasso* (New York: Crown, 1957), 11.

63. Charles Baudelaire, *The Essence of Laughter*, trans. Gerard Hopkins (New York:
Meridian Books, 1956), 110.

64. J. Morreall, "Philosophy of Humor," in *Stanford Encyclopedia of Philosophy* (online),
2012, https://plato.stanford.edu/entries/humor/.

65. Baudelaire, *The Essence of Laughter*, 111.

66. Carl Cederström and André Spicer, quoted in Steven Poole, "*Desperately Seeking Self-
Improvement* Review: How can I be a better person?" *The Guardian*. November 8
2017, https://www.theguardian.com/books/2017/nov/08/desperately-seeking-self
-improvement-review-by-carl-cederstrom-and-andre-spicer.

67. Wendy Simonds, *Women and Self-Help Culture* (New Brunswick, N.J.: Rutgers
University Press, 1992), 215.

68. Patricia Neville, "Helping Self-Help Books: Working Towards a New Research
Agenda," *Interactions Studies in Communications and Culture* 3, no. 3 (2012): 361–79.

INDEX

Abani, Chris, 32, 60
Achebe, Chinua, 40, 55–56, 57
Adams, James Eli, 201
Adler, Mortimer, 22, 36, 247, 248–51, 256
Adorno, Theodor, 30, 32, 39, 128, 142, 183;
    on advice columns, 138, 186–87, 188,
    199; *Aesthetic Theory*, 200; on Beckett,
    199, 200, 225; on culture industry,
    176–77; on do-it-yourself spirit, 91–92,
    181; on instrumentalism, 175, 177, 182,
    199; *Minima Moralia*, 108, 181; on
    Proust, 39, 175, 176, 178–81, 183, 251; on
    "pseudo-activity," 82, 91–92
advice columns, 185–97, 218; early history
    of, 302n37
African Americans and self-help, 31–32,
    234–36
agency, 7, 8, 33, 80, 131, 142, 229, 236,
    244, 256
Alcott, William A., 11
Aimé-Martin, Louis, 46
Alger, Horatio, 50, 144, 187, 193, 264n38
Alleine, Joseph, 9–10
Amazon.com, 25, 47
Amis, Martin, 166
Anderson, Amanda, 80, 253

Anderson, Margaret, 122–23
anhedonia, 140
Anne, Jessica, 104, 106
anti-self-help movement, 33, 104, 109–10,
    125–26, 220
Argov, Sherry, 71, 75
Armitage, David, 252
Asian Americans/Canadians and
    self-help, 230–31, 233–34
Atwood, Margaret, 207
Aubry, Timothy, 8, 23
Auden, W. H., 20, 176
Austen, Jane, 20, 219
authoritarianism, 44, 165, 199, 202; in
    advice columns, 186, 188. *See also*
    fascism and totalitarianism
autosuggestion. *See* hypnotism
Aw, Tash, 37, 39, 44, 68, 71–77, 211, 218
Azikiwe, Nnamdi, 50

Baldwin, James, 60
Ball, Jesse, 2, 211
Balzac, Honoré de, 160
Barber, Karin, 57
Barnard, Rita, 197
Barnes, Djuna, 122, 291n130

Mishra, Pankaj, 217

Mitchel, John, 203, 204

Moaveni, Azadeh, 42

modernism, 4, 19–22, 39, 119–25, 141–44, 183–84; autonomy and, 15, 20, 83, 97–98, 175, 213, 254; Bennett-Woolf feud over, 133, 135–40; common reader and, 146, 157, 171–73; critiques of, 119–21; didactic aversion of, 209–10; difficulty and, 20, 122, 146, 171, 181–83; experimentation and, 21, 61, 83, 92; "great divide" between mass culture and, 149, 295n19; mundane in, 49, 142–43; Onitsha pamphlets and, 60–61, 276n84; Trilling on, 138; Wharton's aversion to, 119–20, 121–23, 143

modernity, 8, 32, 42, 48, 209, 217, 228

Montaigne, Michel de, 20

Moore, Lorrie, 104–6, 229–30, 232

Moretti, Franco, 185

Mulford, Prentice, 131, 141

Musil, Robert, 114, 144

mutual improvement societies, 81–82, 83, 86, 242; French form of, 86–89, 94–96

Myerson, Abraham, 140, 292n144

Naipaul, V. S., 53, 74, 204, 211–12

Nakamura Masanao, 62–65, 69

Narcross, John C., 255

"negative visualization," 109, 117, 119, 144

Nehring, Daniel, et al., 53–54, 68

Neville, Patricia, 42, 77, 258, 263n28

New Criticism, 22, 104, 143, 150, 180, 251–52, 254

Newell, Stephanie, 52, 56

New Nancy School, 16

New Thought, 16–18, 35, 55, 121, 126–28, 131–32

Ngai, Sianne, 29

Ngũgĩ wa Thiong'o, 56

Nicholl, Robert, 46

Nietzsche, Friedrich, 229

Nigeria, 37, 43, 55–58; Onitsha Market pamphlets in, 32, 40, 57–61, 213, 215, 276nn84–85

Nnadozie, Joseph O., 60

Norberg, Jakob, 108, 181

North, Joseph, 251, 253–54

North, Ryan, 2

novels. See literature

Nu, U, 33, 34

Nussbaum, Martha, 148

Obiechina, Emmanuel, 58

O'Brien, Flann, 19, 110–19; The Hard Life, 110–11, 113–14, 119; The Third Policeman, 38, 110, 114–19

O'Connell, Helen, 163, 164

Odili, Frank E., 58

Offil, Jenny, 29

Ogali, Ogali A., 58, 60

Olisah, Okenwa, 57–58, 59, 60

Orientalism, 70, 73, 278n125

Ornatowski, Gregory, 71

Orr, Mary, 280n9

Ovid, 9

Ozaki, Shunsuke, 78

Paramore, Kiri, 66

Parks, Acacia, 242–43

Parnell, Charles, 166–68

Peale, Norman Vincent, 22, 32, 222

Peel, Robin, 120

Percy, Walker, 207

Perelman, S. J., 185, 193

Persall, Paul, 20

"personal inventory-taking," 223–24, 226

Phelan, James, 105–6

Pink, Daniel, 48

Porter, Noah, 182

Posner, Richard, 148

political unrest and, 211; quotations in, 2, 3, 14, 37, 41, 58, 60, 255; propaganda and, 187; race and, 31-32, 52-52, 55-61, 229-231, 233-237; scholarship and, 34–36; social class and, 22, 84, 86, 89, 122, 138, 157, 158; titles in, 176. *See also under* literary fiction

self-help movement in Ireland, 157, 163, 203–4

self-management, 102, 133, 223; Foucault on, 252–53

Seneca, Lucius Annaeus, 25, 224

Shakespeare, William, 20, 22, 39, 41, 60, 116, 216; Japan and, 65, 217; Joyce and, 116, 147, 150–51, 155

Shibusawa Eiichi, 66

Shields, David, 222–23

Shinker, William, 24, 34

Siebers, Tobin, 124–25

Simonds, Wendy, 2, 39, 61, 238, 258

Sloterdijk, Peter, 108–9

Smiles, Samuel: background of, 48–49, 81–82, 84, 86, 280n16; on character, 47–48, 64, 135; on education, 241–42; ethos of, 47–47, 222; influences on, 46; Heti on, 214–15; lists in, 45–46, 84; Naipaul and, 53, 204, 211–12; popularity and influence of, 13–14, 37, 40, 44–55, 62–65, 68, 83, 151, 277n102; quotations in, 14, 41, 255; socialism in, 49; warnings against novels in, 14, 26, 52–53, 74, 219

Smith, Ali, 237

Smith, Zadie, 34

sociétés savantes. *See* mutual improvement societies

Solano, Solita, 122

Sowell, Thomas, 31

Speedy Eric (pseudonym), 60

Spencer, Herbert, 3

Squillace, Robert, 133

Starker, Steven, 12, 130

Steele, Shelby, 31

Stein, Gertrude, 4, 15, 28, 61, 104, 213

Stendhal, 212

Stoicism, 63, 116, 118–19, 217, 223–25, 232

Strayed, Cheryl (aka Dear Sugar), 23, 197–98

Susman, Warren, 48

sustainability, 108–9, 142

Swedenborgism, 16, 289n98

Sweetman, Paul, 211

Svevo, Italo, 16

Synge, John Millington, 163

Taylor, John F., 159

Taylor, Verta, 30–31

"thin culture," 42–43, 54

Thomas, David Wayne, 80, 252

Thometz, Kurt, 60–61

Thorndyke, E. L., 183

Thoreau, Henry David, 70

Thurston, Baratunde, 32, 234, 235–36, 237

Tiede, Todd, 32

Tolstoy, Leo, 115, 165

Toomer, Jean, 124

Toyoda, Sakichi, 62

Transcendentalism, 16, 46, 63, 70

translation, 64–65, 68–70, 72, 210

Trendafilov, Vladimir, 46

Trilling, Lionel, 138, 143, 210

Troward, Thomas, 131

Trump, Donald, 32, 211

Twain, Mark, 110

Ty, Eleanor, 231

unconscious, the, 18, 109, 141

universities and self-help movement, 241–48, 255, 256–57

upward mobility, 7, 33, 45–46, 144, 231, 234, 249

Uramoto, Yuka, 78, 79